CONTEMPORARY
INDIAN PHILOSOPHY

Contemporary Indian Philosophy

Basant Kumar Lal

MOTILAL BANARSIDASS PUBLISHERS
PRIVATE LIMITED ● DELHI

First Edition: Patna, 1973
Second Revised Edition: Delhi, 1978
Reprint: Delhi, 1987, 1989, 1992, 1995, 1999

ISBN: 81-208-0260-8 (Cloth)
ISBN: 81-208-0261-6 (Paper)

Also available at:

MOTILAL BANARSIDASS

41 U.A. Bungalow Road, Jawahar Nagar, Delhi 110 007
8 Mahalaxmi Chamber, Warden Road, Mumbai 400 026
120 Royapettah High Road, Mylapore, Chennai 600 004
Sanas Plaza, 1302, Baji Rao Road, Pune 411 002
16 St. Mark's Road, Bangalore 560 001
8 Camac Street, Calcutta 700 017
Ashok Rajpath, Patna 800 004
Chowk, Varanasi 221 001

PRINTED IN INDIA
BY JAINENDRA PRAKASH JAIN AT SHRI JAINENDRA PRESS,
A-45 NARAINA, PHASE I, NEW DELHI 110 028
AND PUBLISHED BY NARENDRA PRAKASH JAIN FOR
MOTILAL BANARSIDASS PUBLISHERS PRIVATE LIMITED,
BUNGALOW ROAD, DELHI 110 007

PREFACE

This work has been undertaken just to negate the impression that contemporary India does not have a philosophy of its own. In fact, sincere attempts have not been made to present Contemporary Indian Philosophy in the mould of academic philosophy. This is a fact that contemporary Indian thinkers are true to their tradition, but attempts have not been made to highlight such constructive aspects of their thought that bear the mark of original thinking and insight. Their attitude towards tradition is 'reverential', and therefore, they appear to be tradition-tied and dogmatic. Tradition, at times, does become a source of dogmatism in philosophical thinking, but this also is true that a complete and radical breaking away from tradition is impossible. Those who wish to do so become 'homeless' and start looking towards other sources for inspiration. The philosophy that they produce becomes derivative — a kind of moon-light philosophy. Therefore, what is needed is to re-think the thoughts of the contemporary Indian thinkers emphasising both the points of repetition and those of original thinking. The present work claims to serve that purpose in its own modest way.

The work is mainly expository; at times, reflections or critical comments have been made, but they have been made with the sole intention of clarifying some of the complex concepts. For a faithful exposition of a thought or a point of view, its appreciation is necessary, and in order to appreciate a thought-system it is essential to establish some kind of identification with it. That is why the exposition throughout is somewhat sympathetic, even when objections are raised and difficulties apprehended, they serve the purpose of helping the understanding of a difficult notion or an idea.

In India today there are two distinct currents of philosophical activities flowing almost side by side. One is the kind of philosophy in which both the intellectuals and the general people take interest, and the other is the kind of philosophical activity that is purely academic and somewhat 'professorial'. This work has not given due regard to the latter although thinkers like K.C. Bhattacharya and Radhakrishnan can be said to be the representatives of this group. But it is possible to develop a comprehensive view of the philosophical activities that are being pursued in the universities of India by the teachers and students of philosophy. That of course will be a major work in itself and hence will deserve a separate treatment.

The attempt to arrange these thoughts in an academic and systematic manner met with an initial difficulty — the difficulty regarding the selection of topics. Naturally, only such topics were selected which appeared to be 'philosophical' and which, taken together, could give a comprehensive picture of a thought-system.

The work includes roughly the thinkers of the twentieth century with the sole exception of Swami Vivekananda, whose philosophical activities were confined to the late second half of the nineteenth century.

This work does not claim to be fully comprehensive as some of the contemporary Indian thinkers have not been included in it. That is chiefly on account of the fact that any attempt to reduce their thoughts into the academic models of philosophy will necessarily involve repetitions.

My thanks are due to M/S Motilal Banarsidass for consenting to publish the work. I am particularly grateful to Shri Jainendra P. Jain who took personal interest in the project and inspired me to expedite the work.

Department of Philosophy,   Basant Kumar Lal
Magadh University,
Bodh Gaya.

CONTENTS

viii

INTRODUCTION

Characteristics of Contemporary Indian Philosophy

Indian Philosophy today is standing almost at a cross-road. It is anxious to retain the forces of the centuries of its tradition through which it has grown, and yet it cannot afford to overlook the 'scientific facts' and 'the empirical attitude' of the present-day world. It is in such a state of inner conflict that the contemporary Indian thinker develops his system of thought. He tries to escape this predicament by asserting the value of the elements of tradition with a renewed vigour emphasising that these elements are not against the scientific temper of the present-day world. Consequently, what they have been able to evolve is some kind of an east-west-synthesis.

Perhaps, it is on account of this that some people characterise Contemporary Indian Philosophy as 'interpretative and not creative'. But, that raises a question of a more fundamental nature, when is a philosophy just interpretation and when does it become creative ? Is it that a creative philosophy never interprets or is it that there cannot remain any originality in a work of interpretation ? It does not need any argument to show that 'interpretation' and 'creative thinking' are not completely exclusive of each other. Śaṅkara, for example, is a commentator on the *'Vedānta Sūtra'*, and yet he is one of the most original thinkers that the world has ever produced. Moore himself admits that he derives the subject-matter of his philosophy from the thoughts and writings of others, and yet his philosophy is a consistent and continuous attempt at construction. Contemporary Indian thinkers also try to re-interpret some of the ancient ideas derived chiefly from the Upaniṣads (and from the Quran in the case of Iqbal) and yet, in their philosophies we come across some refreshingly new notions and rational demonstrations and similar other attempts at construction. They are, thus, both interpretative and creative — of course within certain limits.

It is said that every philosophy bears the mark of its origin. That is why British Philosophy is generally empirical and

American Philosophy is rooted in realistic and pragmatic considerations. French Philosophy is rationalistic, while German Philosophy is pre-eminently speculative. In that vein, Indian Philosophy can be described as *meditative*. It arises as the result of a kind of meditation on the holy powers of the soul and of Nature. Generally, Indian Philosophy is described as 'spiritual'; by this is meant that it lays emphasis on values that are supernatural and other-worldly. But this description is not adequate because it gives the impression that Indian Philosophy has no concern with this-worldly values. At least Contemporary Indian Philosophy should not be described in that way. It emphasises the ultimacy of, what is called, spiritual values; but it does not do so in a completely one-sided manner disregarding absolutely considerations that are empirical and this-worldly. In fact, the contemporary Indian thinker tries his best to reconcile the two. He explicitly says that spiritual awakening cannot take place in a void — that for spiritual growth the physical nature is not to be rejected but perfected. That shows that it is better to describe the general character of Indian Philosophy as *meditative*. In this context, the word 'meditative' is more comprehensive than the word 'spiritual', because it incorporates in it even the word spiritual. What is being suggested here is that the Indian philosopher comes to discover certain holy powers of Nature and also a capacity of self-transcendence within man himself. He becomes curious and amazed and tries to know more about them. The process that he adopts is one of 'meditative speculation', he meditates upon his experiences of these powers and makes speculations about their nature. That is how philosophy takes its birth. The Indian philosopher is not just a romantic who marvels at the apprehension of the ordinary and derives pleasure therefrom, he is much more than that, as he is able to meditate upon the extra-ordinary powers of both Nature and Man. Philosophy in India invariably arises in some such acts of meditative speculation. It was so with the Vedic seer and also with the Upaniṣadic thinker, and it continues to be so even with the contemporary Indian thinker. Just as *experience* provides the back-bone of every kind of British philosophy, so *meditative speculation* has been the method of the Indian Philosopher throughout history.

This method proceeds in a particular way and follows a particular process. Through some meditative insight the thinker is able to grasp some notion or idea. That becomes an article of his belief, and now he concentrates his meditative capacity in order to find a rational justification for the belief that he has already come to hold. Now, rational demonstrations, arguments, criticisms — all become secondary, because truths are revealed to the thinker in an intuitive insight. That is why the Indian thinkers believe that truth can be known only by some super-rational cognition. Contemporary Indian thinkers also have adopted the same method of meditative speculation, and hence, they also do not attach to rational argumentation that value which is normally attached to it; at least in this regard the Contemporary Indian thinkers are very faithful to the tradition of Philosophy.

Now, we are in a position to outline the characteristics of Contemporary Indian Philosophy emphasising the points that it shares with the ancient Indian Philosophy and also the points with respect to which it appears to be novel and different from the latter.

Ancient Indian Philosophy is said to be based on, what can be called, a tragic sense of life. It somehow believes that life is full of suffering and that the aim of religion and philosophy is to attain freedom from suffering. The Contemporary Indian thinker acknowledges the reality of suffering and speaks about the possibility of an escape from it; and yet he approaches the problem in a different way. He gives to life a meaning and purpose and makes it an aspect of the process of spiritual growth. Some of the contemporary Indian thinkers go to the extent of saying that it is through pain and suffering that life gets a dignity and a human significance.

For the contemporary Indian thinkers the roots of philosophical thinking lie in considerations that are existential. Tagore and Radhakrishnan, in particular, analyse the existential conditions of man, speak of the life of care and anguish — of fear and boredom — and assert that life means living in the midst of and in spite of them. It is true that they also speak about the ultimate escape, more or less, in the manner of the ancient Indian thinkers, but they make a distinction between the *concern* of philosophy and the *ideal* of philosophical thinking. Philosophy is concerned with the existent individual living in the midst of his life-situations, but the ultimate ideal that it recommends is the redemption both of the individual and of the race.

That is why contemporary Indian thinkers accept the reality of the world and also of the bodily aspect of man. Unlike the ancient Indian thinker, who thinks that a complete control of the body, the senses and the mind is essential for spiritual growth, the contemporary Indian thinker recommends that these propensities are not to be killed but perfected. The world is considered as the only field for action and the body as 'the temple of the Divine'. It is by emphasising the reality of these and by assigning to the body and the senses some role in the process of spiritual growth that the contemporary Indian thinkers consider themselves to be close to the empirical and the matter-of-fact attitude of the present times.

Philosophy in India is defined as *Darśana* or *Vision*. It is believed that philosophy is capable of giving a vision of reality. That is how philosophy comes to be associated with the actual and the practical problem of pain and suffering. The ancient Indian philosopher believes that suffering is on account of our ignorance regarding the nature of the real. Because we cannot make a distinction between the real and the unreal, we wrongly develop an attachment for the unreal and the transient and hence suffer. The contemporary Indian thinker views the problem in a different way. He believes that philosophy is an attitude — a way of looking at things. Philosophical knowledge enables us to cultivate an attitude that can adopt an entirely different perspective from the one that we normally adopt. Even though life's situations remain the same, the individual who is able to cultivate such an attitude is not affected by life-situations in the manner in which he used to be affected by them in the past. When a child comes to know what a bank-note is, he does not treat it like any other paper. Mind, for example, in its initial stages of development might have treated a gold-ore like any other stone, but when it came to realise its value, its attitude towards the gold-ore changed. Likewise, when we consider ourselves as separate egos, we take life in one way treating the world as if it is meant only for us. But once philosophical understanding enables us to realise that we are one with all, this separative tendency — this tendency to acquire and to possess — changes. In this way the contemporary Indian thinker puts the old wine in a very new bottle.

This shows that the contemporary Indian thinkers are still struggling with the same old problems that had kept the ancient Indian thinkers engaged. Concepts of karma, rebirth, immortality, salvation etc. continue to stimulate the contemporary Indian mind. Perhaps these thinkers feel that 'problems' do not change, and that they can be viewed and reviewed from newer and newer perspectives. Whatever might have been the reason, the contemporary Indian thinker treats these notions in a manner quite different from that of the ancient Indian thinker. According to the ancient Indian thinker all these notions are beyond the grasp of ordinary experience or of the intellect. That is why these notions appear to be very much abstract — even unrealistic. Contemporary Indian thinkers keep on relating these notions to actual life and experience. *Salvation* or *Sarvamukti* or *Divine Life* are the different names given to the goal of life, but invariably an attempt is made to assess the impact of these ideas on actual life and existence. For example, it is said that one can have flashes of immortality even in this life. Examples of indulgence in the acts of pure joy like music, aesthetic contemplation, rational insight, ethical behaviour etc. are taken, and it is suggested that through these one can have the idea of the state of 'liberation'. For the Vedānta, the most favourite example is that of dreamless sleep, which is not actually a state of experience. It is almost a state of 'experience-iessness'. The contemporary Indian thinker takes examples from the actual experiences of life, and thus succeeds to some extent, in reducing the abstractness of these notions. These experiences, at least temporarily, enable us to forget the burden of mundane existence and lead us to a different world — a world of pure joy. Now, this itself becomes a reason for thinking about the possibility of the attainment of a state in which this joy will be greater and uninterrupted.

From what has been said above, it is clear that the contemporary Indian thinkers share some common beliefs. At least with respect to certain issues there appears to be a general agreement among them. Iqbal, however, presents a difficulty in the way of generalisation because he belongs to a different tradition. Still there is a striking similarity between some aspects of his thought and those of other thinkers.

Some of the prominent issues with respect to which all these thinkers appear to be in agreement are : monism, reality of the world, integral nature of man, dignity of manness, reality of human freedom, importance of intuitive knowledge etc. All these thinkers are monists, but Monism expresses itself differently in all of them. According to some the distinction between Monism and Monotheism is irrelevant; some of them, while asserting the oneness of the Absolute, make God a necessary aspect of the Absolute, and according to some others, the monistic character of reality carries it into the realm of the Indefinite.

Likewise, all of them give to the world a reality and assert the dignity of humanness. They all believe that the ideal of life can be reached only by transcending the finite world, and yet, they all are one in asserting that being in the world or being human is not a misfortune as the ancient Indian thinker took it to be.

Again, they all somehow believe that the apprehension of reality is possible only through some intuitive awareness. This awareness has been named differently by the different thinkers, but they all are at one in believing that the awareness of reality is possible not by sense-experience or by intellectual reasoning, but by a kind of super-consciousness — an intuitive insight into the reality. Not that sense or intellect has not been assigned any role; they have their own functions to perform in their own realms, but they cannot directly apprehend the reality. This special kind of awareness has not been conceived in an entirely abstract manner, it has been shown that it is the consummation of the kind of activities that mind performs. It is demonstrated that everybody is capable of having some intuitive awareness. When, by constant and disciplined practice, one is able to intensify the powers inherent in mind, he can have intuitive cognitions of the reality. Thus, these thinkers assert that this faculty is not a mysterious faculty; it is natural to man, and is inherently present in every individual.

These thinkers have similar views to offer with respect to the notion of human freedom also. This notion of freedom, however, is not ethical or social, it is metaphysical or existential. It is believed that man is free both existentially and metaphysically. An interesting conclusion follows : freedom is both the nature of man and his ultimate destiny. According to these thinkers there is no contradiction involved in it. Man is potentially free, but certain obstacles that he has ignorantly put around himself appear to limit his freedom. He makes efforts to remove these obstacles, because only then the ideal of fully manifested freedom will be realised. These thinkers go to the extent of suggesting that the free individuality of the individual is not obliterated even in the state of realisation.

Thus, the contemporary Indian thinkers believe that Philosophy is essentially tied up with life. Even the ancient Indian philosopher believed in that, but his concern was not the normal civic life, he was concerned with a peculiar esoteric life of escape. The contemporary Indian thinker relates philosophy not to a life of escape, but to this very life. He asserts that even after realising *mokṣa* the work of the individual is not over, he has to continue to be in the world, living in the midst of fellow-men, helping them in making their lives healthier and purer. No man, they say, can be saved unless the race is saved.

This insistence on relating Philosophy to life has placed the contemporary Indian Philosopher almost in a state of quandary. He is eager to preserve the scholarly character of his pursuits, and yet he cannot afford to overlook the demand that Philosophy has to be made closer to life. He is aware that there is a distinction between 'a purely academic philosophy' — the philosophy of the scholar, and a 'philosophy of life and existence' — the philosophy of the wise man. He finds himself in a difficult position. If he chooses to follow the way of the scholar, his 'philosophy' becomes the habitat of a few intellectual adventurers, as a result of which he becomes isolated and is accused of driving philosophy away from life. If he chooses the latter course, the danger is that his philosophy may lose its status and dignity and become 'popular' and commonplace'. The contemporary Indian thinker is very acutely aware of this crisis and seeks a way out by striking a balance between the two. He comes to realise that the two pursuits are not after all completely incompatible with each other — that it is possible for the 'scholar' to be 'the man of wisdom' and vice versa. He comes to see that in the Indian tradition itself the two pursuits are combined in the career of the great thinker, Śaṅkara. He is able to combine in himself both 'scholarship' and 'wisdom of life'. He is able to develop and deliberate upon highly technical doctrines relating to epistemology and metaphysics, and at the same time is able to suggest and work out 'a way of life'. The contemporary Indian thinkers learn this lesson well, and try to philosophise about life and its destiny without letting the scholar in them relax even for a moment. This is noticeable not only in the thoughts of academic thinkers like K. C. Bhattacharya, Radhakrishnan or Iqbal, but even in the thoughts of such popular figures as Gandhi and Tagore. Indeed in the former case the scholarly treatment gets an upper hand, in the latter it remains in the background. But all of them go on substantiating their own views by quoting support from thinkers both of the east and the west, and never miss an opportunity of describing and referring to a relevant point of view borrowed from tradition or history. That is why both the common man and the scholar derive from their writings not only satisfaction but enough 'food' for their own thought. Sri Aurobindo in particular has exercised tremendous influence both on the popular mind and on the scholar. Scholars ever find in his writings a ready treasure-house for their scholarly pursuits — commentaries and dissertations, and likewise, countless individuals have been able to learn 'a way of life' from his teachings. Perhaps it is on account of this that Contemporary Indian Philosophy does not completely fit in the mould of Philosophy prepared by the technical philosophy of the west, where philosophy has become the exclusive pursuit of some academic men of philosophy. They are of the firm conviction that philosophy can neither cultivate a metaphysical world-view nor can outline 'a way of life'. For them, philosophy, broadly speaking, is a 'technique', 'a style of thinking', 'a way of reflection' with the help of which muddles, ambiguities, vaguenesses etc. can be cleared, new insights can be gained and new issues can be raised. For them, philosophy is a purely intellectual pursuit, pursued for the joy of it, and, at best, for the clarification of concepts. The contemporary Indian thinker, while conceding the positive claims of their western counter-part, is not prepared to agree with them in their negative assertions. Indeed for them too, 'clarification' is one of the main functions of Philosophy. But this itself may enable the pursuer to cultivate a particular world-view. He feels that it is possible to combine the two pursuits together, in fact he is of the opinion that every attempt at clarification presupposes a standpoint and a perspective, from which alone that clarification can be relevant or significant. That is why in their writings one comes across both scholarly and highly intellectual analyses and deliberations and also positive suggestions regarding conduct, behaviour and the way of life.

There is one particular point with respect to which there appears to be an implicit agreement among all the contemporary thinkers of India. They are all, in a particular sense, humanists. Some of them combine both humanism and humanitarianism. For example, Swami Vivekananda tries to give to his philosophy a humanistic garb, and at the same time, recommends very strongly humanitarian work and service. But their philosophical humanism is of a particular type. In a very basic sense every standpoint has to be humanistic. The minimum of humanism is inevitable, because the basic equipment for viewing things is itself human equipment. But there is no controversy with respect to this. Humanism these days has come to acquire a definite import, it is scientific humanism. It is based on the realisation that it is man himself who can shape his own destiny. The achievements of science and technology, the ever-increasing successes in controlling and even subduing the forces of Nature have given to man a sort of a self-confidence — a confidence in his own capacities. Consequently he comes to assert that everything concerning man depends ultimately on man himself. As such, he does not feel the need of relying upon any super-natural or spiritual powers. Thus, this kind of Humanism becomes positivistic, secular and this-worldly in its outlook. These days the word

'Humanism' has come to stand for this particular type of doctrine.

Obviously, this doctrine is not compatible with the standpoint adopted by the Contemporary Indian Thinkers. They have an unflinching faith in the ultimacy of spiritual pursuits and ideals. As such, a modern Humanist will be disgusted with the suggestion that Contemporary Indian Philosophy is also humanistic in its outlook.

In fact, the humanism that these thinkers adopt is by far more comprehensive than scientific Humanism. Indeed it incorporates even that within its bosom and says something more. The Contemporary Indian thinkers have succeeded in obliterating the opposition between 'humanism' and 'spiritualism', by suggesting that the former envelops and comprehends the latter. Tagore and Radhakrishnan, in particular, have developed this point by analysing the concept of humanism itself.

Whatever else may be meant by the expression 'Humanism', this much is certain that it is a way of viewing things by relating them to man's concerns. It centres round man, and asserts that the capacities, the characters, the qualities of man have to be given fullest expression. Tagore and Radhakrishnan point out that the concept of *Dharma* literally stands for a 'sort of a bringing out the inmost and the essential nature of the object'. It is in this sense that 'the capacity to produce heat' is said to be the dharma of fire and that wateriness is said to be the dharma of water. In that sense the dharma of man is to bring out the essential and the *inmost* nature of man. In that sense it can be said that giving expressions to that humanistic urges of man is man's Dharma. At this point at least theoretically 'humanism' and 'Dharma' become almost synonymous.

Let us pursue the point still further. What is the essence of man — his inmost nature ? That nature has to be given a full play, but what precisely is that *nature*. Scientific Humanism, as we have seen, asserts that that consists in the aspiration, urges and capacities of man — and that they have to be given fullest expression. But let us analyse the nature of these aspirations themselves. It is at this point that scientific Humanism misses or overlooks one very fundamental aspect of human aspiration. It is true that these aspirations consist in his desires —

in his will to do something. But that is not all, there is yet another aspect of this aspiration. Contemporary Indian thinkers assert that an analysis of human aspiration clearly reveals that it is an ever-going — ever-progressing process. It is never satisfied with the goals it is able to attain. No satisfaction is final, it is always aspiring for more — for going higher and higher. Contemporary Indian thinkers describe it as the perpetual consciousness of the beyond. Tagore calls this aspect of man 'the surplus in man'. This also represents one of the most important and basic aspects of man, and therefore even this must be given full expression. The normal desires have to be given their due, but this aspiration also represents the unique character of man — unique because only man has this kind of aspiration. Therefore, these thinkers recommend that this aspect must also be given its fullest expression ; and that would constitute spiritual pursuits. Spiritualism is nothing but trying to satisfy those urges of man that transcend the normal, physical level. Therefore, if Humanism is allowed full expression, both the kinds of aspirations will have to be satisfied. In that sense spiritualism no longer remains incompatible with Humanism, but becomes an aspect of it. It is in this sense that Contemporary Indian Philosophy, in spite of its emphasis on spiritual ideals, is humanistic.

CHAPTER I

SWAMI VIVEKANANDA

Life

Vivekananda was born on the 12th January 1863 in a well-to-do family of Calcutta. His early life was not very eventful. His initial education, in a sense, was all-round, because he took to physical culture almost as zealously as to intellectual learning. He made his mark not only in literature and music, but also in riding, swimming and wrestling.

He had a good study of Indian scriptures as well as of Western thought. His initial mental frame-work was that of a rationalist and sceptic combined in one.

In 1881, however, he happened to meet Swami Ramakrishna and that proved to be a turning point in his life. He was initially sceptical towards the teaching of his master, but after a brief period of doubt and resistance, he surrendered and accepted Swami Ramakrishna as his friend, philosopher and guide.

After the death of Ramakrishna in 1886, he undertook an extensive travel of almost the whole of India, and thereby acquainted himself with the social and economic conditions of the country. He came to feel that India, in spite of its rich spiritual heritage and very strong cultural history, had not been able to root out poverty, weakness and social evils. He strongly felt the need of bringing about a spiritual revolution, which, he also realised, required a very strong spiritual leadership.

At that very time he came to know that the Parliament of Religions was going to meet at Chicago He decided to go there and to participate in the meet. What happened there is today a household story, but this was a fact that the Parliament of Religions enabled Vivekananda to assume the spiritual leadership of the Indian people.

He travelled extensively even in foreign countries and learnt about their good things. After his return, he founded the Ramakrishna Ashram at Belur, near Calcutta and started, with great vigour, the work of social reform and service. In 1899, he undertook a second journey to the West and breathed his last on the 4th of July 1902, leaving behind an institution and a host of disciples to carry on the good work he had started.

The Influences that shaped his Philosophy

Vivekananda's philosophy arises from the awareness of the social, religious and economic conditions of the Indian masses. He had also a realisation that at least some of the social evils were due to the orthodoxy and superstitions prevalent in the society of the time. He had a deep conviction that this was due to a loss of faith in spiritual values. Consequently, he aimed at, what could be called, a spiritual awakening and accepted with gratitude whatever he could learn from faiths and disciplines emphasising the ultimacy of spiritual values.

The deepest influence upon his thought is obviously of Ancient Hindu Philosophy — especially of the Vedānta. It can safely be said that to a very great extent, Vivekananda also is a Vedantist. The main body of his thought is derived from the Hindu Scriptures — from the Upaniṣads and the Vedānta. His basic belief in the essential unity of everything, that is, in the completely monistic nature of reality, owes its origin to the Vedānta. His doctrine of Māyā, again, is derived from the same source. The distinction between 'an empirical point of view' and 'a transcendental point of view' that he so often makes and to which he refers time and again in order to solve certain apparent contradictions of his thought, is also borrowed from the Vedānta. It is true that Vivekananda always emphasises the need of re-interpreting Vedānta in accordance with the demands and needs of the time; in fact, his philosophy itself is an attempt in that direction, but this remains a fact that some of the basic ideas of the philosophy of Vivekananda are derived from ancient Hindu philosophy — specially the Vedānta.

In a certain sense, Vivekananda is influenced by Buddhist philosophy also. There are at least three ideas in Vivekananda's philosophy for which he remains indebted to Buddhist thought. The first and the foremost is the idea of 'mass-liberation' that Vivekananda envisages; it has a clear similarity with the Buddhistic ideal of Bodhisattva. Secondly, Vivekananda is impressed by the Buddhistic assertion that the raft with the help of which one crosses a river in storm, should be left for the use of others. Buddha himself, even after attaining Nirvāṇa, kept on roaming about and helping others in their struggles against suffering. Vivekananda frankly recognises the worth of such humanitarian and altruistic work. His own missionary zeal for service is influenced by this. Thirdly, some of the Buddhistic ideals, like *Samyak Karmānta* and *Ājīva* have also inspired Vivekananda a great deal.

Along with these Indian influences, he also carried, on his thought, the influence of Christianity. He was impressed by the strength of character, the soul-force that the man of the Cross possessed. He could see that it required a supreme spiritual strength to forgive the oppressor even in the midst of acute physical suffering. From Christianity, therefore, Vivekananda takes up the ideal of service and love. His conviction that man contains within him the spark of Divinity and his optimistic belief in the possibility of man's redemption contain elements that greatly resemble the Christian notion of the Kingdom of God.

There were certain other influences too. For some time he was under the influence of Brāhmo Samāj, and, it can be said that his strong feelings against the prevalent orthodox and superstitious rites were generated under that influence. He also seemed to be influenced by the personality of Dayananda Saraswati. It can be said that Dayananda's emphasis on the indeterminate nature of reality and his practical insistence on the quality of fearlessness had left a deep mark on Vivekananda also. Then, there was the *Gītā,* which, with its emphasis on 'selfless work', was a source of constant inspiration to Vivekananda.

But the profoundest influence, in the light of which every other influence was remodelled and shaped, was that of his master — Swami Ramakrishna Paramahamsa. In fact, the story of the life of Vivekananda would have been entirely different, had he not come under the influence of Ramakrishna. It is said that Ramakrishna brought about a spiritual transformation in the personality and the mental make-up of Vivekananda. Swami Nikhilananda, speaking about this, says, "It was his Master who had taught him the divinity of the soul, the non-duality of God-head, the unity of existence and one more great thing — that is the universality or harmony of all different religions".[1] It is true that Ramakrishna initiated him to spiritual discipline and meditation.

---

1. Swami Nikhilananda, *Vivekananda, a Biography*, p. 53.

His Metaphysical Standpoint

It is difficult to reduce the teachings of a social reformer and a religious teacher into the technical mould of academic philosophy. The reasons are simple : a preacher or a religious teacher does not merely seek to satisfy the intellectual curiosity of man, he appeals to feelings and fancy as well; as such, he does not feel the need of observing the rules of logic. Moreover, one who is basically interested in the practical affairs of life does not have the time to care for discrepancies and contradictions involved in the theory-side of the problem. In the comprehensive sweep and the feeling-approach of the religious teacher, contradictions just melt away.

Even so, an attempt can be made to apply metaphysical epithets to the philosophy of Vivekananda. The philosophy of Vivekananda is idealistic in more senses than one. Idealism may mean either *Ideal-ism*, or *Idea-ism* or *Idealism* as such. There is a difference between the second and the third senses of the term although both can be examples of Metaphysical Idealism. Metaphysical Idealism believes that the reality is ultimately spiritual or mental or ideal in character. Some metaphysical idealists go on to hold that the ideal reality is of the nature of 'Ideas' — ideas either of some mind, finite or Infiinite or Ideas as such, objective and universal. Berkeley may be an example of the first kind and Plato of the other. Vivekananda is not an idealist in that sense. He is an idealist because he believes that the ultimate reality is essentially spiritual in character. He is also an idealist in the sense that he believes in the ultimacy of certain ideal values and recommends that a continuous and persistent effort should be made for the attainment of those values. His 'ideal-ism' is therefore not unrealistic; ideal-ism becomes unrealistic only when the ideal is nothing but a creation of one's imagination. Vivekananda asserts that the ideal that he talks about is a living ideal capable of inspiring and attracting man towards itself.

Vivekananda's idealism is monistic. An idealistic philosophy that is strictly monistic becomes abstract and comes to assert that reality has to be indeterminate. The One, it feels, cannot accept any distinctions or qualifications of any kind within it. Vivekananda very often describes reality in this fashion — in the fashion of the abstract monist. But, at many other places, reality is given a monotheistic description and assertions about God's characters are emphatically made. Now, one is at a loss to decide whether Vivekananda's philosophy is strictly and abstractly monistic or monotheistic. This difficulty that a student of academic philosophy experiences does not present any problems to Vivekananda. He does not perceive any contradiction or opposition between the two. Monism and Monotheism have a reference to different dispositions and attitudes of men, the difference in dispositions does not create differences in truth as such, it is due to the difference in approach to truth. Therefore, Vivekananda freely keeps on oscillating between Monism and Monotheism.

Reality and God

It is somewhat philosophically unusual to treat reality and God under the same head. But, in the philosophy of Vivekananda, they are not distinct concepts. Traditional philosophy treats reality as a metaphysical concept and God as a religious concept. For Vivekananda such distinctions are irrelevant.

In fact, Vivekananda combines, in his thought, Abstract Monism and Theism. He is a Pantheist, and yet God, according to him, is personal. Consequently, we find two currents flowing almost side by side in the philosophy of Vivekananda — one that resembles Advaita Vedānta, and the other that reminds one of the theism of the Bhakti-cult. Vivekananda is almost convinced that these two currents are not really two currents, that they are just two ways of looking at the Reality. But then, an attempt can be made to determine the features of both these aspects of his thought.

Almost like an Advaitin, Vivekananda says that reality is one absolute Brahman. He emphasises the monistic character of reality to such a great extent that he says that reality is one but not a 'whole'. The concept of a 'whole' implies that there must be parts, which, when organised, give the whole.[1] But, according to Vivekananda, Absolute is perfect unity, and therefore the distinction between whole and parts completely vanishes. The concept of Absolute is arrived at by carrying the process of

---

1. He says, "The Infinite is indivisible, there cannot be parts of the Infinite. The Absolute cannot be divided". *Complete Works*, III., p. 7.

abstraction to its maximum possible limit, and that explains its strictly monistic character.

This Brahman, according to Vivekananda, is beyond space, time and causation, and as such it is changeless. Its being changeless does not mean that it remains the same in all points of time. On the other hand, it means that the question of time is irrelevant to it. In fact, all these subtleties of thought arise on account of our ways of apprehending God; in reality 'God is neither outside nature nor inside nature, but God and nature and soul and universe are all convertible terms. You never see two things : it is your metaphorical words that have deluded you'.[1]

That is why the Absolute has been described as indeterminate. You cannot properly attribute qualities to the Absolute. To attribute characters to the Absolute would amount to knowing the Absolute and 'knowing the Absolute' is nothing but a contradiction-in-terms. Absolute is the unknowable, it does not admit even internal divisions.

But, an attempt can be made to give a working-a-near-description of the Absolute. Like Śaṅkara, Vivekananda also says that the Absolute can be described as *Sat-Cit-Ānanda*. The concepts of *Sat* (existence) and *Cit* (consciousness) *are* similar to the *Sat* and *Cit* of Advaita Vedānta, but the concept of *Ānanda* (bliss) has been greatly enriched by Vivekananda. Partly under the influence of Buddhism and partly under the influence of Christianity, Vivekananda makes 'love' the essential core of 'bliss', He asserts that *ānanda* is in love.

This reference to 'love' takes us to the consideration of the other aspects of Vivekananda's philosophy of God — to its monotheistic aspect. Vivekananda asserts that the absolute — the impersonal Brahmaṅ — is looked upon by the mind as the Creator, Ruler, and the Destroyer of the world and as its complete Cause. He is also viewed as supremely good and loving — as one who is constantly taking interest in his creation. Thus, along with the impersonal nature of the Absolute, a belief in personal God also emerges.

In fact, Vivekananda believes that the religious urges and aspirations of man demand satisfaction, and that demand can be met only by a personal God. In Śaṅkara's Advaita Vedānta

1. Swami Vivekananda, *Complete Works*. III., p. 214.

also the concept of God has been given a place, but there God has been conceived as a product of ignorance and Māyā, and as such, is not real from the real point of view—the Pāramār-thika dṛṣṭi; but Vivekananda believes that Absolute and God are not two — that God is not a creation of Māyā. These distinctions surely arise on account of ignorance or our limited ways of apprehension, but knowledge means the realisation of the irrelevance of such a distinction. Metaphysically speaking, reality is absolute Brahman, the same reality viewed from the religious point of view is God. He who is supremely real, is also the object of our devotion and worship.

That is why Vivekananda emphasises the all-pervasive nature of God. God is present everywhere and in everything. "Through his control the sky expands, through his control the air breathes, through his control the sun shines, and through his control all live. He is the Reality in nature. He is the soul of your soul."[1] Again, he says, "...the Absolute is that ocean, while you and I, and sun and stars, and everything else are various waves of that ocean. And what makes the waves different ? Only the form, and that form is time, space and causation all entirely dependent on the wave."[2]

Proofs for God's Existence

Vivekananda has a very deep faith in God, this faith expresses itself in the conviction that it is, in fact, impossible to live without a faith in God. He appears to be very sanguine in emphasising the necessity of God concept. This necessity is almost obvious to him for the simple reason that an outright rejection of God is simply impossible. It is impossible, he feels, to maintain the reality of the world and the soul and to reject the reality of God. God has to be presupposed as the necessary support and ground of both the world and the soul.

This raises a very pertinent question : if the notion of God has a necessity about it, why is it that people of all religions and sects always try to prove God's existence ? Why must we take recourse to rational demonstrations of the existence of God ?

In fact, at times Vivekananda does not feel inclined to make any effort for the demonstration of God's existence. He feels

1. Swami Vivekananda, *Complete Works*, II., p. 236.
2. *Ibid.*, p. 136.

that it is possible to have a direct realisation of God. He is convinced that Swami Ramakrishna had a direct realisation of God. So he thinks that arguments, proofs, demonstrations etc. are not actually needed for establishing God's existence; His existence can be felt and realised.

This does not mean that, according to Vivekananda, rational proofs and demonstrations do not have any value or worth. It is wrong to presuppose that proofs are needed only in cases where direct evidence is not available. In the case of God particularly even if the possibility of direct realisation is there, rational proofs have to be given at least on account of two factors; (a) it is not possible for everybody to have the realisation any day he likes. That requires years of rigorous discipline and meditation. There are only a few seers who have been able to 'see'. Therefore, for the majority, it is the proofs that create initial interest and even faith. One can cling to a doctrine if it appears rationally satisfying to him; (b) the revelations of the few seers have also to be communicated to others. They are invariably obscure and difficult to be translated into the language that the ordinary man understands. Rational proofs and demonstrations serve the purpose of interpreting these truths and also of communicating these truths to the common man.

But, how can God's existence be demonstrated ? Vivekananda believes in the possibility of such a demonstration and follows almost the same procedure that is normally adopted by rational demonstrations of this kind. One would experience some difficulty in joining together Vivekananda's demonstrations of God's existence, because they are unsystematically scattered throughout his writings and speeches. He is, after all, not an academic philosopher, and naturally it is not possible for him to be systematic in the manner of a man of a technical philosophy. But one comes across in Vivekananda's writings demonstrations of both kinds — *a posteriori* and *a priori*. Certain arguments seek to prove God on the basis of his evidences and effects discovered in the world (*a posteriori* demonstration) and certain other arguments seek to prove God's existence on the basis of an analysis of God's concept itself (*a priori* demonstration). Let us now try to enumerate some of these 'proofs' for God's existence as they have been conceived by Vivekananda.

(a) At some places Vivekananda has referred to certain demonstrations that appear to be similar to the traditional teleological proof for God's existence. He says, "The whole of nature at best could teach them only of a personal Being who is the ruler of the Universe; it could teach nothing further. In short out of the external world we can only get the idea of an architect, that which is called Design Theory."[1] This clearly shows that the vastness, harmony and the grandeur of the world lead us to suppose that there must be an architect, an intelligent designer of the Universe.

(b) On occasions, one comes across passages in the writings of Vivekananda that remind us of the causal demonstration of God's existence. He comes to find the evidences of God scattered everywhere, he finds himself unable to account for the 'things' of the world without taking recourse to an all-powerful cause. In the world we come across many things whose origin and movement cannot be accounted for in any naturalistic term. We are not their authors, and as such we are forced to conceive of a Divine Author. Vivekananda says, "A stone falls and we ask, why? This question is possible only on the supposition that nothing happens without a cause....It means that everything in the universe is by turn a cause and an effect. It is the cause of certain things which come after it, and is itself the effect of something else which has preceded it. This is called the law of causation and is a necesary condition of all our thinking."[2] Now this causal series itself leads to a final and ultimate cause — to a cause which, although is the cause of everything, is itself not caused. That, according to Vivekananda, is the Absolute or God. "That which exists by itself alone cannot have a cause. That which is free cannot have any cause; else it would not be free, but bound."[3] Thus starting from the 'things' of the universe, we arrive at the notion of a self-caused cause of the Universe. This can, therefore, be called a causal demonstration of God's existence.

(c) God is also sought to be established from the fact of 'oneness of everything.' Vivekananda says that the universe expresses an essential unity of everything. One has only to pause and contemplate in order to discover that things that look so very different from each other are really and basically one and the same. He says, 'If you go below the surface, you find that

1. Swami Vivekananda, *Complete Works*, I., p. 353.
2. Swami Vivekananda, *Jnana Yoga*, pp. 119-120.
3. *Ibid.*, p. 121.

unity between man and man, between races and races, high and
low, rich and poor, gods and men, and men and animals. If
you go deep enough, all will be seen as only vibrations of the
one, and he who has attained to this conception of Oneness has no
more delusion.'[1] This fact of unity itself is an argument in favour
of the One. There cannot be any other explanation of this unity
except that the reality is one.

(d) A similar demonstration is put forward by arguing from
the fact of 'love'. What is the nature of love? What do we
really love? Vivekananda does not have any hesitation in saying
that we do not really love any 'other,' but we love ourselves.
Love consists in discovering oneself in the object of love. He
says, 'None, O beloved, loves the husband for the husband's
sake, but it is for the sake of the self who is in the husband, that
the husband is loved; none, O beloved, loves the wife for the
wife's sake, but it is for the sake of the self who is in the wife
that the wife is loved.'[2] If love is of this type, then in the act of
love the distinction between 'me' and 'thou' would vanish, and
this carried to its ultimate conclusion, will show that there is
no other, that reality behind everything is just one supreme
principle of love.

(e) Vivekananda also offers proofs based on authority. Times
without number he refers to the ancient Indian Scriptures, to
the Vedas and the Upaniṣads in order to justify his assertion regarding the Absolute. It is true that reference to an authority of
this kind creates logical difficulties, generally it involves an argument in a circle. In order to explain these scriptures they refer
to God and in order to establish God's existence they refer to
these scriptures. This is nothing but arguing in a circle. Vivekananda is aware of this, but he does not perceive any logical
difficulty here. So long as we have not been able to know and
realise God, we can base ourselves and rely on the authority
of the scriptures, but that does not take away from the scriptures
their Divine Origin. The difficulty, thus, is solved in a very simple manner. From the point of view of existence and reality
God alone is there, but from the point of view of our finite knowledge, scriptures appear to be prior, and, therefore, for the sake
of initial knowledge and faith we can safely rely on them.

1. Swami Vivekananda, *Jnana Yoga*, p. 13.
2. Swami Vivekananda, *Complete Works*, III., p, 92.

(f) Vivekananda, at times, uses certain arguments that may be called analogical. At many places Vivekananda takes help from analogies of various kinds to arrive at the notion of God. For example, at one place he takes up the analogy of a beautiful picture. "Who enjoys the picture, the seller or the seer? The seller is busy with his accounts, computing what his gain will be, how much profit he will realise on the picture.... That man is enjoying the picture who has gone there without any intention of buying or selling. He looks at the picture and enjoys it. So this whole Universe is a picture, and when these desires have vanished, men will enjoy the world...."[1] Vivekananda conceives God in the analogy of a painter or a poet or an artist. He admits, "I never read of any more beautiful conception of God than the following: 'He is the Great Poet, the ancient Poet, the whole universe is His poem, coming in verses and rhymes and rhythms, written in infinite bliss."[2]

(g) Vivekananda seeks to prove God on the strength of the necessity of God's notion. Its rejection, according to Vivekananda, is impossible. God's idea is shown to be necessary on various grounds. It is necessary because it is the Truth and Truth is necessary. It is necessary also because it is freedom. The fact of human freedom presupposes the ideal of absolute freedom which is nothing but Divine Freedom. It is necessary also because it is inherently present in man. Vivekananda asserts, "It is the God within your own self that is propelling you to seek for Him, to realise Him. After long researches here and there, in temples and in churches, earths and in heavens, at last you come back, completing the circle from where you started, to your own soul and find that He for whom you have been seeking all over the world, for whom you have been weeping and praying in churches and temples, on whom you are looking as the mystery of all mysteries shrouded in cloud, is nearest of the near, is your own self, the reality of your life, body and soul."[3] God, thus, is necessary, because the very condition of existence involves God.

(h) The proof on which Vivekananda lays greatest reliance is what may be called, an intuitional proof for God's existence.

1. Swami Vivekananda, *Jnana Yoga*, p. 148.
2. *Ibid.* p. 148.
3. Swami Vivekananda, *Complete Works*, II., p. 81.

Vivekananda does not feel the urgency or the necessity of offering regular proofs for God's existence, because there cannot be any better proof than *direct realisation*, and an intuitional argument stands on the secure foundation of direct realisation. Vivekananda is aware that there have been seers of the great Truth, he is also convinced that every body can have that realisation, if he is prepared to follow the path of rigorous religious discipline and meditation. Then, *rational* proofs would not be needed, these proofs are needed only so long as the capacity to have a direct vision is not developed.

Some other Characters of God

It is now apparent that Vivekananda conceives God more or less in the manner of Advaita Vedānta — but with a difference. The difference consists in the fact that Vivekananda is not prepared to accept that theistic descriptions of God are descriptions of God from a lower point of view; in fact, he feels that the Vedantic distinction between Absolute and God is redundant. God, according to him, is the essential unity of everything, and as such, is all-pervasive. Therefore, there is no need for making distinctions of any kind, every body is free to view Him in whatever manner he likes.

God is described as the one eternal principle. This may lead one to suppose that God is the unchanging and abiding principle in the midst of change, but that is not the exact conception of eternity. God is eternal because time and change are irrelevant to it.

God has also been conceived as Supreme Goodness. Goodness, in Vivekananda, does not mean mere moral perfection because from the point of view of God the question of morality is also irrelevant — in God there is no distinction between good and evil. According to Vivekananda, Divine Goodness has two implications. First, it means that God is bliss and happiness. Secondly, it implies that it is possible for every individual to be good if he fixes up the Supreme Goodness as his ideal and inspiration.

This takes us to assert yet another character of God to which Vivekananda has given a unique importance. God, according to him, is a human God. This assertion, far from being anthropomorphic represents a very great truth. It does not suggest that God has been cast in man's image, on the other hand, it suggests that man bears the spark of Divinity within himself. Vivekananda is conscious that one of the greatest justification of God concept is the fact that God is able to satisfy our urges and needs, and is able to provide to our life greater vitality and strength. Therefore, God has to be given some human attributes just in order to make inter-communication possible. Therefore, Vivekananda says, "He has human attributes, He is merciful, He is just, He is powerful, He is almighty, He can be approached, He can be prayed to, He can be loved in return, and so forth. In one word, He is a human God, only infinitely greater than man."[1]

This description of God clearly shows that God is also conceived as the ultimate Ideal of life and existence. It is in and through Him that everything has made its appearance, therefore, the original bond of unity is always asserting itself. Consequently, the aim is to realise the unity once again. In fact. the unity is not actually disturbed, but there is an apparent feeling of disruption. This feeling has to be superseded, and unity has to be re-established. God, therefore, is the supreme Ideal.

This ideal can be reached through LOVE. That is why Vivekananda has made even 'love' a metaphysical attribute of God. Disruption or disunity is an account of the failure to realise the affinity or kinship of everything with everything. This can be realised through love, and so Vivekananda comes to assert that God himself is love and quotes scriptures in support of this.

Vivekananda does not consciously enter into the controversy regarding the personal or impersonal nature of God. In fact, he has described God on both ways and he seems to be convinced that this distinction between a personal God and an impersonal God does not affect God's nature in any way. God is what He is, the distinction between 'personal' and 'impersonal' is the result of our attempts to apprehend God. One takes to the way that suits him, and therefore, it is not proper to reduce God's nature to the nature of our approaches to God. Even so, one feels that Vivekananda is more inclined towards the personal nature of God. The reason is simple. Vivekananda is trying to bring religion within the easy reach of the common man, and he feels that the common man is more inclined towards the personal character of God.

---

1. Swami Vivekananda, *Complete Works*, II., p. 40.

But, this does not take away from Vivekananda his basic Vedantic convictions. He is convinced that properly speaking God cannot be described. Our language is inadequate to represent Him accurately. These attempts to represent the characters of God are nothing but our limited ways of trying to know the unknown. Vivekananda says, "You cannot describe Him by any language. All attempts of language, calling Him father, or brother, or our dearest friend, are attempts to objectify God, which cannot be done. He is the eternal subject of everything.'[1]

Nature of the World : The Cosmos

An attempt to determine the nature of the world naturally raises the question of its origin. Is the world a creation ? This question becomes very significant in the philosophy of Vivekananda because Vivekananda conceives the cosmos more or less in Śaṅkara's way. Śaṅkara believes that in reality there has never been any creation. From the transcendental point-of-view, creation, according to Śaṅkara is unreal. It is true that he also comes to discuss the process of creation, but that has a validity only from a lower — the empirical point-of-view.

Vivekananda tries to strike a balance between the two positions. He has to accept the basic monistic position of Advaita Vedānta, but he somehow gives to the world also a reality. God is the only real principle, creation is God's creation, and, therefore, an aspect of God. It is true that in the state of realisation, the distinction between the creator and the created would not exist, but for all practical purposes, creation has to be conceived as real. This dual character of the world would not present much difficulty to Vivekananda's philosophy of the world — as it would be apparent in due course.

Creation can best be described as the expression of the creator in finite forms. Vivekananda raises the question, 'How has the Infinite — the absolute, become the finite ?' and tries to answer it in his own way. In *Jnana Yoga* he takes help of a figure in order to illustrate his answer to this question.[2]

"Here is the Absolute (a), and this is the universe (b). The Absolute has become the universe. By this is not only meant

1. Swami Vivekananda, *Complete Works*, II., p. 184.
2. Swami Vivekananda, *Jnana Yoga*, pp. 119-120.

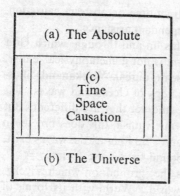

the material world but the mental world, the spiritual world — heavens and earths, and in fact, everything that exists. Mind is the name of a change, and body the name of another change, and so on, and all these changes compose our universe. The Absolute (a) has become the universe (b) by passing through Time, Space and Causation (c)".

This description of creation implies that in Absolute there was no Time, Space or causation. The idea of space cannot be there, because there is no change — no external position of the Absolute. The idea of time cannot be there because there is no 'thought' in the Absolute, and the Absolute being strictly one, the question of the presence of Causation in the Absolute does not arise. Therefore, it has to be realised that all these begin to operate after the creation-process starts.

But then, another question can be raised : wherefrom do Time, Space and Causation emerge ? If they are not in the Absolute, and if creation has to take place through them, then they become independent entities, and this would affect the ultimate monistic conviction of Vivekananda. Vivekananda is aware of this, and so, he solves the difficulty in a very easy manner. He tries to show that Space, Time and Causation are not metaphysical realities, they are mere forms.

They are not metaphysical realities because they are not independent existences. Time is entirely a dependent existence, it changes with every change of our mind. The same time may appear to one as very long, and to another as very short. At times, the idea of time vanishes altogether. In dream, sometimes, one imagines that one has lived for several years, and at other times, years pass just in a second. So time is entirely dependent on our state of mind. It is so with space and causation as well. Spatial dimensions depend on our angles of vision, likewise what is 'cause' from one point of view is 'effect' from another point of view. They are also dependent on our mind. Space, Time and Causation are not independent entities also because they cannot exist all by themselves separate from other things. We cannot have any idea of abstract space or abstract time or abstract causation. Thus, they do not have any independent existence.

They are, therefore, just forms in and through which God makes creation possible. A form is not a metaphysical entity, but, for that matter, it is not false or unreal. Vivekananda illustrates this with the help of the analogy of Ocean and waves. The waves are the same as the ocean, and yet they are different. But when the waves subside, the forms vanish, this does not mean that forms of the waves are illusory. So long as the waves exist, the forms are there, and one is bound to see the forms.

This analogy clearly explains the ground on which Vivekananda asserts the reality of the world. World with its forms of space, time and causation is not a delusion. In realisation these forms may vanish as do the forms of the waves when the waves subside, but so long as the world is there, these forms are there and one is bound to 'see' them.

In fact, the necessity for emphasising the reality of the world over and over again is felt by Vivekananda because of the difficulties felt by Śaṅkara in maintaining the reality of the world. Śaṅkara escapes the difficulty by calling *Jagat mithyā*. Vivekananda not merely asserts the reality of the world, but feels that Vedānta does not intend to say that the world is unreal. He thinks that the word Mithyā has been misunderstood. There are many other scholars of Vedānta who also feel that way. They all feel that in Vedānta the word *mithyā* has been used in a special sense. It means that which has no permanent value — that which is constantly changing and varying — that which is transitory and temporary. That which is *mithyā*, cannot have a fixed or permanent or absolute character. If 'mithyā' is understood in this sense, all difficulties disappear, because in this sense it is not opposite to 'the truth' or to 'the real'. Thus, Vivekananda feels that what Vedānta asserts is not the unreality of the world, but its *mithyātva*, it merely emphasises that *Jagat* cannot have any fixed or absolute character of its own.

This means that creation is not a completed process, world does not come out of God as a finished product. Vivekananda seems to be in favour of, what can be called, perpetual creation. Creation, according to him, is timeless, having no beginning or end in time. The universe is just a manifestation — an expression of God and the question of time cannot be raised with respect to this. He says, 'It is not that this world was created the other

day, not that a God came and created the world and since that
time has been sleeping, for that cannot be. The creative energy
is still going on. God is eternally creating. He is never at
rest."[1]

That shows that Vivekananda has tried to combine the notions
of 'creation' and 'evolution'. Usual theories of evolution find it
difficult to explain the beginning of everything, even Drawin
could not explain how the first living cells came to be. Vivekananda's theory of creation is able to explain the origin of the
cosmos, and he explains the growth of the world in terms of an
evolutionary process. According to him, everything in nature
grows from certain subtle form to its grosser form. The story of
the world is the story of the unfolding of the rudimentary elements into their more clearly expressed forms.

The Doctrine of Māyā

An account of Vivekananda's doctrine of creation has to refer
to the doctrine of Māyā. Vivekananda, in a sense, is a neo-
Vedantist, and as such, the Māyā-doctrine naturally makes its
appearance in his philosophy. It is true that Vivekananda has
borrowed this doctrine from Advaita Vedānta, but his conception of Māyā is not exactly similar to that of Śaṅkara. Like
Śaṅkara, Vivekananda also believes that Māyā is a power of
the Creator; he also thinks that Māyā is the principle of change,
a śakti that makes creation possible. But in Advaita Vedānta,
Māyā is the power that creates illusion, it is that Divine śakti
which has the capacity of deluding man into believing that the
world is real. Vivekananda does not accept this position.
According to him, Māyā does not necessarily mean being illusory
or unreal. In Vivekananda's philosophy Māyā, is conceived
just as a fact about the nature of the world, it seeks to express
the essential characters of the world as it exists.

Vivekananda explains the nature of this fact in a very clear
manner when he says, "......Māyā is not a theory for the explanation of the world : it is simply a statement of facts as they
exist, that the very basis of our being is contradiction, that everywhere we have to move through this tremendous contradiction,
that wherever there is good, there must also be evil, and

1. Swami Vivekananda, *Complete Works*, III., p. 122.

wherever there is evil, there must be some good, wherever there is life, death must follow as its shadow, and everyone who smiles will have to weep, and vice-versa."[1] Māyā, thus, is a convenient name for the fact of 'contradiction' that the Universe so clearly exhibits. Our whole life is a contradiction, a mixture of being and non-being. At times, it appears that one can know everything, and at once he comes across a block or a hindrance which he finds himself unable to cross. His activities appear to move in a circle, and he finds himself unable to go beyond that circle. Vivekananda says, "what you call matter, or spirit, or mind, or anything else you may like to call them, the fact remains the same: we cannot say that they are, we cannot say that they are not. We cannot say that they are one, we cannot say that they are many. This eternal play of light and darkness — indiscriminate, indistinguishable, inseparable — is always there, A fact, yet at the same time not a fact, awake at the same time asleep — this is a statement of fact and this is what is called Māyā."[2]

This description of Māyā has one great advantage in it, it differs from the Vedantic concept of Māyā without contradicting it. The Vedānta says that Māyā is the power of God through which the world — illusion is created. Vivekananda would add that the Power in itself is neither good nor bad, it is neutral. Therefore, Māyā must have a neutral character. Māyā's neutral nature can be retained only if Māyā is conceived as the name for the fact of contradiction apparent in the world.

At places, Vivekananda admits that Māyā has a reality from the lower point of view only. Such admissions are made only when Vivekananda finds it difficult to reconcile the doctrine of Māyā with the doctrine of reality. He is aware that finally all contradictions have to be resolved, and therefore, finally Māyā has to be superceded. But he asserts that the superseding act does not completely cancel or negate that which is superseded. He tries to explain this fact with the help of the analogy of 'Ocean and waves'. Waves, even as waves are nothing but water, and yet they have a name and form. If the waves subside, nothing remains but the ocean, but so long as the waves are rising and falling they have a reality of their own; and even when the waves subside, it is not the waves that have become the ocean,

1. Swami Vivekananda, *Jnana Yoga*, p. 64.
2. Swami Vivekananda, *Complete Works II.*, p. 112.

because the ocean is never separate from the waves. Moreover, the subsiding of the waves does not negate the name and the form that waves as waves had assumed. Likewise, even when Māyā gives way, it gives way only to find that all the time it was lying within the bosom of the Brahman itself, its being superceded does not take away from it its distinctive role that it had been playing so long.

This description of Māyā can also justify the Vedantic description of Māyā where it is described neither as real nor as unreal, nor even as real-unreal. It is described as *anirvacanīya*. Vivekananda also gives a similar description of Māyā when he says that Māyā can neither be defined as existence or as non-existence. Vivekananda also places Māyā somewhere in between Absolute Being and non-being.

Nature of Man

Some anthropologists have claimed that the origin of religious thought lies in some form of animism. The primitive man found himself unable to explain the phenomena of *dream, unconsciousness* and *death*. He was forced to believe that the real man was not the man that was apparently seen moving and living. This crude idea about the mysterious being started taking shape as man's capacity to think and speculate grew. That is why Vivekananda says that this was the main object of inquiry for the Upaniṣads. "...the Kaṭha Upaniṣad begins with the inquiry : when a man dies there is a dispute. One party declares that he has gone for ever, the other insists that he is still living, which is true ?"[1] He himself tries to answer the question by saying, "Two positions remain to mankind. One is to believe with the nihilists that all is nothing, that we know nothing, that we can never know anything either about the future, the past or even the present....Then there is the other position — to seek for an explanation, to seek for the real....In this body which is an aggregate of molecules of matter, is there anything which is real ?"[2]

Vivekananda seeks for the real in his own way. According to him the real in man is a sort of a 'concentration of spiritual

1. Swami Vivekananda, *Jnana Yoga*, p. 21.
2. *Ibid.*, pp. 23-24.

energy' Man, according to him, is *a spirit*. The word 'spirit' has
both a negative import and a positive one. Usually the negative
import is given more prominence, it is believed that the spiritual is not the ordinary, is different from the empirical. Vivekananda would not reject this implication of the word 'spiritual'.
Man is not what he ordinarily appears to be. Over and above
this, Vivekananda also asserts that man is spiritual in positive
terms also — because he represents some aspirations and urges
which only he is capable of having. He has devoted much time
and energy in trying to determine the spiritual dimensions of
man; his emphasis on spirituality is so great that even the bodily
aspects of man get spiritualised.

The physical Nature of Man

Thus, the picture of man that emerges in the philosophy of
Vivekananda is an organised unity of the physical and the spiritual. Vivekananda never undermines the importance of the
physical nature of man. The very fact that man is always asked
to awaken his spirituality presupposes that there is a side of
man that is somewhat different from and yet akin to his spiritual nature. That is his physical nature.

The physical nature of man includes the bodily, the biological
and the psychological aspects of man's nature. In fact, the body
itself represents the physical nature of man. At times, Vivekananda also refers to the subtle body and to some other bodily
centres that are talked about in Tantra Vidyā, but the physical
nature of man can be clearly apprehended even if the structure,
function and the importance of the gross Body are clearly
understood.

Vivekananda believes that even in his physical capacities man
is superior to other beings. Not that he possesses greater strength
than other animals, in strength and sheer brute force many
animals are more powerful than man, many animals possess
keener senses than man; even so, man is physically superior to
them all because his physical nature is better organised and
exhibits a greater unity. His responses to the environmental
factors are not just instinctive or mechanical, he is not merely a
body of reactions, even his physical behaviour generally follows
a plan and a pattern. His responses even to physical stimuli
exhibit a sense of purpose and choice. The presence of the

brain-system in the body distinguishes man from every other species and gives him a unique status in the world.

The Spiritual Nature of Man

This uniqueness of his physical nature is also due to the presence of spirituality in him. Although Vivekananda, at least initially, does not deny reality to the physical side of man, he is convinced that this represents only his inferior nature. His real nature consists in his capacity of going beyond his physical nature. Vivekananda describes the true nature of man as *Soul-Force* or *Ātman*. In his descriptions of the Ātman Vivekananda has freely used even exaggerated expressions. Following the *Gītā* he describes the Ātman thus, "It is the self, beyond all thought, one without birth or death, whom the sword cannot pierce or fire burn, whom air cannot dry or water melt, the beginningless and endless, the unmovable, the intagible, the omniscient, the omnipotent Being, that it is neither the body nor the mind, but beyond them all."[1] Such a description of the real nature of man brings to light at least two essential characters of the Ātman. Firstly, it is clear that, according to Vivekananda, this aspect of man is similar to Divine nature; and secondly, this also is fairly evident that it is not possible for us to give an exact description of this aspect of man — at least in a language that we as ordinary finite individuals are capable of using and understanding. Let us try to explain these two characters more clearly.

Like a true Vedantist, Vivekananda never hesitates in identifying the true nature of Ātman with Brahman itself. His reasons for identifying the two are generally similar to the reasons given by Vedānta. The basic fact to be noted is that unless the two are identified, the strict monistic character of reality cannot be maintained. Soul cannot be said to be an aspect or a part of the One, because in that case the One will become composite having parts or aspects within itself. Souls cannot be conceived also as expressions or manifestations of the Absolute, because even in that case they would become separate realities over and above the Brahman. Then, there is only

---

1. Swami Vivekananda, *Complete Works*, I., p. 141.

one way of conceiving the relation between the two, that the two are basically identical and that their difference is only apparent.

Vivekananda tries to explain the difference between soul's real nature and its apparent nature in various ways. He consistently maintains that apparent diversity in no way affects the true nature of man. The self or soul is one all-comprehending existenee, and it only appears as manifold. He tries to illustrate this idea with the help of various analogies. For example, Look at the waves of the sea, different waves appear to be different, but in reality they are all one, they are not different from the Ocean. Adopting the Vedantic analogy of 'Pratibimba' Vivekananda says that the same sun may shine in its reflections on water kept in different pots, but the different reflections are only apparent — 'reflections' of the sun, the real sun is always the one. "There is, therefore, but one Ātman, one self, eternally pure, eternally perfect, unchangeable, unchanged; it has never changed; and all these various changes in the universe are but appearances in that one self."[1]

Vivekananda admits that normally we do not have an awareness of this identity, but certain experiences and realisations can be taken as pointers towards this. The most usual example of such an experience is the feeling that one is capable of having in the face of adversities and problems — when he persistently tries to fight them out and to solve them. In fact, the very realisation that nature provides almost a challenge to man, and that man can unravel the mysteries of nature, is itself an evidence of his Divine Nature. Another evidence of this fact is the inherent capacity of man to go 'beyond'. If we survey the life of man either in its collective aspect, or in its individuality, we find that there is no upper limit — no boundaries that can be set around him and beyond which he cannot go. His quest for truth, for his activities, knows no bounds. He comes to acquire knowledge, or comes to enrich his personality by doing something good and noble, and yet he can still go ahead. This capability of self-transcendence is itself an evidence of the basic oneness of the Ātman and Brahman.

And yet, Vivekananda admits that it is not possible for us to comprehend the nature of this identity; that requires an extension of consciousness to its farthest possible limits and we can-

1. Swami Vivekananda, *Jnana Yoga*, p. 350.

not do that in the limited spheres in which we live. Our mental capacities, our consciousness through the mind-body mechanism and our embodied existence are inadequate to have a complete understanding of this aspect of man's nature. We have only casual glimpses of our powers — of our superhuman capacities. Our various spiritual pursuits are some of the ways in terms of which we can seek to understand this essential aspect of man's nature.

But, at this point we may raise a question, if the soul is identical with the Brahman, why do we have the experience of the plurality of soul ? If the identity is a fact, then monism is a fact, and a strict monistic system cannot have a place for many souls. This problem is related to many other problems — the problem regarding the plurality of souls, the problem regarding the relation between the two aspects of soul, the problem regarding the relation between mind and body.

In trying to solve this problem, Vivekananda leans on the Vedānta, but with a difference. His solutions are generally similar to the Vedantic solutions of the problem and yet he has given emphasis on some such points which have not been emphasised to that extent by the Vedānta.

Vivekananda unhesitatingly asserts that the apparent plurality of selves and the apparent experiences of births and deaths are only apparent. In reality the question of their being many selves or the question regarding births and deaths is a misleading question. The one Ātman neither comes nor goes, it is neither born, nor does it die, the question of its re-incarnation does not arise. Like the Vedantist, Vivekananda also believes that the Ātman is, in fact, never deluded. In the state of realisation the Ātman clearly becomes aware that plurality of selves is an illusion and that this illusion itself is a sporting play of the Ātman.

In spite of such a description of the Ātman, which appears to be exactly similar to that of Vedānta, Vivekananda asserts, unlike Vedānta, that the finite aspects of man should not be treated as completely false. So long as man ignorantly believes in the reality of the embodied state and in the plurality of selves, this aspect has a reality for him. Therefore, his upliftment would consist not in a complete annihilation of this aspect, but in its being raised and perfected. An ascetic who denounces and freely suppresses his material needs and demands may be a great man, but he also is great who is able to raise his bodily aspects to perfection.

Freedom and Karma

We have seen that the real nature of man is *freedom*. Freedom is not conceived as a character or a quality belonging to the soul, it constitutes the very essence of the soul. A quality or a character is something different from that to which it belongs, but freedom does not belong to the soul, the soul is freedom.

But then, Vivekananda also believes in the *Law of Karma*. He is of the opinion that our actions produce tendencies-karma, in accordance with which our future lives are determined. He, like the ancient Indian thinker, believes that man normally performs his actions out of ignorance. He somehow or other forgets his own true nature, fails to discriminate between the real and the unreal, and consequently performs his actions in the light of his wrong and false notions. Such actions create saṁskāras or tendencies which determine his future nature. Now, a doubt arises : how can Vivekananda maintain at the same time the determining character of karma and man's freedom ? If man's entire personality and actions are determined by his karma-tendencies, then man is *determined*; how can we say that freedom constitutes his real nature ?

Vivekananda is aware of this problem, and solves it in a number of ways. Firstly, he says that freedom does not mean absence of all kinds of determining factors, in that case freedom would be a state of chaos. Freedom, truly speaking, does not mean 'no-determination', it means SELF-DETERMINATION, which suggests that the free agent is determined not by anything else but by himself. If this is understood, freedom and karma no longer remain incompatible with each other. Man's karmas determine his nature, but they are MAN's karmas, his OWN actions create tendencies that bear fruits for the future. Secondly, karma does not contradict man's freedom also because final escape rests ultimately again on man's own actions. By his own good deeds man can win over his ignorance and suffering. That also shows that man is basically free. *Again*, Vivekananda solves this problem more or less in the Vedantic fashion by showing that the apparent incompatibility of karma and freedom is only apparent. The soul — the Ātman, in fact, always remains free — is never in bondage. The apparent state of karma — bondage, is really a delusion created by ignorance, it is merely a *Līlā* in which the soul has become involved. When he would finally win over this delusion he would be amused to find that he was, in fact, never in bondage.

Destiny of the Soul : Realisation of Immortality

Now, it is apparent that according to Vivekananda, freedom represents the essence of the soul, and as such, soul is not really in bondage. The impression that it is in bondage is only apparent. Now, this presents a difficulty, such a description of the soul is difficult to understand, because our awareness of the usual state of the soul creates the impression that soul is the suffering individual, limited in his capacities and action. In fact, such an awareness makes us thoughtful and forces us to think about the ultimate destiny of the soul. Vivekananda is aware that every thoughtful person is confronted with a question like this. But he is convinced that there is no contradiction between these two impressions — between our impression of the soul's limited capacities and the conviction that the soul is, in reality, never in bondage. These points are clarified in Vivekananda's deliberations on the nature of the soul's immortality — the realisation of which, in his opinion, is the ultimate human destiny.

Vivekananda admits that it is not possible to give an exact and scientific demonstration of the soul's immortality, but he also feels that this notion cannot be treated as an unscientific notion — if not for anything else, at least for the fact that this has played a very significant and important role in the history of religion and culture. It has always remained ethically and religiously very significant, and almost in every age and civilization persistent efforts have been made to try to find rational justifications for the doctrine of immortality. Thus, he feels that this notion cannot be brushed aside as a false notion or delusion, because a notion cannot keep on deluding generations after generations and civilizations after civilizations. Referring to the question about the nature of immortality, Vivekananda says, "often in the turmoil and struggle of our lives we seem to forget it, but suddenly some one dies — one, perhaps whom we loved, one near and dear to our hearts, is snatched away from us — and the struggle, the din and turmoil of the world around us cease for a moment and the soul asks the old question, "What after this ? "What becomes of the soul ?"[1]

1. Swami Vivekananda, *Jnana Yoga*, pp. 273-74

The literal meaning of the word 'Immortality' is both its minimum meaning and its most universal meaning. Literally, it means *deathlessness*, by calling the soul immortal, literally we would mean that death is not the 'end' of the soul — that the soul survives death. This negative meaning of the word 'Immortal, is least controversial and universally acceptable. Controversies start when we start giving positive specifications of this state.

Vivekananda also accepts this basic meaning of the word 'Immortal', and in trying to determine its positive characters leans heavily on the Vedānta and on his own realisations. Like the ancient Indian thinker, he also believes that the soul survives death, and that this survival assumes firstly the form of *Rebirth* and finally the realisation of immortality, of complete freedom. Thus, in Vivekananda's thought, rebirth is an aspect of immortality and the ultimate realisation of immortality would mean finally getting out not only of this world but also of the cycle of births and rebirths. Let us try to explain this.

Now, we find that there are two aspects of Immortality, survival and Immortality as such. Survival means merely that death is not the end of life. At this place Vivekananda takes help from his doctrines of ignorance and karma and incorporates them in his doctrine of the soul. The soul, he says, performs actions in ignorance, certain tendencies and saṁskāras are created in accordance with which the next birth is determined.

But, what would be the ultimate nature of immortality ? Is this continuous movement through births and rebirths the ultimate destiny of the soul ? This obviously cannot be so, because birth or the embodied state has been conceived by Vivekananda as a state of bondage. Therefore, the ultimate destiny of man must consist in freedom from this state, true immortality can be attained only when this 'cycle' is finally stopped. The ancient Indian Philosopher believes in this, and Vivekananda also believes in it.

But then, this would mean that immortality is a prize to be won, it is the goal which can be realised only by strenuous and persistent effort. Now, this assertion puts the student of Vivekananda's philosophy in a quandary. Vivekananda repeatedly asserts that the soul is immortal, that immortality represents his essence and constitutes his nature. How can we reconcile the two positions ? If the soul is immortal, what is the sense in saying that immortality is a prize to be won ?

Vivekananda feels that these two positions are not incompatible with each other — and that they can be maintained at the same time.. Firstly, it has to be accepted that without maintaining that the soul is immortal, we cannot maintain also that the soul CAN realise immortality. For the realisation of immortality the soul has to grow — evolve, but nothing which is not already there can even be evolved. This is a fact of experience, having the testimony of science also behind it. The seed, for example, grows into a tree only because the tree is already potentially contained in the seed. The child grows into an adult only because the child is potentially the adult. Thus, it can be said that the soul is able to realise immortality because the soul IS immortal. Immortality is latent in him, soul in ignorance is not aware of it, he has to be made aware, the latent element of Immortality has to be fully manifested. That would be the realization of Immortality. Vivekananda says that it is like finding the lost necklace on one's own neck. All the time he searches for it in all directions, and it is there with him. Secondly, the nature of evolutionary growth also is in favour of this. From the lowest protoplasm to the most perfect human being there is but one life. Immortality is also the consummation of the growth of man, and, therefore, we shall have to believe that it is the same basic being which expresses itself from the beginning to the end. Vivekananda says, "the whole of the manifestation of this one series, from the protoplasm upto the most perfect man, must be the very same thing as cosmic life. First it got involved and became finer, and out of that fine something; which was the cause, it has gone on evolving, manifesting itself, and becoming grosser...there is nothing new, there will be nothing new. The same series of manifestations are presenting themselves alternately like a wheel coming up and going down."[1]

Evidences in its Favour

Although Vivekananda is confident that Immortality is the utlimate truth about the soul, he offers certain evidences in its favour also. Immortality is not to be proved, it has to be discovered, but man's intellect, which at least initially suspects and

1. Swami Vivekananda, *Jnana Yoga*, p. 278.

doubts everything, has to be convinced by evidences placed
before it. They are not actually proofs, but they serve the
purpose of generating an initial conviction. Another thing to be
taken note of in this connection is that all these evidences serve
the modest purpose of demonstrating that death cannot be the
end of existence. They do not prove anything about the positive
nature of Immortality. They are evidences in favour of deathlessness.

One of the most popular evidences offered to support Immortality is the argument based on the simplicity of the soul. This
argument has been used by almost all the supporters of the
doctrine of Immortality — Ancient Indian Philosophers and Plato
alike. They say that the soul is immortal because it is simple.
Vivekananda also lays emphasis on this argument. He says that
what is liable to destruction is invariably something composite,
because destruction means breaking the whole into its parts. The
soul being simple is partless, and therefore, the question of its
destruction does not arise.

Another — a very certain evidence of the soul's immortality
comes from the analysis of the power and capacities latent in
man. Man's potentialities appear to be infinite. In the hours of
need and emergency man is able to do even the impossible. He
has the capacity of going beyond every task that he is faced with.
That is why the story of man's growth is a story of continuous
progression, a continuous onward march. If that is so, will it
not be bad logic to say that at a particular point suddenly the
soul's life comes to an end ? The fact of continuous and onward
growth and development constrains us to believe that the process
continues even after death.

Our yearning for mukti, the desire to win over death is also
taken as a sign of our immortality. Our desires do have an
object, it is true that some of our desires are not fulfilled, but
that does not mean either that these desires are fantastic or
that the objects of these desires are unreal. Genuine desires
have always something real as their objects. That shows that our
desire for immortality itself is an evidence of immortality. And,
no body can say that this desire is unreal, because we always
have a yearning to win over death, we always long for more of
life. Therefore, we have got to accept that there is an actual
object of this desire for immortality.

In fact, Vivekananda feels that it involves almost a contradiction to think of the soul's mortality. The soul is the embodiment of a forceful life, it is actually leading a powerful life. How can then it be involved in death which is the negation of life ? That is why, no individual can ever imagine his own mortality. If any body tries to think about his own perishment, he will find the thought queer, if not entirely absurd. Vivekananda says that "even to imagine my own annihilation I shall have to stand by and look on as a witness."[1] This inability on our part to imagine our own mortality is itself an evidence of the fact that we are after all immortal.

Nature of the Liberated

Vivekananda, more or less, in the manner of ancient Hindu Philosophy, says that it is only when man is able to pass beyond the cycle of births and rebirths that he is able to attain immortality. Births are guided by the *karma* performed by the self, by actions again the activity of body-producing karma can be stopped. Particular kinds of karma cause birth, a different kind of karma will stop this process. Now, two questions arise : (a) What would be that kind of action that would stop this cycle and enable the soul to attain immortality ? and (b) What happens after immortality is attained, that is to say, what is the nature or the status of the soul after it has attained immortality ? Let us consider the second question first.

Birth is the association of the soul with the body. This is bondage and this causes suffering, This association again is on account of ignorance, this ignorance being the ignorance of the real nature of man. Naturally, therefore, in the state of immortality all this would be transcended. It would be a final transcendence of the process of birth, and hence a freedom from body-bondage. Again, it would be a state in which suffering will finally come to an end, and again, it would be a state of knowledge and not of ignorance. Freedom from the chain of births, freedom from suffering, knowledge, realisation of the free character of the soul — these would be the aspects of the soul in the state of immortality. Over and above these, Vivekananda also says that this state would be a state of pure joy and bliss. It

1. Swami Vivekananda, *Complete Works* IV., p. 254.

does not merely provide a negative happiness of freedom from miseries, it is a state of positive joy.

We can say that in describing the nature of the liberated, Vivekananda is trying to incorporate in his account almost all description of the *mukta* that he comes across in the various systems of Indian Philosophy. But, his description is closer to that of Vedānta in so far as he makes 'joy' an essential aspect of immortality.

Vivekananda also speaks of the possibility of the realisation of immortality in the embodied state itself. The distinction between 'Jīvan-mukti' and 'Videha-mukti' is maintained even by him. His description of the jīvan-mukta is also, more or less, like the vedantic description of it. The jīvan-mukta, although in body, ceases to identify himself with the body. Consequently, his actions are no longer directed by the needs of the body and the senses. He acts in a dispassionate manner, he is no longer interested in having things for himself. Possession, acquisition etc. will not regulate his behaviour. He performs his activities and yet is not affected by them. In this way he continues in his embodied existence so long as the karmas determining the body are not completely exhausted. Then he attains the state of bodyless immortality.

At this point, a question may be asked : this question has become important in Contemporary Indian Philosophy on account of the fact that thinkers like Sri Aurobindo and Radhakrishnan have made this point prominent. They speak of the possibility of a Divine Life or Sarvamukti (Universal redemption) in which all souls would be liberated. Therefore, they say that attainment of individual immortality is not the *ultimate* human destiny, it is realisation of the redemption of all, and as such, every liberated individual has to work to expedite the process of universal redemption. These thinkers say that no one is really saved unless every one is saved. Now, the question is, Does Vivekananda believe in the possibility of universal redemption ? Does he suggest that every jīvan-mukta has to keep on working till every one is saved ?

Vivekananda does not appear to be very clear at this point. He does speak of the immense value of altruistic work, but, at times, one feels that even doing good to others and doing service to mankind are taken to be means for the individual's own realisation. But, at other times, he talks of universal deliverance and praises the ideal of Buddhistic Bodhisattva, thus indicating that there is the possibility of sarvamukti. But this much is certain that he never intends to make individual liberation a step towards sarvamukti. These two are not inconsistent with each other, but they are not necessarily two stages of the same process. It is possible for every one to attain immortality, but that does not mean that one's attaining immortality is a means towards the immortality of others. By my own efforts — knowledge and action, love and service — I may realise immortality. I may show the way to others also, but he can realise immortality only through his own efforts. Therefore, according to Vivekananda the ultimate destiny of an individual is the realisation of immortality. He may help others in their spiritual growth towards immortality, but that does not mean that his redemption would be final only when a universal redemption takes place.

Ways of Realisation

But, how can the soul realise immortality ? What is the process of this realisation ? This process can be described in one word, it is *yoga*. What is yoga ? This word normally is associated with two kinds of meanings. It may mean *union* or it may stand for a kind of a *discipline*. Vivekananda uses the term in a very comprehensive manner, and therefore, incorporates both these meanings in his sense of the word yoga. Thus, the path leading to the realisation is the path of *Discipline* and *Union*. It would consist of certain disciplines — such disciplines that would enable the pursuer to have the feeling of union. These disciplines might relate themselves to cognition, or to feeling or to action or to a synthesis of all the three. Vivekananda favours the last, but his synthesis, although comprehensive, is of a particular type. He does not say that there is only one kind of yoga incorporating all these in it, on the other hand, he says that all these — the way of cognition, the way of feeling, the way of karma — are themselves different ways for the realisation of immortality. They are not inconsistent with each other, they are NOT *rival* ways, they are complementary to each other. Vivekananda is so comprehensive in his outlook that he includes even 'yoga' in the popular sense (as meditation through postural adjustment) as one of the alternative ways. Before emphasising

their synthetic or complementary characters it is better to have
an idea of these ways.

i *The Way of Knowledge (Jñāna Yoga)*

The way of knowledge is based on the realisation that bondage
is due to ignorance. Ignorance, according to Vivekananda, is the
ignorance of the real nature of things, it is the inability to distinguish between the real and the unreal. This lack of discrimination is ignorance, and therefore, knowledge has to be discriminatory, it must have an awareness of the distinction between the
real and the unreal. Self-knowledge, knowledge of the Brahman,
knowledge of the unity of everything — all these are different
names of the discriminatory knowledge mentioned above.

Such a knowledge cannot be had merely through study or by
listening to the words of wise teacher. They are also necessary,
but they would not rise above the level of mere information,
unless one is able to realise what he has been able to gather
through study or through his teacher. For such a realisation, he
must be able to meditate upon the truths learnt. This requires
the practice of concentration on the nature of the truths learnt.

Concentration is not an easy process. It requires that the self
should direct his entire energy on the object of concentration.
The energy of the soul is wasted through its body-activities.
through the senses and the motor organs. Energy must be withdrawn from them so that it may be utilised for the purposes
of knowledge. That means that the senses and the body have to
be kept in control, sense-gratification must be stopped, body must
be kept under restraint, even the mind must be brought under
control. This practically amounts to the suppression of bodily
desires, it means that the demands of the senses have to be
curtailed almost ruthlessly.

This is, what can be called *Renunciation*. Vivekananda says
that renunciation is a necessary stage in the practice of Jñāna-
yoga. Renunciation demands getting rid of all selfishness and
controlling the body, the mind and the senses. This is called
vairāgya. But, according to Vivekananda, there is a positive side
of renunciation also, it is being impelled by nothing else but the
longing to know the Brahma. This positive aspiration for knowledge is an essential condition of Renunciation.

After this, concentration can be practised. The entire energy of the body can be concentrated in the direction of knowledge. In the initial stages of concentration one can choose any form — he may even try to understand the various Divine characters. In course of time this concentration will become intenser, and the individual may attain the stage of complete concentration or samādhi, in which all kinds of distractions would melt away, in which even the distinction between the self and the Brahman will not remain, and he will have a realisation of oneness, of perfect unity. This is the Jñāna-mārga.

ii *The Way of Devotion* (*Bhakti Mārga*)

This is the way of knowing God through intensity of feeling. Vivekananda says that strong emotions have the capacity to awaken and activate the potential powers of man. As such, it is possible to activate it so much that man is able to know God himself. Ordinary emotion can be converted into powerful feelings, ordinary love can be converted into Divine Love or Supreme Devotion, this is the Bhakti Mārga.

Devotion or love, according to Vivekananda, is natural to man. The only point is that ordinarily the object of our love is the finite object which is transitory, perishable and, in the last analysis, unreal. Love, in this sense, is not pure love but attachment. The Bhakti-mārga is the way of pure love in which the object of love or devotion is not the finite or the limited, but the Supreme. This love will be universal love, love for all, because this will be based on the realisation of oneness of everything. He says that it is possible to realise God simply by 'loving' we may go on extending the scope of our love, so as to make it more and more comprehensive till it becomes truly universal.

Vivekananda is able to determine the steps through which the Bhakti-yoga progresses towards the realisation of the Supreme. The first stage is the stage of external worship. The ordinary man is not able to concentrate on the subtler expressions of God, and hence he begins his worship in a gross manner. In this stage, idols and images, representations of Gods and Goddesses, incarnations — even prophets and God-men — are all objects of devotion and worship. Idol-worship is the most popular form of external worship. Then, in the next stage, prayer and repetition of God's name, chanting of religious hymns and singing the songs of God's glory would become prominent. In the third stage, this kind of prayer is transcended, and in its place a sort of a silent meditation starts. Vivekananda says that in this stage there exists for the devotee nothing but God. Then, in the final stage even this distinction vanishes, the devotee becomes almost one with the Supreme. This is a kind of inner realisation — a vision of the omnipresent God. It is a feeling that there is nothing besides Him. Thus, external worship, prayer, repeating of God's name, meditation are all stages of Bhakti, through which the devotee attains a realisation in feeling of the essential oneness of everything.

Vivekananda says that this mārga is the most convenient and the most popular of all the ways. It is natural to man, and it does not require any special aptitude or capacity or resources which other ways require. That is why this appears to be the easiest also.

iii *The Way of Action (Karma Mārga)*

Vivekananda says, "Karma-yoga ... is a system of ethics and religion intended to attain freedom through unselfishness and by good works. The Karma-yogi need not believe in any doctrine whatsoever. He may not ask what his soul is, nor think of any metaphysical speculation. He has got his own special aim of realising selflessness, and he has to work it out himself."[1] Such a description of karma-yoga shows that it emphasises firstly the importance and value of action, and secondly of unselfishness.

The first emphasis shows that it does not recommend asceticism or a flying away from the world. Man has to remain in the world, in the midst of evil and good, and pain and suffering. And he has to work, — has to keep on working as well as he can.

The second emphasis is still more important. The Karma-yogi has to work for unselfishness, which means that his work has to be non-attached. He has to work as if he is a stranger to the world, he must not allow any work to dominate over him or to bind him. Vivekananda says that one must work like a

---

1. Swami Vivekananda, *Karma Yoga*, pp. 131-32.

master and not like a slave. If one allows personal or selfish considerations to regulate his actions then he has become a slave of his desires. One must be unattached. Vivekananda seems to be very much impressed by the *Gītā*-ideal of Niṣkāma-karma The secret of action is that one must not expect any-thing in return of the action done. One must assume the per-manent role of a giver, in which everything given is a free offering to the world.

Vivekananda very reverently takes the example of the life of Lord Buddha, who, after attaining Nirvāṇa, kept on working throughout his life. His works can be taken as the ideal of non-attachment. He did not fly away from the world, he remained in the midst of men, kept on working for the good of men and expected no return. Vivekananda says, "He works best who works without any motive, neither for money, nor for fame, nor for anything else; and when a man can do that, he will be a Buddha, and out of him will come the power to work in such a manner as will transform the world. This man represents the very highest ideal of Karma-yoga."[1]

Now, a question arises: how can this lead to the realisation of immortality ? Vivekananda answers this question in a very simple manner. Immortality is the realisation of oneness of every thing, it is complete freedom from all kinds of bondage. A continuous doing of selfless work, or constant practice of non-attachment in all actions of life enables a man to rise above his self, and to have a feeling of oneness with everything. Moreover, bondage is bondage of self — of personal motives and desires. Unattached action is evidently a transcendence of this kind of bondage. Thus, through selfless work one's mind becomes pure and he is able to identify himself with all. This is the realisa-tion of Immortality.

iv *The Way of Psychology* (*Rāja Yoga*)

Rāja-yoga is the way to the realisation of immortality by con-trolling the mind and the body. This control is not like the control recommended by the Jñāna-yogī, it is controlling the mind and the body by subjecting them to certain physical and mental disciplines. Patañjali laid the foundation of such a yoga in his

1. *Ibid.*, pp. 142-43.

Yoga-sūtra, and according to some, it is the surest — the most direct and the quickest method for attaining salvation. That is why they call it *Rāja-yoga,* the king of all yogas. By definition, its aim is the realisation of unity with God. It is believed that this mārga consists in a ruthless suppression of all hindrances that create difficulties in the way of realisation.

Rāja-yoga is the way of physical and mental discipline. It is based on the pre-supposition that bondage is due to the distracting activities of the body and the mind. They waste the energy of the soul and dominate over it. Therefore, they must be brought under control so that the energy wasted by them may be saved and directed towards the Supreme. But, to control the body and the mind, a direct and forceful method has to be adopted. That is why in Rāja-yoga a plan of physical and mental disciplines has to be worked out. That would involve certain *yogic exercises* of the psycho-physical nature. Even here the final stage is that of concentration, but the conviction is that perfect concentration cannot be practised unless the psycho-physical organism is put completely at ease and under complete control of the individual.

Vivekananda is aware that this method is not for the weak, as it requires an immense faith in oneself and also physical and mental strength. It gradually enables the yogī to acquire certain excellences and powers, and finally the yogī is able to practise complete concentration leading to the realisation of unity with the Divine.

A Final Note on the Four Kinds of Yoga

Although Vivekananda describes these four ways differently, he says that they are different ways for the realisation of the same goal. These four different ways are recommended in view of the fact that men differ in their temperaments, dispositions and capacities. It is quite possible that a particular person is incapable of following the Jñāna-mārga, and finds the way of Devotion convenient and to his liking. Therefore, Vivekananda feels that one can choose the path he likes. If one follows any one of these paths with sincerity and earnestness, he will be able to reach the goal.

Moreover, these paths are not completely exclusive of each other, in fact, in certain respects they overlap. It is not that the man of 'Devotion has nothing to do with the way of knowledge, he also performs certain acts of self-sacrifice. These ways, therefore, are not divided in water-tight compartments. Vivekananda gives perfect liberty to the individual for choosing and pursuing the course that he likes best. The only thing is that there must be a very strong and intense sincerity and a sense of purpose. Vivekananda asserts that realisation requires a very radical regeneration of the individual; he must be transformed morally, religiously and spiritually. Therefore, whatever be the way, the entire energy of the soul has to be put into it.

Religion, its Nature

Religion as a necessary aspect of life

Vivekananda says, "of all the forces that have worked and are still working to mould the destiny of the human race, none certainly is more potent than that, the manifestation of which we call Religion."[1] He asserts that religion is a necessity of life. Ordinarily only those things are regarded as necessary for life which satisfy the daily and the outward needs of life. Food, clothing, shelter etc. are examples of, what can be called, physical or materialistic needs. But, they are not the only needs of life. This is clearly proved from the fact that they alone do not fully satisfy man, even in the midst of comfort and luxury man craves for something higher — something better. This craving is his religious craving, without seeking satisfaction for which he cannot live.

Vivekananda demonstrates in a number of ways how religion has to be regarded as a necessary aspect of life. Those who do not consider this as necessary do so because they identify religion with some of its expressions which appear to them as not necessary in any way. But, the fact that there is a longing of a higher kind — a longing for something that the physical environment cannot satisfy — shows that religion is a necessary aspect of life. Secondly, there appears to be an element of inevitability in religion, it cannot be given up. Trying to give up religion will itself become a religion. That also proves its necessity. Thirdly, the historical fact of the survival of religion itself is an evidence of its necessary character. Political or social organiza-

1. Swami Vivekananda, *Jnana Yoga*, p. 1.

tions remain prominent for some time, and then they pass out; but religions have continued to live through all circumstances — even adverse and hostile ones. Religion has never been vanquished. Whenever it appears that religion is being suppressed, it reappears in some form or the other. What can be a better demonstration than this of the fact that Religion is a necessary aspect of life.

Origin of Religion

Vivekananda is interested in the problem of the origin of religion not so much to find an exact solution of the problem as to determine the general nature of the origin, because that will have a bearing upon the nature of religion itself.

He feels that two theories regarding the origin of religion have gained acceptance among scholars. One is the Spirit-theory of religion, and the other believes that religion originates in the apprehension of the extra-ordinary or the super-natural. One party maintains that animism or some form of spirit-worship like ancestor-worship is the origin of religion, the other party maintains that religion originates in the awareness of the tremendous power of the forces of Nature. Thus, one party says that ancestor-worship is the beginning of religion, the other says that Nature-worship is the beginning.

Vivekananda says that if we compare the two views, we find that there is a common element in both of them, an element which is more fundamental than either of them, and which, in reality, expresses itself in them both. Vivekananda calls that element *"the struggle to transcend the limitations of the senses."* This is the reason behind both ancestor-worship and Nature-worship. Man remains active throughout his life, and suddenly he dies. The primitive man could offer no explanation for this phenomenon because his senses could not apprehend the realm beyond death. He wanted to have a glimpse of what remained there after the body was dissolved. Ancestor-worship was an expression of that wish. Likewise, Nature-worship was an attempt to understand the working behind the forces of Nature — a phenomenon that was not evident to the senses. Thus, it is clear that in both the cases an attempt had been made to go beyond the capacity of the senses. Vivekananda takes the specific examples of dreams and says that it is quite probable that the first glimpse of religion might have come through dreams. If mind can go on

working in the state of sleep, which also is apparently almost a
state of temporary death, there is no wrong in supposing that it
can go on working even when the body is dissolved for ever.
That, according to Vivekananda, might have suggested to man
the idea of the soul and its immortality. But, even here dreams
provide an occasion — a way — to man for going beyond the
limitations of the senses. Thus, we find that all the available explanations for the origin of religion, like animism, fetishism,
Nature-ism etc., somehow presuppose the basic fact — namely that
religion originates in man's attempt to go beyond the senses.
He experiences an uneasiness within when certain phenomena
appear to him as beyond his ordinary capacity of understanding. His religious activities are expressions of that feeling of
uneasiness. The primitive man used to live like any other
animal, his activities were confined to such activities only that
could satisfy his instinct, appetite and senses. But, when, unlike
other animals, he started transcending his sensuous existence,
religion was born. This appears to Vivekananda as the most
satisfactory, the most basic and the most comprehensive explanation of the origin of religion.

Nature of Religion

Vivekananda is aware that no description of religion can be
exact. The various difinitions that have been given are not
wrong, but they invariably miss one or the other aspect of religion. Therefore, the best way to appreciate the nature of
religion is not to try to define it but to highlight such aspects of
religion without which it would be difficult to call a religious act
religious.

At the very outset, two aspects of religion have to be distinguished : the inner and the external. The external is not superficial or entirely redundant, but it has a value in a particular way.
But, even this becomes truly religious when it gets the sanction
of the inner aspect of religion. Therefore, the essence of religion
can be discovered not so much in the external nature of religion
as in its inner aspects. Religion, according to Vivekananda, is
a growth from within, it is inherent in the very constitution of
man, and therefore, the nature of religion can be known by
analysing the religious sense.

Vivekananda describes this sense, more or less, in the manner
of a psychologist. He says, firstly, that this is universally

present — even the atheist has it — and secondly, that like all other mental aspects, it has all the three elements in it, the cognitive elements, the feeling elements and the conative elements. It is true that these elements are never present in equal proportion or degree, but the nature of religion is determined by the preponderance of this element or that. For example, where there is a preponderance of feeling, religion tends to be mystical or emotional, where emphasis is laid on knowledge, religion becomes intellectual and abstract, and where volitional elements become prominent, religion becomes practical and ritualistic. But, the true religious consciousness tries to harmonise all these aspects by organising them into a unity.

A very important characteristic of religion, according to Vivekananda, is that it invariably has a super-natural content. This element of super-naturality gives to it a uniqueness and distinguishes it from all other forms of intellectual discipline. What is the nature of the super-natural content? It may be anything — a personal God or the Absolute or a supernatural Law or anything of this kind. This element, however is, the object of religious aspiration and hence represents the core of religion.

It has been said that religion is an attempt to transcend the limitations of the senses. Vivekananda adds further that religion transcends not only the limitations of the senses, but also the power of reasoning or of pure intellectual deliberation. It is only when one goes beyond these that he comes face to face with such facts which senses could never have apprehended and intellect could never have reasoned out. That is why religion at times is described as trans-empirical and trans-rational.

This brings us to consider a very interesting fact regarding the nature of the contents of religion. Religious facts are not like concrete facts discovered by the sciences, they are, more or less, *abstractions*. "In all the highly organised religions they take the purest form of Unit abstractions, either in the form of an Abstracted Presence, as an Omnipresent Being, as an Abstract Personality called God, as a moral Law, or the form of an Abstract Essence underlying every existence."[1] Even in those religions where attempts are made to preach religion without referring to the super-sensuous abstractions, have been used and given different names like 'the Moral Law', 'the Ideal Unity'

---

1. Swami Vivekananda, *Jnana Yoga*, p. 8.

The Ideal of Humanity' and so on. All these concepts are abstractions, we nowhere come across the ideal humanity, but we are asked to believe in it, otherwise progress will become impossible. Therefore Vivekananda says, "Thus, this one fact stands out from all these different religions, that there is an ideal Unit Abstraction, which is put before us, either in the form of a Person or an impersonal Being, or a Law, or a Presence, or an Essence."[1]

It is true that, at times, Vivekananda clearly says that religion is awakening of spirituality in man, or that it is the realisation of Divinity. Both the expressions 'Divinity' and 'Spirituality' are used in very broad senses. The word 'Spirituality' comprehends everything that transcends the sensuous and the intellectual. Therefore, to say that religion is a spiritual pursuit is just to emphasise that it begins in an awareness of the inadequacy of sense and reason. Man finds himself unable to tackle many of the things he comes across, he fails to understand some of the 'mysteries' of Nature. This produces in him a consciousness of his own limitation and imperfection. In an attempt to supersede this sense he starts leaning on some super-natural element. This is religion. What is the nature of this supernatural element ? Vivekananda is broadminded enough to say that it can be anything — a God, or an impersonal principle, or the Absolute Reality, or the Destiny, or the Law, or anything of this sort.

There is yet another characteristic of religion that appears to Vivekananda as important. Religion does have a value and significance for the individual, but it has a social content also. Usually, a distinction is made between morality and religion by saying that morality serves social purpose and religion has a value that transcends even the social. Vivekananda feels that religion provides a secure foundation and an ultimate sanction to morality also. Without this sanction, ethics will ever remain blind and chaotic. Doing good is all right, but sooner or later we must come across the question, 'why should we do good?' There must be an ideal, and the ideal must be somehow universal, otherwise, again, there will not remain any ethics, as the ethics of one group will conflict with that of the other. Religion provides that universal ideal, and thus is able to justify ethics. Moreover,

1. *Ibid.*, p. 9.

a religious sense which somehow bases itself on an awareness of unity of everything makes ethical practice both convenient and easy.

Vivekananda feels that Religion has a value in a different way also. It is the greatest and the healthiest exercise that the human mind can do. This struggle to get beyond the limitations of the senses and reason, this pursuit of the Infinite itself is the purest pursuit that man can imagine. It brings satisfaction, it enables the individual to rise above the ordinary evils and ills of the world, and to enjoy peace and bliss. That is why religion appears to be the greatest motive force that moves the human mind. No other ideal can captivate human mind as religion does.

But, it is necessary to distinguish between the true religion and what may be called, institutional religions. In fact, objections against religion arise because people identify religion with institutions. Sects and institutions set unnecessary limits to religion. Vivekananda says that true religion must be above these separative and disruptive tendencies. *True love must be universal.* This, according to Vivekananda, represents the essence of true religion. He says, 'when we come to the real, spiritual, universal concept, then, and then alone, religion will become real and living, it will come into our very nature, live in our every movement, penetrate every pore of our society and be infinitely more a power of good than it has never been before."[1] But, before explaining this further let us first try to determine the contents of religion, because religion has to be universal in all its cotents.

According to Vivekananda there are three aspects or contents of religion : *Philosophy, Mythology and Ritual.* Every religion has these three contents. Philosophy seeks to represent the whole scope of that religion, 'setting forth its basic principles, the goal and the means for reaching it'. Mythology consists of legends relating to the moral and spiritual adventures of men and supermen. Vivekananda says that mythology *concretises* philosophy by making the imaginary lives of men and supermen the mode or vehicle for conveying the philosophical ideas. Ritual is made up of forms and ceremonies that serve the function of both keeping men engaged religiously and of organising them in powerful religious organizations.

It is true that every religion has its own philosophy, mythology and ritual, this also is true that conflicts of religions arise on

1. Swami Vivekananda, *Jnana Yoga*, p. 19.

account of the fact that different religions have different philosophy, mythology and ritual. The truly universal religion must rise above these petty differences, and must seek to have universality even with respect to these three basic contents of religion. But, can we have a really universal philosophy or a really universal mythology or a really universal ritual? Vivekananda has his own doubts. But then, how can religion be really universal?

Nature and ideal of Universal Religion

It is a historical fact that there have been various religious (or spiritual) organizations having different religious codes and beliefs. This also is a historical fact that they have been quarrelling against each other almost throughout history. Each religious sect has claimed its exclusive right to live on the ground that it considers its own doctrine and its own organization superior to any other. The peculiarity about this is that in spite of open and even bitter conflicts, most of the major religious sects have at least continued to live. These internal and external conflicts, instead of weakening these sects, have added vitality to them and have enabled them to expand and to live.

This fact appears to Vivekananda as significant. This shows that conflicts are only apparent, and that they do not affect the inner vitality or the core or the essence of religion. In fact, Vivekananda admits that sects and conflicts have to be there. If everybody thinks the same thought, there remains actually nothing to be thought. "It is the clash of thought, the differentiation of thought, that awakes thought...whirls and eddies occur only in a rushing, living stream. There are no whirlpools in stagnant, dead water"[1] Variation is the sign of life, it must be there.

But then, a question arises, 'how can all these varieties be true? how can opposite opinions be true at the same time?" On an answer to a question like this would depend the fate of a universal religion. A universal religion, if really universal, must satisfy at least two conditions; first, it must open its gates to every individual, it must admit that no body is born with this or that religion; whether he takes to one religion or the other must ultimately be left to his inner likes and choice. In this sense by individualising religion we really universalise it. Secondly, a really universal religion must be able to give satisfaction and

---

1. *Ibid.*, p. 379.

comfort to every religious sect.   After all, the universal religion
has to supersede the conflicts of these sects, and, therefore, must
appear satisfying and reasonable to them all.   We have seen that
variety is inevitable, that all these various minds and attitudes
have to be there.   Therefore, if there is going to be an ideal
religion — a really universal religion, it must be broad and large
enough to supply food to all these minds.

Does a religion of this kind exist ?   Or, is it possible to have
religion of this kind — a really universal religion ?   Vivekanada
believes that *such a religion is already there*.   We are lost so
much in the external conflicts of religion that we fail to notice
its presence.   Vivekananda demonstrates this in a very clear
manner.   He says, *firstly*, that a simple insight into the natures
of different religions will show that they are not actually contradictory to each other. They are, in fact, supplementary to each other.
The truth of religion is so comprehensive that different religions
concentrate only on one aspect or on a few aspects of religion. They
concentrate their energy on their chosen aspect in such a vehement
manner that they come to assume that there are no other aspects.
But, in reality, each religion takes up an aspect of religion and
develops it. Therefore, every religion is adding to the rich variety
that religion is capable of generating, and it is also adding to the
development of religion in its own way. Its interpretation may be
partial, but, as Vivekananda says, man never progresses from
error to truth, but from truth to truth, from lesser truth to higher
truth.   *Secondly*, Vivekananda wishes to make it clear that there
may be contradictory points of view of the same thing.   If we
take photograph of the same object from different angles, no two
photographs will be alike — they may even give opposite impressions; but they are photographs of the same object.   Likewise,
we view truth in our own ways, colour them from our own points
of view, understand and grasp them in our own peculiar ways of
understanding and grasping.   This, then, will make a difference
between man and man, and this explains the contradictory character of the different views.   But, all the same, they are basically
views of the same reality, and hence supplemenary to each other.

Thus, the Universal religion already exists.   Just as the universal brotherhood of man is there, although some men fail to notice
it, so universal religion is there although some of us are not
aware of it. But, what can be its nature ? Does it comprehend the
common elements of all religions ? Has it succeeded in discovering

some such aspects of religion that would give comfort to every one ? Vivekananda is aware that this is a difficult — almost an impossible task. Different religions emphasise different qualities of religion and, as such, it is not possible to find the common elements. Islam, for example, lays émphasis on *universal brother-hood*, Hinduism on *Spirituality*, Christianity on *self-purification for entering into the kingdom of God*. It is difficult to compare these and, therefore, the tenets of Universal religion would not be the common characters of different religions. Vivekananda is not dismayed by this because he recognises the natural necessity of variation. By universal religion he does not mean a religion that will have one universal philosophy, or one universal mythology or one universal ritual. They may all differ from sect to sect or even from individual to individual, and yet the universal religion is there.

The elements of universal religion would consist in recognising that there may be various and different ways of approach to the religious object. It gives perfect liberty to the individual in this regard. But at the same time, the spirit of universal religion demands that every approach must be large-hearted enough to have a respect for the other ones. The one *watch-word* for Universal religion, according to Vivekananda, is *acceptance*. Acceptance is not just tolerance. Tolerance is negative in its import, it implies, at least at times, that something is being allowed in spite of its being wrong. Vivekananda recommends positive acceptance. That is why he says that he can worship in any form with any individual or sect. He says that he can enter and offer his prayers anywhere, in a temple, or a church, or a mosque, or any other place. The believer in the universal religion has to be broad-minded and open-hearted, he would be prepared to learn from the scriptures of all religions, and keep his heart open for what may come in the future.

Such an attitude enables Vivekananda to discover at least one such element which can be said to be common to all religions in a general way, and which, consequently may represent the essence of universal religion. That common point is *God*. Even things that are apparently different, may be similar in a particular sense. Man and woman are different, but as human beings they are alike. As living beings, men, animals and plants are all one. In that way, although different religions talk of different aspects of the Truth, as aspects of the same Truth, they are all one. According to Vivekananda, that Truth is God. In Him we are all one. The word 'God' is being used in its most comprehensive sense, it may be the Personal Omnipotent and Good God, or it may be described as the Universal Existence or the Ultimate Unity of the universe. Every religion, consciously or unconsciously is struggling towards the realisation of this unity or God. Therefore, this may be said to represent the *Ideal* of Universal Religion.

Another characteristic of universal religion is that it has to be acceptable to all minds. It has to satisfy the largest possible proportion of mankind, and, therefore, it must be able to supply food to all the various types of mind. Therefore, Vivekananda says that the ideal religion must harmoniously balance all the aspects of religion namely, *philosophy, emotion, work,* and mysticism. "And this religion is attained by what we, in India, call Yoga — union. To the worker, it is union between men and the whole of humanity, to the mystic, between his lower and Higher Self, to the lover, union between himself and the God of Love, and to the philosopher, it is the union of all existence. This is what is meant by Yoga",[1] and, the aim of yoga is union, realisation of oneness. Vivekananda says, "Religion is realisation, not talk, nor doctrine, nor theories...it is being and becoming, not hearing or acknowledging; it is the whole soul becoming changed into what it believes."[2]

1. Swami Vivekananda, *Complete Works, III,* p. 419.
2. *Ibid.,* p. 432.

CHAPTER II

RABINDRANATH TAGORE

Introduction

A student of philosophy is invariably faced with a difficulty when he is trying to apprehend a thinker who is also a poet. The procedure that is followed in philosophy is that of gathering evidences first and then of making deductions from those evidences. A poet-philosopher is not interested in arguments and logic, he is a visionary, and therefore, communicates the truths that are revealed to him directly through his poetic images. But then, it is the business of the student of Philosophy to go beyond the poetic images deep into the poet's realisation in order to pick up the truths and to gather the evidences. There is the danger of error, but, "if you shut your door to all errors, truth will be shut out."[1] With care an insight has to be cultivated — an insight into the poet's mind, feelings and realisations.

The outward life of Rabindranath was not very eventful. Excepting the award of the Nobel Prize and the founding of the 'Shantiniketan', the external events of his life were, more or less, normal. But, this was an index of a very powerful and dynamic life being lived within. His *Reminiscences* themselves speak not so much about the external happenings of his life as about his urges and aspirations, feelings and realisations. Therefore, an attempt to determine the nature of his thought and beliefs is, in fact, to tell the story of his life.

General Philosophical Standpoint

In India, Philosophy is called '*Darśana*', which means 'vision' — 'vision of the real'. Rabindranath takes this meaning of the term 'philosophy' rather literally. That is why in his thought there is a very great emphasis on 'personal realisation'. In *Religion of Man* he says, 'I have already made the confession that my religion is a poet's religion. All that I feel about it is from vision and not from knowledge. Frankly, I acknowledge that

1. Rabindranath Tagore, *Stray Birds*, 130.

I cannot satisfactorily answer any question about evil or about what happens after death. Nevertheless, I am sure that there have come moments in my own experience when my soul has touched the Infinite and has become infinitely conscious of it through the illumintion of joy."[1] This creates another difficulty for the student of Philosophy. He is trained to read the thoughts of a thinker in terms of certain accepted epithets and concepts. But, it may not be possible for him to apply his traditional philosophical models to the 'personal realisation' of a seer of truth, and therefore, a logical interpretation of such a thought may not be very accurate. "The meaning of the living words that come out of the experiences of great hearts can never be exhausted by any one system of logical interpretation."[2] But, in spite of this difficulty, it is worthwhile to try to determine the ideas of Tagore's philosophy in terms of accepted and academic philosophical concepts.

The greatest influence that Tagore's thought bears upon itself is of ancient Indian thought — of the Upaniṣads and the Vedānta. His early education and the ways of his upbringing implanted in his mind the ancient Indian ideals. But that influence was not accepted by the poet in an abstract fashion. Naturally, therefore, he came under the influence of Vaiṣṇavism and the teachers of the Bhakti-mārga. The lyrical outbursts of the saints like Dādu, Ravidās, Nānak and Kabīr touched the poetic elements of the philosopher. Finally, the *Gītā* showed the way by reconciling the abstract and impersonal nature of the Upaniṣadic Brahman with the personal God of the bhakta. This enables the poet-philosopher to have a vision and come out with a firm faith in a God who is also the omnipresent reality — the Brahman. Apparently this may not appear to be self-consistent to a student of Philosophy, but in Tagore's philosophy the apparent inconsistency of the reality, conceived as both personal and impersonal, somehow evaporates.

In the light of this, it can be said that his philosophy is a peculiar and yet a religious synthesis of Abstract Monism and a particular type of Theism. Reality, according to him, is one. He identifies this reality with personal God. This identification of impersonal reality with personal God gives interesting results.

1. Rabindranath Tagore, *The Religion of Man*, p. 107.
2. Rabindranath Tagore, *Sadhana*, p, viii.

Now, all attempted descriptions of his thought assume a validity. Tagore can rightly be called 'an idealist' or 'a spiritualist' he can again be described both as a 'monist' and a 'theist'. That is why many commentators on Tagore say—and say so ·legitimately that Tagore's philosophy oscillates between *Śaṅkara's Vedānta* and *Vaiṣṇavism.*

Different people have tried to describe the general character of Tagore's Philosophy in different ways. Hirendranath Datta calls it the philosophy of *Concrete Monism.*[1] It is monism because reality is conceived as one, and it is concrete because the one reality is not an abstract principle negating completely the reality of the many, but is a concrete whole comprehending the many within its bosom. Radhakrishnan says, "we do not know whether it is Rabindranath's own heart or the heart of India that is beating here."[2] He says further, that his philosophy is the "ancient wisdom of India restated to meet the needs of modern times."[3] It is apparent from these statements also that Tagore's philosophy is an attempt to revive the ancient ideals of life; but then, they have been re-stated in accordance with the needs of the present times. The traditional philosophical notions of India have been brought out by Tagore from the dark abyss of abstractions, where they were lying all the time, into the open to be viewed in the light of the present philosophical beliefs. That is the reason why a philosopher like Radhakrishnan himself describes his philosophy thus, "He [Tagore] gives us a human God, dismisses with contempt the concept of world-illusion, praises action overmuch and promises fullness of life to the human soul."[4]

At times, Tagore is also described as a *mystic*. That is probably because Tagore does not formulate his beliefs on the strength of logical speculation, on the other hand, he comes to have them through his poetic insight, which is, more or less, the insight of a seer. In this way, Tagore's philosophy can be described in various ways, and what is interesting about it is that all these descriptions do throw some light on the general nature of his thought.

---

1. Hirendranath Datta, "Rabindranath as a Vedantist", *Visva Bharati Quarterly*, May/Oct 1941.
2. Radhakrishnan, *The Philosophy of Rabindranath*, p. vii.
3. *Ibid.*, p. 3.
4. *Ibid,*, p. 4.

Reality and God

It is safe to say at the very outset that by the terms 'reality'
and 'God'; Tagore does not mean two different entities. Here,
both these expressions are being used only as a precautionary
measure against a possible misunderstanding that may wrongly
be created. In metaphysical context, a distinction between 'God'
and 'reality' is maintained. For Tagore such a distinction is unnecessary. Although, at times, one gets the impression that Tagore
also is using the two expressions differently, but on a closer analysis it would appear that such impressions are created only because the poet cannot be philosophically precise in his writings.

There are descriptions in Tagore that create the impression
that Tagore's Absolute has been conceived almost in Śaṅkara's
manner. He asserts that everything is a manifestation of the
Absolute. In *Gītāñjali* he says, "Thou art the sky and thou art
the nest as well."[1] Again, there are passages in Tagore's writings that clearly indicate that his position is fundamentally
different from that of Śaṅkara. In fact, in his lecture on 'Universal Man', Tagore examines Śaṅkara's standpoint and distinguishes it from that of his own.

Perhaps it is on account of this that Tagore rarely uses the
word 'Absolute' for the Absolute. The expressions that have
been most frequently used are : *The Universal Man, The Supreme
Person, The Supreme Spirit, The Infinite Personality* etc. Such
expressions naturally refer to a *theistic God*. And yet, God has
also been described as formless and featureless. He is called
Satyam, ānandam, śivam and *sundaram*. He is conceived as the
only ONE as the only reality, as the basic postulate of everything. These descriptions are the descriptions of the vedantic
Brahman. Once again, we are constrained to believe that
Rabindranath somehow is both an abstract Monist and a Theist.
Let us try to amplify this idea still further.

On the basis of a comprehensive survey of Tagore's metaphysical beliefs it can be said that the final metaphysical position
of Tagore is that of a *theist*. Abstract Monism and also the
concept of a nirguṇa Brahman are sometimes openly ridiculed
by Tagore. That is why some critics of Tagore accuse him of
falling under the influence of Christianity and of neglecting the

1. Rabindranath Tagore, *Gitanjali*, 67.

Vedantic ideals. But such accusations are not well-founded. Tagore can never even imagine that he is in any way contradicting Vedānta, on the other hand, he is firmly of the opinion that the theistic emphasis is not so much on account of the influence of Christianity as on account of other influences. The influence of Christianity might have been there, but it is almost insignificant in comparison to the tremendous influence which philosophers like Rāmānuja and saints like Dādu and Kabīr had on his theistic convictions. All these influences, and above all his own realisation led him to think that there must be a Supreme Person guiding and controlling the universe. That is why he conceives God as a person. God, according to him, is not merely an abstract hunt-out of the metaphysician. [HE is the concrete ideal of man's life and aspirations.

Tagore has a very sound — a human reason for believing in a personal God. Man, he finds, cannot be interested in anything with which he cannot have an actual inter-communion. Man cannot take an active and living interest in the unapproachable Brahman because that is merely an abstract principle. He says, "Just as the physiology of our beloved is not our beloved, so this impersonal law is not our God."[1] Tagore thus feels that God has to be brought nearer to man. The declaration of 'that thou art' is not enough, the throb of the 'that' must be felt within. 'Man can take interest in the Absolute only when it is humanised.'[2] Like the Baul singers of Bengal who do not profess anything about the Brahman and sing in the glory of God, Tagore also calls his God 'The Man of his heart' — his 'Jivan-Devatā.'

The strongest evidence that Tagore has to offer for this is that God can be realised only in a powerful experience — in a forceful and positive concentration of our being, while the Absolute can be apprehended only negatively. Tagore's prophet is Zarathustra who is a picture of forceful and positive vision — "who emancipated religion from the exclusive narrowness of the tribal God, the God of the chosen people and offered it to the Universal Man."[3] The relationship between man and God can only

---

1. Rabindranath Tagore, *The Religion of Man*, p. 114.
2. P.T. Raju, Idealism of Rabindranath Tagore, *Visva Bharati Quarterly* Nov '39/Jan '40, p. 205.
3. Rabindranath Tagore, *The Religion of Man*, p. 80.

be a relationship of intense love — of an all-comprehensive and powerful feeling of oneness. Such a relationship is possible only if the 'lover' and the 'loved one' are conceived as *personal*. Our God then has to be God and man at the same time and "if this faith be blamed for being anthropomorphic, then man is to be blamed for being man."[1]

Tagore never hesitates in attributing personality to God. The Upaniṣadic descriptions of the Brahman have been taken note of, but *'personality'* remains the most important character of the Supreme Man. He says, "Reality is the expression of personality, like a poem, like a work of art."[2] That is why, in sorrow and in suffering, when 'existence becomes tasteless and unmeaning', when man feels acutely the need of consolation, love and strength — he looks towards the Supreme Person. His God is his last hope, and it is this hope that sustains his life and gives him strength. Therefore, the object of his love — his God — must be one with whom an emotional relationship — a relationship of hope and love and faith — is possible. Tagore feels very strongly about this kind of emotional bond between man and the totality. He says that man is not a mere stranger in the world, resting, so to say, in a wayside inn. Man, on the other hand, lives in a world which he takes to be his own, with which his life appears to be essentially bound. That is why he must have a faith in the reality of a God which would satisfy this emotional urge of man. Tagore says, "My world is given to a personal me by a *personal* Being."[3]

This personal Being has naturally been designated as the "Jīvan-Devatā". The Jīvan-Devatā at once reconciles the metaphysical demand with the emotional need, it is the meeting point of the Vedantic Absolute and the theistic God. Jīvan-Devatā has been conceived as the supreme principle of love and it is believed that in *love* all these distinctions somehow melt away. "In love at one of its pole you find the personal, at the other the impersonal. At one you have the positive assertion 'here I am', at the other the equally strong denial, 'I am not', without this ego what is love? And again only with this ego how can it be possible?"[4]

1. *Ibid.*, p. 130.
2. Rabindranath Tagore, *Personality*, p. 66.
3. *Ibid.*, p. 19.
4. Rabindranath Tagore, *Sadhana*, pp. 114-15.

In fact, a clear picture of Tagore's conception of Jīvan-Devatā would emerge only after having an idea of his philosophy of man because in his scheme God and man go together. Man is called the spark of the Divine and the Supreme is conceived as the ideal which man has to realise, This ideal, consequently, can not be an impersonal and indifferent Absolute. His presence has to be felt everywhere because He also is an actual participant in the drama that is perpetually going on.

And yet, the attribution of personality does not limit God. Tagore is not prepared to accept that Divine Personality can, in any way, be a limitation of God. Personality is a limitation only when it is a finite personality, a personality of wants and defects. But the Divine Personality is 'infinite' personality — not subject to finitude and limitations. Tagore feels that it is not proper to ascribe the characteristics of our finite personality to the Infinite.

Infinite Personality is conceived as comprehending the finite ones and yet being unaffected by the finiteness of the finite personalities. Rabindranath says, "there is a point where in the mystery of existence contradictions meet, where movement is not all movement and stillness is not all stillness, where the idea and the form, the within and without, are united, where infinite becomes finite without losing its infinity."[1] Such a notion may not appear to be self-consistent to a logically-oriented intellect, but Rabindranath feels that the realisation of the infinite Personality is superlogical. It transcends logic only because without finite intellect we cannot have a clear and complete picture of the Infinite.

This also, in an indirect way, shows that the question of the limitation of Infinite Personality cannot even arise. Its reality cannot be comprehended by the finite personality. Finite personalities are individual centres, whereas the Infinite Personality is the 'Universal Man', as Tagore calls it; and its element of Universality makes it rise above limitedness. Tagore says, "The world for me is both individual and universal. My world is mine, but it is also yours. It is not in my own individual personality that reality is contained, but in an infinite Personality."[2]

1. Rabindranath Tagore, *Personality*, p. 44.
2. *Ibid.*, p. 58.

Proofs for God's Existence

Tagore does not feel the necessity of offering regular proofs for the existence of this Supreme Person. He is not in favour of making God an object of too much intellectual and abstract argumentation. God is the postulate of existence, therefore, proofs are not necessary. His being, again, has to be realised — felt within. It cannot be an object of logical demonstration. Rational proofs will not be able to comprehend the Divine Unity. Therefore again, proofs are not necessary.

But, Tagore is also aware that in ordinary discourse — in day-to-day life — rational proofs and logical demonstrations do play a part. In the absence of personal realisation, proofs do generate some kind of an initial tendency towards belief. In awareness of this, Tagore, at times, does offer some arguments which may be treated as proofs. Some of them resemble the traditional proofs for God's existence, and some bear the mark of Tagore's own insight.

One of his most favourite proofs to which repeated references have been made is, what is traditionally known as the *Teleological Proof* or the *Argument from Design*. The poet is himself a lover of beauty and order, naturally an argument based on evidences of order and harmony appears to him as fascinating. In the *King of the Dark Chamber*, Janārdan says, "Look at the nice order and regularity prevailing all over the place — how do you explain it without a king?"[1] Another reference to this argument is made in the *Creative Unity*. He writes, "we feel that this world is a creation, that in its centre there is a living idea, which reveals itself in an eternal Symphony played on innumerable intruments, all keeping perfect tunes."[2] These references show that Tagore feels that the examples of order and harmony that we find in the universe constrain us to believe in a creator — a being capable of creating this ordered cosmos. The universe appears to Tagore as a symphony in which all notes are being played in harmony. This cannot be explained without postulating a 'Music-maker' behind it. A student of philosophy can easily notice that this is a particular version of the Teleological proof of God's existence.

1. Rabindranath Tagore, *The King of the Dark Chamber*, p. 9.
2. Rabindranath Tagore, *Creative Unity*, p. 35.

The same argument has been used elsewhere in a different way. Tagore feels that the world exhibits a wholeness and unity in spite of the apparent facts of contradictions. If we analyse apparently contradictory things, we would find that even there there is a unity. This appears to Tagore as very significant. For example, the banks of a river apparently provide boundaries to the river, and, in that sense, put a limitation to the sideward expansion of the river. But, a little reflection will show that a river is a river on account of its banks. It is the banks that give to the river an onward push and make it flow and live.[1] Likewise, in spite of the fact that we shut our eyelids every second, we get a continuous and unbroken picture of what our eyes perceive.[2] Such facts are not rare, they exhibit the truth that there is a unity behind even apparently contradictory facts. That shows that there is a principle of unity — a God-behind creation who is ultimately responsible for the unity evident in the creation.

Tagore suggests that it is on account of a wrong point of view that we get a distorted picture of the world and fail to realise that there is a being guiding and controlling everything. Almost like Spinoza he says that truth lies not in ordinary consciousness, not in the consciousness of fragments, but in the consciousness of the whole. In the strings of a violin there is a greater possibility of discordant notes being produced than of melodious music being played. Everybody can strike the strings and produce a sound, but only a few talented ones can play upon it. But does that mean that the violin is manufactured for producing discordant notes? This analogy shows that from the fragmentary point of view we fail to perceive the unifying hand of the Supreme Being behind all discords and disharmony. Those who cultivate the power to realise the whole, those who have been able to see the fragmentary nature of the fragmentary point-of-view and have been able to develop the power to look at things from the point-of-view of the totality will realise Him, the Unity-giver.

Rabindranath finds a different type of evidence for God's existence in the fact of joy inherent in every aspect of creation. Every individual has within him the capacity to feel this joy.

1. Rabindranath Tagore, *Sadhana*, p. 47.
2. *Ibid.* p. 50.

How can this be explained unless the creator is believed to be the living principle of joy himself ? This joy could have been explained differently if this joy had meant mere pleasure satisfying a particular individual in a particular point of time, but this joy appears to have a universal element in it transcending its particular expressions. Pure joy appears to Tagore as having no other explanation except the fact that it is Divine.[1] He gives examples of saints who have confirmed this to be a fact. He writes, "Dadu, Ravidas, Kabir and Nanak ... had glimpses of the world of unity ... they babble like babes of the joy of their vision of Him, of the ecstasy into which His music has thrown them."[2]

Again, God is presupposed as the object of love, hope and aspirations. Tagore feels that certain basic urges of ours require satisfaction and also explanation. These urges can have no other explanation than the explanation in terms of the Supreme. No body can deny that man, at times, specially on some crucial moments of his life, feels a dire need of some super-human solace and hope and strength. Religions evolved merely to satisfy that human need. This restlessness, this longing for the unknown is a fact. This becomes apparent, for example, when some near one is on his death-ded. Now, what can be the explanation for this longing? There must be an object of this longing, and our explanation would be inadequate if that object is just a finite or ordinary object, because the longing is for the extra-ordinary, the super-human. Why must this foolish heart recklessly launch its hope on the sea whose end it does not know?"[3] The question itself suggests the answer — this longing for the unknown is a fact and is due to the fact that the unknown, although unknown, is the reality behind the universe. Unless we believe in this we cannot explain this longing adequately.

Although the proofs mentioned above look like rational demonstrations of God's existence, Tagore is convinced that such

1. In *Fruit Gathering*, Tagore says, "I will meet one day the life within me, the joy that hides in my life, though the days perplex my path with their idle dust. I have known it in glimpses . . . I will meet one day the joy without me that dwells behind the screen of light . . . and will stand in the overflowing solitude where all things are seen as by their creator."

Fruit Gathering, XXI.
2. Rabindranath Tagore, *The Religion of Man*, p. 228.
3. Rabindranath Tagore, *Lover's Gift and Crossing*, "Crossing," 30,

proofs are not at all necessary. God, according to him, can only be realised. Glimpses into His nature can be had in any kind of spiritual experience — aesthetic, moral or religious. Being a poet he again and again refers to aesthetic experience — to artistic sensibility, to music — just to show how these experiences enable a man to realise Divinity for a few moments. That is why he prefers to describe God by using many artistic similies; for example, God has been called *'an artist-par-excellence, a lover, a singer with the universe as his song,* the *Music-maker,* and so on.

Creation

Tagore believes in the reality of creation, and so, has given a definite view on the nature of creation. His account of creation is, more or less, theistic even though it has a humanistic significance also.

God is the ultimate reality, and as such, He is the basis of the universe. What, then, is the explanation of the Universe? Creation is, in a sense, the manifestation or the expression of the Absolute. This expression is almost necessary in the sense that there is no sense in conceiving a creation-less God — a God who just is, but does not create. God, according to Tagore, finds himself by creating.

The reason for Creation is *joy*. Using the Indian concept of 'Lila' Tagore says that creation is the 'līlā' of the creator. He creates in the fulness of joy — just to find himself in the play of joy. It is on account of this that the act of creation does not give rise to any kind of duality. It is in the nature of joy to create another only to absorb it finally in the consummation of joy. Creation, thus, is separate from the creator, and yet united with him. It is separate because it has been created, but it is still united because both the creator and the created are aspects of the joy of creation. Rabindranath says, "This joy whose other name is love, must by its very nature, have duality for its realisation. When the singer has his inspiration, he makes himself into two, he has within him his other self as the hearer and the outside audience is merely an extension of this other self of his. The lover seeks his own other self in his beloved. It is joy that creates this separation in order to realise, through obstacles, the union."[1]

1. Rabindranath Tagore, *Sadhana*, p. 104.

Now, it can be said that there is a sense in which creation is
necessary. It is necessary in spite of the fact that creation is a
free act of the creator. Joy, for its fulfilment and play needs creation. These two elements appear as inconsistent with each other,
how can a 'free' act be 'necessary' at the same time ? Tagore is
aware of this difficulty and therefore tries to escape from it in a
number of ways. He would say that creation is necessary
because it is the expression of joy. He says, "Our Master himself
has joyfully taken upon him the bonds of creation, he is bound
with us for ever."[1] That he has wilfully taken up this 'bond'
shows that creation is a free act, but there has to be an expression of the joy inherent in the Brahman, in that sense creation
is necessary. The Infinite requires the finite for the fulfilment
of love. In another way also this apparent inconsistency is
sought to be removed. It is said that the One wanted to appreciate its unity in diversity, and there was creation. This shows
that creation is a free act. But that does not make creation
something different and separate from the Creator. "The Infinite and the finite are one as song and singing are one."[2]
That shows that creation is necessarily an aspect of the Brahman,
it is inseparable from Him. In that sense it is necessary.

Such a conception of creation raises another question of a
fundamental nature — Is creation real or is it merely an appearance ? Passages from Tagore can be quoted to show that the
world has been conceived as an illusion, more or less, in
Śaṅkara's way. But such passages occur generally in the ethical
context, they do not appear to have any metaphysical basis.
Most often these passages occur when Tagore is found recommending a withdrawal from finitude and a consequent extension
of one's consciousness. From the metaphysical point of view
it is fairly clear that Tagore believes that creation, although a
manifestation or an appearance of the Absolute, is not false or
illusory. It is real just as appearance is real.

At this point it is better to make a mention of Tagore's
idealistic conviction. According to him, "what we call nature is
not a philosophical abstraction, not cosmos, but what is revealed to man as nature."[3] In *Personality* he says, "It is almost a

1. Rabindranath Tagore, *Gitanjali*, 11.
2. Rabindranath Tagore, *Personality*, pp. 56-57.
3. Rabindranath Tagore, *The Religion of Man*, pp. 114-15.

truism to say that the world is what we perceive it to be. We imagine that our mind is a mirror, that it is more or less accurately reflecting what is happening outside us."[1] He illustrates this with the help of various examples. If we change the focus of our mind, the forest might appear as running, the waterfall as standing still and even the painful as pleasurable. Science does not appreciate this because the scientific standards are impersonal. "She [Science] tries to do away altogether with the central personality in relation to which the world is a world."[2] But at this point, a doubt may be raised. The idealistic assertion may imply that whatever is perceived is merely an appearance. Tagore will accept this, but he will not be prepared to accept that the world becomes unreal on that account. The appearance is of the reality, the One appears as creation and therefore, even the appearance is real. Tagore says, "When you deprive truth of its appearance it loses the best part of reality."[3]

Doctrine of Māyā

Tagore has introduced the concept of *Māyā* also in his philosophy of God and the world. Although the concept has been taken from the Vedānta, it has been conceived in the light of Tagore's conception of the nature of creation. Māyā, more or less, in the Vedantic fashion, has been conceived as the principle that brings about the appearance of Creation. Māyā, according to Tagore, is ignorance on a universal scale, it is the 'principle of the cosmic error.' 'It is the mist and not the sun.' Truth, according to Tagore, stands for unity, Māyā stands for separateness.

Tagore explains the nature of Māyā with the help of an analogy.[4] A savage gets some bank notes from somewhere. He does not know their value, and so they are completely useless for him. One who knows, one who considers the bank notes in relation to the bank, that is, considers them not in their separateness, perceives a value in them. Likewise, if the creation is viewed as the creation of the creator, there would appear a value in creation. But, if the forms of the universe are viewed independently and apart from Him whose forms they are, then

1. Rabindranath Tagore, *Personality*, p. 47.
2. Rabindranath Tagore, *Personality*, p. 50.
3. *Ibid.*, p. 51.
4. Rabindranath Tagore, *Sadhana*, p. 80.

we would get a false picture of the universe, and then, the universe will not appear to have any significant value for us. This is Māyā — the tendency to see from the wrong point of view.

This Māyā is not really a separate entity. It does not exist by itself, nor does it limit God's infinity. Tagore explains this point with the help of an analogy of the Chess-player. The Chess-player puts upon himself certain restrictions with regard to the moving of the chess-counters. "It is not that he cannot move the chess-man just as he pleases, but if he does so then there can be no play."[1] Likewise, if God assumes his omnipotence and starts doing everything in an arbitrary or whimsical manner, then there would be no play — no game of joy. He, therefore, must willingly set limits to his will and power. This *self-imposed* limitation *of God is Māyā* . "It is like a father settling upon his son some allowance within the limits of which he is free to do what he likes."[2]

This shows that the principle of Māyā is not altogether an illusory principle or a delusion. Tagore gives to this principle a reality of its own. It is, in a sense, a power of God. Only this has to be remembered that its reality is like the reality of error. It has a reality, but it has to be superseded. "Error, by its nature, cannot be stationary, it cannot remain with truth, like a tramp it must quit its lodging as soon as it fails to pay its score to the full."[3]

P. T. Raju has explained this point, and in that connection, has clarified the nature of Māyā itself as it has been conceived by Tagore. He says that Māyā has been conceived by Tagore not exactly in the way of Śaṅkara. According to Śaṅkara, Māyā *neither 'is' nor 'is not'* for Tagore it is *both 'is' and 'is not'*. It has being because finitude which is produced by Māyā, is a matter of experience, it has non-being because when infinity is realised it vanishes. Māyā also gives knowledge, but that is not final knowledge, it requires a going beyond Māyā to attain the final realisation. Tagore says, "The mystery is like the darkness of night, it is great. Delusions of knowledge is like the fog of the morning."[4] The darkness of the fog cannot be as profound as the darkness of

1. Rabindranath Tagore, *Sadhana*, p. 86.
2. *Ibid.*
3. *Ibid.* p. 48.
4. Rabindranath Tagore, *Stray Birds*, xiv

the night. That is why Māyā is called the mist and not the sun. The sun, here, is the sun of ultimate knowledge which can remove the darkness of the night of ignorance by piercing through the mysteries of creation.

Degrees of Reality

Talking about the mysteries of creation, we come to consider the problem of, what is called, 'the degrees of reality'. Scholars seem to be in agreement in saying that Tagore believes in it in a general way. The Supreme has been conceived as the unity of the manifold. The most frequently used analogy for this is that of Music. Music comprehends diverse notes, it is an organised symphony — a unity of these distinct notes, and yet, each note in itself cannot be called music. Likewise, God is everything, but everything is not God. 'God has many strings in his Sitar, some are made of iron, others of copper and yet others are made of gold.'

Thus, we see that Tagore does believe in the fact of 'gradation'. He believes that some aspects of the world are superior and some inferior. On many occasions, for example, Tagore talks about the superiority of man over other aspects of creation. The worm is superior to the clod, the animal is superior to the worm, and man is superior to them all. Man has been, at times, described as the *golden* string of God's Sitār. It is on account of his superiority that man resembles his creator in many respects and is able to organise his affairs consciously.

But one thing has to be borne in mind. The question of the degrees of reality would be relevant to the realm of creation only and not to the realm of the Supreme. The Supreme is one and therefore, the question of something being less or more in it would not arise. It is in the realm of creation that something appears to be more akin to the reality proper and something as less similar to it. Thus, it is in this realm that we can talk of any kind of gradation or of something being more real than something else.

Nature of Man

Tagore conceives man in such a manner that without affecting the Godness of God, he gives to man also a special dignity and uniqueness. Tagore is often described as primarily a philosopher of humanity perhaps on account of the fact that in his philosophy man has been given a very key status. Metaphysically speaking, he is in many respects God-like, and yet he is very much a creature of this world.

Tagore traces the history of evolution of life and shows that with the advent of man evolution itself strikes a different note. Before man appeared on earth, evolution proceeded, more or less, in a mechanical manner. The physical forces, the mechanical laws of *aggregation, adjustment, co-ordination* and *heredity* controlled completely the course of evolution. Almost mechanically the species went on entering into the realm of competition and were selected or rejected according as they succeeded in adjusting themselves to the demands of the environment.

But, with the advent of man there appears a significant change in the nature of the evolutionary process. The responses of every other product of evolution are determined by the environmental factors and the physical forces, their patterns of response and behaviour can be rigidly determined and forestalled. But, man is not a tool in the hand of the physical forces. It is with the appearance of man that this rigidity — this pattern of behaviour changes. Man somehow has the capacity to play a part in evolution, he has the power to change the pattern of his behaviour and responses. His responses are not automatic, they cannot be pre-determined.

It does not mean that Nature and physical forces do not have any determining influence on man. Tagore does not say this. He also accepts that many of the human mechanisms like the eyes or the ears have developed in accordance with the laws of evolution, but there is a difference. Eyes and ears, for example, work mechanically, but they determine the man only in the sense in which a trigger determines explosion or the crystal determines the rainbow colours. That is to say, they are also, in a sense, control ed by man's own inner power and decisions. In man they cannot function as mechanically or instinctively as they do in the case of other animals.

Tagore tries to analyse the nature of this change that characterises the evolution of man and comes to find that this change is from determinism to freedom and from the physical to the inner. Evolution changes its course and nature in the evolution of man because at this stage it partially goes beyond the mechanical and the physical level and enters into a 'spiritual' level — in which this new species of evolution assumes a basic inner

freedom. This change, therefore, is because of a peculiarity with
which man appears on the earth — the *surplus* in him, which is
the capacity of going beyond himself. This surplus enables him
to transcend his limitations from which other animals can never
free themselves. Tagore says, "the most imortant fact that has
come into prominence along with the change of direction in
our evolution is the possession of a spirit which has its enor-
mous capital with a surplus far in excess of the requirements
of the biological animal in man."[1] "As an animal he is still
dependent on nature, as a man he is a sovereign who builds his
world and rules it."[2]

The account of the origin of man brings to light at least
two important factors regarding the nature of man, firstly, man,
continues to have that biological and physical nature whioh he
has received from evolution, and secondly, he has within him a
spiritual nature which makes him unique and gives to him some
amount of freedom. The first can be called the biological or
physical aspect of man, and the other can be designated as the
'Surplus' in man or as the Infinite aspect of man. Man then is
finite-Infinite.

i *The Finite-Infinite Nature of Man*

Tagore says that an insight into the nature of man clearly reveals the fact that there are two essential aspects of his nature, a
lower one and a higher one. Even self-analysis can testify to this
fact. The most usual way of describing this is to say that man
is finite-infinite. He combines in himself the physical nature with
the spiritual nature. "He is earth's child but heaven's heir."
Tagore describes this very clearly when he says, "At one pole of
my being I am one with the stocks and stones. There I have to
acknowledge the rule of universal law. That is where the foundation of my existence lies....But at the other pole of my being
I am separate from ali. There I have broken through the cor-
don of equality and stand alone as an individual."[3]

Thus, we can safely say that there are two aspects of the self —
the physical and *the spiritual*. The physical is deteminable in terms
of biological, physiological and psychological facts, the spiritual is

1. Rabindranath Tagore, *The Religion of Man*, p. 43.
2. *Ibid.*, p. 44.
3. Rabindranath Tagore, *Sadhana*, p. 69.

expressed in longings and aspirations that are not rooted in these considerations — that are aspirations of a higher kind. Positivists, Scientists and persons with an exclusively empirical bent of mind emphasise the first aspect of man suggesting that man is not a mysterious creature — that he can be known in scientific terms. Their reason for saying so is the consideration that the physical is accessible to them, whereas the spiritual does not appear to be scientifically determinable. Then, there are certain cynics and ascetics who believe that the finite aspects of man are unreal and hence are like fetters around the true nature of man — his spiritual aspect.

Tagore feels that both these points of view are one-sided and narrow and, therefore, defective. The empirically oriented thinkers who reject the spirituality of man by calling it imaginary or fantastic are blind to truth. They do not realise that there are many aspects of reality that are not open to scientific insight. There are things that the scientific insight does come across but is not able to explain. For example, scientific or physical explanations cannot explain as to why we should be thrilled by a work of art, by a sweet music. They cannot determine the reasons for love and compassion. Similarly, there are many aspirations and urges of higher kind which are facts of our life but which transcend the capacities of our usual ways of explanation. Therefore, it is not proper to deny the reality of the higher self.

Likewise, Tagore is critical of those thinkers also who deny the reality of the finite self. The finite self represents the self which lives and moves in the world; how can it be illusory ? Moreover, Tagore says that a rejection of the finite self will naturally mean a rejection of the Infinite self also, because it is in and through the finite that the Infinite is sought to be realised. If the finite self is rejected, self would become contentless, and hence there would not remain any basis even for the Infinite self.

There is another essential characteristic of man which Tagore seeks to emphasise by calling him finite-infinite. The finite-infinite man is, in fact, the *individual-universal* man. Every individual has his own individual peculiarities on account of which he is different from other individuals. These constitute his individual characters. But he also has a nature which he shares with all and on account of which he has a feeling of kinship with every other individual. This is the *Universal* in him. His individual peculiarities are the aspects of his finite self and his universal

nature is the infinite aspect of his personality, This also shows
that man is finite-infinite. In order to have a clear idea of this
it would be better to determine the nature of these two aspects
separately.

ii The Finite Aspect of Man

It is now clear that by finite aspect of man's nature Tagore
means that aspect of man which can be explained in terms of
natural and environmental factors. In other words, it can be
said that the psychological individual is the finite man.

In order to give an idea of the nature of the finite man Tagore
lays emphasis on *three* aspects of man's finite nature. *Firstly*,
he says that in his finite existence man shares some of the qualities and characteristics of the animal world. He is also determined, to some extent, by the stimuli coming from the environment. He has some instinctive and mechanical ways of action
and behaviour. Like other animals, he is also conscious of
his self, and many of his actions are guided by the motives of self-
satisfaction or self-preservation. Like animals he also quarrels
with others for the satisfaction of his needs and desires. These
dispositions and activities are expressions of the finite aspect of
his nature. *Secondly*, even in his finite existence man possesses
certain characters that distinguish him from other living beings.
For example, all his senses are keenly developed and are under
the control of the self. He can withdraw them, place them at
any point and can train them to work in a particular manner.
Moreover, the possession of mind is a unique privilege of man.
On account of this his reactions to environmental factors become
very different from those of other aspects of nature. The animals, for example, have to accept and surrender to the forces
of Nature like rain, flood, fire, storm etc., man, on the other
hand, just by dint of his physical capacities, evolves methods for
meeting the challange of these forces. So, even in his finite nature
man is evidently superior to other aspects of existence. That is
why animals can be tamed by man. Tagore says, "The elephant's
trunk, the tiger's paws, the claws of the mole have combined
their best expressions in the human arm"[1] *Thirdly*, the finite
nature of man itself gives evidence of the spiritual potentialities
of man. An analysis of human desires shows that they are not

1. Rabindranath Tagore, *The Religion of Man*, pp. 40-41.

always ego-centric, they aim at the realisation of some social good. Some of the yearnings of the finite self — like aesthetic sensibility — indicate that the finite self also is constantly trying to excel itself. Moreover, the finite self, even if it wishes to maintain its aloofness and separateness, will not be able to do so. It will always be impelled towards others, it will always have a realisation of a bond or kinship in between others and itself.

Now, we are in a position to determine some of the prominent characters of the finite self — characters that control and regulate the finite existence of the self.

Firstly, it can be said that the considerations that guide the finite self are by and large the considerations of the embodied existence. Man spends his energy in trying to meet the demands and needs of the body. Food, clothing, shelter, means of comfort, and similar other considerations guide his life and activities.

That is why Tagore says that one of the foremost tendencies of the finite self is towards *acquisition*. The finite self derives immense satisfaction by 'possessing' or 'acquiring'. His love and struggles, his associations and conflicts are all guided by his desire for acquisition. That is why no amount of wealth or property or possession can quench his thirst. Just as he succeeds in procuring something for himself he develops a longing for more or for something else. In a sense this keeps man in bondage because acquisitions means having an attachment for the purely physical. But, in a different sense, this is also indicative of spirituality present in man, because even this extends the limits of one's own limited existence.

Another very prominent aspect of the finite existence of man is a very keenly developed ego-sense. This may assume various forms — that of self-assertion or of vanity or of pride, but one thing is fairly certain that such activities seek to satisfy man's ego. He may tend to be even unreasonable in order to satisfy his ego-sense, he may become even desperate and vindictive if his ego-sense is injured. A survey of the life of an individual can clearly show that all activities in the finite realm are ego-directed — desires, motives, other activities — all directly or indirectly spring from egoistic considerations.

That is why the finite self wishes to maintain his uniqueness at all cost. It gives a peculiar satisfaction to the individual to think that he is either superior or at least distinctly different from every other individual. Every man considers himself to be the wisest on earth, he will subject the actions of every other to his individual scrutiny and will judge them as right or wrong in that light. That the uniqueness or distinctiveness of the self is considered by the finite individual as his most precious possession is proved by the sufferings he undergoes or sins that he commits in order to preserve it.

The finite self, again, is an organisation of desires. Some of the desires are physical and bodily and some of them go beyond the individual; but the entire activities of the finite individual can be reduced to certain basic desires. One of the most normal desire is for bodily comforts — for the satisfaction of the needs of the body. Desires for food, drink, comfort etc. come under this head. Then, there is the general desire of the physical system as a whole. We are not always conscious of this because this does not refer to the satisfaction of any particular or immediate desire. It is desire for the body as a whole — for the preservation and maintenance of the body, the desire to maintain the general health of the bodily system. Then again, there may be a desire of a general or social nature — the desire to be socially prominent, the desire to be somehow loved and admired or the desire to be powerful in society. These, according to Tagore, are the different kinds of desire that go to constitute the finite self. It is for the fulfilment of these desires that the finite individual performs his activities.

Such a description of the finite self shows that the finite self is the natural or the ordinary man. Tagore emphasises the fact that this represents a real aspect of man. Although this aspect appears to be somewhat inferior — of a lower nature, it does not become false or unreal on that account. If the finite nature of man is not taken to be real then there would not be any basis for maintaining the reality even of the infinite self. In the finite self itself lies the root of the infinite self, it is the finite self that grows and develops into the Infinite.

iii *The Infinite Aspect of Man's Nature*

The infinite aspect of man's nature has been variously described by Rabindranath Tagore, it has been called the 'Universal' in man, the 'Surplus' in man, the element of Divinity present in man, and so on. Tagore is aware that it is difficult to determine precisely the nature of this aspect of man, but he refers to many kinds of experiences of life that bear witness to this fact. Whenever we have an evidence of this, whenever we feel impelled to

do something good and undertake suffering and sacrifice to do
it, we have a realisation of the element of Divinity present in us.
Tagore says, "We have seen men conquering pain by undaunted
prowess, plunging into fiery ordeals only to march forward with
triumph. What striving is this ? This power that lies behind
is neither physical nor mental, it belongs to the inward self where
man is united with his God."[1]

The most obvious character of the infinite aspect of man is that
it constantly impels the individual to go beyond. There is nothing
which can finally arrest his energy — there is no goal in life that does
not, at the same time, induces man to go ahead. There is, again,
no task which is completely impossible for man. He may attempt
and fail, but even failures prompt him to make renewed efforts.
This element of man has truly been called 'the surplus' in man.
This creates in him a feeling that he is destined to be something
higher, that he is not what he ordinarily appears to be.

It is again, on account of the infinite aspect of his nature that
man has a yearning for *mukti* or immortality. No other creature
can aspire for immortality, but man somehow has this feeling in
spite of his obvious experience of the phenomenon of death. He
somehow feels that death cannot be the end of life. Many of
his actions are based on this conviction. How is this so ? Tagore
raises this question and himself provides the answer. He says,
'What is it in man that asserts its immortality in spite of the obvious fact of death ? It is not his physical body or mental organization. It is that deeper unity, that ultimate mystery in him which,
from the centre of this world radiates towards the circumference,
which is in his mind, yet grows beyond his mind, which, through
the things belonging to him expresses something that is not in
them, which, while occupying his present overflows its banks of
the past and the future. It is the *personality* of man conscious
of its inexhaustible abundance, it has the paradox in it that it is
more than itself, it is more than as it is seen, as it is known, as
it is used. And this consciousness of the Infinite ever strives to
make its expressions immortal and to make the whole world its
own."[2]

It is again on account of the presence of this aspect of man that
man feels attracted towards nature. The physical man cannot
have any feeling of kinship with nature. But man is thrilled by

1. Rabindranath Tagore, *Personality*, p. 38.

the beauties of nature, overawed by the sublime powers of natural forces. He somehow feels that in spite of his experience of Nature apparently working against his plans and projects, Nature is not, after all, alien to him. This feeling, coupled with his resolute tendency to defy nature and to subdue it for its own purposes, can be an evidence of nothing else but of the presence of an element far beyond the finite.

This aspect of man's nature, according to Tagore is basically *creative*. The finite self responds to stimuli more or less in mechanical and pre-determined manner, and yet there is inherent in man a creative capacity which is an expression of the tendency to express oneself. By creativity Tagore does not mean the mere capacity to construct something new. Creativity is the capacity of having and giving expression to novel ideas, it is the power of having new and original visions. In that sense, man has an artist hidden in him. This aspect of man has also been described as the *artist* in man.

It is on account of his infinite nature that man's personality is *dynamic* and *ever-growing*. Growth is not a mechanical or repetitive process, it follows from the character of creativity; it means progress by carrying the past along with oneself and yet creating and adding something fresh and new at every stage. Had man been simply the body, his growth would have meant the physical development of his body. But, his personality does not grow merely in that manner, it incorporates an inner growth also which is an evidence of the fact that infinite aspect of man's nature is essentially active.

Another important characteristic of this aspect of man's nature is *freedom*. Man enjoys some amount of freedom even in the physical realm, but that, according to Tagore, is like the freedom inside a cage. The physical man is basically limited by the limitations of the physical body. The freedom that characterises the infinite nature of man is spiritual freedom, the freedom to break the shackles of the finite body and to aspire for the realisation of oneness or unity. Perfect freedom, according to Tagore, lies in a perfect harmony of relationship — in the realisation of the Universal within the individual.

But, the most basic and perhaps the most important character of this aspect of man is that all its expressions and activities are expressions of *Joy*. Joy, according to Tagore, is inherent in the soul and whatever is considered to be beyond the physical is

nothing but an expression of joy. Man's natural urge for realising the Truth, the Good and the Beautiful is an expression of
joy. It is on account of the element of 'joy' present in man,
that whenever he rises above the mere physical he is able to
forget the worries and anxieties of life. It is joy that makes him
realise his affinity with Nature, it is joy again that makes him
moral or religious or noble. Joy is both the condition of his
spiritual growth and also its ultimate goal. So far as man forgets his infinite nature and becomes a slave to the bodily aspect
of his life, his joy is reduced; and as he goes on asserting the
higher aspects of his life his joy goes on increasing. 'Joy' thus
constitutes the higher — the spiritual aspect of man's nature.

It is on account of this that Tagore calls this aspect of man's
nature as 'Jivan-Devatā'. It is the 'Lord of life' because it gives
'joy' of existence, because it stands for both the possibility and
realisation of all that which man is constantly trying to attain.
Jīvan Devatā is God in man, the element of Divinity present in
man, and as such, it is this element that makes him God-like.

iv *Soul and Body*

Roughly speaking, 'body' represents the finite side of man's
existence and 'soul' stands for the infinite aspect of man's nature.
Just as Tagore believes in ther eality of both these aspects, he
believes that both the soul and the body are real.

Tagore never suggests that the body is an illusory or false aspect of man's life. On the other hand, it has been conceived as
the temple of the Divine. But, as this analogy also suggests, a
distinction has to be made between 'the temple' and 'the Divine'.
We must not make the mistake of mistaking the temple for the
Divine. The temple may have a reality of its own, but in order
to realise the Divine attention has to be withdrawn from the
temple to the Divine.

So, Tagore says that although body has a reality of its own,
we must remember that it only represents the lower aspect of
man's nature which has to be transcended in order to attain the
higher nature — that of the soul.

The body, thus, can be viewed in two ways. If we give exclusive emphasis on the body, we are imprisoning the soul in the
body. The body in that sense may be compared with a 'jewelled
chain' which may be beautiful to look at, but which is a 'chain'

all the same'. But, if we view at the body as providing an occasion and a base for spiritual discipline, body becomes an aspect of the game of joy that man has to play. Tagore says, 'Heaven is fulfilled in your sweet body, my child, in your palpitating heart."[1] The whole point can be made clear with the help of an analogy that Tagore has made use of.[2] If we weigh a pitcher full of water we feel its weight, but the same pitcher does not appear to be heavy if we balance it in a river. What is the difference ? In the former case emphasis is laid on the *pitcher* full of water, in the latter case emphasis is on *water*, the pitcher now becomes insignificant and the water inside the pitcher becomes an aspect of the great reservoir of water all round. Likewise, if we lay emphasis on the body, the soul encompassed in the body is lost sight of. But if we view at the body as an aspect of the Infinite, even the body becomes a partner in the joyous game of the Spirit.

Nature of Religion

Rabindranath initially was a Brāhmo-samājī. Later on he developed a religion which combined some elements of Brāhmo Samāj with some elements of orthodox Hinduism. Finally, he came to believe in, what he called, 'the Religion of Man'.

Whatever be the influences or the determinants that shaped Tagore's views on religion, the fact remains that Tagore explicitly believes that religion cannot be confined to any group or sect or tribe or nation. Man picks up that particular form of religion that suits him, but in the final analysis religion transcends all such particular forms.

Ordinary religions, according to Tagore, are just aimless wanderings. The aim of true religion is the realisation of one's kinship with everything. Religion, according to him, is a sort of homesickness. Like a flock of homesick cranes flying night and day back to their mountain nests, the religious man is also on his sacred voyage to his eternal home. In the *Gītañjali* the poet bursts out in a religious fervour, "No more sailing from harbour to harbour with this my weather-beaten boat...now I am eager to die into the deathless."[3]

---

1. Rabindranath Tagore, *Lover's Gift and Crossing*, "Crossing" 49.
2. Rabindranath Tagore, *Sadhana*, p. 157.
3. Rabindranath Tagore, *Gitanjali*, 100.

That is why Tagore does not favour asceticism. Man has to
realise his kinship with everything, he has to cultivate a universal
feeling of love. How can this be possible if he runs away from
the world ? He says, 'Deliverance is not for me in renunciation. I
feel the embrace of freedom in a thousand bonds of delight...
No, I will never shut the doors of my senses. The delights of
sight and hearing and touch will bear thy delight."[1] In the
Gardener he is still more explicit when he says, "No my friends,
I shall never be an ascetic, whatever you may say .... no
friends, I shall never leave my hearth and home and retire into
the forest solitude...... if its silence is not deepened by soft
whispers. I shall never be an ascetic."[2]

Religion, thus, is not an escape; it is life and existence. But,
Tagore insists that true religion must not be confused with, what
is called, 'Institutional religion'. A particular person may be
a Hindu or a Christian — it is a matter of accident. In fact, the
forms and ways, in which these religions are practised, mislead
the believers. Tagore says, "It should be remembered that
religions or churches or religious organizations are not the same.
They are to one another as the fire is to the ashes. When the
religions have to make way for religious organization it is like
the river being dominated by sand beds, the current stagnates
and its aspect becomes desert-like."[3]

Tagore sincerely believes that religious organizations have
almost debauched religion. They take away from religion their
life-spirit and instead, emphasise only the superficialities of religions. True religion preaches freedom, whereas religious organizations make religions a slave of their own institutions. Ridiculing the attitude of the religious organizations of the Hindus,
Tagore says, "The same blindness which impedes them to rush
to bathe in a particular stream, renders them indifferent to the
sufferings of their unknown fellowmen. God does not appreciate
this prostitution of his most precious gift."[4]

Thus, the institutional religions, according to Tagore, are
dogmatic and false. What distinguishes the true religion from

1. Rabindranath Tagore, *Gitanjali* 77.
2. Rabindranath Tagore, *The Gardener* 43.
3. Rabindranath Tagore, *A letter, The Modern Review*, Sept. 1917,
p. 335.
4. *Ibid.*

the false ones ? The true religion must have the qualities of *Spontaneity* and *naturality* in it. There cannot be any compulsion about it, there are no fixed limits set around it. It is free and spontaneous in every individual. Tagore says, "In dogmatic religion all questions are definitely answered, all doubts are finally laid to rest. But the poet's religion is fluid, like the atmosphere around the earth where light and shadow play hide and seek...it never undertakes to lead anybody anywhere to any solid conclusion; yet it reveals endless spheres of light, because it has no walls around itself."[1]

From this it follows that religion expresses the essential element of all things. There is a sense in which even physical objects have a religion. "Dharma is the innermost nature, the essence, the implicit truth of all things", as for example, "only when the tree begins to take shape that you can come to see its dharma."[2] Tagore says, "In my language the word religion has a profound meaning. The wateriness of water is essentially its religion, in the spark of the flame lies the religion of fire. Likewise, man's religion is his innermost truth."[3]

What is the innermost truth of man ? Man's religion has been described as the spontaneous expression of the essential and inner aspect of man. What is the essential aspect of man ? Tagore says, "Man possesses an extra-awareness that is greater than his material sense — this is his manhood. It is this deep abiding creative force which is his religion."[4]

Now, this can be said that, according to Tagore, religion consists in man's capacity of self-transcendence. Man has a self-awareness, which reveals to him the fact that he has a capacity of going beyond himself — of constantly pushing himself ahead towards higher and higher regions. This is a distinct and essential peculiarity of man. Therefore, his religious life must consist in a constant exercise of this capacity. That is why Tagore clearly says, "If there is any philosophy of religion in my writings, it amounts to this : to realise the relationship of perfect love between the Supreme Soul and the souls of all created beings is indeed true religious sense — this love that holds duality

1. Rabindranath Tagore, *Creative Unity*, p. 16.
2. Rabindranath Tagore, *Sadhana*, p. 74.
3. Rabindranath Tagore, *An Article*, Indu Datta, tr. *Tagore Testament*, p. 37
4. *Ibid.*

on one side and non-duality on the other, union as well as separation and bondage along with freedom."[1]

The aim of Tagore's religion, therefore, is the realisation of onenesss of the individual soul with the Supreme Soul, and this realisation has to be a realisation in love and joy. Explaining this point, P.T. Raju says that just as wateriness is the religion of water, the Supreme Man is the religion of the finite man.[2] Another point to be taken note of in this connection is that the Supreme Self with whom union is sought to be established is not an abstract principle. He is the 'God of Humanity' the Supreme Personality. Thus, we find that the innermost essence of man is the presence of Divinity in him. Therefore, religion is nothing but an attempt to realise this Divinity.

That is why a religious life means a life of 'self-denial for self-realisation'. Tagore is never tired of using the analogy of 'the oil and the lamp'. So long as the lamp keeps its oil confined in its store, there is no light. The lamp sacrifices the store of its oil and thereby is able to realise its function, in fact, in that sacrifice lies the justification and the reality of the lamp. Likewise, religion demands a sacrifice of the narrow aspects of the individual self in order to gain its true aspect — its Divinity. Thus, "Religion consists in the endeavour of man to cultivate and express these qualities which are inherent in the nature of man, the eternal, and to have faith in them."[3] In such a religious life the human personality finds its worth and essence. The modern man has forgotten this, and, therefore. is miserable. If one loses sight of this, if one forgets the religious sense, his life loses the sense of direction and purpose. Tagore says, "Upon the loss of this sense of Universal Personality, which is religion, the reign of machine and of method has been firmly established and man, humanly speaking, has been made a homeless tramp."[4]

Now, it can be said that in Tagore's thought it is difficult to distinguish between religion and philosophy, they have the same end to realise. Philosophy is the 'vision of the real' and the aim of religion is to realise 'man's unity with the Divine.' Both mean one and the same thing. That is perhaps the reason why

1. *Ibid.*, p. 67.
2. P.T. Raju The Idealism of Rabindranath Tagore, *Visva Bharat Qly.* 1939-40, p. 213.
3. Rabindranath Tagore, *The Religion of Man*, p. 144.
4. Rabindranath Tagore, *Creative Unity*, p. 125.

Tagore calls his religion *the Religion of Man'*. It can very well be described as universal religion also, because it throws its gate open to every individual.

There is a danger inherent in the excessive use of the expressions like 'realisation of one's true nature', 'unity of the self with the Divine' etc., such descriptions tend to make religion abstract and un-practical. Tagore is conscious of that, therefore he recommends the rule of *love* in religion. The realisation of the Infinite cannot be brought about at once. One should begin with love and in love itself would lie the consummation of his efforts. Tagore feels that one should try to give up the narrow outlook of life that merely feeds his ego. The individual should extend his consciousness in love to nature and to men, and in this act of love itself he would come to the realisation of unity.

Love, sacrifice, sincerity, innocence — these constitute a religious life. Tagore is so impressed by the powers of 'innocent love' that he thinks that in the useless wisdom of institutional religions religion loses itself. Speaking analogically he says, "From the solemn gloom of the temple children run out to sit in the dust, God watches them play and forgets the priest."[1]

Human Destiny

The account of religion, as given by Tagore, itself suggests what, according to him, is the ultimate human destiny. It is the realisation of unity — the realisation of Divinity, it is comprehending, in an act of supreme love, nature and everything else, it is the realisation of the Universal within.

But, what is the nature of this realisation ? Does this realisation make man entirely different from what he has been so far ? Is the individual completely lost in the One ? Is this merely a negative state of painlessness ? Does this realisation give rise to a realisation of the illusoriness of the universe ? What, after all, is the nature of the state thus realised ? All these questions are very relevant specially because ancient Indian Philosophy has given much thought to all these problems. Moreover, unless these questions are answered one would fail to have an idea of the ultimate goal of life or of the state the realisation of which is the end of religious activities.

1. Rabindranath Tagore, *Fire-flies*, 23.

An analysis of our normal life shows that death almost puts an end to all our activities. We do not know what happens thereafter. That is why materialists and positivists take death to be the end of life. But, according to Tagore, death is not the end of life, it is not even the negation of life, it is a positive aspect of life which gives to life a significance and a value. Man is afraid of death because he is not able to perceive its real meaning, ignorantly he takes it as something alien to its nature, as putting an end to what his life stands for. But, if death is understood in its proper perspective, we shall find it to be a stage that gives to life an onward direction. Death, according to Tagore, serves another human and spiritual purpose also, it is a supreme lesson in 'giving away'. Life can realise its proper function only when it gives up its narrow egoistic outlook. Death gives away life itself — puts an end to whatever man considers as his 'own' in life. Thus, death plays an important role in the spiritual process of the extension of consciousness.

Death, thus, may be an end of *this* life, it is not the destiny of man, it is a phase — a stage of his existence. That shows that Tagore somehow believes in the process of *Re-birth*. The entire Indian tradition believes that soul progresses through the cycle of births and re-births, each stage being determined by the tendencies and karma performed in the past. Tagore does not explicitly deal with the problem of Re-birth, because he feels that it is futile to try to determine the forms of life that soul would assume after death. But according to him, this much is certain that soul survives death and continues to live till his ultimate destiny is attained.[1]

That means that even Re-birth is not the destiny of man, it is merely a stage through which soul has to pass. The ultimate destiny is the realisation of immortality, of complete freedom. The spiritual progress of man is from bondage to freedom. The embodied state is a state of bondage as all its powers are body-determined. As we go on unfolding the powers and the freedom of the soul by rising above the bodily and by trying to realise our essential affinity with all, we are progressing towards immortality — towards the realisation of complete freedom.

---

1. Tagore explains this point poetically when he says, "Thou hast made me endless, such is thy pleasure. This frail vessel thou emptiest again and again and fillest it with ever fresh life." *Gitanjali*, 1.

In the background of our normal existence we can try to determine the characters of this state of freedom. It can be said that in this state all the fever and fret of our normal embodied existence come to an end. The discord, conflicts and contradictions of life are quietened, and there emerges a fully harmonious existence. Knowledge, love and actions do not go against each other, there is a perfect inner concord among them all. This is a state in which man rises completely over his egoistic life and has a realisation of the essential unity of everything. He feels one with nature, one with everything. This enables him to rise above even the distinction between pleasure and pain, and good and evil, because these distinctions arise only when we believe in the distinction between me and thou, or between mine and yours. This, according to Tagore, is the feeling of the presence of 'Him' all round, this is the realisation of Divinity — and this is the ultimate human Destiny.

That shows that man after attaining his ultimate destiny does not suddenly wake up and find himself in an entirely different world. In fact, when one is able to realise 'God' within himself, the changes that occur are chiefly inner. What changes is the point of view — the way of looking at things — the manner of viewing nature and fellow-beings. The liberated man does not become an entirely different individual — a separate unit. On the other hand, his self-centred out look gives place to love and joy. He enters into the 'ocean' of joy, as it were, which is boundless, which knows no shores. Tagore says, "Where is the further shore ? Is it something else than what we have ? Is it somewhere else than where we are ? Is it to take rest from all our works, to be relieved of all the responsibilities of life ? No, in the very heart of our activities we are seeking for our end. We are crying for the across, even where we stand."[1]

But, this means that the individual somehow remains an individual even after attaining his ultimate Destiny. Does Tagore mean to say that the individuality is retained till the end ? This question is important because some systems of Indian Philosophy have held that in realisation the individual loses its individuality and is lost in the One. Some have believed that losing of the individuality in the Absolute itself is the ultimate

1. Rabindranath Tagore, *Sadhana*, p. 162.

human destiny. Although, at times, Tagore talks in such a manner that one gets the impression that he also believes that the ultimate destiny is the realisation of complete identity with the Brahman. Such descriptions are generally expressions of poetic inaccuracy. The general trend of his writings suggest fairly clearly that he is in favour of retaining the individuality till the end. For example, he gives a very direct and clear account of the problem when he says, "In India, there are those whose endeavour is to merge completely their personal self in an impersonal entity which is without any quality or definition; to reach a condition where mind becomes perfectly blank, losing all activities. Those who claim the right to speak about it say that this is the purest state of consciousness, it is all joy and without any object or content. This is considered to be the ultimate end of yoga, the cult of union, thus completely to identify one's being with the infinite Being who is beyond all thoughts and words.........Without disputing its truth, I maintain that it may be valuable as a great psychological experience, but all the same it is not religion,.........and man is more perfect as a man than where he vanishes in an original indefiniteness."[1] He appears to be so much convinced that he does not feel the need of asserting even this — that the soul, in realisation, becomes free from the cycle of births and re-births. Usually, the Indian Philosopher conceives liberation as freedom from re-birth — from the tendency to be re-born. Tagore thinks that such a concept might affect the distinctness of human personality; and therefore he comes to suggest that even that is not necessary. He gives a very illuminating solution of the problem. He suggests that in liberation God and man become partners in the game of 'joy'. Now, they would play the game in whatever manner they would like to play it. If it would be necessary for the souls to re-appear in order to pursue the game of joy, the souls, in all probability, would assume births again. Thus, it cannot be decided from before as to how the game would be played in the state of realisation. The ultimate human destiny is the realisation of complete freedom, and so, those who realise this state perform all activities with complete freedom and in fullness of joy.

---

1. Rabindranath Tagore, *The Religion of Man*, p. 117.

The Problem of Evil

The presence of Evil in the world presents a problem to every theistic account of the universe. Tagore is also faced with that problem. Specially when he speaks about a state of joy and freedom as the ultimate human destiny, he is obliged to take up and solve the problem that evil presents. Are not evils facts of life ? Do they not keep man encircled in the cobweb of suffering ? Can man attain realisation unless he makes himself free from the shackles of evil ? Tagore feels that problems like these do deserve a consideration.

Tagore does not hesitate in accepting evils as facts of life. Our experiences of life confirm their reality. Evil is an imperfection, and as such, it has to be there in creation, because creation itself is a limitation of God. All created beings are finite and limited, and therefore, evils which naturally follow from finitude and limitation have to be there. Thus, the problem is discussed in awareness of the fact that in an imperfect creation evils are inevitable.

What, then, is the problem of evil ? Evil presents a problem to the theist because he finds it difficult to reconcile its presence with the creator-God, who is omnipotent, omniscient and good. The problem before him is; how can evil be there in the creation of such a God ? But, the problem does not present itself to Tagore in that form, because he does not accept the very assumption of the problem thus conceived. He does not feel the necessity of accepting that the creation of an omnipotent and good God cannot be imperfect. On the other hand, he feels that creation as creation has to be imperfect.

Does that mean that evil is a necessary factor of existence ? Does he mean to say that evil presents a problem because it is *inherent* in existence — because existence itself is evil ? Tagore feels that this is going to the other extreme and being unnecessarily pessimistic. "If existence were an evil, it would wait for no philosopher to prove it. It is like convicting a man of suicide while all the time he stands before you in flesh. Existence itself is here to prove that it cannot be an evil."[1]

Now, it is clear that, according to Tagore, evil is a fact of the finite existence, and yet, existence itself is not an evil. What

1. Rabindranath Tagore, *Sadhana*, p. 53.

then is the problem of evil ? Tagore says that evil presents a
problem only when we come to think that it is a permanent
and final aspect of existence. If we view at evil in that way, we
get the uneasy feeling that it cannot be dispensed with. But,
Tagore asserts that that is not the correct way of looking at
evil. The finite aspects of creation or of man are all real, but
they have to be superseded. Going beyond them is not rejecting their reality, just as crossing a mile-post is not rejecting the
reality of that mile-post. Thus, evils are facts, but they are not
the ultimate facts.

Tagore says that evils must not be viewed as the very antithesis of good, just as imperfection is not the opposite of perfection. It is on account of such an outlook that evils appear as
ultimate. It is because we concentrate on the evil as it is seen —
without relating it to other aspects of life, that is to say, because
we look at it as an isolated and separate fact, that it appears as
ultimate. But, truth cannot be known by a fragmentary or a
piecemeal point of view, Truth lies in the consciousness of the
whole, therefore, the proper perspective to see the truth of a
thing is to relate it to the whole. If imperfections are viewed
that way they would not appear as denials of perfection. "In
fact imperfection is not a negation of perfection, finitude is not
contradictory to infinity, they are but completeness manifested
in parts, infinity revealed within bounds."[1] Viewed in this way,
imperfection or evil is merely a stage leading to perfection
or good.

This point can be explained clearly with the help of an analogy. We watch a child trying to walk. In the process he falls
again and again, even gets hurt. If we view it in that way, the
sight would appear as cruel. But, if we realise that the failures
and falls are but necessary stages or steps towards his eventually-
learning to walk, the whole sight is a source of joy to us. Likewise, let us take the example of the phenomenon of death.
Death is an evil if it is viewed as a separate incident affecting a
particular individual. But, if it is viewed in relation to the whole
it would appear not as an evil but as an aspect of the perfect
plan of the universe. Had the phenomenon of death been not
a fact, every man and, for that matter, every living being would
have continued to exist eternally. Existence, then, would have

---

1. Rabindranath Tagore, *Sadhana*, p. 48.

become like a life in hell with the awareness that every one has to live eternally with the supply of food, shelter, space etc. continually decreasing.

Evil, then, is an impermanent aspect of our finite existence. Its nature is like that of error, which we always come across in our intellectual life, and yet which is always impermanent. For example, if we survey the history of the growth of scientific knowledge, we find that it always progresses through mistakes. Every time a mistake is committed, something new comes up removing the mistake. That shows that error is essentially impermanent. So is evil. Again, this analogy itself throws light on another relevant point. Although in the history of scientific growth errors have been by far more numerous than the discovery of truth, no body remembers the mistakes of science. It is the truths discovered that are remembered. Likewise, evils may be many, but they are aids in the process of the attainment of good. What is then to be remembered is good, not evil. Evil, thus, cannot arrest the progress of life. The direction of progress is from evil to good. Evil, then, is merely a stage to be superseded, an occasion for the disciplining of the life's ways.

The real problem of Evil, then, is this : 'How is one to expedite or help this progress from evil to good or from imperfection to perfection', 'how can evil be transformed into good ?' Evil appears as evil on account of a limited and short-sighted point of view. That point of view has to be changed. Even a selfish individual undergoes pain and sufferings and faces hardships just to satisfy some selfish ends. Pain or suffering is an evil, but he willingly and joyfully undertakes pain because he does not view at pain in isolation — as a separate fact, but he views at it in relation to the whole scheme or project of his own. Now even pain becomes a source of joy to him. Likewise, evil is evil when we view at it from the point of view of our limited ego. That has to be changed to a whole point of view. *The consciousness of the self has to be changed into a soul-consciousness.* That precisely is the way to realisation of human destiny.

Ways of Realisation

i *Soul-consciousness and self-consciousness*

The ultimate human destiny is the realisation of the universal in the individual. That means that the individual must go beyond his egoistic existence and try to realise the universal. This idea is explained technically by Tagore by using the expressions *self-consciousness* and *soul-consciousness*. The ordinary man in his embodied existence is the self, he can realise his true nature by becoming a *soul*. The *self* is the narrow egoistic existence of the individual, the *soul* is the existence of the individual as an aspect of the universal. That is why Tagore says that for realisation of one's true nature consciousness has to be extended beyond the ego, the consciousness of the self must make room for soul-consciousness.

This idea can be made clear with the help of an analogy. The shell of the egg is, in a sense, a sort of a cage, it imprisons the life of the chick. Only when the shell is broken through that the chick knows the world. So long as it is in the shell, it has a limited existence, but once it comes out of it, breaks through it — transcends it — it comes to know life. Likewise, so long as an individual is confined to his selfish or egoistic world, he cannot know life, he cannot have a glimpse into the nature of the reality. But, once he goes beyond this narrow existence, he is on the way. Only then he would be able to realise the worth of existence.

ii *The Way*

The ordinary man, as we have seen, is the self, soul-consciousness is his goal. But, how would he enlarge his consciousness ? What is the way of awakening from self's slumber to soul-consciousness ?

It cannot be 'logic', nor, what usually goes in the name of, knowledge. Worldly wisdom or logic may, at times, be of use; but they can never be the means of attaining soul-consciousness. Intellect may be the proud possession and the tool of the scholar, but it cannot give us an insight into the nature of reality. It gives only a broken view of reality. For example, intellect can count the petals, classify the scent and describe the colour of the rose, but that is not knowing the rose because these do not constitute the roseness of the rose. Just as grammar is not literature and prosody not a poem and knowledge of the theory of music not music, so the intellectual view of things is not the real view.

In fact, even in intellectual life we go on avoiding details by trying to reduce them to simpler and smaller organizations.

Tagore illustrates this with the help of an analogy of 'Truth and Facts'.[1] The apple falls from the tree, the rain comes down to the earth, the magnet attracts iron — we can go on burdening our mind with such facts. But, once the law of gravitation is understood, all these individual facts become insignificant and irrelevent; mind no longer feels the weight of too many facts and feels almost liberated. Thus, we see that even intellect strives to attain unity, although the unity discovered by it is partial in so far as it is departmental — confined to particular departments of nature.

The unity that is the goal of life is not partial, but all-comprehensive, and therefore, it can be attained not through intellect but through *vision*. Vision is defined as "a sudden spiritual outburst from within."[2] It is a sudden outburst and hence immediate. Naturally, its function cannot be analysis, it grasps its object as a whole. When we get a vision of the reality we are not intellectually aware of the details, we have a realisation of the unity within us, of a unity that comprehends the universe.

Now, one may say that the explanation given above has not actually explained anything and has merely substituted the word 'vision' in the place of 'soul-consciousness'. How, after all, are we going to have that vision?

Tagore answers the question in one word — *Love*. It is only through love that our consciousness can be enlarged. The soul has been described as a lover always in search of the beloved. The union will be possible only when soul *intensifies* his love. But, this word is not as simple as it appears to be. Love has been defined as *comprehension*. Comprehension is comprehending 'all' in a unity. Tagore says, "When love prepares your seat, she prepares it for all. Where the earthly king appears, guards keep out the crowd, but when you come, my king, the whole world comes in your wake."[3] In love, again the sense of difference is obliterated. "The meaning of this is that whomsoever we love, in him we find our own soul in the highest sense ... because in them we have grown larger, in them we have touched the great truth which comprehends the whole universe."[4] Love,

1. Rabindranath Tagore, *Sadhana*, p. 26.
2. Rabindranath Tagore, *The Religion of Man*, p. 6.
3. Rabindranath Tagore, *Lover's Gift and Crossing*, Crossing 59.
4. Rabindranath Tagore, *Sadhana*, p. 29.

therefore, is identifying oneself with the object of one's love, and the discovery of oneself outside his own self is a source of joy. Therefore love *is* joy. The ideal of love is the state of perfect joy. That shows that love demands a going beyond the egoistic impulses. So long as 'I', 'me' and 'mine' continue to guide man, he cannot love. In the *King of the Dark Chamber* the queen sees the king only when she gives up her egoistic pride.

Love must be distinguished from attachment. Attachment centres round the ego, and hence it always has a motive or a purpose behind it. True love does not seek to satisfy any egoistic motive. "For love the questions 'how', 'why' 'what for' etc. do not exist. Love is its own reason, its own goal and is its own responsibility."[1]

There is yet another aspect of love. Love presupposes sacrifice. Love and sacrifice go together, without the one the other loses its function. This character is important, because in the act of love, with which man begins his spiritual journey, giving up and sacrificing of all personal considerations constitute the first step.

Here, one may raise a point of suspicion by suggesting that the description of love, as given above, applies only to 'perfect love'. Our experience of life tells us that love begins with pain and sorrow. Tagore is aware of this, but he is also confident that this does not reduce either the power or the importance of love. He says, "Trust love even if it brings sorrow ... let sorrowful love wake in your eyes."[2] He thinks that love may bring pain with it, but this pain is able to bring out the secrets of man's innermost being.

This description of love, as it has been outlined above, is more or less, theoretical. How is love to be practised? Tagore admits that love has its practical side also. Love, according to him, is not mere sentimentality or an emotional attitude towards its object. The lover must not merely feel for his beloved, love demands some actions on his part. Theoretical side of love stands for certain feelings for the object of love, its practical side refers to certain corresponding actions springing from and expressing the feelings of love.

1. Rabindranath Tagore, *Prem, Shantiniketan,* 1st series.
2. Rabindranath Tagore, *The Gardner,* 27.

Man can conveniently begin by trying to have a sympathetic attitude towards others, by trying to develop a loving relationship with others. Even here the first step may be 'love for the near ones'. It is true that generally our love for our childern, friends and near ones prevents us from extending our love to others; but evidently this is also going beyond oneself and therefore, a discipline. Moreover, how many of us really love our near ones? Do we not merely pose to do so and all the time love only ourselves? That shows that love for the near ones also, in its own limited sense, is a step onwards, is going beyond the egoistic self. The process of sacrifice starts here. In loving his own people man at least starts casting his bonds off.

This love may further be extended to include, in its grasp, others also. With such a widening of love, the process of self-sacrifice also becomes intenser. The initial acts of self-sacrifice may be painful and reluctant, they are like the sacrifice that even the selfish man at times makes. But, as the process changes into habit 'self-sacrifice' becomes natural and a source of joy. Tagore says, "It [initial sacrifice, more or less under compulsion] is like plucking fruit when it is unripe, you have to tear it and bruise the branch. But when a man loves, giving becomes a matter of joy to him like the tree's surender of the ripe fruit."[1]

Tagore recommends that our acts of love and sacrifice, whose scope we keep on widening, must be expressed in suitable actions performed for the good of others. To work for the good of others does not necessarily mean to be a utilitarian, because the utilitarian's love for others is based on personal consideration. Tagore's maxim has a metaphysical foundation. To work for all would mean the recognition of the metaphysical unity of all and to work under that recognition. This would no longer remain a life of the finite, it would be living in the Infinite. That is so because soul finds its freedom in action. Action for others gives him a freedom in the outside world, and that is a prelude to his finding freedom within.

It is interesting to find that this has been designated by Tagore as *Realisation in Action* in addition to, what he calls, *Realisation in Love*. These are not actually separate ways of realisation, nor are they entirely different from each other. Tagore feels that any process that enables an individual to extend his conscious-

1. Rabindranath Tagore, *Sadhana*, p. 77.

ness beyond his ego and towards the universal is a way of realisation. This is possible in love, and therefore there is a possibility of *Realisation in Love*. This is possible also through action, and therefore, there is the possibility of *Realisation in Action*. Aesthetic sensibility may also be of help, and so he talks about *Realisation of Beauty*. These are all aspects of the same process, they all lead to the same goal — *The realisation of the Infinie*.

Tagore has a reason for laying an emphasis on 'Realisation in Action'. Activity is the play of joy, it involves voluntary giving for the sake of joy. Even the self-centred man, who is otherwise lost in his egoistic designs, at times, craves for moments of joy. During those moments he also gives and makes sacrifices freely. Therefore, Tagore recommends that the aspirant for mukti must practise this kind of 'sacrifice' in all his acts. "Just as the joy of the poet in his poem, of the artist in his art...of the wise man in his discernment of truth; ever seeks expression in their several activities, so the joy of the knower of Brahman, in the whole of his everyday work, little or big, in truth, in beauty, in orderliness and in beneficence, seeks to give expression to the Infinite."[1]

The two ways, *Realisation in Love* and *Realisation in Action* that have been discussed so far, refer to the aspirant's relation with the outer world primarily, but the aim is to realise unity within. For this, some inner discipline and insight also have to be cultivated. Tagore is a poet, and naturally, he feels that the 'sense of beauty' has also a specific function to perform.

This is almost a truism that an object becomes a burden when it ceases to be an object of joy for us. Ordinarily an object is taken on its utility-value, the moment it ceases to serve any purpose it ceases to interest us. The reason is simple. The object is considered in relation to the ego and in terms of its egoistic and pragmatic uses. But, if somehow we develop the capacity of seeing the object not from the point of view of use or utility, but from the point of view of their beauty, we shall take a positive step towards going beyond the egoistic self. *Realisation of Beauty*, therefore, is a way to the realisation of the Infinite; this capacity is not alien to our nature, it is inherent in us; we have merely to develop it.

---

1. Rabindranath Tagore, *Sadhana*, p. 131.

According to Tagore, 'Beauty' is everywhere — in every example of order and harmony there is beauty. That does not mean that the word 'ugliness' should be abolished from our language. Ugliness lies in "the distorted expression of beauty in our life and in our art which comes from our imperfect realisation of Truth."[1] Awareness of Beauty, therefore, is based on an awareness of Truth. That is why Tagore talks about Realisation of Beauty. He recommends that man should lead a life of nature "tending trees, feeding birds and animals, learning to feel the immense mystery of the soil and water and air."[2] He further talks about the cultivation of the aesthetic sense and about developing the artistic sensibility.

Music, according to him, is the purest form of art, the most direct expression of beauty. Tagore feels that the manifestation of the Infinite in the finite forms of creation is itself a music, silent and visible.[3] This world is a song which is never separated from the Singer. Every aspect of the universe is a note of this music, and therefore, every aspect of the universe reflects the Infinite. Art, music, cultivation of the aesthetic sense — these are the ways through which the aspirant for realisation can approach the object of its aspiration.

Tagore talks about *Spiritual Yoga* also. But, he does not speak about the usual things that are normally associated with the word Yoga. For example, he does not talk about *āsana*, or about the different yogic postures. Yoga is taken in the sense of a discipline that demands sacrifice and renunciation. Renunciation consists in one's giving up of his possessions and in his sacrificing his egoistic impulses. This does not mean that the lower self — the lower aspect of man's nature — has to be killed altogether. It has to be raised higher — made more perfect. What is needed is the disciplining of the self — not its annihilation. In this respect Tagore's view is similar to that of ethical perfectionism. He cleary says, "The renunciation is not in the negation of the self, but in the dedication of it."[4]

This *Yoga*, therefore, is "the daily process of surrendering ourselves, removing all obstacles to union and extending our

1. Rabindranath Tagore, *Sadhana*, pp. 140-41.
2. Rabindranath Tagore, *The Creative Unity*, p. 201.
3. Rabindranath Tagore, *Sadhana*, p. 142.
4. Rabindranath Tagore, *The Religion of Man*, p. 182.

consciousness of him in devotion and service, in goodness and in love."[1] "Thus to be conscious of being absolutely enveloped by Brahman is not an act of mere concentration of mind. It must be the aim of the whole of our life. In all our thoughts and deeds we must be conscious of the Infinite. Let the realisation of this truth become easier every day of our life, that none could live or move if the energy of the all-pervading joy did not fill the sky. In all our action let us feel that impetus of the Infinite energy and be glad."[2] This is what he calls, the *Realisation of the Infinite*.

Tagore's Humansim

An account of Tagore's philosophy would not be complete without making a mention of his humanistic beliefs. His humanistic attitude pervades all aspects of his thought, and yet, he does not allow it to fall down to the status of narrow anthropomorphism.

There is a sense in which Tagore humanises not only nature and objects, but also God. In the book *Religion of Man*, while describing the purpose of the book he says, "The idea of the humanity of our God, or the divinity of man, the Eternal, is the main subject of this book."[3] This appears to represent the basic idea which Tagore tries to develop in so many ways. At times, man is raised higher to the status of God, at other times, God is brought down to man in so far as divinity is said to be discernible in the heart of man. Tagore's God is somehow God and man at the same time and he asserts that "if this faith be blamed for being anthropomorphic, man is to be blamed for being man."[4]

In fact, the humanism of Tagore is just the application of the belief that feeling anything as human — in the human way is a source of joy. It is the human mind that reveals the meaning and significance of things. Tagore's 'Idealism' is humanistic. He says, "It is almost a truism to say that the world is what we perceive it to be. We imagine that our mind is a mirror, that it is, more or less, accurately reflecting what is happening outside

1. Rabindranath Tagore, *Sadhana*, p. 149.
2. Rabindranath Tagore, *Sadhana*, p. 149.
3. Rabindranath Tagore, *The Religion of Man*, p. 17.
4. *Ibid.*, p. 114.

us."[1] If we could adjust the focus of the mind the forest might appear as running, the pleasurable may appear as painful. This speaks of the primacy of the human point of view. The one effort of man's personality is to transform everything with which he has any true concern into the human. For example, the description of the beauty of sunrise has its eternal interest in us because, in fact, it is not the sunrise that catches our interest, but the fact of sunrise in relation to our interest or aesthetic sense.

This is why we always find a human touch in the writings and poems of Tagore. If a river is described, a ferry at once appears, if a scene or a landscape is painted, a human form must remain there; when a flower is presented, it is presented as bringing a message for the human soul; when the beauty of the rainy night is being described, the rains have to fall on 'the spire of the temple rising above the undefined mass of blackness grouped around the village huts'; and if the quietness of solitude is pictured, its peace has to be intensified with joy by the rising notes of a faint song. The outer world, according to Tagore, is nothing but 'a cradle for the human spirit'. That is why in Tagore's thought the notions of 'life', rhythm, beauty, harmony, order, love, delight, music etc. have become important. All these are human concepts, they become meaningful when they are related to human values. In fact, most of the analogies that Tagore uses to describe nature are related to man's disposition and urges and feelings. For example, in the *Lover's Gift and Crossing* he says, "O, listen to the secrets of the world, I know that lily is pale for moon's love. The lotus draws her veil aside before the morning sun and the reason is simple."[2] Or again, in the same series of verses he says, "The world to you is like an old woman's chant at her spinning wheel — unmeaning rhymes crowded with random images."[3] Such similies and analogies are not rare, and they all are indicative of the intensely human disposition of the poet-philosopher.

It is on account of such a disposition that he feels that an intellectual approach to Nature and to problems of life has to be cold and indifferent approach, because intellect surveys a thing from a distance and n a dispassionate manner. An approach with the heart

1. Rabindranath Tagore, *Personality*, p. 47.
2. Rabindranath Tagore, *Lover's Gift and Crossing*, Lover's Gift 17.
3. *Ibid.*, 24.

full of feelings and interest is a human approach. The philosopher usually neglects this, but a philosopher who is also a poet,
makes truth live in the form of beauty and thereby establishes a
personal bond between man and objects. That most probably is
the reason for Tagore's humanistic convictions. Tagore himself
admits this when he says, "I have great faith in humanity. Like
the sun it can be clouded, but never extinguished....We are
waiting for the time when the spirit of age will be incarnated in
a complete human truth and the meeting of men will be translated into the unity of man."[1]

1. Anthony Soars, Ed., *Lectures and Addresses of Rabindranath Tagore,*
p. 146.

Chapter III

MAHATMA GANDHI

Life

Mahatma Gandhi was born at Porbandar on the 2nd of October 1869. His ancestors were *Vaiśya* by caste and profession, but his father, uncle and grandfather were service-holders. His father was, for some time, prime minister in the court of Rajkot and also in Vankaner. Although his parents were orthodox Vaiṣṇavas, they were enlightened enough to make all necessary arrangements for giving modern education to their children. Mohandas Karamchand Gandhi grew in a mixed but balanced set-up. He was initiated into religious and moral traditions, and yet his mind was sufficiently open to the changing needs of the time.

His early educational career was uneventful except for his association with one of his friends who tempted him to evil like meat-eating, smoking etc. These experiences had a good effect as they aroused in Gandhi the ever-present moral sense. In 1888, he was sent to England for legal studies. His father was dead by then, and he could receive his mother's permission for going abroad only after taking a vow in the presence of his mother not to touch meat and not to keep bad company. In fact, later on this vow became for him a symbol of resolute will and came to convince him that sincere determination for doing anything good was bound to succeed. In England, besides his legal studies, he also came to acquaint himself with the great and good things of the West. He returned to India in 1891 after qualifying as a barrister-at-law. After staying in India for a very brief period he went to South Africa to work in the case of an Indian merchant there. His stay in South Africa and his bitter experiences of various acts of racial discrimination committed by the white people of that place changed the entire course of his life and action. There, for the first time, he started his moral experiments of trying to conquer evil by love. He started passive resistance by openly defying immoral laws and thus started putting to practice his moral and religious ideas.

With his unique experiences of South African moral and political adventures, he came to India, determined to make efforts for the independence of India by applying the technique of Satyāgraha. He also had taken a decision to work for the social reform of India by trying to remove such social evil as untouchability, social disparity etc. He was also convinced that his methods of non-violent Satyāgarha,which had succeeded in solving smaller problems of life, could also be effectively used for solving greater problems like, 'political slavery'. The life of Gandhi from 1920 to 1948, when Gandhi attained his martyrdom, has become almost a household story, and hence is not to be repeated here.

Influences that shaped his thought

It is true that Gandhi's thought has an originality and a freshness about it, but it carries on it the stamp of a number of influences. One of the earliest influences that provided to Gandhi's thought its backbone was that of ancient Hindu tradition. He had grown up in a family and in a tradition that had always respected orthodox Hindu ways of religion and worship. At a very early age he had studied the *Gīiā* and the *Rāmāyaṇa*, and also the Vaiṣṇava and the Jaina literatures. These studies sharpened his moral sense and kindled his religious insight.

While in England he got an opportunity of being acquainted with some of the intellectuals of the time and also with Christianity. It is said that when he saw the statue of Christ at St. Peters in Rome, he burst into tears. He had a tremendous respect for the life and personality of Jesus, and thus was able to incorporate in his thought some of the original sayings of Jesus Christ. For that he was, in some respects, indebted to Tolstoy, who in his *The Kingdom of God is within you*, gave almost a new interpretation to Christianity. Tolstoy left his mark on the mind of Gandhi in various ways, specially his emphasis on the power and dignity of suffering gave to Gandhi an inspiration for developing his own notion of Satyāgarha. Likewise, the great American thinker Thoreau also influenced Gandhi a great deal. His idea of civil disobedience revealed to Gandhi the possibility of using non-violence as a technique for solving even the major problems of social and political life. Besides these he had also a first-hand knowledge of Zoroastrianism and Islam and also of the works of Ruskin and those of some of the theosophists of the time. All these influences were taken and deliberated upon. Gandhi carried on experiments after experiments on moral, religious and existential issues both in his inner life and in outward existence; and his thought is nothing but a product of the series of experiments that he carried upon.

God and Truth

Gandhi's Theism

A student of Philosophy finds it extremely difficult to reduce Gandhi's philosophy of God to any of the accepted philosophical models. Gandhi did not have any training in academic philosophy, for him the distinction between Pantheism and Theism was not even relevant; but this can be said that Gandhi's theistic beliefs were, more or less, of the 'Vaiṣṇava' type. His early initiation into the Vaiṣṇava cult, and the influence of the family-atmosphere in which he grew, implanted on his mind the rudiments of the idea of a theistic God.

Vaiṣṇavas in India are thiests *par excellence*. They respect the authorities of the Vedas and the Upaniṣads and, at times, draw their inspirations from them. But, in a general way they are not inclined to accept that advaitic trend of thought and belief that has become very prominent in India. The great Advaita Vedantist, Śaṅkara, emphasised the reality of *Nirguṇa Brahman*, and came to think that the world which apparently looked real, was metaphysically merely an illusion created by ignorance of the individual. Naturally therefore, the Advaita Vedantist never felt the need of a Creator or a God. If the reality is essentially one, if the perception of the many is a product of an illusion — producing ignorance, then both creation and the creator become unreal.

The Vaiṣṇava thinkers, on the other hand, accept the reality of the world, and therefore, believe in a God as the creator and preserver of the world. There is yet another, a more significant, point of difference between the Advaita Vedantist and the Vaiṣṇava thinker. According to the former reality is an attributeless, indeterminate Brahman, and therefore, salvation consists in the knowledge of this reality. Reality, being *Nirguṇa*, cannot be approached in the devotional manner, because devotion presupposes inter-personal relations. Therefore, the only way that the Advaita Vedantist recommends for attaining liberation is the way of knowledge. Vaiṣṇava thinkers conceive God in a theistic manner, and as such, God becomes a personal God.

Now, they feel that a cold and dispassionate way of knowledge will always fail to establish a feeling relationship with God, and therefore, will always maintain a 'distance' from Him. God, according to these people, has to be felt and realised, and therefore, the way of feeling and devotion is the only way to salvation. Not that they deny the role of importance of knowledge altogether, but they somehow feel that devotion and emotional surrender are the essential requirements for salvation. This is the chief reason why the Vaiṣṇava-cult is popular in India, it advocates a simple path that can be taken up by every man.

Gandhi's philosophy of God also is strictly theistic in character. It is true that at times Gandhi, more or less like an Advaitist, talks of the nirguṇa character of the real. But that is so because he feels that the academic distinction between 'saguṇa' and 'nirguṇa' is irrelevant for the beliefs and practices of a true believer. In fact, he feels that God is needed not merely for the satisfaction of reason or intellectual curiosity, but also for providing strength and solace. A faith in God must enable an individual to be in peace with the world. He says, ".....He is no God who merely satisfies the intellect, if He ever does. God to be God, must rule the heart and transform it."[1] This is possible only where an inter-personal relationship is possible, and only when God is conceived as a person. Gandhi was deeply impressed by the life and practices of the saints of the Bhakti-cult, and therefore, it was not difficult for him to arrive at the conception of a personal God. He was helped in arriving at this notion of God by his studies of the Bible and the Quran.

The theistic current of Gandhi's thought at once meets with a difficulty when God and Truth are sought to be identified with each other. Truth is an impersonal principle, God as conceived by Gandhi is a person — how can the two be identified ?

Truth is God

To find a solution of this problem it is essential to enter into the thought-system of Gandhi. Gandhi was aware of the difficulty, and therefore, he very often tried to make his standpoint clear. He says, "In my early youth I was taught to repeat what in Hindu scriptures are known as one thousand names of God.

---

1. *Young India* 31-12-31, 427.

But these one thousand names of God were by no means exhaustive. We believe — and I think it is the truth — that God has as many names as there are creatures and therefore, we also say that God is nameless, and since God has many forms we also consider Him formless, and since He speaks to us in many tongues, we consider Him to be speechless and so on ... if it is possible for the human tongue to give the fullest description, I have come to the conclusion that for myself God is Truth."[1]

An interpretation of this passage will bring to light the reasons for Gandhi's saying that God is Truth. Firstly, this assertion is the result of a search for a name or a category for the universal reality, that is God, which appears to defy all description. Secondly, God is described as Truth because God alone is real. Truth, according to Gandhi, is not an attribute of God, but God is Truth. Truth, according to him, is derived from the word '*sat*', and '*sat*' means 'is'. And so, by calling God Truth, what is being asserted is that God alone is.

But later on, Gandhi, instead of asserting the previous statement 'God is Truth', came to assert the statement 'Truth is God'. Normally, such conversion presents logical difficulties. From the statement 'all men are mortal', we cannot pass over to the statement 'all mortals are men'. Such difficulties are practically removed when the subject and the predicate are identified with each other. Therefore one can say that there is nothing peculiar or extraordinary in shifting the emphasis from 'God is Truth' to 'Truth is God'. But, Gandhi's reasons for bringing about this change are not as simple as that. He says, "But deep down in me I used to say that though God may be God, God is Truth above all. ...But two years ago I went a step further and said Truth is God. You will see the fine distinction between the two statements, viz. that God is Truth and Truth is God. And I came to the conclusion after a continuous and relentless search after Truth. ...".[2]

This shows that there is a very strong reason for bringing about this change. One reason for this change is that the word Truth is not as ambiguous as the word God. Nobody understands exactly the same thing by the word 'God', God may be pantheistic, theistic, polytheistic, or even deistic. But, the

1. *Young India*, 11-10-28, 310.
2. *Ibid.*

word 'Truth' is always clear in its significance. Again, there is yet another, a more fundamental reason, for suggesting this change. Gandhi is able to realise that it is possible to rationally doubt — even to deny — the existence of God, but that it is self-contradictory to attempt to deny Truth. Reason can raise arguments against the possibility of God's existence, but reason cannot reject Truth. There have been many sceptics and non-believers in the world, but even they cannot deny truth. In fact, Truth provides a common platform to both the theist and the atheist. Truth is the only factor which is completely universal and comprehensive. Gandhi says that an atheist would resent strongly if he is described as a God-fearing man, but he would gladly accept his own description as a 'Truth-fearing' man. This, more than anything else, leads Gandhi to assert the primacy of Truth. Blind religious notions about God have done immense damage to mankind, and therefore, the emphasis has to shift from God to truth. He says, 'I don't care for God if He is anything but Truth.'

What is Truth ? In the logical sense of the word 'Truth', truth is considered to be a property of judgment, but, in the metaphysical context Truth is conceived differently — it is conceived as right knowledge, as knowledge that corresponds to reality. In Indian metaphysics, at times, Truth is conceived as self-illuminating as revealing itself. Gandhi somehow combines all these meanings of the word 'Truth' and then comes to identify Truth with God. In fact, in doing so he relies on, what can be called, the popular meaning of the word 'truth'. Popularly a distinction between 'Sat' and 'Satya' is not made. Gandhi explicitly asserts that the word 'Satya' is derived from 'Sat', and this leads him to identify Satya with reality.

But, a student of philosophy may raise a doubt : how can the two be identified with each other ? Truth is the picture of reality grasped by human mind. How can the picture of reality be identical with reality itself ? But, Gandhi seems to have solved this difficulty in his own peculiar way. The distinction between 'knowledge of an object', and 'the object of knowledge' is based on, what is known as, the Dualistic theory of knowledge. Now, there are many religious philosophers and intuitionists who reject this theory and come to assert that knowing is being. The influences that shaped Gandhi's thought — viz., The Upaniṣads, Christianity, thoughts of Tolstoy etc. — had also similar ideas about knowledge. Naturally, Gandhi does not find any difficulty in identifying Truth with reality. Therefore, Gandhi says. 'My uniform experience has convinced me that there is no other God than Truth ... the little fleeting glimpses, therefore, that I have been able to have of Truth can hardly convey an idea of the indescribable lustre of truth, a million times more intense than that of the sun we daily see with our eyes. In fact what I have caught is only the faintest glimmer of that mighty effulgence."[1]

There are certain interesting implications of Gandhi's assertion that Truth is God. These implications have both a pragmatic value and a religious value. One very significant implication of this assertion is that the object of worship is not God but Truth. This can very well become a basis for a really universal religion. because 'worship of Truth' is one thing that can bring persons of every caste, creed and nation together.

In the initial stages of his experiments he was a firm believer in the ultimacy of God, but, in course of time he came in association with many sincere and thoughtful persons who honestly believed that the traditional idea of God was open to criticisms on account of its being a defective notion. But, even their rejection of God was based on a sincere desire to know the Truth. Gandhi at once came to realise that reason could reject anything but not Truth. He could see that all religious believers of all kinds and even the atheists could be brought together under the banner of Truth. 'Truth appeared to him as the only force that could unify even conflicting ideas and ideals. That led him to say, "If it is at all possible for the human tongue to give the fullest description of God, ... then we must say that God is Truth .... But I went a step further and said Truth is God. ... I never found a double meaning in connection with truth, ... Hence the definition 'Truth is God' gives me greatest satisfaction."[2]

This explains Gandhi's catholic attitude and his assertion that a sincere love and worship of Truth will bring together Hindus, Muslims and even Marxists and Atheists. That is why Gandhi says that there are no atheists in the real sense of the term.

1. Mahatma Gandhi, *My experiments with Truth*, p. 615.
2. *Young India*, December, 31, 1931.

Proofs for the existence of God

Critics of Gandhi often point out that Gandhi does not give due regard to 'reason' in formulating his ideas about God. The basis of such a criticism is the fact that Gandhi most often talks about 'the inner voice' or 'the voice of the conscience'. This also is a fact that Gandhi appears to be convinced about the veracity of his beliefs simply on the testimony of his own inner voice. In fact, at times he even ridicules reason for all sorts of fantastic cobwebs that it keeps on weaving. Writing in the *Young India* he says, "Rationalists are admirable beings, but Rationalism can be a hideous monster when it claims omnipotence for itself. Attribution of omnipotence to Reason is as bad a piece of idolatry as the worship of stick and stone believing it to be God. I plead not for the suppression of reason, but for a due recognition of that in us which sanctifies reason."[1]

But, this only proves that Gandhi does not place the ultimate emphasis on rational demonstration of God's existence. He is convinced that God can be known only in a state of inner realisation, that God's knowledge can only be revealed to an individual in some sincere and sacred inner experience. Even so, at times, Gandhi does talk about evidences of God's existence. A student of philosophy who is acquainted with the traditional proofs for God's existence, can very well find elements of such proofs in Gandhi's writings.

The *causal argument* for the existence of God makes its appearance, more or less, in the form of Descartes' Cosmological proof. Gandhi argues in the following manner : we exist, our parents have also existed, and the parents of our parents have also existed. This question can be extended further and further, and thus, it can very legitimately be asked, 'who originates the whole of creation ?', who is the 'parent' of the whole universe ? Gandhi feels that one can reasonably arrive at the concept of God in this way. God can be concieved as the 'parent' of the whole universe. This process of arriving a tthe concept of God very well resembles 'the causal proof', which starts with the universe, seeks for its cause and arrives at the concept of God.

One can find traces of, what is called, the Teleological proof for God's existence, in the following kind of references that

1. *Young India.*, December 1926.

Gandhi frequently gives. At various places Gandhi talks of the order and the harmony of the universe. He also says that there is a Law governing the universe. Then he argues that the order, harmony and the Law cannot be explained unless an intelligent Law-giver is presupposed. If the cause is not a unity, we cannot find unity in the universe. He says, 'I subscribe to the belief or the philosophy that all life in its essence is one .... This belief requires a living faith in a living God who is the unltimate arbiter of our fate."[1]

But, the proof that appears to be most convincing to Gandhi is the Moral proof. In fact, Gandhi values this proof very much and very frequently makes a reference to this. He seems to be convinced that the voice of conscience carries a dependable testimony for God's existence. Conscience, according to him. represents the Divine in man. It has an awareness of the good and the bad. It sanctions the good and condemns the bad. It creates an exalting feeling when the good is done and it pricks whenever a wrong step is taken. The peculiarity about this inner voice is that whenever it speaks it speaks with an authority. Its voice appears to be obligatory. One is constrained to feel that obedience of the dictates of this voice is one's duty. Now, for Gandhi there seems to be no other explanation of this call of conscience except the fact that it is a representative of a Being who is at once the embodiment of Supreme Goodness. He clearly says, "I have no special revelation of God's will. My firm belief is that He reveals himself daily to every human being but we shut our eyes to the 'still small voice."[2]

Then, at times, a reference is made to a kind of proof that can be called "Pragmatic proof." Gandhi believes that a belief in God's existence is necessary because God satisfies a very important aspect of our life. If we survey our life we find that, over and above the wants and needs of everyday existence, we do have an urge of a different kind which cannot be satisfied with the usual materialistic fulfilments of life, and which demands a spiritual satisfaction. We become keenly conscious of such an urge in the moments of anxiety and crisis, when we feel forsaken by all the worldly and materialistic ways of life. Then we clearly realise that we are in need of a supreme object

1. N. K. Bose, *Selections from Gandhi*, p. 26.
2. *Ibid.*, p. 10.

of love, by having a faith in which, we can derive strength, solace, peace and even happiness. This supreme object of love is nothing but God. Therefore, Gandhi says, "He who would in his own person test the fact of God's presence can do so by a living faith. And since faith itself cannot be proved by extraneous evidence, the safest course is to believe in the moral government of the world and therefore in the supremacy of the moral law, the law of truth and love."[1]

But, the fact remains that, according to Gandhi, proofs cannot serve the function of producing a faith in the existence of God. Gandhi is aware that God can be felt through actual experience. He does not outline the condition or the nature of such an experience. At times, of course he does refer to moral sense and to moral experience; but that also is done not to outline the nature of experience, but to provide a way for testing one's religious faith. Thus, it is apparent that, according to Gandhi, God not only transcends senses, but also defies rational proofs. God is a matter of inner realisation and faith.

Some other Characters of God

Gandhi never misses an opportunity of trying to describe the characters of God. The characters mentioned by him are generally theistic, but they bear the mark of Gandhi's basic conviction, namely that 'Truth is God.'

Gandhi conceives God as all-pervasive. God is the reality in which everything lives and moves. In conceiving God in this manner Gandhi is almost identifying the metaphysical reality with the theistic God, and in the process, he is also identifying character of all-pervasiveness with that of omnipresence. He says, "There is an indefinable mysterious power that pervades everything. I feel it, though I do not see it. It is this unseen power that makes itself felt and yet defies proof, because it is so unlike all that I perceive through my senses".[2]

God is also, at times, described as Law. Although this description creates the impression that God is an impersonal principle, Gandhi rises above such an impression when he says that God's Law and God are not different from each other. God him-

---

1. *Young India*, October 11, 1928.
2. *Young India*, October 11, 1928.

self is the Law. To say that God rules everything means simply that his Law abides.

Gandhi very often calls God 'Love'. The full implication of this description of God will be clear only when Gandhi's conception of Love and Ahiṁsā is fully grasped, but one thing seems to be fairly evident that there can be no other way of apprehending God than the way of Love. God is present in every one of us, and therefore, by a gradual process of extending love we can love everybody and thereby God himself. This kind of love demands a kind of a self-sacrifice — a sacrifice of the egoistic and selfish ways for the love and the good of others. Gandhi says, "I have but shadowed forth my intense longing to lose myself in the external and to become merely a lump of clay in the Potter's divine hands so that my service may become more certain because uninterrupted by the baser self in me."[1]

Nature of the World

It is difficult to outline precisely Gandhi's view on the nature of the world, because his remarks on the nature of the world are both casual and too much scattered. Yet, an attempt can be made to organise his thoughts into a full-fledged account of the nature of the world. Nature, according to Gandhi, is the expression of God, is an evidence of the all-pervasive reality. He says, "God manifests himself in innumerable forms in this universe and every such manifestation commands my reverence."[2]

This description of Nature has two implications : one metaphysical and the other practical. Although Gandhi does not like either to raise or to answer the question regarding *the why* of creation, it is apparent that metaphysically speaking the world is an expression of God, and as such is both real and finite. It is real because it is *God's creation*, it is finite because it is not itself God. Even a casual survey of the course of the evolution of the universe will show that the universe is real, although finite. Gandhi tries to gather the results of the studies and researches of different sciences and comes to find that there is a Law governing every movement and every development in

1. *Young India*, 17-11-1921.
2. *Young India*, 26-9-1929.

every part of the universe. "All things in the universe including
the sun and the moon and the stars obey certain laws. Without
the restraining influence of these laws the world would not go
on for a single moment."[1] "Gandhi perceives in the inexorable
laws of nature nothing but the force or the will which maintains
the world in harmony and order, and saves it from destruction.
This force for him is nothing but God, and the laws are nothing
but the ways of the working of that force."[2] That gives to the
world its reality. This is also apparent from the consideration
of the fact, which is more or less, confirmed by the sciences,
that there is a continuity among the various forms of life and
existence. Sciences have shown that the world exhibits a gradual
progress — a continuous process of growth. What is the end
towards which this onward march of Nature is progressing ?
It can be nothing else but God himself who is the perfect and
the ultimate ideal of everything. Thus, God is the beginning of
the world and also its end. This gives to the world its reality.

This emphasis on the reality of the world has a practical implication also. If the world has a reality, then it is suicidal to
deny the reality of anything. Gandhi would never favour a
'denial of the will to live', on the other hand, in accordance
with his conviction he recommends a return to Nature. Nature
does not merely appear to him as full of poetic charms, he also
perceives in it a field for action. Gandhi feels that Nature provides to man a 'Karma-sthala' — a field for action, where man
can discipline his soul by leading a religious and moral life.
That is the reason why Gandhi, at times, talks of the beauties
of Nature — of the solemn silence of forests and hills and of
the majesty of the snow-clad Himālayas and at other times, he
recommends an actual return to nature just to derive benefits
of the actual healing power of Nature. His deep love for
Naturopathy, his recommendations to take plenty of air and
water and to walk barefooted are some of the evidences of his
love for Nature.

Even so, the world is finite. It is finite because it is not infinite, and it is not infinite because there cannot be two infinites.
That the world is finite is shown to be a fact by referring to
the forces of destruction and disharmony present in the universe.

1. *Young India*, 23-1-1930.
2. D.M. Datta, *The Philosophy of Mahatma Gandhi*, p. 60.

Gandhi is not blind to the discordant notes evident in the world. The presence of such elements does not negate the reality of the world but merely proves its finitude and limitedness. Neither Nature nor man is free from imperfection, and so, what is required is an attempt to transcend this finitude and imperfection.

Nature of Man

In the history of philosophy, there have been many thinkers who have given thought and attention to the question regarding the nature and the status of man. Some of these thoughts are influenced by Psychology and some of them are expressions of metaphysical insight. Freud and the Freudians, for example, try to paint a complete picture of man on the basis of their analysis of unconscious urges and impulses. Some other psychologists, taking their clue from these thinkers, seek to reduce man to some original and native impulses, desires and emotions. Then, there are thinkers like Hobbes who seek to determine man in terms of a social drive of a self-centred nature. Man basically is conceived as a selfish individual, who, for the sake of his own pleasure, feels the need of making adjustments with others, and consequently enters upon, what can be called, a social contract. Then, there are certain sociologists who try to explain the nature of man entirely in terms of social conditions. According to them man is essentially and basically a social creature; apart from society he cannot even exist. These people, therefore, emphasise the importance of social factors and seek to reduce man entirely to his social conditions. Then, there are some metaphysicians who believe that explaining the nature of man means discovering the common and essential characters of man. Aristotle, for example, describes man as a rational animal suggesting that this description represents the characters that every man necessarily shares with every other man. Then again, there are some Humanists and Existentialists who appear to be convinced that the description of man in terms of his class-characters cannot be an exact description of man for the simple reason that in the case of man his peculiarities are by far more important than the common characters. Every individual man is unique in his own way, and as such, posseses certain characters that are peculiar to him alone. According to the Existentialists, in particular, no description of man can be adequate unless it gives due regard to the peculiarities of man. Thus, these have been some of the prominent conceptions about the nature of man in history of thought.

But, Gandhi would say that these pictures of man are superficial and partial because they do not emphasise the basic truth about man. It would appear to Gandhi that these pictures of man, are in fact, pictures of the apparent man only. Gandhi feels that all such accounts of man are based on partial or superficial analysis of man's external behaviour and conduct. It does not mean that the bodily aspects of man do not have any reality or that the apparent picture of man is essentially a false picture. Gandhi is aware of the importance and value of this aspect of man, but he believes that there is another aspect of man which is much more basic, which gives nourishment even to the bodily aspect and which is, more or less, neglected or forgotten by all psychological or psychoanalytic or sociological theories about human nature. This, according to Gandhi, represents the true nature of man.

Gandhi feels that man is a complex being. The bodily man is the apparent man, his body is natural in so far as it is akin to other objects of nature. The body grows and decays according to the laws of Nature. But, this aspect of man represents merely the physical aspect. Man is not merely a physical being. He has many other characters which are not just physical. He has consciousness, reason, conscience, will, emotion and similar other qualities. He has an aesthetic sense, a feeling-sensibility, and an insight into the nature of good and bad. These are not just physical activities, these are all expressions of the real man — of the *spirit* or *soul* present in him.

In fact, Gandhi's conception of the nature of man is based on his metaphysical conviction. Gandhi, metaphysically speaking, is a monist, he believes in the reality of one Supreme God. As such, he has to believe that whatever we come across is an expression of the one God. Man, therefore, is also an expression of that one reality. Thus, both the bodily and the spiritual aspects of man are expressions of God, Even so, Gandhi feels that the spiritual aspect of man represents man's superior and true nature simply because it is akin to Divine nature.

Gandhi accepts that every individual is a mixture of the bodily and the spiritual. He also believes that initially the bodily and the physical aspects were more predominant and that the spiritual went on becoming more and more prominent as the evolutionary process progressed. Evolution, according to him, is a change from the physical to the spiritual, aiming ultimately at the complete realisation of spirituality, that is, Divinity. This also shows that in spite of the fact that the bodily aspect of man also has its own importance and value man's essential nature consists in his spirituality.

Thus, it is apparent that there is an element of Divinity present in every man. This is expressed in various ways. The presence of reason, conscience, free-will etc. is an evidence of the presence of this element in man. Gandhi asserts that if these Divine elements are used in the right manner, man can bring heaven on this earth.

In fact, the most illuminating description of this aspect of man that Gandhi very frequently gives is that it is the aspect of the essential goodness present in every man. Although outwardly man appears to be selfish and even brutish, inwardly and essentially he is good. He says, 'I refuse to suspect human nature. It will, is bound to, respond to any noble and friendly action."[1] "In the application of the method of Non-violence, one must believe in the possibility of every person, however depraved, being reformed under humane and skilled treatment"[2] This is possible only because of the essential presence of such an element in man that is responsive to spiritual stimulation — an element which is itself spiritual.

This belief in the essential spirituality and goodness of every man leads Gandhi to believe further in the essential unity of mankind. He says, 'I believe in absolue oneness of God and therefore also of humanity... though we have many bodies, we have but one soul. The rays of the sun are many through refraction, but they have the same source."[3] This unity is expressed both in the life of an individual and in social life. The spiritual law is constantly working behind all kinds of activities, individual, social, economic and political, and is, in fact, running through and unifying them all. He clearly says, "I believe in *advaita*. I believe in the essential unity of man, and for that matter of all that lives."[4]

1. *Young India*, 4-8-20.
2. *Harijan*, 22-2-42.
3. *Young India*, 25-9-24.
4. *Young India* 4-12-24.

Karma and Rebirth

Gandhi believes in rebirth also. This belief is obviously a product of his extreme respect for Hindu beliefs and tradition, But, there is a significant sense in which Gandhi's faith in the possibility of rebirth carries the distinctive mark of his own personality and genius. In Hinduism rebirth is, more or less, a metaphysical doctrine, a belief postulated for explaining mysteries of life prior to birth and after death. While Gandhi is not going to deny this, he does not feel the need of entering into the details and subtleties that the concept of rebirth involves. On the other hand, he gives a moral interpretation to this doctrine by emphasising the pragmatic and ethical value of this belief. He feels that by believing in the possibility of rebirth one is able to make adjustments with life. This belief enables man to be loving, kind, moral and benevolent even in the midst of his bitter experiences of jealousy, hatred and strife. It is true that life is not a bed of roses. It involves strife, struggle, hardship and consequently suffering. Most often an individual tends to break down in the face of all this. But, a belief in rebirth opens out before him new vistas and new possibilities. He comes to realise that this world is not the end of everything and that acts done in this life have implications for future lives also. Evil and suffering experienced in this life are not final, This realisation enables man to face this life with strength and in a dignified manner. Belief in the possibility of rebirth, therefore, becomes a condition for a pious, moral and noble living.

A belief in rebirth goes side by side with a belief in Karma. Hindu thought has given tremendous importance to the doctrine of Karma. It is taken to be both a metaphysical and a moral law. Metaphysically speaking, this law explains births and formation of bodies. Our present life and body are on account of our past Karmas. It is believed that our Karmas create tendencies in accordance with which our subsequent bodies and capacities are built. The Law of Karma is also conceived as a moral law. It is considered to be another name of the moral maxim 'as you sow so you reap'. The ancient Indian seers have suggested that man's bondage and suffering are due to his own wrong actions done in the past and that right and good deeds performed in this life will bear fruit in future and will enable man to make himself free and liberated.

Gandhi also has referred to both these aspects of Karma, he also describes the metaphysical status of man in terms of his Karmas, more or less, like a metaphysician. According to him, "every individual is unique because of his peculiar physical and mental inheritance and equipment. What an individual now is, is the effect of his actions — his habits of thinking, feeling, speaking and acting in the past. Man makes himself through all these diverse activities, internal and external. They appear to be so insignificant separately, but taken together they create the tremendous forces that shape his health, character, and his entire destiny."[1] But, for Gandhi, the moral significance of the Law of Karma appears to be more important because it is consistent with his moral convictions and also with his kind of faith in rebirth. The realisation that one's own Karmas determine the future nature and status of an individual creates the further realisation that it is man himself who is the maker of his own destiny. Now, it is for an individual to consider whether by his own acts he is going to make himself a good man or an immoral man. Gandhi thinks that such a realisation will creat a sense of responsibility in man. He will now know that it is almost obligatory for him 'to raise himself by himself' so that he can fully express and realise the Divinity latent in him.

Non-Violence (Ahimsā)

An account of Gandhi's theory of Truth necessarily takes us to the consideration of his views on the nature of Non-violence. Gandhi himself says, "I have nothing new to teach the world. Truth and Non-violence are as old as the hills. All I have done is to try experiments in both on as vast a scales ar I could. In doing so I have sometimes erred and learnt by my errors. Life and its problems have thus become to me so many experiments in the practice of truth and non-violence. . . .In fact it was in the course of my pursuit of truth that I discovered non-violence."[2] Explaining more clearly the transition from the notion of Truth to that of Non-violence he says, "*Ahimsa* and Truth are so intertwined that it is practically impossible to disentangle and separate them. They are like the two sides of a

1. D. M. Datta, *The philosophy of Mahatma Gandhi* p. 77.
2. N. K. Bose, *Selections from Gandhi* p. 13.

coin, or rather a smooth unstamped metallic disc. Who can
say, which is the obverse, and which the reverse ? *Ahimsa* is the
means; Truth is the end. Means to be means must always be
within our reach, and so *ahimsa* is our supreme duty. If we
take care of the means, we are bound to reach the end sooner
or later."[1]

Let us first try to determine the Gandhian sense of the word
'Ahimsā'. Not that Gandhi is using this word in some special
sense which is entirely different from its traditional or customary sense, but, Gandhi has emphasised certain aspects of
Ahimsā which have not been given that importance by any other
believer in Ahimsā. On account of such emphasis there has
emerged a Gandhian sense of the word, which, although similar
to its usual sense, has some distinctive features of its own.

In Gandhi the word Ahimsā has both a negative and a positive import. The positive aspect of its meaning is more fundamental for Gandhi, because it comprehends the negative aspect
also and represents its essence.

The usual meaning of Ahimsā is non-killing. Most often its
meaning is made broader by emphasising that non-killing is
merely one example of Ahimsā. Ahimsā, then, is conceived as
non-injury. In any case, Ahimsā is conceived as the opposite of
himsā. Gandhi accepts this and adds much more to its content.
He also accepts that *himsā* means causing pain or killing any
life out of anger, or from a selfish purpose, or with the intention
of injuring it. Refraining from doing all this is *Ahimsā*. In fact,
in conceiving Ahimsā thus Gandhi seems to be influenced by
Jainism which recommends the practice of Ahimsā in thought,
speech and action. According to it, even thinking ill of others is
himsā. Not only this, Jainism demands that one should not
only commit himsā himself, he should not cause himsā or permit himsā to take place. Gandhi's negative requirements of
Ahimsā are not as rigid as that, because Gandhi is aware that
it is not possible to observe non-violence in as strict and rigid
manner as Jainism demands. He is aware that in certain cases
himsā is unavoidable, as for example, in the processes of eating,
drinking, walking, breathing etc. It is impossible to sustain one's
body without injuring other bodies to some extent. Gandhi in
fact, openly recommends killing under certain circumstances.

1. *Ibid.* pp. 13-14.

He says, "Taking life may be a duty. We do destroy as much life as we think necessary for sustaining our body. Thus, for food we take life, vegetable and other, and for health we destroy mosquitoes and the like by the use of disinfectants etc., and we do not think that we are guilty of irreligion in doing so . . . for the benefit of the species we kill carnivorous beasts . . . even man — slaughter may be necessary in certain cases. Suppose a man runs amuck and goes furiously about sword in hand, and killing anyone that comes in his way, and no one dares to capture him alive. Anyone who despatches this lunatic, will earn the gratitude of the community and be regarded as a benevolent man,"[1] He makes this point still clearer when he says, "I see that there is an instinctive horror of killing living beings under any circumstances whatever. For instance, an alternative has been suggested in the shape of confining even rabid dogs in a certain place and allow them to die a slow death. Now my idea of compassion makes this thing impossible for me. I cannot for a moment bear to see a dog or for that matter any other living being, helplessly suffering the torture of a slow death. I do not kill a human being thus circumstanced because I have more hopeful remedies. I should kill a dog similarly situated, because in its case, I am without a remedy. Should my child be attacked with rabbies and there was no helpful remedy to relieve his agony, I should consider it my duty to take his life. Fatalism has its limits. We leave things to Fate after exhausting all the remedies. One of the remedies and the final one to relieve the agony of a tortured child is to take his life."[2] Thus, it is apparent that Gandhi considers it almost a virtue to take life under certain conditions. In fact, he feels that under conditions similar to the examples given by him, continuing to live itself is pain and that, therefore, non-killing amounts to prolonging pain and agony. Thus, Non-injury itself has been conceived in a slightly different manner by Gandhi.

He is of the opinion that *killing* or *injury to life* can be an act of violence only under certain conditions. These conditions are *anger*, *pride*, *hatred*, selfish consideration, bad intention and similar other considerations. Any injury to life done under these motives is *hiṁsā*. Thus, the negative meaning of Ahiṁsā is

1. *Young India*, 4-11-26.
2. *Young India*. 18-11-26.

'non-killing or non-injury', but this presupposes that a non-violent act is free from hatred, anger, malice and the like.

But, for Gandhi, the positive aspects of Ahiṁsā are much more basic than its negative characters. Aniṁsā is not merely refraining from causing injuries to creature, it stands for certain positive attitudes towards other living beings that one must cultivate.

In working out the positive principles of Ahiṁsā Gandhi proceeds under a basic conviction, namely that Ahiṁsā represents one of the basic and essential qualities of mankind. That does not mean that violence does not have any place in life. In fact, even in preserving one's existence one has to commit hiṁsā of one kind or the other, and yet *Ahiṁsā* is considered to be the law of our species. This is apparent from the fact that even when violence appears to do some good, the good that results is very temporary. Nothing permanent can be built on violence. History teaches us that those who have, even with sincere and honest motives, ousted the greedy and the dishonest by using brute force against them, have, in their turn, become a prey to those very evil things with which the dishonest persons had suffered.

This particular belief of Gandhi is expressed in his oft-quoted assertion that *Ahiṁsā is natural to man.* He illustrates this in various ways. If we survey the course of evolution we shall find that although in the initial stages *brute force* appeared to be dominant, the progress of evolution is towards Ahiṁsā. In fact, in the case of every species it can be seen that no animal or creature eats or devours or destroys its own offsprings. In the case of man, in particular, this fact is still more evident. Man is both body and spirit. Body can represent physical power and therefore can, on occasions, do hiṁsā; but man's true nature consists in his spiritual aspects. Man as spirit is essentially non-violent. A simple evidence of this is the fact that while body or the senses can be injured, the soul can never be injured. Hiṁsā, therefore, is alien to man's nature. The moment the spiritual side of man is awakened, his non-violent nature becomes apparent.

In fact, in its positive aspect Ahiṁsā is nothing but *Love.* Love is a kind of feeling of oneness. In an act of love one identifies himself with the object of his love, and this cannot be possible unless there is an effort to free mind from every such disposition that prevents the spontaneous outflow of Love.

Therefore, Ahimsā demands a sincere effort to free mind from feelings like anger, malice, hatred, revenge, jealousy etc., because these create obstacles in the way of Love. *Love*, according to Gandhi, is the energy that cleanses one's inner life and uplifts him, and as such, love comprehends such noble feelings as benevolence, compassion, forgiveness, tolerance, generosity, kindness, sympathy etc.

To love, of course, is a very difficult discipline. It is easy to hate, but it requires supreme energy and strength to love. The task becomes still more difficult when one is required to love a person who is ordinarily to be regarded as an opponent. Therefore, Gandhi says that non-violence is meant for the strong and not for the weak. This can be demonstrated in a very simple manner. Gandhi believes that violence is essentially an expression of weakness. One who is inwardly weak develops a sort of a fear and out of fear starts arming himself against real or imaginary enemies. Violence may have the appearance of strength, but it is born out of fear and is, therefore, a sign of weakness. Only he can be truly non-violent who has conquered fear. The capacity to kill is not a sign of strength, the strength to die is the real strength. Only when one has this strength in him that he can claim to have risen above fear and is able to practise non-violence. "A helpless mouse is not non-violent because he is always eaten by the pussy. He would gladly eat the murderess if he could."[1] In fact, "Non-violence pre-supposes the ability to strike."[2] One who is practising Ahimsā *has* the strength to overpower his adversary, and still he practises ahimsā because ahimsā ' is a conscious and deliberate restraint put upon one's desire for vengeance."[3] In fact, the really strong wins not by brute force, but by *fearless love*. "Non-violence does not mean meak submission to the will of the evil-doer. It means pitting of one's whole soul against the will of the tyrant. Working under this law of our being, it is possible for a single individual to defy the whole might of an unjust empire."[4]

Non-violence again is conceived as a gospel of action. It is not an attitude of indifference or passivity. It is true that the

1. *Harijan*, July 20, 1935.
2. *Young India*, 12-8-1926.
3. *Ibid*.
4. *Young India*, 11-8-1920.

seeds of non-violence lie deep down in the heart, but they are expressed and given shape in actions. Therefore, Non-violence is a dynamic process involving continuous and persistent deliberations, efforts, strains and actions. It is true that non-violence requires extreme patience on the part of one who is using this method, but this patience is not a sign of inactivity, it is an expression of a conscious and inner effort to force the so called opponent to see and realise his own mistake.

This is why it is said that non-violence involves sacrifice and suffering. Sacrifice, according to Gandhi, is an indispensible companion of Love. Love demands a going beyond, a self-transcendence. Only he can love who is selfless, who only believes in "giving" and not in taking. Gandhi says, "Love never claims, it ever gives. Love ever suffers, never resents, never revenges it self."[1] This is self sacrifice and this involves suffering. "The test of love is *tapasyā* and tapasyā is self-suffering."[2] Gandhi feels that suffering is the surest way of getting victory in the battles of life. If we quietly suffer wegive time to the opponent for his anger to calm down. He will then come to realise his mistake. Of course, one presupposition of conscious suffering is that there must be a 'love' for even the opponent and also a faith in the essential goodness present in him. Without this suffering would be in vain. That is why suffering is conceived as an aspect of Love. The essence of love, according to Gandhi is not enjoyment, it is suffering.

Gandhi also feels that non-violence conceived as love and conscious suffering can give full protection to one's self-respect and sense of honour. In fact, the non-violent man does not bend, it is the opponent who has to bend. He, infact, practises forgiveness in the maximum degree, and in the process the opponent is almost put to shame.

It is the firm conviction of Gandhi that Ahimsā can be practised universally. It is a power which can be wielded equally by all — children, young men and women or grown up people of all places and times. It does not involve the use of any external object, it only demands a sincerity of purpose and a purity of intentions, and as such, it can be practised by every body — even by societies or nations.

1. *Young India*, 9-7-25.
2. *Young India*, 12-6-22.

But there is one supreme condition attached to the practice of Ahiṁsā. It cannot be practised unless one has a living and unflinching faith in God. The practice of Ahiṁsā requires an inner strength, which can only be generated by a living faith in God. A sincere faith in God will make man see that all human beings are *fellow-beings* and essentially one. Thus, the love of God would turn into a love of humanity, which alone can make possible the practice of Ahiṁsā. It is as a result of the realisation of the unity of mankind that one will be able to love his fellow-beings. Faith in God, therefore, is the most fundamental condition for the practice of Ahiṁsā.

The Technique of Ahiṁsā — Satyāgraha

Gandhi is aware that a theoretical emphasis on the value and importance of Truth and Non-violence would lead us nowhere unless a way is shown for the practice of Ahiṁsā. That takes him to develop a *technique* of Ahiṁsā, to which he gives the name of *Satyāgraha*, which is translated in English as *Truth-force*, or even, at times, as *Soul-force* or *Love-force*, Gandhi, through out his life went on making newer and newer experiments with this technique and thus succeeded in giving to it some definite shape. In order to be able to appreciate its nature it would be better to begin with the description of this technique in Gandhi's own words. Describing the nature of Satyāgraha Gandhi says, "Its equivalent in the vernacular rendered into English means Truth-Force. I think Tolstoy called it also Soul-Force, or Love-Force and so it is. Carried out to its utmost limit, this force is independent of pecuniary or other material assistance, even in its elementary form of physical force or violence. Indeed, violence is the negation of this great spiritual force which can only be wielded or cultivated by those who will entirely eschew violence. It is a force that may be used by individuals as well as by communities. It may be used as well in political as in domestic affairs. Its universal applicability is a demonstration of its permanence and invincibility. It can be used alike by men, women and children. It is totally untrue to say that it is a force to be used only by the weak, so long as they are not capable of meeting violence by violence. This superstition arises from the incompleteness of the English expression [Passive Resistance]. It is impossible for those who consider themselves to be weak to apply this force. Only

those who realise that there is something in man which is superior
to the brute nature in him, and that the latter always yields to it,
can effectively be passive resisters. This force is to violence and,
therefore, to all tyranny, all injustice what light is to darkness."[1]
An attempt to explain clearly the ideas contained in this lengthy
passage taken from the writings of Gandhi will bring to light the
salient features of Satyāgraha.

One thing seems to be obvious, and it follows from the very
etymology of the word 'Satyāgraha'. Truth according to Gandhi,
is God, and Satyāgraha is '*āgraha*' of 'Satya' and thus, it means
holding fast to truth. It, therefore, demands a deep sincerity and
a vigorous love for Truth. It works on the conviction that Truth
represents the will and the ways of God. Therefore, the path
of Truth has to be followed in a vigorous manner for no other
consideration except the fact that it is God's way — that it is the
way of Truth. In this sense the doctrine of satyāgraha is strictly
rigoristic.

This means that Satyāgraha is essentially based on *love*. In
fact, Satyāgraha appears to Gandhi almost as a religious pursuit.
It rests on a religious belief that there is one God behind every
thing and being, and as such the same God resides in every one
of us. This is the basis of Love, and unless one has this basic
love for mankind he cannot practise the technique of Satyāgraha.

There is yet another religious presupposition of Satyāgraha.
In fact, all rigoristic ethical doctrines, somehow or other, believe
that there has to be another life, otherwise, they would not be
able to explain the strictly rigoristic character of their belief.
Gandhi also feels that a belief in rebirth is almost a pre-condition
of Satyāgraha. Satyāgraha demands selfless and sincere pursuit of
Truth without having any consideration of any advantage or gain,
But, one will be able 'to walk on such a sharp 'razor's edge' only
if he somehow believes that he will get the fruits of his good
work, if not in this life, in subsequent life. He says, "with the
knowledge that the soul survives the body, he [the satyāgrahī] is
not impatient to see the triumph of truth in the present body."[2]

Gandhi describes Satyāgraha as a force against violence,
tyranny and injustice. All these evils arise on account of a
neglect of the 'truth' that is all-pervasive and all-comprehending

1. N.K. Bose, '*Selections from Gandhi*, pp. 218-19.
2. *Speeches and Writings*, Madras 1934, p, 504.

Therefore Gandhi says that if we start resisting evil with evil, violence with violence, anger with anger, then we are only adding fuel to fire. The most effective force against these evils can be the one which would force them to evaporate, and that can be done only by Satyāgraha.

This is possible only because satyāgraha creates conditions for the anger of the opponent to spend itself out. It gives ot the opponent a chance to see and realise his mistake and thereby to mend his ways. It is based on the conviction that there is an element of essential goodness in every man because man contains divinity within himself. Evils result because this element is either pushed to the background, or is clouded by passion, hatred and anger. What is, therefore, required is to awaken this aspect of man. The moment this element of goodness is aroused, the individual himself will realise the wrong that he had been doing.

The Satyāgrahī can do this by subjecting himself to suffering for the sake of Truth. Ahiṁsā is conscious suffering. The Satyā-grahī, therefore, suffers and thereby converts the opponent. Gandhi says, "Nations, like individuals, are built through the agony of the cross and in no other way. Joy comes not out of infliction of pain on others, but out of pain voluntarily borne by oneself."[1]

That is why Satyāgraha has been described as a method of *conversion* rather than a method of coercion. Coercion implies violence, it may not be physical violence, but it is at least mental violence. The aim of satyāgraha is not to embarrass the wrong-doer. It does not appeal to fear, it does not proceed in terms of threats. It appeals to the heart and to the good sense of the wrong-doer. Its intention is to bring about, what Gandhi calls, a *change of heart*. It fact, satyāgraha is based on the pre-supposition that there are no 'enemies' or 'opponents', but that there are only wrong-doers. A wrong-doer will also develop some kind of a resistance if he is physically forced to be otherwise, but if he is made to see and realise the wrong, he will himself repent and change.

Therefore, Satyāgraha is based on love. There must be *love* even for the opponent. Distrust or hatred of any kind will prevent the success of Satyāgraha. There must be a 'trust' in the goodness of the opponent and a love based on the realisation that he is also one of us. Gandhi goes on to add that there must also be a *respect* for the opponent. Satyāgraha seeks to persuade the wrong-doer to give up his wrong, and this can be done very effectively when the wrong-doer is also approached with love and respect.

Satyāgraha also demands extreme patience on the part of the satyāgrahī. A wrong-doer cannot see his wrong at once, he will take time to win over his anger and hatred. The Satyāgrahī must wait patiently for the good sense of the wrong-doer to be aroused.

Gandhi distinguishes *Satyāgraha* from *Passive Resistance* with which it is usually confused. Firstly, Satyāgraha is not a passive state; in fact, it is more active than violence. Secondly in passive resistance, there is an element of force, it does not completely forbid the use of violence. In fact, in it there remains the scope for the use of arms on particular occasions. In Satyāgraha, on the other hand, violence is completely forbidden even in the face of very adverse situation. Thirdly, "In passive resistance there is always present an idea of harassing the other party and there is a simultaneous readiness to undergo any hardship entailed upon us by such activity, while in *Satyāgraha* there is not the remotest idea of injuring the opponent. *Satyāgraha*, postulates the conquest of the adversary by suffering in one's own person."[1] Fourthly, in passive resistance laws are disobeyed and as such the impression is created that passive resisters do not have respect for law. In *Satyāgraha*, on the other hand, there is invariably a very great respect for the higher Law — the Law of Truth and God. In fact, the entire process of Satyāgraha is initiated by such a respect. Fifthly, while there is no scope for love in passive resistance, hatred has no place in Satyāgraha, but is a positive breach of its principle and function. Passive resistance is based on a feeling of dislike (if not of complete hatred) for the opposite party. Satyāgraha is based on a feeling of love. Sixthly, Passive resistance tends to compel the other party to do a thing, there is an element of coercion in it. It does not seek to change men's heart. The Satyāgrahī essentially appeals to the mind and heart of men with the sole aim of bringing about a conversion. The essence of Satyāgraha is to liquidate antagonism, not the antagonist.

1. N. K. Bose, *Selections from Gandhi*, p. 221.

Thus, Satyāgraha is based on the conviction that through love, ahiṁsā and conscious suffering the forces of evil can be neutralised, because this is the Divine way, the way of Truth. Gandhi believes that this technique is universal in its application. It can be practised by children and adults, by men and women, by individuals and communities and by societies and nations. It can be put to use on all possible fronts — in domestic life, in social relationship or in political situations. Its universality is derived from the fact that it is the way of God.

Requirements of a Satyāgrahī

But, Gandhi is aware that although it is possible for every body to use this technique, it cannot be followed in a loose or casual or insincere manner. It requires a very strict moral and religious discipline, Gandhi has, in course of his numerous references to this subject, mentioned a number of qualities and characters which a Satyāgrahī must possess. Some of the basic ones can be enumerated and emphasised here.

1. A Satyāgrahī must be basically honest and sincere. It implies honesty of purpose and sincerity of effort. Without this a Satyāgraha will remain satyāgraha merely in name.

2. A Satyāgrahī must not have any mental reservations, he must be open-minded. Gandhi feels that a change of heart can be brought about only when the other party, is approached open-mindedly, with no 'second' or 'hidden' ideas or motives.

3. A Satyāgrahī must be a disciplined soldier. Truth alone should be his master and conscience his guide. He should be loving, but firm.

4. This means that a Satyāgrahī must be completely fearless. He must not fear anything worldly — even death. Gandhi says that one who has not conquered fear cannot follow the way of Satyāgraha effectively.

5. Fearlessness leads to another virtue, sacrifice. A Satyāgrahī must be prepared for the greatest possible sacrifice. He has to be completely selfless, and no sacrifice is great for him. He must be prepared to undergo any amount of suffering for the sake of Truth and for the good of others.

6. Suffering and Sacrifice have to be undergone in an attitude of simplicity and humility. If a Satyāgrahī becomes

arrogant and starts feeling that he is doing something great, his satyāgraha would go in vain. Humility, according to Gandhi, is one of the prime virtues of a Satyāgrahī.

7. Gandhi asserts that a Satyāgrahī is required to practise truthfulness and non-violence not only in his actions, but also in thought and speech. He admits that this is not possible all at once, but asserts that constant discipline and sincere effort wolud be of great help.

8. A Satyāgrahī must be firm in his dealings and behaviour. He must not yield to pressure, he must not give way to greed and dishonest persuasions. He must have a strength of character and a resoluteness of will. Honesty and Integrity must be his ideal.

9. There must be a conformity between the thought and action of a Satyāgrahī. Gandhi knows that the absence of this character gives rise to many kinds of evils. Moreover, it reflects the disintegrated and disorganised character of the person concerned. A Satyāgrahī has to win the confidence and love of the adversary, and therefore there must be a co-ordination between what he thinks and says and what he does.

10. Gandhi also recommends that the Satyāgrahī must learn to put on restraints upon his own self. He gives practical tips and hints for such practices. One of the effective suggestion in this regard is the practice of *Fasting*.

11. He also recommends the cultivation of some of the essential virtues of life. The virtues most often mentioned are the ones that ancient Indian philosophy has emphasised — viz. Asteya (Non-stealing), Aparigraha (Contentment), Brahmacarya (Celebacy) etc.

12. The Satyāgrahī must also have *tolerance* in him. Gandhi is not happy with this word, but for want of a better word he uses it. He says that a Satyāgrahī has always to deal with *adversaries*. If he does not have tolerance, he will lose self-control, and thus, will upset the way of Love.

13. The Satyāgrahī is also required to observe other ordinary virtues of life like punctuality and order. These, according to Gandhi, are forms of Discipline that help in the cultivation of the power of self-control.

14. The most fundamental requirement is that a Satyāgrahī must have a living faith in God. In fact, the entire principle of Satyāgraha is based on the conviction that there is one God and also on the faith that there is an element of Divinity present in everyman. A faith in God, therefore, is the religious pre-requisite of the life of a Satyāgrahī.

Gandhi feels that a true Satyāgrahī who has been able to fulfil the requirement mentioned above can work wonders. He alone can face the might of an army or even of an empire. Great powers also would bend before the *Truth-force* of a single Satyā-grahī. Describing vividly his own idea of how Satyāgraha can meet a violent army in a non-violent manner, Gandhi says, "At the risk of being considered a visionary or a fool I must answer the question in the only manner I know. It would be cowardly of a neutral country to allow an army to devastate a neighbouring country. But there are two ways common between soldiers of war and soldiers of non-violence, and if I had been a citizen of Switzerland and a president of the federal state what I would have done would be to refuse passage to the invading army by refusing all supplies. Secondly, by re-enacting a. Thermopylae in Switzerland, you would have presented a living wall of men and women and children inviting the invaders to walk over your corpses....Imagine these men and women staying in front of an army requiring a safe passage to another country. The army would be brutal enough to walk over them, you might say. I would then say that you will still have done your duty by allowing yourself to be annihilated. An army that dares to pass over the corpses of innocent men and women, would not be able to repeat that experiment. You may, if you wish, refuse to believe in such courage on the part of the masses of men and women; but then you would have to admit that non-violence is made of sterner stuff. It was never conceived as a weapon of the weak, but of the stoutest hearts."[1]

Kinds of Satyāgraha

Although Gandhi believes that Satyāgraha is one simple technique which can be used differently in different situations, in

---

1. *Young India*, 31-12-31.

actual practice it has assumed different forms. Therefore, the impression is created that there are many kinds of Satyāgraha.

Some of the prominent kinds of Satyāgraha that have been used not only by Gandhi or his followers but also by believers in other kinds of theory (viz. the communists) are the following:

1. Negotiation
2. Arbitration
3. Agitation and Demonstration
4. Economic Boycott

5. Non-cooperation
6. Civil Disobedience
7. Direct Action
8. Fasting

To this list are also added some other measures that have become popular in course of time:

9. Strike
10. Picketing

11. Dharnā
12. Non-payment of Taxes. etc.

All these are not favoured equally by Gandhi. In fact, some of these are even condemned by him. He is aware of the possible perversions of the way of Satyāgraha. He says, "Indiscriminate resistance to authority must lead to lawlessness, unbridled licence and consequent self-destruction."[1] He knows that all these methods would fail if the intention is not pure and if these are not taken resort to in a spirit of love. Therefore, he recommends that a Satyāgrahī must first exhaust all other means before he resorts to Satyāgraha. He must constantly and continually approach the constituted authority, he must appeal to public opinion, educate it, state his case calmly and coolly before everybody, and only after he has exhausted all these avenues that he should resort to Satyāgraha. People, at times, just to get quick returns take resort to some of the forms of Satyāgraha. Gandhi is completely against this. Explaining this by taking the example of *non-payment of taxes* he says that this may produce quickest possible results. But, he feels that we must not resort to non-payment of taxes because of the possibility of a ready response. The readiness of this kind, according to him, is a fatal temptation. Such non-payment will not be civil or non-violent, but it will be criminal and fraught with the greatest possibility of violence. Likewise, ridiculing the present form of 'Dharnā' he says, "Some students have revived the ancient form of barbarity in the form of *sitting dharna*. I call it barbarity because it is a

1. *Young India*, 2-4-31.

crude way of using coercion. It is also cowardly because one who sits dharnā knows that he is not going to be trampled over. It is difficult to call the practice violence, but it is certainly worse. If we fight our opponent, we at least enable him to return the blow. But when we challenge him to walk over us, we are *knowing* that he will not, place him in a most awkward and humiliating position."[1] Even with respect to Non-co-operation he says that extreme caution is necessary in resorting to it. "Non-co-operation, when its limitations are not recognised, becomes a license instead of becoming a duty and therefore becomes a crime."[2] In such cases, Satyāgraha, according to Gandhi, becomes Durāgraha. In fact, the moral and religious requirements of Satyāgraha are very strict and rigorous, any deviation would distort the whole process. It has to be based on sincerity of purpose and on an essential love for the other party. Of course, Gandhi concedes that the use and application of the technique of Satyāgraha would vary from person to person. He accepts Satyāgraha as a universal principle, but admits the practical limitations of its complete operation. But, he lays down a fundamental and essential condition for its use: that is the recognition of the existence of a soul — of a good nature in every man. This recognition must not only be a kind of an intellectual understanding, it must be a living faith on which our life and conduct can unhesitatingly be based.

The forms of Satyāgraha that Gandhi seems to favour most are *Disobedience, Non-co-operation, Direct Action* and *Fasting*. *Disobedience* is considered to be a protest against unjust laws. Gandhi, in this regard, seems to be influenced by Thoreau and accordingly feels that it is morally proper to be right and true than to be law-abiding. He resorted to this technique chiefly in South Africa when he protested against the unjust, discriminatory and racial laws. *Non-co-operation*, according to Gandhi, is essentially a cleansing process, it affects the Satyāgrahī more than the other party and is able to give to the Satyāgrahī a power to face evil and to endure suffering. Non-co-operation, as Gandhi conceives it, amounts to a kind of a refusal on the part of the exploited to be exploited. Gandhi feels that the exploited is also to be blamed for being exploited because he has allowed himself

1. *Young India*, 2-2-21.
2. *Young India*, 29-12-21.

to be exploited. Non-co-operation, therefore, is refusal on the part of the exploited to succumb to the forces of exploitation. 'Swadeshi' is an example of this kind of Satyāgraha. *Direct Action* is conceived as an open and mass rebellion. Although the word rebellion has associations with violent ways, 'Direct Action' is essentially non-violent. It is also open in the sense that there is no secret about it. The QUIT INDIA call given by Gandhi in 1942 was an example of this kind of Satyāgraha. But, the most effective form of Satyāgraha, according to Gandhi, is *fasting*. Fasting works in a double way, it aims at self-purification and also by honestly choosing the way of death it can mend even the obstinacy of the other party. But, Gandhi feels that this should be treated as the last weapon of the Satyāgrahī and should be resorted to only at the last moment — only when other means of persuasion have failed. Fasting concentrates the energy of the soul and forces the opponent to see reason. He says, "It is my firm belief that the strength of the soul grows in proportion as you subdue the flesh."[1] He further says, "My religion teaches me that whenever there is distress which one cannot remove, one must fast and pray".[2]

Philosophy of End and Means

In every ethical thought that seeks to reflect upon the nature and standard of morality, the problem regarding 'Means and End' becomes a very significant problem. In fact, traditional ethical thought has tried to relate these two concepts to the concepts of 'Right' and 'Good'. The word 'good' even etymologically has a reference to 'end' and the word 'right' means 'according to law'. Being 'in accordance with law' has a necessary reference to the ways of operation and behaviour, and therefore, to means. That is why sometimes it is suggested that if 'right' and 'good' have a necessary relation with each other, there is a relation between means and ends also as they are conceived in the light of the concepts of 'right' and 'good'. Some thinkers have gone to the extent of suggesting that in case the means is *right*, the end has to be *good*.

Gandhi also conceives 'end' and 'means' in somewhat similar

1. *Young India*, 23-10-24.
2. *Young India*, 25-9-24.

manner, with the difference that he takes these concepts much more seriously. In fact, these two concepts have become 'central' in his thought, in so far as the relationship that is conceived to exist in between the two concepts has very important implications for Gandhi's notions of Truth and Non-violence.

Gandhi's assertion that End and Means are intimately related with each other is a common-sense assertion. But, he goes beyond common-sense when he says that 'means' and 'end' are convertible terms in his philosophy of life. This assertion is not to be taken too literally because it merely throws light on the essentially inseparable character of the two. The end is the 'goal', and the means is the 'way' of the realisation of the goal. Means cannot be separated from the end just as 'the way' cannot be separated from the 'goal'. Explaining the relation between the two Gandhi says, "The means may be likened to a seed, the end to a tree; and there is the same inviolable- connection between the means and the end as there is between the seed and the tree."[1] One implication of this description is that means somehow contains in it, (of course in an implicit manner) the possibility of the end, just as the seed contains in it the energy that is expressed in the form of the tree.

This raises the question regarding the justification of end and means in terms of each other. Does the end justify the means ? Are we permitted to attain good ends by whatever means we can ? Should means also be essentially good if a good end is to be realised ? Is purity of means an essential aspect of the way of the realisation of a good end ? These are precisely the questions which engage Gandhi's attention in his philosophy of means and end.

In arriving at his views on the matter, Gandhi, as usual, is determined by his basic metaphysical conviction regarding the essential spirituality and unity of everything. Spiritual unity is the ideal of life, the goal or the end of every activity. A spiritual end cannot be attained by any non-spiritual means. That means that a good end cannot justify any and every means. If a good end is to be attained, it is also essential that the means adopted for the realisation of the end is also good.

That is why Gandhi gives very great importance to 'means'. He says, "They say 'means are after all means.' I would say

1. *Hind Swaraj*, p. 39.

'means are after all everything.' As the means so the end. There is no wall of separation between means and end. Indeed the Creator has given us control (and that too very limited) over means, none over the end. Realisation of the goal is in exact proportion to that of the means. This is a proportion that admits of no exception."[1] He illustrates this further by showing that adoption of a particular means makes very great difference in the nature of a work. Even when the end is the same and only the means are different, the character of the work will differ in accordance with the nature of the means. "If I want to deprive you of your watch, I shall certainly have to fight for it, if I want to buy your watch, I shall have to pay you for it, and according to the means I employ, the watch is stolen property, my own property, or a donation. Thus, we see three different results from three different means."[2] This shows that Gandhi is almost convinced that ends do not *justify* the means and that purity of means is an essential condition of realising good ends. A wrong means will adversely affect the character of a work.

There is a logic behind this. If we examine the nature of a work or a project, we find that the end of the work is always beyond our control. End is the ideal, and therefore, is not yet within our reach or grasp. What we have at our disposal and control is the means. We can change or adjust or manoeuvre only means and never the end. Goodness or badness of an act depends upon my doing it, and in doing anything we are concerned *only* with the means. Therefore, it follows that the means has to be the right one. Clarifying his stand on the point Gandhi says, "Though you have emphasised the necessity of a clear statement of the goal, but having once determined it, I have never attached importance to its repetition. The clearest possible definition of the goal and its appreciation would fail to take us there, if we do not know and utilise the means of achieving it. I have, therefore, concerned myself principally with the conservation of the means and their progressive use. I know if we can take care of them attainment of the goal is assured. I feel too

---

1. *Young India*, 17-7-24.

2. *Hind Swaraj*, p. 40,. also in B.S. Sharma, *Gandhi as Political Thinker*, p. 44.

that our progress towards the goal will be in exact proportion to the purity of our means."[1]

Gandhi's philosophy of End and Means has a direct relation with his doctrine of Truth and Ahiṁsā. Truth is the ideal of life, it is the goal towards which we must strive. But what would be the nature of this striving ? What would be the way to approach Truth ? That, according to Gandhi, is Ahiṁsā. Therefore, for Gandhi, Truth is the end and Ahiṁsā is the means. We cannot attain Truth by any other way. On some such considerations Gandhi, even while recommending that swarāj was the 'end' of the Indian People, always insisted on the adoption of non-violent ways for the realisation of swarāj. He clearly said, "let there be no manner of doubt that swarāj established by non-violent means will be different in kind from the swarāj that can be established by armed rebellion."[2] "Violent means will give violent swarāj. That would be a menace to the world and India itself."[3] Thus, Gandhi's uncompromising and straight recommendation is that if the end of Truth is to be attained, the means has to be pure, has to be the means of Ahiṁsā,

Religion and Morality

In a philosophical account of the thoughts and beliefs of a particular thinker 'religion' and 'morality' ought to be dealt with separately because, philosophically speaking, the two concepts are basically different. Moral values are essentially this-worldly, they are concerned with life as it is lived. Religious values have a reference to the 'beyond'. It is quite possible for the two to co-exist, but conceptually they are different. In Gandhi's thought, however, they almost overlap. Gandhi believes that true religion and true morality are *inseparably* bound up with each other. He would unhesitatingly reject any religious doctrine that conflicts with morality. He would be prepared to accept even unreasonable religious sentiment if it is not immoral. He says, "As soon as we lose the moral basis, we cease to be religious. There is no such thing as religion over-riding morality. Man for instance cannot be untruthful, cruel and incontinent and claim to have God in his side."[4]

1. N.K. Bose *Selection from Gandhi*, p. 36.
2. *Young India*, 2-3-22.
3. *Young India*, 1-7-724.
4. *Young India*, 24-11-21.

But then, for philosophical understanding the two can be treated separately.

(A) *Religion*

i. *What is Religion ?*

The basic conviction of Gandhi is that there is one reality — that of God, which is nothing else but Truth. His religious ideas are also derived from that conviction. If truth is God, sincere pursuit of Truth is religion. Religion is ordinarily defined as devotion to some higher power or principle. Gandhi is not against such a description of religion, he only qualifies it further by saying that that higher principle being Truth, devotion to Truth (or God) is religion. He tries to give an outline of what he means by religion in the following lines. He says, "Let me explain what I mean by religion. It is not the Hindu religion... but the religion which transcends Hinduism, which changes one's very nature, which binds one indissolubly to the truth within and which ever purifies. It is the permanent element in human nature which counts no cost too great in order to find full expression and which leaves the soul utterly restless until it has found itself, known its maker and appreciated the true correspondence between the Maker and itself."[1]

An explanation of the passage quoted above brings to light the salient features of Gandhi's views on the nature of religion. *Firstly*, religion is the expression of the permanent nature of man. The animal and brutish aspect of man's nature is not its permanent aspect, the permanent aspect is the aspect of Divinity — the element of essential goodness present in every man. *Secondly*, religion has the character of purifying and elevating one's nature. Gandhi believes that true religious spirit has the capacity of changing one's nature because it is the expression of the good elements present in man. *Thirdly*, religion has the power of arousing in man a sense of spiritual restlessness — a kind of a thirst — which enables the individual to cultivate and develop a sense to the right and the good, and makes him a truly moral man. *Fourthly*, religious aspiration is based on a desire and a cognitive urge to know 'the beyond'. It has somehow the feeling that the ultimate religious ideal is nothing but the realisation of God. *Fifthly* and finally, religion involves a conscious

1. *Young India*, 12-5-20.

and sincere love and striving for Truth. Without this all other characters of religion would be ineffective. Therefore, Gandhi says that there is no religion higher than Truth and Righteousness.

ii. *The Way of Religion*

For Gandhi, religion is not just a theoretical concept that seeks to satisfy intellectual curiosity and urges, it is, for him the way of life, a practical necessity. In fact, he feels that a religion which takes no account of practical affairs and does not help to solve them is no religion. He believes that true religion has to be practical. Therefore, he says that religion should pervade every aspect of our life — even political life. Religion is the belief that there is an ordered moral government of the universe; and as such, this belief must have practical bearings for all aspects of life.

What would be the way of the realisation of the religious ideal ? As for Gandhi there is no difference between religious ideal and metaphysical or moral ideal, the religious way is also the way of Truth — *Satyāgraha*. The ideal is the 'realisation of God'. One is right on the way if he is following the path of Truth and Non-violence. Even so, Gandhi does make a mention of such exclusively religious practices as *prayer, surrender to God's will by subordinating one's body and mind to the call of Truth, self-sacrifice, renunciation, love and tolerance* etc.

Prayer, in particular, appears to have a very great importance and value for him. Specially in hours of crisis Gandhi used to retire in silent meditation and prayer, and invariably after such an experience he used to come out with renewed vigour, strength and conviction. Prayer, according to Gandhi, is not *asking,* it is a longing of the soul. Prayer is the only way of bringing about peace, harmony and order in our life. He says, "Prayer is the very soul and essence of religion, and therefore, prayer must be the very core of the life of man, for no man can live without religion."[1] But, at this point a question may arise, which Gandhi has been able to anticipate. "But why pray at all ? Does not God, if there be one, know what has happened ? Does He stand in need of prayer to enable Him to do His duty ? No, God needs no reminder. He is within everyone. Nothing happens without His permission. Our prayer is a heart search. It is a reminder

---

1. *Young India,* 23-1-30

to ourselves that we are helpless without His support. No effort is complete without prayer — without a definite recognition that the best human endeavour is of no effect if it has not God's blessing behind. Prayer is a call to humility. It is a call to self-purification to inward search."[1] Prayer, thus, makes us purer and brings us nearer to God. Through prayer we are able to gain strength and prepare ourselves to share the sufferings of others.

Religion demands the awakening of the spiritual aspects of man, For that it is essential to subdue and to put a check on the bodily and the sensuous aspects of man. This requires a ruthless curtailing of all our selfish motives — an attempt to reduce ourselves to zero. This a kind of self-sacrifice and renunciation. But this renunciation is not escape. Gandhi does not believe in flying away from the world. True renunciation means renouncing of the selfish and the personal for the good of others. Gandhi recommends that the religious man must practise renunciation by living in the midst of men.

That would mean that he will have to cultivate and develop a cold, indifferent and detached attitude towards worldly gains and losses. Gandhi, following his philosophy of means and end, recommends that a certain way of practising this kind of renunciation is to do one's duty and work without caring for — or without even thinking of — the fruits or consequences of his actions. Gandhi, in fact, is following the path of 'Niṣkāma Karma' as shown by the *Gītā*. Gandhi calls the *Gītā* his *guru* and tries to follow the Karma-mārga as preached in the *Gītā*. Renunciation, therefore, means selfless action for the good of humanity. In fact, the religious recommendation is that the fruits of one's effort are to be left to God, they are his concern not ours.

iii. Attitude towards living Religions

Religion, according to Gandhi, is more or less, a way of life, and as such is the personal concern of the individual who has to choose his way of life. But, if an individual has the freedom to take to the religious way of his own liking, he must also have a tolerance and a respect for the points of view that others might have chosen for themselves. Therefore, he recommends that the attitude towards different religions must be one of tolerance and respect. In his own case it is much more than that. Although

1.   *Harijan*, 8-6-35.

sometimes an impression is created that he has a special liking
for Hinduism, his attitude towards other religions is one of reverence. He was born in a Hindu family and so the way and the
atmosphere· in which he grew and developed implanted in his
mind the elements and tenets of Hinduism. Naturally, the *Gītā*
and the *Rāmāyaṇa* became his two invariable companions.

But he made a study of many great religious scriptures — of
the *Bible* and the *Qurān*—and he came under the influence of a
number of saints and religious teachers. All these led him to
believe that different religions are the different ways of apprehending *the Truth*.

Gandhi believes that every religion contains good precepts and
noble teachings, he also finds that some of the interpretations
and commentaries have degraded religion and distorted it. He
also finds that almost every religion has given rise to some fana-
tic and unreasonable practices. Therefore, his conviction is that
all religions are good as well as bad, basically good — good in
conceiving its ideal, but bad in giving rise to hatred, crusades and
fanaticism. The experience of communal riots in India streng-
thened his belief. Therefore, he suggests that religions — historical religions — must not be allowed to cross the limits of *reason-
of 'sober reason*', as he calls it. He is convinced that this element
of 'rationality' will be able to bring about, what can be called,
'a fellowship of all religions' or, 'the kingdom of God' — a christian expression which he also approvingly uses on various
occasions.

His attitude towards all historical religions can be summed up
in his own words. Describing his attitude on the matter as early
as in 1921, he says, "After long study and experience, I have
come to the conclusion that (1) all religions are true, (2) all religions have some error in them, (3) all religions are almost as dear
to me as my own Hinduism, inasmuch as all human beings should
be as dear to one as one's own close relatives. My own veneration
for other faiths is the same as that for my own faith, therefore
no thought of conversion is possible. The aim of fellowship
should be to help a Hindu to become a better Hindu, a Mussal-
man to become a better Mussa.man, and a Christian a better
Christian. Our prayer for others must be NOT "God, give him the
light thou hast given me," BUT "Give him all the light and truth

he needs for his development". Pray merely that your friends
may become better men, whatever their form of religion."[1]

This shows that in spite of the fact that he does not attach
much importance to historical religious institutions, he has profound respect and reverence for all religions How he hopes to
combine rationality with religion can be well illustrated by the
manner in which he remembers *Christ — the Saviuor*. He says,
"God did not bear the cross only 1,900 years ago, but He bears it
today, and He dies and is resurrected from day to day. It would
be poor comfort to the world if it had to depend upon a historical
God who died 2,000 years ago. Do not then preach the God of
history, but show Him as He lives today through you."[2]

iv. *Attitude towards Hinduism*

In trying to determine Gandhi's attitude towards Institutional
religions, it is essential to make a mention of his attitude towards
Hinduism in particular. He himself describes his attitude in this
way, 'I can no more describe my feeling for Hinduism than for
my wife. She moves me as no other woman in the world can.
Not that she has no faults. I dare say she has many more than I
see myself. But the feeling of an indissoluble bond is there.
Even so I feel about Hinduism with all its faults and limitations.
Nothing elates me so much as the music of the *Gītā* or the
Rāmāyaṇa of Tulasīdāsa, the only two books in Hinduism I may be
said to know."[2] On account of such an attitude towards Hinduism Gandhi is at times, accused of being partisan to Hinduism.
But Gandhi tries to make it clear that his love for Hinduism is
not a 'bias' for Hinduism.

He says that every individual is born in a cultural environment,
the traditions of which become important and significant for him.
Birth may be an accident, but the traditions and heritage that
birth brings with it are very significant. It is unnecessary — and
perhaps futile too — to try to negate or ignore them. What is
required is the proper development of the traditions. Gandhi feels
that his initial education and the manner of his upbringing along
with the religious traditions of his birth created such conditions
that Hinduism suited him best. He feels that everybody is free

1. Sabarmati 1938, D. M. Datta, '*The Philosophy of Mahatma Gandhi*
p. 49.
2. *Young India*, 11-8-1927.
3. *Young India*, 6-10-1921.

to cling to the religion of his choice, and Gandhi's choice was for Hinduism.

Gandhi has definite views with regard to some of the important Hindu doctrines, some of which he openly condemns, some he likes and approves and some others influence and determine his own thought. For example, condemning UNTOUCHABILITY he says that Hinduism has sinned in giving sanction to untouchability. He goes on to say that the Hindu practice of untouchability degraded us to the extent that we have become *pariahs*. Again, speaking against *animal sacrifice* he says that such acts cannot be approved in spite of the fact that animal sacrifice finds a place in the Vedas, because they are against the fundamental principles of Truth and Non-Violence.

In spite of these references, it can safely be said that his religious ideas are influenced by Hinduism. In fact, even the attitude of tolerance that he recommends for other faiths is derived from Hinduism, specially from the *Gītā* wherein the value of other ways and paths has also been recognised.

His idea of God itself is derived from some kind of Vaiṣṇava Theism. The Hindu ideas of *Incarnation*, *Idol Worship*, *importance of heredity* etc. have all found explicit mention in the writings of Gandhi, with the difference that they have all been coloured in the light of the personal convictions and experiences of Gandhi. One particular Hindu idea that has been approvingly mentioned times without number is the idea of *Varṇa* along with the *Varṇāśrama Dharma*. Gandhi regards Varṇāśrama as a healthy division of work based on birth. The present idea of caste, according to him, is a perversion of the original system. Varṇa, according to Gandhi, does not admit the superiority or the inferiority of any varṇa over any other, it is purely a question of duty. It simply means that one has to perform the duties that his forefathers had been performing. In fact the original recommendation was based on the consideration that man is born with some specific missions, obligations and duties. He must do his share of work for the preservation and growth of his species. One is not born for the purpose of amassing wealth, because there would be no limit to it and consequently man will forget the basic mission which he has to fulfil in life — namely, that of awakening his spiritual elements. Gandhi finds this system to be advantageous in many ways. It is advantageous economically, because it involves a division of labour. It ensrues hereditary skill, and as such limits undesirable competition. It has all the advantages of trade-unions and above all it reduces the possibility of individual poverty or pauperism to the minimum. Socially speaking also this system succeeds in promoting social cohesion, if of course it is not abused. Even politically and religiously this system had worked well, because every community used to manage its internal affairs through its varṇa-system. But somehow, the system disintegrated and gave rise to many castes. Gandhi feels that the present caste-system with the existing innumerable divisions and with the artificial divisions imposed upon it, is the very antithesis of varṇāśrama. In fact, Gandhi tries to incorporate Varṇāśrama in his socio-political scheme.

(B) *Morality*

i. *Religion and Morality*

It has been said earlier that morality represents the core — the essence of religion. According to Gandhi, true religion and true morality are inseparably bound up with each other. Religion is to morality what water is to the seed that is sown in the soil. Just as water causes the seed to sprout and grow so religion causes moral sense to grow and develop.

There is a very logical reason for this. For Gandhi the religious ideal is the realisation of Truth or God. God is the essential unity of everything. Now, if this unity is to be realised, one must go beyond oneself — beyond one's selfish consideration and love others. This act of self-transcendence is nothing but morality. God can be discovered by trying to find Him in His creation, and that would be possible only by loving all and by serving all. This is morality. Therefore, D. M. Datta observes, "The path to the realisation of the True self or God, therefore, lies through the love of others and the performance of duties towards others as love demands. Morality thus becomes the essence of religion."[1]

ii. *What is Morality ?*

Ethical philosophers have analysed the concept of morality and have been able to see that the question of morality can be

---

1. D.M. Datta, *The Philosophy of Mahātma Gandhi*, p. 83.

raised only with respect to such actions which have the quality of being called either good or bad. Instinctive actions or reflex actions which are more or less automatic, fall beyond the scope of morality. That is why it is said that only voluntary actions can be called moral. Voluntary actions are voluntary, that is to say, they are the results of the free decision of the doer. Therefore, they can be either good or bad.

One would be amazed to find that Gandhi's description of moral actions is quite close to the academic description of it. He clearly says that no action which is not voluntary can be called moral. So long as we act like machines, there cannot arise any question of morality. If we call an action moral, it means that it has been done consciously and as a matter of duty. Any action that is dictated by fear or by coercion of any kind ceases to be moral. It also follows that all good deeds that are prompted by hope of happiness in the next world cease to be moral.

In another sense, Gandhi's description of 'morality' is not so close to its academic description. Academically even actions that can be described as 'bad' are moral because they are voluntary, but according to Gandhi, moral actions would include only good actions. In ethical philosophies of the academic type the opposite of 'moral' is 'non-moral', but in Gandhian philosophy the opposite of 'moral' is 'unmoral'. Whatever is good and virtuous is moral, a sense to the good and the bad is the moral sense, and trying to live in accordance with the dictates of this moral sense is *Morality*.

But, if the good consists in doing good to others, it would involve sacrificing one's personal motives for the good of others. That means that *Self-transcendence* or *Love* constitutes the essence of morality. Love, according to Gandhi, is Divine; it makes performance of duty not only a convenience, but also a duty. But, *Love* at times, tends to be blind. This may lead to dogmatism and even to barbarism and fanaticism. Therefore, Gandhi says that morality does not consist in loving blindly, it is loving with the full consciousness and *knowledge* of love. Love in ignorance tends to become sensuous and narrow, knowledge will break its bonds and barriers. A good action requires and is based on a knowledge of its factors, conditions, motives etc. Knowledge, therefore, is an essential aspect of morality.

Morality thus is obeying the voice of the conscience with the full knowledge of the conditions that make this call imperative or obligatory. In fact, morality, according to Gandhi, is nothing but *satyāgraha*. The requirements of morality are nothing but the requirements that a true Satyāgrahī has to meet.

iii. *The Cardinal Virtues*

The virtues approved and recommended by Gandhi are nothing different from the requirements laid down for a true satyāgrahī. Only he can be truly moral who has voluntarily chosen for himself the way of Satyāgraha. Therefore, Satyāgraha is the highest morality. Even so, Gandhi has given special emphasis on some of the virtues of life — which, according to him, are essential for a pious and moral life. These virtues have nothing new about them, but the emphasis that has been put on them is both novel and morally expedient.

Traditional Indian philosophy has also emphasised the need of some cardinal virtues which everyone should try to practise. In fact, all the systems of Indian philosophy except Cārvāka believe that the world is being governed by a moral law, and that the nature of the world is moral. They believe that every kind of action — good or bad — produces some tendencies and effects which the doer has to face or suffer. This is the belief in 'Law of Karma" which, in terms of morality, changes into the maxim. 'As you sow, so you will reap'. This being so, it is very essential that only such actions are performed which generate good tendencies. Herein comes the need of developing certain basic virtues, which would enable an individual to be on the right path. Indian Ethics talk about *five* such virtues : they are Non-violence (*Ahiṁsā*), Truthfulness (*Satya*) Non-stealing (*Asteya*), Non-acceptançe or Non-possession (*Aparigraha*), and Chastity (*Brahmacarya*). Gandhi admits all these, and adds some more. The only difference is that Gandhi interprets these virtues in his own way — in the light of his own experiences. His one consideration is that these virtues must be interpreted in an up-to-date manner so that they may be consistent with the needs of the time and the conditions of existence prevalent at the time.

Before elaborating these, one general remark with regard to the practice of these virtues has to be made. Gandhi asserts that these virtues are to be practised not only outwardly, but in *thought*, *speech* and *action*. The aim of ethical activities is attainment of *purity*, and complete purity can be attained only when a person is virtuous not only in deeds but also in thought and speech.

(*a*) *Ahimsā* according to Gandhi is the most important virtue. Its nature has already been made clear. The moral aspect of Ahimsā is nothing but tolerance and love. It also lays down the maxim that all persons are equal. Therefore, for the realisation of God, love for every being is a necessary condition. Gandhi regards Ahimsā as the highest virtue (*ahimsā paramo dharmah*), and, among other things, the reasons for his preference are the following :—(a) No virtue can be practised unless all beings are allowed to live. We cannot do any duty to any fellow being unless he lives, (b) all the other virtues presuppose love. All virtues require some amount of self-sacrifice and this is not possible without love.

(*b*) *Satya* (*Truthfulness*) — Truth is conceived as God, and therefore, Gandhi says that regard for Truth or truthfulness is a virtue. How can we know Truth ? And, without knowing Truth how can we have regard for Truth ? Gandhi is aware of the difficulty. He admits, more or less, like the ancient Indian Philosopher, that Truth is in fact self-revealing, but that we have become blind on account of our ignorance. Ignorance, according to Gandhi, is not natural or necessary to the self. We, somehow cloud our capacity for knowledge. Gandhi says that moral degradation or perversion of one kind or another causes ignorance. He explicitly mentions the six deadly enemies which cause prejudice, malice and ill-will to arise, on account of which the person is unable to see or feel the Truth. These deadly enemies are *lust, anger, greed, infatuation, pride* and *falsehood*. Therefore, in order to practise *Satya* one must constantly endeavour to free oneself from these evils, one must cultivate moral purity and courage and must not allow these enemies to cloud his vision.

Gandhi is also aware that in the present-day world falsehood appears to be more paying and beneficial. By speaking lies people do get success. Gandhi is aware of it, but very logically he demonstrates the superiority of Truth over falsehood. He says that even when falsehood appears to be succeeding it does so only by passing under the garb of Truth. Only that falsehood succeeds which, for the time being, appears as the Truth. Only when falsehood is presented as the 'Truth', that it works and gains success. That shows that it is truthfulness and not false-hood that has the intrinsic power of goodness.

There is one condition regarding the speaking of the Truth which Gandhi accepts because of its pragmatic value. Even in accepting this Gandhi is trying to be faithful to the ancient Indian teaching. The condition is that the truth should be spoken in a pleasant way. If the truth is expressed in a blunt, rough and unpleasant manner, it may be socially injurious as it might give rise to anger and quarrels. In fact, in the ancient Indian philosophy there is a maxim which says, 'speak the truth, speak the pleasant; but do not speak the unpleasant truth', Gandhi seems to be influenced by the element of practicality contained in this maxim. Therefore, he says that truthfulness has to be practised, that it is an art which has to be developed by rigorous and constant discipline and practice.

(c) *Asteya (Non-stealing)*— There are two senses of the word Asteya, it popularly means the observance of the rule of not taking away the belonging or the property of anybody unless it is given by that person. But, there is a stricter and a more rigorous meaning of the word 'asteya'; it forbids the keeping or holding in possession of such things that are not needed. Gandhi uses the word Asteya in both these senses. In fact, in conceiving the nature of this virtue he is influenced by Jainism which believes that stealing is also a kind of hiṁsā. Property is, in fact, outer life, because bodily existence depends upon property. Therefore, to rob one of his property is to take away his outer life. Non-stealing is a virtue also because stealing is not compatible with the highest virtue of 'love'. Therefore Gandhi recommends that a truly moral individual has to take a solemn vow to cultivate the virtue of non-stealing.

(d) *Aparigraha (Non-acceptance)*—Whereas non-stealing is nega-tive in its import, non-acceptance has a positive significance. This, for Gandhi, means contentment — being contented with the necessities of life and not to pine for more. Aparigraha is non-possession. Gandhi feels that the tendency to possess things is at once the cause of all evils. Therefore, one must cultivate the discipline of living with what one has. Gandhi, of course, is aware that it is not possible to practise this virtue in the abso-lute way, because absolute non-possession is impossible in life; even the body is a possession — the things needed for the pre-servation of the body are also 'possessions', and therefore, so

long as we are alive we cannot completely do away with possessions. Even so, *aparigraha* has to be practised to the best of
one's capacity because this does away with the cause of rift in
social life and provides a solid foundation for a universal love to
flourish.

(e) *Brahmacarya* (*Celibacy*) — The word Brahmacarya etymologically means 'living in the Brahman'. Popularly it means
abstinence from sexual relations or at least physical control
over the organ of generation. In fact, the ways of the ancient
Indian life were such that a student for the first twentyfive years
of life was required to devote his energy to study and learning.
He was called a Brahmacārī, because he was. required to gain
knowledge about reality, God and the world. A Brahmacārī,
thus, was forbidden to indulge in sexual relations. On account
of this the word 'Brahmacārī' came to have the association (of
celibacy) that popularly goes with it.

Gandhi uses the word Brahmacarya both in its popular sense,
and in its traditional sense. He emphasises the importance of
sexual control, but adds that Brahmacarya is more than that.
It is putting a check and restraint over all the senses and the
mind. Senses often delude us and misguide us. Immorality is
basically born out of a desire to satisfy the demands of the
senses. Therefore, we must cultivate a discipline by which we,
instead of being led astray by the senses, may be able to keep
the senses under control. In fact, even sexual control cannot be
practised unless senses are put in check. For example, Gandhi
feels that our food-habits have to be changed. The 'palate' is
responsible for our taking delicious and rich food, which, in its
turn, causes sexual urge to arise. Therefore, Gandhi experiment-
ed with different kinds of food, just in order to evolve a food
pattern, which, without reducing the health-value of food, would
not allow amorous and undesirable urges to arise. The name
'Brahmacarya' is given to a discipline of this kind.

These five virtues are the five virtues recommended and approved by ancient Indian Ethics. Over and above these, Gandhi
recommends a few more from his own side.

(f) *Abhaya* (*Fearlessness*)— We have seen that fearlessness
is conceived as an essential condition for the practice of Ahiṁsā.
It is a difficult discipline because it requires not only a conquering
of ordinary fear, but also a freedom from such fears as the fear

of starvation, humiliation, physical violence and even death. Gandhi repeatedly asserts that cowards can never be moral. Fearlessness, therefore, is the virtue of having moral courage even in face of adversity and danger.

(g) *Faith in God* — Gandhi believes that none of these virtues can be practised unless one has a faith in the ultimate goodness of God. Unless one sincerely believes that the ultimate nature of the universe is moral, he will not feel the need of cultivating any virtue. The practice of 'love' also presupposes this faith. The faith in God, therefore, is not only a religious faith, it is a postulate of morality, a condition for a moral and virtuous life.

Social and Political Ideas

Gandhi called himself a 'Practical Idealist'. He is an idealist on account of his theoretical views — on account of the fact that he believes in an 'ideal' that is through and through spiritual. But, he is a practical philosopher because he always tries to put his ideas into practice. Naturally therefore, he comes to develop some views regarding society, state and similar other institutions. He tries to show in a concrete manner that his religious and moral views are not merely fanciful flights of the speculative faculties of a thinker — that they could be put to use and practised. He tries to show that society and state can very well be shaped in accordance with his philosophical and religious views.

Before any attempt is made to outline the social and political views of Mahatma Gandhi, one thing has to be borne in mind. Gandhi reflects on the problems relating to society and state not with the intention of a theorist. He is not interested in finding out the basis of social organisation, or in evolving a theory of the state. His ideal is a practical one — that of introducing certain reforms in social and political set up. Therefore, his analysis of social and political problems are 'normative', they always suggest an 'ought', they invariably refer to an 'ideal' — to the same basic ideal of Truth and Non-violence around which the entire thought-system of Gandhi is built. Gandhi, for example, would not discuss in detail the process that might have led to class-formation, but he would discuss and highlight the process and the way through which such a system could become a healthier system.

i. Society

The first question with which every social philosophy begins is the question regarding the formation of society. Gandhi does not feel the need of entering into the problem regarding the origin of society, he would be prepared to accept any rational conjecture about class-formation. For example, Gandhi would not be opposed even to the Hobbesian view, which believes that society was a result of some kind of contract entered upon by individuals who saw that it was not possible for them to have everything for selves and that some kind of understanding with others was essential for a healthier and more peaceful life.

Gandhi derives a moral from this and similar other accounts of the origin of society — a moral which at once becomes the ethical basis of society. The or gin of society lies in man's realisation that complete selfishness has no place in life. Only when man thought of putting some restraints on his brutish and selfish ways that society came into existence. Thus, the very origin of society lies in the man's conscious effort to transcend his egoistic ways — to rise above his selfish motives. Moreover, this also seems to be fairly plausible that the initial contract might have been entered upon only to avoid strife and quarrel. That means that the very reason that led to the formation of society was to avoid violence. Thus, Gandhi has been able to find out the very basis of society, it consists in *Non-violence* and *self-sacrifice*. Even today, whenever we decide to have small groups or societies to serve certain common ends, these factors remain at the root. We have to sacrifice, at least to some extent, some of our personal considerations and we have to decide that we shall avoid inner strife and violence as far as possible.

Form this, it naturally follows that in a society there cannot remain any opposition between 'individual good' and 'social good.' If the very origin of society lies in self-sacrifice, then there has to be a harmony between our personal considerations and the good of the society. This can be accounted for in a very simple manner. When man was in the completely brutish stage his ways of existence were not different from those of animals. But, when he decided to form groups and tribes his ways became different. His profession also, by that time, had changed from hunting to animal-rearing and agriculture. Even in society he had to care for his food and shelter, and for that he had *to work* in co-operation with others.

Gandhi feels that it is 'work' that distinguishes man from other animals. This 'work' relates every man with every other member of his society and serves the end of satisfying not only his personal needs but also the needs of others.

Work, thus becomes the basis of social organization. Even the modern sociologists admit that *Labour* — which is nothing different from work — is the basis of social organization. But, they have developed their theories in terms of 'struggle', whereas Gandhi, although starting from the same point of work or labour, develops his theory in terms of *love* and *cooperation*.

iii. The Natural Classes or the Varaṇas

From this it follows that a healthy social life must be based on sincere feeling of co-operation and division of work. Gandhi believes that there should be an inner arrangement inside a society for enabling every member to do his share of work for the betterment of the society. He believes that the ancient classification of Hindu society into four Varṇas had been made in that spirit. He says, "I believe that every man is born in the world with certain definite limitations which he cannot overcome. From a careful observation of those limitations the law of varṇa was deduced. It established certain spheres of action for certain people with certain tendencies. This avoided all unworthy competition. Whilst recognising limitations, the law of varṇa admitted of no distinctions of high and low. On the one hand it granted to each the fruits of his labour and on the other it prevented him from pressing upon his neighbour. This great law has degraded and fallen into disrepute. But my conviction is that an ideal social order will only be evolved when the implications of this law are fully understood and given effect to."[1] This passage makes it quite clear that Gandhi does not approve of the present-day Hindu caste-system. In fact, it is a pereverse or degraded form of the original *varṇa* in so far as it has distorted the very spirit of *Varṇa*. Varṇa does not mean that somebody is born high and some low, varṇa does not give superiority to anybody simply by birth. Varṇa is *class* not *caste*. The original varṇa-distinctions were based not on the distinctions of high and low, but on the capacities, skill and power inherent in an individual, and also on the principle of 'division of work'. According

---

1. B. S. Sharma, *Gandhi as a Political Thinker*, p. 121.

to it, an individual was a brahmin not because he was born a brahmin, but because he was brought up in an atmosphere that enabled him to perform the duties of a brahmin. Similarly, Kṣatriyas or Vaiśyas or Śūdras were known by their respective names on account of the specific duties that they used to perform. It was quite possible for a Śūdra to change his varṇa by successfully performing the duties of a different varna. Moreover, only because one varṇa performs a kind of duty, which, from a superficial point of view, appears to be a better kind of duty than the duties of another varṇa, the former does not become superior to the latter. All kinds of work are important and equally essential for the society, and therefore, all kinds of work are equal.

Gandhi makes this point very clear by saying that varṇa prescribes duties and obligations only, it does not confer any *privileges* on any varṇa or individual. The performance of hereditary functions does not give and 'birth-right' to an individual, it merely means that the kind of duty that he has to perform in the society has already been settled. The factor of heredity is also significant, because it avoids the possibility of rift and strife ensuing from making fresh distribution of work everyday. In fact, Gandhi asserts that if a brahmin born of brahmin parents fails to reveal the attributes of a brahmin, he ceases to be a brahmin.

That is why Gandhi invariably relates the doctrine of varṇa to that of *Varṇāsrama Dharma*. The notion of Dharma is emphasised very much. Dharma stands for duties and Gandhi says that every varṇa has specific and definite *duties* or *Dharmas* attached to it. To the fourfold divisions of class (Brahmin, Kṣatriya, Vaiśya and Śūdra) are added the fourfold divisions of the life of an individual — the four Āśramas (Brahmacarya, Gṛhastha, Vānaprastha, and Sannyāsa). Gandhi believes that if these divisions are understood properly and their implications are fully realised, then a strong and moral society can be built on their basis.

iii. Bread Labour

Now, it is sufficiently clear that Gandhi wants every man to be treated as equal. Consequently, he comes to think of certain ways for preventing and eradicating social inequality; the doctrine of *Bread Labour* is one of them. This idea was suggested to Gandhi through various sources. The writings of Tolstoy and

Ruskin along with the suggestions made in the *Bible* and the *Gītā* suggested this idea to Gandhi. The *Bible* says, 'Earn thy bread by the sweat of thy brow' and the Gītā says that he who eats without labouring for it eats stolen bread. Gandhi feels that this idea can be useful also in bringing a feeling of equality among the members of a society.

By 'Bread Labour' Gandhi means that in order to live man must work. It is essential for every man to realise the dignity of labour and to think that at least for earning his own bread one must do some manual work. It is true that every individual cannot do all kinds of manual work. Moreover, if every individual is required to do every kind of work, then the doctrine of varṇa would fall down. Gandhi is aware of this, therefore, he does not say that every body should go to the field. Any man can choose for himself that work that he can do, he can spin or weave or do carpentry or any other thing. There is at least one thing that every one can do, he can be his own scavenger. In fact, by doing manual work one would be able to keep his body also fit.

One may say that mental work is also work or labour Why should, then, it be insisted that a person doing mental work must also do manual labour. Gandhi says that such an attitude causes social distinctions to arise because people doing mental work consider themselves superior to persons who do merely physical work. But, if the person engaged in mental work also does the work of sweeping and cleaning and does some other things also like spinning or gardening, the distinctions would vanish because the work of cleaning or sweeping would not then be considered inferior.

There is one condition attached to Bread Labour; in fact, this condition is a universal condition as it is the supreme condition of morality itself. Everyone must take to Bread Labour voluntarily. There is no question of any compulsion. Compulsion gives rise to discontent and revolt. Social life has to be a life based on love and willing co-operation, and so, the doctrine of Bread Labour can be socially beneficial only when individuals take to it voluntarily.

iv. *Equality of Wages*

Another recommendation that Gandhi makes in order to prevent social inequality is the one regarding *quality of wages*.

This doctrine provides the basis of the economic structure of society. It is only on account of differences in wages that inequality of all kinds results. People getting higher wages consider themselves superior, professions carrying better emoluments are considered to be better kinds of profession. But, Gandhi thinks that all kinds of work are equally sacred, they are all equally necessary for society. The basis for the division and distribution of work should be the aptitudes and capacities of the individual and not wages. Therefore, he recommends that every worker should get the same wages. The lawyer or the doctor or the teacher should get the same emoluments that should be given to a sweeper or a scavenger. As soon as this is given shape men will start choosing their professions not in terms of wages, but in terms of their aptitudes and capacities. This would increase social efficiency. Gandhi is aware that the equality of wages is a difficult ideal to realise, but he is confident that any step in this direction is a step in the right direction.

v. *Labour, Capital and the Doctrine of Trusteeship*

The doctrine of Labour and equality of wages takes us on to consider the relationship between labour and capital. Gandhi holds that labour is superior to capital, and as such is able to give to the person doing labour a kind of dignity. In this respect his views resemble those of Marx. But, unlike Marxism, he would not recommend an overthrow of the capitalists by force. He is not in favour of inciting labour against capital. Unlike Marxism he does not believe that class-struggle is the key and the basic principle of social development. He believes that society has to be based on love and mutual trust and not on struggle. As a devout believer in the ways of Ahimsā, he would not permit any violent struggle or fight even against the capitalists. Society, in spite of everything, must be based on moral considerations. Class-struggle will breed distrust and hatred, and once these forces are let loose, they will go out of control; and this will have a disastrous effect on society.

For this Gandhi introduces the doctrine of the Trusteeship of the rich. Gandhi believes that even the rich people — the so called capitalists — are after all human beings, and as such they also have in them an element of essential goodness that every man necessarily possesses. It that element is aroused and if the capitalists are also won over by love, they would be persuaded to believe that the wealth in their possession should be utilised for the good of the poor. The rich people should be made to realise that the capital in their hands is the fruit of the labour of the poor men. This realisation would make them see that the good of the society lies in using capital and riches for the good of others and not for one's personal comforts. Then, the capitalists would function only as *trustees* for the poor. They would then keep all surplus wealth in *trust* and this would guarantee both economic solidity and economic equality.

Thus, it is apparent that Gandhi's doctrine of Trusteeship is based on a sense of morality and love. This doctrine is nothing but a sincere working out of the doctrine of Non-possession. The rich also must be made to realise, through a loving process, the merit of Non-possession. A critic of Gandhi might say that this doctrine is based on the assumption of honesty on the part of the rich. But, this is no criticism of Gandhi because Gandhi's entire beliefs are based on the presupposition that every man inwardly is good. He has tired to demonstrate this in various ways and he does not want to exclude the capitalists from that. Even they are good people, only their good sense has to be aroused.

vi. The Economic Basis of Society

Now, we are in a position to give an outline of the economic basis of society. Gandhi is aware that complete economic equality is an unattainable ideal. The factor of individual difference is very important, men do differ in their capacities and talents. Therefore, even if equal opportunities are given to individuals, and even if wages are given at the rate of 'equal wages for equal work', the output will differ from individul to individual, and some would earn more and some less. If rigidly economic equality is enforced, then, it will be completely artificial, it will take away from men initiative for work and change them into nothing but machines.

Therefore, the economic basis of society must be a moral one, society must be based on love and trust. This would naturally prevent economic exploitation. A good individual, whose inner moral sense has been aroused, would love to share his 'thing' with others, would see the merit of contentment. Thus, even for economic reform Gandhi recommends cultivation of a strnog moral sense and a love for others,

vii. *Against too much of Industrialisation*

Gandhi feels that the growth of a moral society is prevented by an over-emphasis on industrialisation. Gandhi has been able to perceive that such an attitude has given rise to many kinds of ills and evils both at the social level and at the political level. It is on account of an excess of industrialisation that such international evils like exploitation of the undeveloped countries, colonial expansion, war among nations etc. make their appearance. Smaller countries are exploited for procuring raw-materials and stronger countries get involved in repeated wars just in order to maintain industrial superiority. Then, even on the national level too much of industrialisation leads to many kinds of unrest and disruptions. It is on account of industrialisation that a permanent rift between capital and labour is created. Moreover, by substituting machines for human labour industrialisation creates problems of unemployment also.

But, the strongest reason why Gandhi is against too much of industrialisation is the fact that it poisons the very spirit of man. It makes life mechanical and artificial and seeks to reduce even man to the status of a machine. It lets loose a process of dehumanisation. The result is that man loses the zest for life. He seeks an escape by indulging in purely sensuous pursuits like drinking, gambling and the like. Consequently, he loses his moral sense, and, in fact, his soul itself. Gandhi reflects with horror on the possible consequences of such a process and therefore recommends a life that would make human existence meaningful and would give to man real happiness and peace.

viii. *Men and Women in Society*

A survey of Gandhi's social ideas makes it clear that Gandhi aims at the establishment of a society in which peace and happiness will reign supreme. He feels that this would be possible only when men and women realise their status and duties in society. It is a fact that women today are trying to compete with men in every walk of life by imitating the ways of men. Gandhi is also aware that men are not prepared to give up their sense of mastery over women. This appears to Gandhi as unfortunate. He feels that in an ideal society duties and functions are distributed not only among the different varṇas, but also among men and women. Both men and women have the same soul, and therefore are equal. The work assigned to one is not inferior to the work assigned to the other. Man, by nature, is physically strong, and therefore he puts in hard labour to support and protect the family. Women, by nature, are loving, and therefore, they are equipped by nature to play the role of a mother and the caretaker of the home. Both these duties are equally important and necessary; this must be realised by both men and women.

Therefore, Gandhi recommends that the goal of marriage must be the same as the goal of life itself. Marriage must also be a means for realising a spiritual life. "The ideal that marriage aims at is that of spiritual union through the physical. The human love that it incarnates is intended to serve as a stepping stone to divine or universal love."[1] That is why he says that the object of sexual relation must be nothing else but preservation of race, that is, getting a child. Therefore, married life must be a training in spiritual love, the husband and wife must cultivate a sense of companionship and a pattern for co-operative living.

ix. *Nature of Gandhi's Political Ideas*

Gandhi's political views, in a sense, differ fundamentally from other political theories in so far as he makes even politics subordinate to ethics and religion. Usually politics is considered to be the game of the clever. Even deception, dishonesty, telling lies etc. are considered to be political achievements if they are resorted to skilfully. Gandhi tries to introduce morality in politics, and that he does by presupposing that even political activity is an aspect of the spiritual pattern that guides the world. He works out his political ideas strictly in accordance with his religious and metaphysical beliefs. All men are essentially one, and there is an element of essential goodness present in every man, and therefore, even in politics distrust, hatred, immorality etc. should not have any place. *Satyāgraha* remained Gandhi's political weapon also. Even in politics he made experiments and successfully worked on the conviction that hate and violence could be conquered by love and suffering.

x. *Political Freedom : Swarāj*

Gandhi admits that for the realisation of the ideal state political freedom is one of the essential pre-conditions. That was why

1. N. K. Bose, *Selections from Gandhi*, p, 273.

he had launched a non-violent struggle in order to gain political freedom for India. The word that he prefers to use for political freedom is *swarāj*. Traditionally this word has come to mean 'own Government or self-rule', but Gandhi uses this word in a much profounder sense. His meaning of swarāj includes its usual meaning and adds something more. He says, "As every country is free to eat, to drink and to breathe, even so is every nation free to manage its own affairs, no matter how badly."[1] Along with this he further extends the meaning of swarāj by saying that the *sense* of swarāj must be felt and realised by every individual of the state. According to him the e is a difference between "mere independence" and 'swarāj'. If a country gets self-rule and the few powerful ones take up everything in their own hands and neglect the poor masses, it is not the Swarāj of Gandhi's dream. He takes particular care to emphasise this. He says, "The Swarāj of my dream is the poor man's swarāj. The necessities of life should be enjoyed by you in common with those enjoyed by princes and monied men."[2] "The Swarāj of my dream recognises no race or religious distinction ...Swarāj is to be for all. ...."[3] "I hope to demonstrate that the real swarāj will come not by the acquisition of authority by a few, but by the acquisition of the capacity by all to resist authority, when abused. In other words, swarāj is to be attained by *educating the masses to a sense* of *their capacity to regulate* and control authority."[4] These self-explanatory extracts from Gandhi's writings make it abundantly clear that real Swarāj means that every individual should have a feeling of freedom. In fact, the ultimate aim of every activity, according to Gandhi, is the realisation of spiritual freedom. Swarāj is a step towards it, because it enables an individual to realise at least political freedom.

xi. The State and the Individual

The idea of political freedom raises the question regarding the relation between the state and the individual. This problem has become very important in the recent times in view of the fact that sociological theories have started emphasising the primacy

1. *Young India*, 15-10-31.
2. *Young India*, 26-3-31.
3. *Young India*, 3-9-25.
4. *Young India*, 29-1-25.

of community and have started saying that the individual apart from the community does not have any value. Gandhi, without undermining the importance of the society and the state, assigns to the individual also a very important place. In fact, he feels that the individual, in a sense, is more basic than the society or the state, not only because he is prior to society and the state, but also because he is the unit around which social and political organizations are built

Gandhi feels that no progress or growth can ever be possible unless the individual is allowed to grow. The state derives its existence and strength from individuals, and therefore, it is the function of the state to see that sufficient scope is created for security, peace and all-round development of the individual. Gandhi suspects that even self-rule may, by its acts of omissions and discrimination, may prevent the growth of individuals. For Gandhi the highest goal of life is moral; conscience or ethical consciousness has to be developed in all individuals. Therefore, no nation can hope to prosper unles all its individuals are morally pure. The state should see that the individuality of the individual is not sacrificed at the altar of the whims of those few who lead the government.

In fact, Gandhi recommends that it is one of the supreme duties of an individual to exercise moral pressure on the state by the method of non-violent non-co-operation whenever the state is found indulging in acts of exploitation and discrimination. Gandhi seems to be convinced that even a single individual can force the might of a nation to bow down before its moral strength.

This description of the relation between the state and the individual should not lead one to suppose that Gandhi, as against the Communists, is through and through in favour of the supremacy of the individual. His emphasis is on moral purity. Morality originates in self-sacrifice, therefore, a purely moral individual will not be selfish and individualistic. He will recognise his duties, he will know that the existence of the state depends upon the mutual co-operation of individuals. According to Gandhi, the allegiance to the state is based on a sincere dependence on the moral sense. Therefore, in a state the individual should not talk of his rights, he should talk about his *duties*.

In fact, according to Gandhi, the relation between the state and the individual is one of *co-operation* and *non-co-operation;*

it is co-operation with the laws of the state so long as the state seeks to move along moral lines, but it is non-co-operation with the laws of the state if the laws are against the rules of ethics.

xii. Decentralisation

If the relation between the state and the individual is to be such that individual's initiative is to be promoted, then it is obvious that power should not be centralised in the state. Centralisation of capital or power, according to Gandhi, would lead to exploitation. Moreover, centralisation cannot be maintained or defended without resorting to force or violence. Centralisation leads to concentration of power and capital in a few hands, and therefore, there emerges the possibility of its misuse. On account of all these reasons, but chiefly on account of his conviction that individual liberty and initiative alone can pave the way to progress, Gandhi recommends *decentralisation* as a necessary political measure.

But then, this means that this process has o be carried to its maximum limit. Therefore, Gandhi recommends, what can be called, a *village republic* as the ideal form of decentralised political and social system. He says that the ideal system which can give maximum opportunity for individual initiative and growth is the *Panchayat System* having self-contained villages based primarily on agriculture and cottage industry. This system presupposes voluntary co-operation on the part of every individual. "In this structure composed of innumerable villages...... life will not be a pyramid with the apex sustained by the bo tom. But it will be an oceanic circle whose centre will be the individual always ready to perish for the village, the latter ready to perish for the circle of villages, till at last the whole becomes one life composed of individuals......the outermost circumference will not wield power to crush the inner circle, but will give strength to all within and derive its own strength from it."[1]

xiii. Ideal State and Sarvodaya

Gandhi has tried to analyse and determine carefully the outline or the salient features of the ideal Government that he wishes the state to have. In fact, he feels that our aim should be to concentrate on the means for bringing about a good, peaceful

1. *Speeches*, p. 276, B. S. Sharma, *Gandhi as a Political Thinker*, p. 92.

and happy state in which every individual would be able to get equal opportunities and comforts, but he does not want to enter into the details of the forms of that ideal state. He is aware that during the recent times so many 'isms' and so many names of possible forms of government have become current that it is unwise and unnecessary waste of time to try to enter into the controversy regarding the nature of the ideal state.

Gandhi's idea of the ideal state is the idea of the *Village Republic.* We have seen that he favours a system of self-contained villages. He thinks that in the representative form of government there is the likelihood of individuals and small villages being ignored and neglected. A country is a big 'thing', it extends over a very large area, and so, it is not possible for the centralised form of government to do justice to and to keep sustained interest in small, remote and far-off areas. The best way out, then, is to make villages autonomous at least for things necessary for day to day existence. Every village should be self-contained at least with respect to daily necessities of life, like food, clothing, basic education, health, sanitation and similar other things. Even this system can have a *Panchayat* for smooth and effective running of things. But, the primary aim of Panchayat also should not be legislation of laws. Legislation should be resorted to only when necessary. The normal basis of this Panchayat type of government has to be a moral one. The village republic must be based on strict moral sense and a feeling of mutual co-operation. This system will be the system of perfect democracy because this would ensure complete individual liberty and will promote individual initiative. It will be a state based on love, trust, non-violence and a keenly developed moral sense. This will have the additional advantage of taking |away the very root of rivalry and fight, because in such a system, no panchayat can afford to have any surplus wealth or power. Naturally, there will not remain any reason for lust or greed and consequently life will be more peaceful, and there will remain no scope for exploitation of any kind.

In fact, in conceiving this form of the socio-political set up Gandhi is moved by the considerations of *Sarvodaya.* Sarvodaya etymologically means 'the betterment of all', and that precisely it is. Usually Sarvodaya is compared and contrasted with Utilitarianism. Utilitarianism is the doctrine that believes in the greatest good of the greatest number. But, Sarvodaya is more comprehensive and more altruistic than Utilitarianism. Utilitarianism is after all a hedonistic doctrine, its standard somehow is *pleasure*. Moreover, it is ultimately based on considerations that are selfish, it is ultimately for the good of oneself that others are taken into consideration. Sarvodaya, on the other hand, is based on 'love', it proceeds on the faith that a *sarvodayī* will also be prepared for maximum possible self-sacrifice for the good of others. The end of all activities, social or political, has to be nothing else but the upliftment of everybody. This can be possible only when no individual is neglected or overlooked, and this, in its turn, will be possible only in the panchayat system, which, through its small village units will be able to pay attention to every individual of the village.

Utilitarianism, again, is essentially limited in its scope. There cannot be a really universal philosophy of Utilitarianism because the talk of utility itself precludes the possibility of its universality. It necessarily has a reference to particular societies. Thus, what may be considered to be utilitarian for one society may not be so for another. Sarvodaya, on the other hand, is based on the belief that there is an essential unity behind everything. The forces of disruption that create distinctions between 'I' and 'Thou' are all rooted in selfish considerations, whereas the realisation of oneness is the supreme condition for the effective following of ethical principles. The system of village republic is based on such a consideration. It is true that a perfect realisation of oneness is not possible in this life, but *true spiritual life consists not in attaining the ideal, but in constantly striving and aspiring for it*. The life in the village republic will be an example of such a spiritual living because every man of a Panchayat will have a bond of affection for every other, and consequently will not develop a sense of having a possession. Even land will be considered as belonging to everybody. Gandhi says, "Real socialism has been handed down to us by our ancestors who taught, 'All land belongs to Gopal, where then is the boundary line ?' Man is the maker of that line and he can therefore unmake it. Gopal literally means shepherd; it also means God. In modern language it means the state, i.e. the People".[1]

In a state like this police, military, and courts of Justice will have a character different from the one they have in the present-

1. *Harijan*, 2-1-37.

day states. In fact, Gandhi feels that in a completely non-violent society there should not be any need of the present type of police or military or law-courts. But it is not possible to have a completely non-violent society all at once. Therefore, so long as imperfections and immorality remain, police and law-courts would be needed. But, Gandhi says that their character and pattern should be different, they should not consider themselves to be the masters of the people, they should be real servants of society dedicated to the task of reforming the wrong-doer. In fact, Gandhi feels that in a state of his conception there would not be much problem, because the possibility of crime will automatically go down. Whatever little acts of crime would be committed would be tackled with love. He is convinced that such a police would get spontaneous help from the people. Likewise, military should also be engaged in promoting the ways of non-violence. Use of arms would not be normally permitted, even the aggressor can be met with an army of satyāgrahīs. But so long as people are not reformed, police and military in their usual senses will have to be retained. He feelingly says, "Alas ! in my *Swarāj of today*, there is room for soldiers." "I agree too that a sudden withdrawal of the military and the police will be a disaster if we *have not acquired* the ability to protect ourselves against robbers and thieves."[1]

xiv. Education

As Gandhian political system is based on the consideration that there is an element of goodness essentially present in every man, there is the need of a proper education which would be able to bring out this element of goodness. The state has to prepare individuals [for the village-republic, or for making possible the emergence of the ideal government. Therefore, individuals have to be trained and educated in such a manner that the ideal is reached conveniently. Therefore, the goal of education, according to Gandhi, should be moral education or character-building and the cultivation of a conviction that one should forget everything selfish in working towards great aims.

Therefore, Gandhi defines education in this way, "By education I mean an all-round drawing out of the best in child and man —

1. B. S. Sharma, *Gandhi as a Political Thinker*, p. 113.

body, mind and spirit."[1] "I hold that true education of the intellect can only come through a proper exercise and training of the bodily organs, e.g., hands, feet, eyes, ears, nose etc. In other words an intelligent use of the bodily organs in a child provides the best and quickest way of developing his intellect. But unless the development of the mind and body goes hand in hand with a corresponding awakening of the soul, the former alone would prove to be a poor lop-sided affair. By spiritual training I mean education of the heart. Proper and all-round development of the mind, therefore, can take place only when it proceeds *pari passu* with the education of physical and spiritual faculties of the child. They constitute an indivisible whole. According to this theory, therefore, it would be a gross fallacy to suppose that they can be developed piecemeal or independently of one another."[2]

Thus, Gandhi is not in favour of the present-day system of education that is prevalent in India. Such an education merely imparts instructions, or makes man literate, but literacy is not education. Every individual is born with certain basic and inborn tendencies and capacities. The aim of education should be to bring out such inherent capacities of every individual. This would be possible only when theoretical imparting of instruction is combined with practical training. Gandhi, like Dewey, perceives the value of learning by doing, and therefore recommends that education should begin with the learning of some crafts like: carpentry, poultry, spinning, weaving or any other similar handicraft. By actually doing manual work while learning, the individual will develop interest in his work and will be able to give out his best. This is what is known as *Basic Education*. In this type of education the child is taught how to manipulate things by actually allowing him to do the thing himself. He comes to learn why a thing is done in a particular way and not in a different way. One advantage of this system would be that unlike the present-day prevalent system of education, the individual will find that the things that he learns are of actual use in life. That is why Gandhi is completely dissatisfied with the higher education that is imparted today in Indian universities. A scholar, after completing his studies, enters into the

1. *Harijan*, 31st July 1937.
2. *Harijan*, 8th May 1937.

life-field only to find that there is absolutely no relation between what he had learnt and what he has to do. Therefore he says, "We have up to now concentrated on stuffiing children's minds with all kinds of information, without ever thinking of stimulating and developing them. Let us now cry a halt and concentrate on educating the child properly through manual work, not as side activity, but as the prime means of intellectual training. You have to train the boys in one occupation or another, round this special occupation you will train up his mind, his body, his handwriting, his artist c sense, and so on. He will be the master of craft he learns."[1]

There is yet another advantage of this kind of education; this kind of education will become the spearhead of a silent social revolution. It will bring the city-life and village-life closer, and thus will eradicate the evil of class-difference. It will prevent the decay of village-culture and the lust for city-life, and thus will lay the foundation of a just social order giving equal opportunity and initiative to every individual. Moreover, as this system will make individuals skilled in their own arts, they will be masters of their own destiny, and will not become the object of exploitation of the privileged people. That is why Gandhi conceives 'Basic Education' as having far-reaching consequences.

xv. Swadeshi, Nationalism, Internationalism

One of the most important concepts of Gandhi's political views is the concept of Swadeshi. The word Swadeshi literally means 'belonging to one's own country'. Gandhi also means, more or less, the same thing by this word and yet this word has assumed in Gandhi's thought a special significance simply on account of the emphasis that has been laid on it and also on account of its very comprehensive use. Gandhi has applied this notion in almost every sphere of life — social, political and economic.

Ordinarily Gandhian interpretation of the swadeshi is given a political colour and is taken as the basis of 'Nationalism'. But, in Gandhi swadeshi has both a positive and a negative sense. Positively it provides a political and economic principle which can be viewed as having a nationalistic tinge, negatively it gives out a basis for inter-nationalism.

1. *Harijan*, 18th September 1937.

The broad meaning of swadeshi is 'the use of all home-made things to the exclusion of foreign things'. But, this is too broad a definition of swadeshi. Properly speaking the use of home-made things to the exclusion of foreign things is recommended only under a condition, only when such a use is necessary for the protection and growth of home-industry. If the use of foreign things is beneficial, and does not adversely affect the cottage industry, then, swadeshi will not be insisted upon. Gandhi is aware that even swadeshi, like any other good thing, 'can be ridden to death if it is made a fetish'. That is a danger that must be guarded against. To reject foreign manufacturers merely because they are foreign and to go on wasting national time and money in trying to promote such manufactures for which the country is not suited would be a folly and a negation of the spirit of swadeshi.

Swadeshi, therefore, is not a narrow parochial doctrine, on the other hand, it is based on the recognition of human limitations and capacity for work and service. We have to provide food, work and employment to our immediate neighbours, and therefore, we shall have to work for what can guarantee these to all of us. The Swadeshi-doctrine, therefore, is a doctrine employed for the protection of home-industry. It, in no way, suggests that the use of foreign goods must be discarded at all cost.

Such an attitude would presuppose a feeling of hatred or at least a dislike for everything foreign, and such a feeling is against the spirit of Ahiṁsā. Swadeshi is also one of the ways of non-violence and therefore, a true believer in swadeshi will not harbour any ill-feeling towards foreign things. Gandhi would be prepared to buy from any part of the world things that are needed for the growth of his country, but he would insist on the use of swadeshi when such foreign things are sought to be imported that hamper the economic status of home-industry. For example, any article is swadeshi if it protects the interest of the people even if the capital and talents are foreign and are under the effective control of the country. For example, even if *Khadi* is promoted by the use of foreign capital and talent, it is swadeshi. Gandhi would be prepared to import medicines, useful tools, technical instruments etc. without hesitating even for a second. Swadeshi, thus, is not an outright rejection of everything foreign, it of course is based on a feeling of concern for the economic and political stability of one's own country. Thus the notion of swadeshi raises the question of nationalism and internationalism.

Gandhi's insistence on swadeshi raises a very genuine doubt in the minds of many : is it not a fact that by insisting on swadeshi Gandhi is contradicting himself ? On the one hand he asserts that there is an essential unity of everything, and at the same time he is preaching 'love for one's own country', that is, love for only one aspect of mankind. Gandhi is aware of this and he solves this problem in his own way. He says that nationalism and internationalism are not essentially opposed to each other.

The first requirement of love is self-transcendence, going beyond the individualistic considerations of the self. This process goes on extending itself from family to society, from society to nation, from nation to humanity and so on. In fact, Gandhi feels that the act of love has to be particularised in order to be effective. The general love for everything, at least in the beginning, will have no apparent significance unless it is localised. Just as there cannot be a friendship except between this and that individual, so there cannot be any love unless it is for something. Love of the nation, or swadeshi, therefore, has to be there. Nationalism is a merit.

And yet, it is neither against Inter-nationalism nor does it create any obstacle in the way of love for mankind in general. Gandhi believes that a man can serve his neighbours and humanity at the same time, the condition being that the service of neighbours is in no way selfish or exclusive and does not involve any exploitation of any human being. Talking about his own patriotic feelings or nationalism he says, "My patriotism is both exclusive and inclusive. It is exclusive in the sense that in all humility I confine my attention to the land of my birth, but is inclusive in the sense that my service is not of a competitive or antagonistic nature."[1] In fact, if I do not carry ill-will against any country and if I do not do anything against any country, my nationalism is not against inter-nationalism. Nationalism in itself is neither an evil nor against inter-nationalism, it becomes an evil when it is based on narrowness and selfishness.

1. B. S. Sharma, *Gandhi as a Political Thinker*, p. 116.

According to Gandhi, nationalism, in reality is a pre-condition of inter-nationalism. The question of inter-nationalism arises only when nationalism becomes a fact, that is, only when people have already organised themselves into different nations and are prepared to act as one unit. There must, therefore, be a healthy inter-dependence among different nations, which would be possible only when a feeling of love — a sense of inter-nationalism is developed in the different nations. Gandhi says that true inter-nationalism presupposes the reality of national units and also the recognition of the fact that all nations are equal. The moment we start making distinctions between big and small nations, inter-nationalism will be disturbed. Another requirement of inter-nationalism is that every nation must appreciate and realise the value and importance of non-violence. Gandhi recommends that every nation should go for disarmament voluntarily.

Thus, it is apparent that the rule of love, which Gandhi applies to man, he applies also to nations. Just as man is asked to be loving, kind and friendly to others, so nations are also asked to be loving and friendly to other nations. Inter-nationalism is an extension of nationalism, which is nothing but the extension of man's self-sacrifice and love. "The individual, being free, sacrifices himself for the family, the latter for the village, the village for the district, the district for the province, the province for the nation, the nation for all."[1]

---

1. D.M. Datta, *The Philosophy of Mahatma Gandhi*, p. 160.

CHAPTER IV

SRI AUROBINDO

Life

Aurobindo Ghosh was born on the fifteenth of August 1872 at Konanagar, West Bengal. He got his early education in the Loretto Convent School of Darjeeling, and was taken to England at an early age of eight. In the early part of his stay in England he was put under the care of an able teacher, named Drewett. In 1885 he was sent to St. Paul's School in London. In school he developed a special fascination for some classical languages like Greek and Latin and also for some European languages. He learnt them all, and even tried to compose verses in Latin and Greek.

After completing his studies he appeared for the I. C. S. examination, was successful in the written test, but could not qualify in the riding test. In 1893 he came back to India and joined the Baroda State Service. There he found enough leisure to read ancient Indian Philosophy.

Somehow he was not satisfied with the type of life he was leading at Baroda, and was drawn into a political career. He remained in Baroda for about ten years, after which he devoted himself to political work. This was a brief phase of his life, which came to an end in 1908 with his arrest. It is said that during the period of his imprisonment he came to feel that he was destined to pursue a different course of life. A kind of a spiritual change brought about the transformation and the hectic political worker took to the ways of a Yogi. In April 1910, he shifted to Pondicherry, and stayed there till he gave up his mortal remains in 1950. He founded an Ashram at Pondicherry with the sole aim of putting to practice some of the spiritual and yogic ideas that he had come to think about. Only after a few years, one of his eminent disciples, Mira Richard, took upon herself the task of the management of the Ashram, and in course of time became almost the symbol of the Ashram, She has been both literally and figuratively 'the Mother' of the Ashram.

Sri Aurobindo's personal influence and magnetism combined with the vast and profound literature that he produced succeeded in winning over a very great number of disciples, who continue to spread his message and teaching. Even after his death (on the 5th December 1950) his Ashram continues to be a centre of learning and spiritual discipline.

The Philosophical Background

Sri Aurobindo's philosophy carries on it the stamp of a number of influences. He had studied western philosophy and literature at an early age and was well acquainted with the comprehensive systems of some of the Greek philosophers like Plato and Aristotle. He was also well-acquainted with some of the idealistic philosophies of recent times. Hegal, Whitehead and the vitalist Bergson seem to have exercised some influence on the mental make-up of Sri Aurobindo He had also studied the ancient Indian philosophies including the *Darśanas* — particularly those of Advaita Vedānta and Yoga. But, relied chiefly on his own vision, contemplation and reason. One feels that in the inner realisation of Sri Aurobindo all these influences were reviewed and re-organised, and what resulted was a new, synthetic and comprehensive vision of reality.

It is difficult to give an exact philosophical description of this vision, in fact, no accepted philosophical epithet can be applied to this. In a broad sense, Sri Aurobindo's philosophy can be called idealistic. It is idealistic firstly because it conceives reality as spiritual, it is idealistic also because it fixes up an ideal for mankind towards which all our efforts have to be directed. But, his idealism cannot properly be called 'Monism' of an abstract type or 'Theism' of a personalistic variety. The best name that can be given to Sri Aurobindo's philosophy is the one given to it by Haridas Choudhary. He says, 'The philosophy of Sri Aurobindo may aptly be described as integral non-dualism (Pūrṇa-advaita), or integral idealism (Pūrṇa-vijñana), or just integralism (Pūrṇavāda).''[1] This non-dualism is different from rationalistic Monism which is based on a conceptually formulated, determinate principle of unity. In fact, in a philosophy of integralism, reality has to be indeterminate, even monism cannot be attributed to it. It can only suggest that reality can

1. Haridas Choudhary, ed. *The Integral Philosophy of Sri Aurobindo* p. 19

be apprehended in some spiritual — supra-rational — insight.
It is called 'integral' because it both accepts and sublimates the
opposition between the lower nature and the higher nature, or
between matter and spirit. The opposition between the two is
transcended as a result of the operation of a super-conscient
creative force, the Mother.

The Two Negations

In order to appreciate the implications of the word 'Integralism' it is necessary to examine Sri Aurobindo's assertions regarding the two negations — *'The materialistic denial and the
refusal of the ascetic'* Aurobindo is aware that Materialism and
Spiritualism are the two prevalent and rival theories which have
attemped to explain the world in their own ways. Aurobindo's
philosophy synthesises or integrates the two. He says, "The
affirmation of a Divine Life upon earth and an immortal sense
in mortal existence can have no base unless we recognise not
only eternal spirit as the inhabitant of this bodily mansion, the
wearer of this mutable robe, but accept matter of which it is
made, as a fit and noble material out of which He weaves
constantly His garbs, builds recurrently the unending series of
his mansions."[1]

According to him the materialist of course has an easier
case, it is possible for him to deny the spiritual and to arrive at
a readily convincing doctrine — a monistic doctrine emphasising the monism of matter or of force. But, Aurobindo feels that
such a materialistic monism cannot last long. The assertions of
the materialists are chiefly based on the testimony of the senses.
But, senses are essentially limited in their scope and application.
Things that senses can know are insignificant in comparison to
things that senses cannot know. The modern materialist claims
to have the sanction of science behind it. Materialism is said to
be essentially scientific in nature. The ultimate units of Materialism are the ones that have been scientifically discovered. But
Sri Aurobindo feels that even the 'Scientific sanction' cannot
justify the materialistic denial. Intellect which has tried to find
the solution of all problems in 'matter' has not succeeded in getting satisfying answers, most often it ends up with such elemen-

---

1. Sri Aurobindo, *The Life Divine*, p. 8.

tary and atomistic principles, which are, more or less, 'theoretical constructs' and are practically unknowable. Moreover, Aurobindo thinks that the materialistic emphasis on 'Science' has almost overlooked a more basic fact — 'The scientific spirit'. What is 'scientific spirit'? It is the spirit which knows no halting place, which is perhaps aware of the limitations of the intellect and which asserts that every solution found is only a step ahead — is only a condition of raising newer issues. This appears to Sri Aurobindo as highly significant. Therefore, he says that science also is constantly and persistently pointing towards a *beyond*. There is no finality about scientific conclusions, and therefore, the materialistic denial of the non-material becomes in the last analysis precarious and self-contradictory.

The spiritualistic negation is also equally onesided and partial. Sri Aurobindo says that the ascetic is also as emphatic in his denial of the material as the materialist is in his rejection of the spiritual. The justification or logic that is put forward by one party is met by an equally cogent logic advanced by the other end. "If the materialist is justified from his point of view in insisting on Matter as reality, the relative world as the sole thing of which we can in some sort be sure and the Beyond as wholly unknowable, if not indeed non-existent, a dream of the mind, an abstraction of thought divorcing itself from reality,... so also is the Sannyāsin. enamoured by that *Beyond*, justified from his point of view in insisting on pure spirit as the reality, the one thing free from change, birth, death and the relative as a creation of the mind and the senses, a dream, an abstraction in the contrary sense of Mentality withdrawing from the pure and eternal knowledge."[1] These Sannyāsins claim to have direct knowledge of the Supra-sensible realities. They think that the higher consciousness is not hampered by and is free from distractions, and as such, is capable of giving more certain knowledge than the senses. Aurobindo says that this knowledge leads these ascetics to deny the reality of the materialistic world. That is why the Indian ascetic comes to discover the concept of 'Cosmic illusion' or 'Bhrama'.

But, Sri Aurobindo feels that these ascetics, in their exclusive onesidedness, overlook a simple fact. If reality is spiritual, then even matter is spiritual, and as such an outright rejection of the

1. Sri Aurobindo, *The Life Divine*, p. 18.

material is evidently fallacious. The fact is that Matter and
Spirit, according to Sri Aurobindo, are like the two aspects of
the same thing. If matter is to ascend to the spirit, there must
be a corresponding descent of the spirit in matter. The material cannot be completely false; even if it has to be spiritualised, it has to be given some status and reality. Ancient Indian
philosophy, specially the Vedānta has committed that mistake,
it does not realise that every evolution must have a corresponding involution. Sri Aurobindo, therefore, tries to work out an
integral view in which both spirit and matter are given their dues.

Reality — Saccidānanda

This spirit of reconciliation becomes the guiding principle of
Sri Aurobindo's metaphysics. He conceives reality as supremely
spiritual and yet he manages to assign to matter a place in it. He
himself admits, "Since, then, we admit both the claim of the Pure
Spirit to manifest in us its absolute Freedom and the claim of
Universal Matter to be the mould and condition of our manifestation, we have to find a Truth that can entirely reconcile these
antagonists and can give to both their due portion in life and
their due justification in thought."[1] He is able to discover such
a principle in the Vedantic concept of *Brahma*, with the difference that many of the aspects of Brahman which had not been
emphasised fully by the Vedānta, are highlighted by Sri Aurobindo. He is able to see that the principle of Brahman, in spite
of being spiritual can accommodate in its bosom the principle of
Matter also.

In order to appreciate this point fully it is essential to analyse
the way in which Sri Aurobindo arrives at his concept of
Brahman. He first comes to feel that in the cosmic consciousness there is a meeting place of matter and spirit where matter
becomes real to the spirit and the spirit becomes real to matter.
In this consciousness, there is at least an attempt to rise above
the separation of the material and the spiritual. But this cosmic
consciousness tends towards a transcendental consciousness,
which initially is nothing but the consciousness of *the unknowable*. The unknowable, in spite of being the unknowable,
appears to us as something supreme, wonderful and ineffable,
which continually formulates itself to our consciousness and

1. Sri Aurobindo, *The Life Divine*, p. 26.

continually escapes the formulation that it itself has caused to be made.

This shows that as our consciousness goes on extending its scope it comes to have a feel of the unknowable. This unknowable is not a malicious magician playing tricks upon us and deceiving us. This is the view that we get of the reality from our perspective. Even when we extend our consciousness to its farthest limits and have a feel of the omnipresent reality, it still is unknowable. This omnipresent reality, which from our limited perspective is the unknowable, has been called *the Brahman*. Sri Aurobindo accepts that we *do not have a knowledge* of the *Brahman*. In fact, he admits that initially there must be an element of *faith* in this omnipresent reality. Our human way of apprehension, which cannot work without proceeding in terms of dualities, has to support itself on an act of faith, a kind of faith which somehow has a rational sanction also. He says, "This creed is given, indeed to humanity to support it on its journey, until it arrives at a stage of development when faith will be turned into knowledge and perfect experience...."[1]

In order to understand the nature of the reality, it is essential to consider the levels or the cords of *Being* as they have been conceived by Sri Aurobindo.

While Sri Aurobindo does talk about the different cords of Being, he does not intend to create the impression that reality is plural in nature. Reality, according to him, is essentially one, but creation depends upon the twofold principle of unity and multiplicity. Creation is the expression of the essential unity of reality, but it is an expression in terms of manifoldness. The cords of being, therefore, are the expressions of reality viewed from the point of view of creation.

He talks about *eight* such principles. They are *Existence, Consciousness-force, Bliss, Supermind, Mind, Psyche, Life* and *Matter*. The first four belong to the higher hemisphere and the last four to the lower hemisphere. The lower hemisphere seeks to represent the stages that evolution has been able to reach, and the higher hemisphere seeks to represent the stages into which evolution is going to enter. The two hemispheres are not opposite in nature, in fact, aspects of the lower correspond to those

1. Sri Aurobindo, *The Life Divine*, p. 33.

of the higher hemisphere. For example, Mind is a subordinate power of supermind, life is a subordinate power of the energy aspect of reality — of consciousness-force. Likewise, "Matter is the form of substance of being which the existence of Saccidānanda assumes when it subjects itself to this phenomenal action of its own consciousness and force."[1] In fact, Sri Aurobindo believes that "the divine descends from pure existence through the play of consciousness force and Bliss and the creative medium of Supermind into Cosmic Being, we ascend from Matter through a developing life, soul and mind and the illumination medium of supermind towards the divine being."[2] The knot between the two hemispheres is where mind and supermind meet with a veil in between them. This description shows that the higher hemisphere, which the lower hemisphere also seeks to reflect, consists of *a triune principle* with supermind as Supreme Truth — consciousness. Supermind is not an entity having a status of its own — a status different from the status of Existence, Consciousness-force and Bliss. Therefore, the best way to represent reality is to describe it in terms of these three principles. That is why Sri Aurobindo describes reality as *Saccidānanda*. Saccidānanda is nothing but a common name for the triune principle of Existence, Consciousness-force and Bliss. Sri Aurobindo says, "We start, then, with the conception of an omnipresent Reality of which neither the Non-being at the one end nor the Universe at the other are negations that annul, they are rather different status of the Reality, obverse and reverse affirmations. The highest experience of this Reality in the universe shows it to be not only a conscious Existence, but a supreme Intelligence and Force and a self-existent Bliss."[3] Let us try to explain their nature.

i. The Pure Existent

In Vedānta existence is conceived to be a universal and ineffable reality, but there the evidence advanced in support of this is that an analysis of the three aspects of life (waking life, dream, and the state of dreamless sleep) reveals the universal and undeniable status of existence. Sri Aurobindo also assigns to 'the Pure existent', more or less, the same status, but his way

1. Sri Aurobindo, *The Life Divine*, p. 212.
2. *Ibid*, p. 243.
3. *Ibid*, p. 32.

of demonstrating this is somewhat different. He analyses (a) the apprehensions of the first philosophical insight and (b) also that of Pure reason and comes to find Existence as pure, universal and boundless energy. He says that when we free ourselves from our personal and egoistic considerations and view at the world in the spirit of a curious enquirer with dispassionate and inquisitive eyes we somehow, at least initially, come to feel before us the presence of a boundless energy — of infinite activity expressing itself in limitless space and eternal time. We come to find that there is an infinite existence transcending our egoistic domains, seeking to fulfil some inapprehensible aims of its own. The first realisation is of an infinitely extended world pitted against ourselves. Thus, there emerges a duality, and we, in ignorance, begin to assert this duality by making ourselves important.

But then, reason starts making further reflections and this infinite existence which originally appeared to be "the other", reveals itself in a different way. Sri Aurobindo feels that science also helps in this rational apprehension of reality. It shows that this boundless energy and movement comprehend both the smallest and the largest, that this movement is so immense and infinite that it is not possible to bind it in terms of our measures of space and time. Space and time create their own limitations, and the Pure Existent cannot be bound by any limiting factors. Thus, pure reason comes to evolve the concept of 'the truly boundless', it is boundless not because it is infinitely extended in space and time, but because it is beyond space and time.

In this way philosophical insight comes to have a glimpse of the Pure Existent. It is infinite and boundless *not* in terms of space and time, but in the sense that the question of space and time cannot be raised with respect to this. One advantage of this concept is that it enables our apprehension of existence to rise above the duality of 'I' and 'the other', which presents itself to our first insight into the nature of reality. Now even the 'I' becomes an aspect of the Pure Existent. When we look at existence, time and space disappear, and with their disappearance, the duality caused by them also disappears.

Sri Aurobindo admits that it is not possible to describe the Pure Existent adequately; in fact, it is not describable in purely intellectual terms. He clearly says, "If this indefinable, infinite, timeless, spaceless Existence is, it is necessarily a Pure Absolute.

It cannot be summed up in any quantity or quantities, it cannot be composed of any quality or combination of qualities. It is not an aggregate of forms or a formal substratum of forms. If all forms, quantities were to disappear, this would remain."[1]

Thus, it is apparent that, in talking about the Pure Existent, Sri Aurobindo makes a distinction between (a) what is revealed of Pure Existent to our insight — to our attempts to *see* the world and (b) what pure reason is able to conceive about it The former is the picture of Existence in terms of space and time, the latter transcends spatial and temporal distinctions. The former pictures Existence as actually existing, the latter forms a concept of Existence. But, finally Sri Aurobindo reconciles the two pictures by suggesting that these two pictures are in fact, the results of the two different ways of looking at Pure Existence. Our initial insight views at it in the forms of space and time, and therefore, it appears as boundless energy — as infinite *movement*. Our rational analysis, on the other hand, seeks to go beyond it and consequently comes to conceive of it as the *Absolute* behind the movement in space and time. Therefore, Sri Aurobindo says, " ... we say that the pure existence *is our Absolute* and in itself unknowable by our thought although we can go back to it in a supreme Identity that transcends the terms of knowledge. *The movement*, on the contrary is the field of the relative and yet by the very definition of the relative all things in the movement contain, are contained in and are the Absolute."[2]

ii. Consciousness-force

We have seen that, according to Sri Aurobindo, strictly speaking, "the Absolute is neither Being nor Becoming, neither One nor Many, but is beyond both Stability and Movement. Unity and Multiplicity are, in fact, our mental representations of the Absolute."[3] But, we have also seen that our insight into the nature of reality reveals itself as boundless energy — as infinite existence. Sri Aurobindo feels that these two ways of apprehending the Absolute are not opposed to each other. The Absolute may appear as *Pure Existence* and also as *Force*. He agrees with

1. Sri Aurbindo, *The Life Divine*, p. 72.
2. *Ibid.*
3. S.K, Moitra, *The Philosophy of Sri Aurobindo*, p. 13.

the ancient Indian assertion that Force is inherent in Existence. Speaking figuratively Sri Aurobindo says that we have to accept the double fact of both '*Śiva*' and '*Kālī*'.

Now, two questions arise : — (a) What precisely is the relation between the Pure Existent and the Force, and (b) what is the nature of this Force ?

The first question is significant in view of the fact that this force is not *conceived as representing the essence* of Existence. It is possible for us to conceive of an Existence free from force. Had this force been the essence of Existence, the question of their inter-relation would not have arisen, but that is not so. Therefore, the question arises: how can a force alien to the nature of Existence come to take place in it ? If 'Śiva' and 'Kālī' are both to be admitted in Sri Aurobindo's scheme of reality, the question regarding their inter-relation has to be raised.

Sri Aurobindo says that Force is *inherent* in Existence in the sense that there is a relation of inseparability between the two. Although it is possible to think of Pure Existence apart from this Force, actually they are inseparably related with each other.

But, Force admits of two possibilities, it can be at rest or in motion. Sri Aurobindo says that this Force also has in it the double or the alternative potentiality of rest and movement, of *self-concentration in Force* and of *self-diffusion in Force*. But this gives rise to a further problem. "Why should this possibility of a play of movement of Force translate itself at all ? Why should not Force of Existence remain eternally concentrated in itself, infinite free from all variation and formation ?"[1] Sri Aurobindo solves this problem in a very simple way — simply by saying that even this is inherent in the nature of Force. In fact, he asserts that the question 'why' cannot be raised at all, because the Force of Existence, by its very nature passes through the alternative modes of self-concentration (rest) and self-diffusion (motion).

Now, we can try to answer the second question regarding the nature of this Force. Is this Force an unconscious energy, an unintelligent power, a chemical force or is it a conscious energy ? Sri Aurobindo unhesitatingly asserts that it has to be conscious. In fact, Sri Aurobindo is able to prove both the facts namely that Force has to be consciousness and that consciousness,

1. Sri Aurobindo, *The Life Divine*, p. 79.

by its nature is a force. Sri Aurobindo examines the nature of all levels of Existence and comes to show that at all levels every movement or dynamism reflects a conscious energy. He takes the word consciousness not in the sense of human consciousness, but in a very comprehensive sense. He says, 'It (consciousness) is no longer synonymous with mentality but indicates a self-aware force of existence of which mentality is a middle term, below mentality it sinks into vital and material movements which are for us subconscient; above it rises into the Supramental which is for us the superconscient. But in all it is one and the same thing organising itself differently."[1] Thus, this conscious Force is conceived as one comprehensive principle comprehending the material, the vital, the mental and also the supramental. Sri Aurobindo calls it the *cit*, and feels that ancient Indian Philosophy—specially the Vedānta has itself given to the word 'Cit' such a comprehensive meaning.

One very illuminating idea introduced by Sri Aurobindo in his conception of the consciousness-force is that *Cit* is the root principle of creation. He calls it *The Mother* and conceives it as the Divine Śakti which is the principle behind the world-process. It is this Śakti that creates and sustains the universe.

Thus, it is obvious that by conceiving the creative principle of the universe as a conscious energy Sri Aurobindo is able to avoid the difficulties connected with the concept of 'Unconscious Teleology.' The moment the creative energy is conceived as conscious, there remains no difficulty in explaining the order, harmony and purpose present in the universe.

iii. The Delight of Existence: Bliss

The Absolute, as conceived by Sri Aurobindo, is not only *sat* and *cit* it is also *ānanda*. "Brahman is infinite Bliss or the infinite delight of the creative play of the force".[2] Sri Aurobindo is aware that Brahman conceived as Existent and as conscious Force may be conceived as a 'complete notion' so that there may not remain any need for the Supreme Reality — the Absolute — to express itself in different forms. He himself raises the question, "Why should Brahman, perect, absolute, infinite,

1. Sri Aurobindo, *The Life Divine*, p. 83.
2. Haridas Choudhary, ed., *The Integral Philosophy of Sri Aurobindo*. p. 38

needing nothing, desiring nothing at all, throw out force of consciousness to create in itself these worlds of forms?[1] One may say that the Absolute has the potentiality of creation, but that does not remove the difficulty. What causes this potentiality to be realised? The Absolute is not limited or bound or compelled by any thing, it does not lack or want anything. What then causes the Absolute to move and to give expressions to its potentialities? Sri Aurobindo feels that *Delight* can be the only reason for creation. There can be no other explanation of this than the fact that it is for the sheer joy of the thing that the Absolute expresses itself in various forms. He says. "It is Ānanda out of which this world is born. It is Ānanda that sustains it and it is Ānanda that is its goal and consummation."[2] This is the ancient Vedantic explanation of creation and Sri Aurobindo also accepts this. He describes creation as the ecstatic dance of Śiva, and as such the purpose of creation can be nothing else but the *joy* of the dancing. This joy or bliss is also as universal and ineffable as Pure Existent or Consciousness-force. Just as a negation of Existence or Consciousness cannot be thought of so a rejection of the universal Bliss is unthinkable. "Absolute of conscious Existence is illimitable bliss of conscious existence; the two are only different phrases for the same thing"[3]

According to Sri Aurobindo the self-delight or Bliss of Saccidānanda is limitless. It is capable of infinite variety, it is expressed in every aspect of existence and conscious activities. Just as conscious force expresses itself in infinite forms, so also in everything that is, there is the delight of existence which constitutes the essence of every activity.

Sri Aurobindo is aware that an emphasis on the Bliss-aspect of Saccidānanda naturally raises the problem regarding 'Evil'. If the universe is an expression of the delight of Brahman and if the Brahman itself is *sat, cit* and *ānanda* then naturally the question arises: why should there be pain and evil in the universe? Sri Aurobindo is aware of the importance of the problem and is also aware that the presence of pain and evil presents an obstacle in the way of conceiving the universe as an expression of joy. But,

1. Sri Aurobindo. *The Life Divine*, p. 86.
2. Sri Aurobindo, *The Life Divine*, p. 67.
3. *Ibid.*, p. 86.

in his characteristic manner Sri Aurobindo is able to show
that the presence of pain and suffering does not, in any way,
contradict the delight of existence.[1]

Nature of Creation : The World-Process

So far we have been trying to determine the nature of the
reality—of Saccidānanda. But, the fact of creation demands an
explanation specially in view of the fact that the Absolute is
conceived as absolute and infinite, as the Supreme that lacks
nothing. Naturally, the question regarding the 'why' and the
'how' of creation would be raised.

In fact, Sri Aurobindo conceives creation as a double-process,
it is firstly a *descent* of the spirit into the worldly forms and
then it also implies an *ascent* of the worldly forms to its original
higher status. Sri Aurobindo is aware that all talks about spiritual regeneration and growth would presuppose two things : (a)
Firstly it would presuppose that the ideal can be reached, and
that there can be no better guarantee to this than the fact that
the *ideal* really is a part of our nature, although somehow we
have forgotten about our own selves. (b) Secondly it would
imply that there has been a descent of the spirit into the world
because ascent presupposes descent. We cannot rise upto the
status of the spirit unless spirit somehow has descended down
to us. In the case of 'knowledge', for example, this process can
be illustrated just only to make possible an analogical understanding of the whole idea. In so far as we attain knowledge we
ascend to it, but *knowledge* has descended down to us. Likewise,
spiritual transformation presupposes the descent of the spirit—
which is nothing but the origin of creation.

Creation, thus according to Sri Aurobindo, is a process of
descent and *ascent*, of *involution* and *evolution*.

i. Descent or Involution

The description of the involutionary aspect of creation, as
given by Sri Aurobindo, follows, more or less, the same pattern
that we come across in the Vedantic description of creation, with
the difference that the terms, concepts etc. bear the stamp of Sri

1. For Sri Aurobindo's solution of the problem see *The Life Divine*, the
subsection on the 'Problem of Evil'.

Aurobindo's own insight. In the Vedānta, creation is described as a result of avidyā. On account of ignorance we come to regard the world and our apparent self as the only realities. It is, therefore, a result of a kind of a forgetting of the true nature of reality. In the advaita Vedānta it is said that in reality there was never a creation, and that this cosmic delusion is nothing but a sporting and joyous act — a *Līlā*.

More or less in the same vein, Sri Aurobindo describes creation as the *plunge of the Spirit into Ignorance*. Ignorance, according to Sri Aurobindo, is the power of Divine consciousness to *withhold itself partially*. Ignorance is not a separate power, it is a part and parcel of Divine consciousness itself. It is not a negation of Divine knowledge. In fact, on the one extreme is the supreme Divine consciousness and on the other extreme is the possibility of *complete nescience*. Ignorance is in between the two, and this is the realm of the created world. Thus, the Absolute itself puts itself partially in check and decides to descend into ignorance, this is creation.

But, the first question that naturally arises is : 'why should Absolute choose to create out of ignorance ?' Can he not create out of knowledge ? And, if he must create out of ignorance, is it not a limitation of its power ? Sri Aurobindo is aware of the possibility of such a doubt. Therefore, he says, that the Absolute can create out of fullness of its self-knowledge. But, that is only a higher creation — a greater world which only seers and sages can see and feel. The question of creation is normally raised with respect to the lesser world — the world in which we live and move. *This* creation is through ignorance. "Infinite consciousness in its infinite action can produce only infinite results ; to settle upon a fixed Truth or order of Truths and build a world in conformity with that which is fixed, demands a selective faculty of knowledge commissioned to shape finite appearance out of the infinite reality."[1]

Such a conception of the world distinguishes Aurobindo's standpoint from that of Advaita Vedānta in so far as such a description of creation does not make the world essentially unreal. World has been given a status and a reality by Sri Aurobindo. To understand this fully it is necessary to outline Sri Aurobindo's views on Māyā.

---

1. Sri Aurobindo, *The Life Divine*, p. 108.

ii. Māyā and Līlā

In fact, these two *words* answer the questions 'how' and 'why' with regard to the world. To the question 'why' creation?' the answer is 'Līlā, and to the question 'How creation ?' the answer is through Māyā. Although these apparently look exactly like Vedāntic answers to these questions, Sri Aurobindo conceives them not exactly in the Vedānta's way but in his own way.

Creation, according to Sri Aurobindo, as also according to the ancient Indian seers is nothing but an expression of joy. Delight is the secret of creation, Delight is the root of birth, Delight is the cause of remaining in existence, Delight is the end of birth and that into which creation ceases. 'From Ānanda', says the Upaniṣad, 'all existents are born, by Ānanda they remain in being and increase, to Ānanda they depart."[1] Therefore, it can be said that creation is nothing but a joyful game—*a Līlā.* The world of which we ourselves are also parts appear even to most casual and obvious insight as a movement of Force, and this Force also appears to be consciously creative — as creating and giving expressions to newer and newer forms. But the moment we reflect upon the purpose and reason of this force and the creation of these forms, we come to realise that the entire rhythm of the universe is an expression of delight. When we come to realise it, we become one with it. This delight of world-process *in relation to the Saccidānanda* is called *Līlā.* Sri Aurobindo says, " ... if we look at the world existence rather in its relation to the self-delight of eternally existing being, we may regard, describe and realise it as Līlā, the play, the child's joy, the poet's joy, the actor's joy, the mechanician's joy of the Soul of things eternally young, perpetually inexhaustible creating and re-creating Himself in Himself for the sheer bliss of that Self-creation, of that self-representation—Himself the play, Himself the player, Himself the playground."[2]

This world, created for the sake of joy is Māyā. Sri Aurobindo tries to determine the process by which Saccidānanda turns Himself into the phenomenal world. He is also aware that it is not quite reasonable to suppose that Saccidānanda does all this, more or less, like a magician simply by moving his magic-wand.

1. Sri Aurobindo, *The Life Divine*, p. 95.
2. *Ibid.*, p. 96.

He perceives *a rule of Law* — a definite pattern or process in creation. To this law he gives the name *Māyā*.

Māyā has been traditionally conceived in two distinct ways. "Māyā in its original sense meant a comprehending and containing consciousness capable of embracing, measuring and limiting, and therfore formative, it is that which outlines, measures out, moulds, forms in the formless, psychologises and seems to make knowable the unknowable, geometrises and seems to make measurable the limitless. Later the word came from its original sense of knowledge, skill, intelligence to acquire a pejorative sense of cunning, fraud or illusion, and it is in the figure of an enchantment or illusion that it is used by the philosophical systems."[1] Thus, in the first sense, it is a power, constructive and creative, and in the second sense it is a delusion-poducing mechanism.

Sri Aurobindo does not feel inclined to accept the second meaning of the word Māyā, because that reduces the world to the status of an illusion. He clearly says that the world is not unreal; even if it were a dream, it would be real as a dream — real to itself in the present. We cannot even say that the world is unreal because it does not have absolute existence; for, although different worlds may come and pass out, *world as such* — world in relation to itself — is real. We cannot, with certainty, think of a time when there would be only an absolute existent-consciousness without having any world.

Therefore, Sri Aurobindo accepts the first meaning of the word 'Māya'. Māyā is the power that creates the world — a power of Saccidānanda which can comprehend, contain and measure out forms of the world out of the Infinite Existence. Sri Aurobindo describes this in a very suggestive language by saying that it is by Māyā that "out of the *Supreme Being* in which *all is all* without barrier of separative consciousness, emerges the *phenomenal being* in which *all is in each* and *each is in all* for the play of existence with existence, consciousness with consciousness, force with force, delight with delight."[2]

But, there is a sense in which Sri Aurobindo incorporates the other meaning of Māyā also. Māyā can be described as cosmic illusion if it is viewed in relation to the supremely real. The world

1. Sri Aurobindo, *The Life Divine*, p. 95.

2. *Ibid.*, p. 108.

may be called Māyā because it is not the *essential truth* of infinite existence. The deluding Māyā, he says, has first to be em-
braced and then overcome. He makes the whole point clear when
he says, "We may, if we choose, call them therefore, illusions of
the infinite consciousness, thus audaciously flying back a shadow
of our mental sense of subjection to error and incapacity upon
that which, being greater than mind, is beyond subjection to
falsehood and illusion."[1]

iii. Ascent or Evolution

Now, we are in a position to explain Sri Aurobindo's account
of ascent or Evolution. Evolution presupposes involution, in
fact, evolution is possible only because involution has already
taken place. The eight stages or cords of being (enumerated and
explainend earlier) involve both these processes. It is on account
of the descent of the spirit in Matter, Life and Mind that these
ascend to the higher regions of the spirit. Matter can envolve
into life only because life itself has involved in it, life can ascend
to mind only because there has been a descent of mind into life
already, the entire lower hemisphere can ascend to the higher one
only because the higher is already in the lower one. Sri Aurobindo
feels that the lower cannot evolve into the higher unless the
higher is already in it because evolution cannot proceed out of
nothing, because it cannot violate the principle of 'nothing out
of nothing'. Therefore, he conceives evolution as the reverse
process of involution. He says, "...Spirit is a final evolutionary
emergence because it is the original involutionary element and
factor. Evolution is an inverse action of the involution: what is
an ultimate and last derivation in the involution is the first to
appear in the evolution. What was original and primal in the
involution is in the evolution the last and supreme emergence."[2]

Evolution, as conceived by Sri Aurobindo, has a distinctive
character of its own, which, in a sense, comprehends all other
forms of evolution. The nature of evolution has generally been
conceived as *repetitive* or *emergent* or as *mechanical* or *teleological*. Repetitive theories of evolution suggest that evolution is a
process in time that gives out, more or less, the same kinds of
forms. Evolution goes on bringing out the same kinds of entities —
repeating the same kinds of beings of existence. As against this

1. *Ibid.*, p. 96.
2. Sri Aurobindo, *The Life Divine*, pp. 759-60.

the theory of emergent evolution believes that at every stage of evolution something new emerges or comes out. Mechanical theories of evolution seek to explain everything in terms of antecedent conditions, whereas, teleological theories relate everything to some goal or purpose which the evolutionary process seeks to realise. Sri Aurobindo's *Integral Theory of Evolution* comprehends the relevant features of all such accounts, and thus can claim to be more comprehensive and rationally satisfying than any of these theories.

Evolutionary growth, according to Sri Aurobindo, is a triple process, it involves processes of *widening, heightening* and *integration*. In a simpler language it means that at first it involves an extension of scope and the incorporation of co-existent forms, then it involves a development and growth towards higher forms. But, in this process nothing is to be completely rejected, everything finally has to be integrated. The process of widening, therefore, means providing greater scope for the operation of every new element or principle. The second process of heightening means ascent from one step or grade to another higher grade. But the most important character of the evolutionary process is *integration*. Evolution is not growing from the lower grades to the higher ones — superseding and rejecting the lower ones as they are crossed. On the contrary, it implies that the lower ones are uplifted and transformed. Integration in the philosophy of Sri Aurobindo means *ascent through descent*. The higher descends into the lower and transforms it completely, in that way the lower ascends to the higher. For example, if we reflect upon the nature of *matter* prior to the evolution of mind and then upon its nature after the evolution of mind the whole point would become clear. When matter evolved into mind, in fact, the nature of 'the material' was also changed. Matter no longer could be viewed in the manner in which it was viewed before. S.K. Moitra tries to make the whole idea clear with the help of a very apt analogy when he says, "The usual view of evolution, which looks upon it as a mere ascent from the lower grade to the higher grade, may be compared to the march of an army which advances without keeping its line of communication with the base intact. And, we may compare Sri Aurobindo's concept of evolution with the march of an army which advances with the whole force, keeping all its lines of communication perfectly intact."[1] One very important reason for emphasising this fact of integration is that only if evolution is conceived in this way that one can talk about the possibility of a Divine life or Sarvamukti. It is quite possible for an individual aspirant to grow spiritually and to attain salvation, but universal redemption can become a fact only when evolutionary growth is conceived as a cosmic process integrating all its aspects and grades.

Now that the general nature of the process of ascent is known we can try to determine the prominent points or aspects of this evolutionary process. Creation, we know, is the descent of the spirit into ignorance, and, therefore the starting point of evolution must be complete absence of knowledge or *complete Inconscience*, and the goal must be *complete knowledge*. In between the two lies the realm of *ignorance*. What are the prominent aspects of evolution in this realm of ignorance ? Sri Aurobindo says that evolution in this realm has passed through matter, life, psyche and mind and has reached so far the realm of mind. Life evolves in Matter and therefore is 'matter-bound'. Mind evolves in Life, and therefore, it is both 'matter-bound' and 'life-bound'. Now mind is waiting to ascend to tne higher stage by entering into the spiritual or super-mental stage. That evolution is yet to take place. This, according to Sri Aurobindo, is going to be the next and the final stage of evolution.

This is a rough description of 'cosmic evolution' as conceived by Sri Aurobindo. But, Sri Aurobindo does not view at evolution merely in the cold, dispassionate manner of a scientist. The process of evolution has not merely to be scientifically described, because we are ourselves involved in it and also because the next stage of evolution is going to take us into the spiritual realm. We can expedite this process of impending spiritual transformation by our efforts also. After all, by our own efforts we have reached the mental stage, and so we can also strive to transform the mental into the higher form — the supramental. Therefore, in Sri Aurobindo's theory of evolution we come across, along with the description of cosmic evolution, a description of the evolution of the individual also. Evolution, according to Sri Aurobindo, is as much individual as cosmic. In fact, he recognises the immense importance of the individual and feels that the individual is the medium through which spirit

---

1. S.K. Moitra, *The Philosophy of Sri Aurobindo*, pp. 66-67.

reveals and discloses its being. Therefore, the ascent of the individual will not symbolise but also help and expedite cosmic ascent. Therefore, the integral theory of evolution attempts to describe the basic features of individual's evolution also. This becomes one of the distinctive charateristic of Sri Aurobindo's theory of evolution. (This problem will be discussed in detail under the heads Supramental transformation and Yoga.)

The Four Theories of Existence

In order to be able to appreciate Sri Aurobindo's metaphysical position in a better way, it would be worthwhile to have a look at the four theories of Existence that he himself enumerates and examines. He says that metaphysical philosophy is an attempt to determine the fundamental realities and principles of being as distinct from the apparent phenomenal process which are the manifestations of the realities behind. But, Sri Aurobindo lays down a very significant condition for metaphysical thinking : its aim and method should be consistent with the truth of being that we see; after all metaphysical theories are evolved for the explanation of the phenomenal world. Therefore, they must be consistent with our experience, otherwise, metaphysics will remain only an empty play of intellect without having any content.

Viewing metaphysics in this way Sri Aurobindo comes to discover four theories of existence. They are, (1) *The Super-Cosmic,* (2) *the Cosmic or the Terrestrial,* (3) *the Supraterrestrial or the Other-worldly, and* (4) *the Integral or the Synthetic.* The last one, according to him, is represented in his own metaphysical theory. Let us first explain the other three outlining their merits and defects.

(*i*) *The Super-Cosmic theory* — According to this theory the Absolute alone is real. Its monistic character is so emphatic that in such a theory the reality of everything else, even of man tends to suffer. In the extreme forms of such a theory even human existence does not have any real meaning, it is conceived as a mistake of the soul or a delirium of the will to live or as an error or ignorance which somehow overcasts the Absolute Reality. Sri Aurobindo places Advaita Vedānta under this

---

1. *Ibid* p. 96.

category. We can also include the metaphysical theories of Bradley or even of Spinoza as falling under this group, because according to them also the Super-cosmic Absolute or the substance is the only reality.

Sri Aurobindo criticises this theory on the ground that it reduces world to the status of an illusion or a dream or an image. It also takes away from man his reality. Moreover, it reduces the universe to a static block-universe and leaves no room for 'becoming' of any kind. It, thus, is not consistent with experience whose explanation it seeks to provide. Sri Aurobindo criticises this theory on the ground that it is extremely onesided and partial.

(*ii*) *The Cosmic or the Terrestrial theory* — This theory is the exact opposite of the Supracosmic. It considers cosmic existence as real. It goes further and accepts the cosmic reality as the *only* reality. Ordinarily, it keeps itself confined to the material universe. God, if at all it exists, is also a changing phenomenon, and if God is not conceived as existent, then Nature is taken to be an eternal process of change and becoming and this life as the only field of action. Man is conceived to be the highest possible form of evolution and change. Nothing is conceived to be permanent except *becoming* or continuous change. Such a view is found most commonly in the western tradition. All forms of naturalistic philosophies — Materialism and Positivisim — can be said to have advanced cosmic-terrestrial views. Cārvāka, in Indian philosophy, can also be roughly described as a representative of this school.

Sri Aurobindo criticises this view again on the ground that it is one-sided. If the Supra-cosmic theory is on the one extreme, this theory is on the other extreme. Its defect lies in the fact that it fails to notice the possibility of the beyond. It completely overlooks the fact that our material existence is extremely poor and inadequate. Such a theory, in the long run is neither intellectually nor emotionally satisfying. It overlooks the fact that every individual is capable of certain nobility of being — of going beyond the terrestrial.

(*iii*) *The Supraterrestrial theory* — It believes both in the reality of the world as well as in the reality of something higher. That is to say, in a rough way, it tries to reconcile the Supracosmic and the cosmic-terrestrial views because it admits the reality of both the 'material cosmos' and 'the transcendent world'. It believes that the earth is a place for a temporary sojourn of the soul, but it also believes that behind the mortality of the bodily life of man there is the soul's immortality. In a sense theistic philosophies and religion would fall under this category, because they all, while recognising the reality of this world, believe in the possibility of a higher world in which soul in its immortality can enter.

It is a fact that this theory seeks to reconcile the first two theories because it makes a room for the reality of all the three aspects of the metaphysical realm the cosmos, the individual beings and the transcendent world. But, Sri Aurobindo feels that even this theory suffers from the same kind of error from which the Supracosmic theory suffers. It believes that there is a higher realm of being — heaven or paradise or something of that sort in which man can enter and find his salvation. But, the present state of man of the world is conceived as a fallen state — as a state of bondage which has to be transcended. Therefore, in a sense this theory also preaches acosmism and reduces man almost to the status of an unreality. Another defect of this theory, according to Sri Aurobindo, is that it rules out completely the possibility of the opening up of higher consciousness in this life and world, because it believes that that is possible only in a different — a higher world. Sri Aurobindo, on the other hand, believes that Divine Life may appear on this earth itself.

(*iv*) The defects of the three theories mentioned above lead Sri Aurobindo to develop his own metaphysical theory, which, in his opinion, is truly *synthetic or integral*. He believes that for a really synthetic theory the reality both of the cosmos and the higher realm has to be maintained. Even the material has to be conceived as an aspect of the Divine, and it must be realised that the attainment of the higher realm would mean a transformation of everything including the material, the vital and the mental. Sri Aurobindo tries to evolve such a theory which maintains the ultimacy of the spiritual or the higher realm and yet makes even the earth-life an aspect of the Divine plan. He says, "Earth-life is not a lapse into the mire of something indivine, vain and miserable, offered by some Power to itself as a spectacle or to the embodied soul as a thing to be suffered and then cast away from it : it is the scene of the evolutionary unfolding of the being which moves towards the revelation of a supreme spiritual light and power and joy and oneness, but includes in it also the manifold diversity of the self-achieving spirit."[1] Such a theory is really synthetic and integral because it synthesises both the Supracosmic and cosmic-terrestrial theories in an obviously more harmonious manner than the Supraterrestrial theory.

Nature of Man

We have traced the general course of evolution and we have been able to establish also that evolution is going to take its final leap into the realm of the spiritual. But, so far evolution has passed from the state of complete inconscience to the grade of the mental, in the process passing through matter, life and psyche. In man the mental grade is best represented, and in man, therefore, lies the possibility of the next step of evolution — the transition to the supramental level. As such, Sri Aurobindo undertakes to explain the nature of man.

Sri Aurobindo feels that the man that is known to us and is evident to our senses, is not the real man — at least he is not the complete man. Somehow we do not normally have the capacity to know ourselves in our true perspective. Sri Aurobindo says, "we are composed of many parts, each of which contributes something to the total movement of our consciousness, our thought, feeling, action;...but we are aware only of their confused and pell-mell results on the surface."[2] The confused or inadequate knowledge of man is on account of the fact that there are, in reality, two aspects of man's being — one external and the other inner. The external is apparent to us, it is that aspect of our being that constitutes our waking-conscious existence. There may even be a subconscient aspect of our life where we do not have any waking consciousness, which is nothing but 'an obscure mind full of obstinate saṁskāra, impressions and associations, fixed notions, habitual reactions formed by our past." But, this aspect is not the inner aspect of our being, it has to be distinguished from the inner or the *subliminal* parts of our beings consisting of the inner physical, the inner vital and the inner mental aspects. These are not obscure or ill-oragnised. External or surface consciousness is not always aware of this subliminal self or the *caitya Puruṣa* because it is veiled from it. In this

1. Sri Aurobindo, *The Life Divine*, p. 606.
2. Sri Aurobindo, *Lights on Yoga*, p. 15.

Caitya self or inner being of man is revealed the *central being*, which the Vedānta has described as the Ātman. Sri Aurobindo explains this very clearly when he describes man in the following words, "The being of man is composed of these elements — the psychic behind supporting all, the inner mental, vital and physical, and the outer — quite external nature of mind, life and body which is their instrument of expression. But *above all is the central being (Jīvātmā),* which uses them all for its manifestation, it is a portion of the Divine Self."[1]

In fact, Sri Aurobindo divides the central being of man into two aspects : the upper and the lower. The upper is the Jīvātmā and the lower is the Psychic being — the subliminal self or the Caitya Puruṣa. The upper is that aspect of man which is prior to human evolution, which transcends the process of ascent, but the lower represents the true man *in the process of evolution.* When man is in the world — is viewed from the point of view of evolution, a distinction between his outer aspects and his inner aspects is made; and the inner aspects represent his subliminal self.

It is necessary to distinguish this aspect of man from the Jīvātmā. The Jīvātmā is conceived as the spark of the Divine, as the human version of Parmātmā, and as such it transcends the individual expressions of life and mind in individual men. The Psychic being, on the other hand, is almost a deputy of the Jīvātmā expressing itself in individual life and existence and supporting it. That is why Sri Aurobindo says that the psychic being is inside the evolutionary process, whereas the Jīvātmā is beyond evolution. Sri Aurobindo distinguishes between these two aspects of man in yet another way. Everything being an expression of the Divine, both the Psychic being and the Jīvātmā are also expressions of the Divine, but, whereas there can be relation of *identity-in-difference* between the Psychic being and the Divine, the Jīvātmā can merge itself *in identity* with the Divine. Here we come across a very illuminating interpretation of the Vedantic utterance — '*Tat Tvam Asi*'. *Thou* is both different and identical with *That* if 'Thou' represents the Psychic being; but '*Thou*' is identical with '*That*' if 'Thou' represents the Jīvātmā.

Thus, we find that there are three aspects of Man according to Sri Aurobindo : the surface or the outer soul, the inner

1. *Ibid.*, p. 23.

soul or the Caitya Puruṣa and the Divine soul or the Jīvātmā. The first is akin to our physical nature, the second and third are akin to our spiritual nature. The second is the spiritual aspect of man in evolution, the aspect which is going to change and get transformed. The third is the potentiality of Divinity that has to be finally expressed.

The question of birth or decay or destruction can be raised only with respect to the outer self. The Caitya Puruṣa is the subtle soul and therefore beyond birth or perishment. Its function is to carry man to spiritual heights by kindling the fire that is already there. It is imperishable, and as such endures through births and is ever active in expediting the Divine transformation. This takes us to consider Sri Aurobindo's account of Rebirth.

Philosophy of Rebirth and the Law of Karma

Sri Aurobindo's account of Rebirth and Karma is not merely an old wine in a new bottle, it contains strikingly original ideas, which, although in certain respects similar to the traditional Indian notions about Karma and Rebirth, significantly differ from them in so far as they emphasise certain elements that carry the mark of Sri Aurobindo's original insight and freshness.

Sri Aurobindo tries to assign to the notion of Rebirth a place in his general scheme of evolution. He asserts that Rebirth is an aspect of the general process of evolution and ascent. We have seen that evolution has reached the level of the mental and is waiting for its next leap into the level of the Supramental. The human individual is an embodiment of the level that evolution has reached so far. The evolving principle passing through the material and the vital has entered the level of the human. Naturally, birth is a vehicle or a way through which the process of evolution can be pushed ahead. Sri Aurobindo says, "It is conceivable that the Eternal may have actually chosen to manifest or rather to conceal himself in the body; he may have willed to become or to appear as an individual passing from birth to death and from death to new life in a cycle of persistent and recurrent human and animal existence."[1]

But, at this point a doubt may be raised. Birth relates to an individual, how can it serve a cosmic purpose? How can an

---

1. Sri Aurobindo, *The Life Divine*, p. 672.

individual's coming into an association with a body be useful or helpful in the universal process of ascent? In other words, how can such an individual phenomenon be an aspect of the universal process of evolution? Sri Aurobindo is aware of the tremendous importance of this question, and so, he has very clear views on the matter. He says that evolution has to be both cosmic and individual. Soul has not completed its task by merely developing into humanity; it has still to develop that humanity into its higher possibilities. The general level that evolution has reached is the level that it has reached both at the universal level and at the individual level. Therefore, if evolution has to go beyond the human level, it must do so both universally and individually. In fact, universal or cosmic evolution will have no significance if it does not incorporate in its scheme even individual evolution.

Sri Aurobindo is aware that it is perhaps not impossible for the Supreme to work out the cosmic scheme without including in it the principle of re-birth. In fact, re-birth cannot be a necessary condition of cosmic existence, because the individual to be born is not prior to cosmic existence, on the other hand, he himself is an aspect of this. Sri Aurobindo admits this, but he adds that once the fact of creation or involution is accepted, that is, once it is accepted that creation is the descent of the spirit — or a plunge of the spirit into ignorance, this also has to be accepted that this descent will assume names and forms. This explains the emergence of the individuality and then as a corollary, even this has to be accepted that every single life will involve succession of individual lives. Individuals, then, would be conceived as following individuals in the manner of waves following waves, the sea remaining the same.

Thus, Sri Aurobindo feels that the individual is a medium through which creation discloses itself. Therefore, the individual has to be given time and opportunity to grow. For this he has to assume a body. It is in this embodied state that the individual can do whatever he can do for expediting the next step of evolution. He must therefore be born and re-born till the spiritual task is performed and the spiritual goal is reached. Sri Aurobindo clearly says, "In a phenomenal universe so created, the separative form becomes the foundation and the starting point of all its life-actions; therefore, the individual Puruṣa in working out its cosmic relation with the One has in this physical world to base himself upon the form, to assume a body, it is the body that he must make his own foundation and the starting-point for the development of his life and mind and spirit in the physical existence. That assumption of body we call birth, and in it only can take place here the development of self and the play of relations between the individual and the universal and all other individuals; in it only can there be the growth by a progressive development of our conscious being towards a supreme recovery of unity with God and with all in God."[1] Birth, then, is a necessity of the manifestation of the self on the physical plane and is a necessary aspect of the growth of the individual towards spirituality.

Sri Aurobindo is cautious enough to emphasise that it is not merely birth, but a succession of human births that is necessary for evolution. The same reasons that necessitate birth explain re-birth also. The spiritual possibilities may not be exhausted in one birth. For example, in the present birth, man has reached the mental level, there are many intervening stages to be crossed before the super-mental level is reached. It may not be possible, as is apparent from our experience of this life, to cross and go beyond those levels in one life. Therefore, births have to be succeeded by re-births. "If there is an evolution of consciousness in an evolutionary body and a soul inhabiting the body, a real and conscious individual, then it is evident that it is the progressive experience of that soul in Nature which takes the form of this evolution of consciousness: rebirth is self-evidently a necessary part, the sole possible machinery of such an evolution...."[2]

Another aspect of the problem of re-birth remains to be considered. What is the mechanism of re-birth ? Does the soul enter into a body immediately as it leaves the previous body or does it wait somewhere in some form before it is given a new body. In the history of religious thought we come across both kinds of answers to the question. On the one hand, there is the belief, vague enough but fairly general that death is followed immediately by the assumption of a body. On the other hand, there is the old religious dogma of a life after death in hell or in heaven or in some other world, which the soul acquires as a

1. Sri Aurobindo, *The Life Divine*, p. 674.
2. Sri Aurobindo, *The Life Divine*, p. 651.

result of his own deeds. It is also believed that only when the soul fully exhausts the effects of his deeds in the previous life that he is sent to another terrestrial life and is given a body. Sri Aurobindo considers both these solutions of the problem in detail and comes to feel that it is not proper to give a very precise or a near-certain answer to the question in hand. He feels that whether a particular soul would get a new body immediately or whether it would continue in some existence for some time before assuming a body would depend on the tendencies and efforts generated by the soul itself. In certain cases we may suppose that there is an attachment so strong as to compel the soul to hasten towards the assumption of a body, or again, we may suppose that in these cases the life-span and the life-experiences have been so brief and incomplete as to compel the soul to an immediate re-birth for the continuance of the process. In certain other cases it may be supposed that re-birth is not assuming a body immediately after death, it is assumption of a new personality that may continue to have a supraphysical existence without assuming a body. It may be believed that these souls have been able to acquire sufficient power over their own nature-formation so as to be able to continue in existence without the support of a material body. Sri Aurobindo gives thought to the nature of this supraphysical existence. Without entering into that it can be said that the problem has been very rationally solved by Sri Aurobindo because he does not try to fix up or rigidly determine the course of re-birth. Whether a soul would assume a body immediately or would wait in some super-physical existence would depend on the soul's capacity and power. Any attempt to solve this problem conclusively, that is, any attempt to determine the course of the process of re-birth is futile.

An account of the problem of re-birth would be incomplete without referring to the problem of *Karma*. Sri Aurobindo is aware of this, specially because he knows that the Indian tradition has tried to explain re-birth and tendencies present in every birth strictly in terms of this law. In the Indian tradition this law has been conceived both as a metaphysical law and as a moral law. From the metaphysical point of view it explains the metaphysical status of an individual in every birth. Man's past and present Karmas determine his future birth and its happenings. As a moral law it lays down the maxim of 'as you sow so you reap'.

Sri Aurobindo in a general way accepts the importance of Karma both in the metaphysical and the moral contexts. He admits that it is quite reasonable to accept both the metaphysical character and the moral aspect of this law. "Man's being, nature, circumstances of life are the result of his own inner and outer activities, not something fortuitous and inexplicable : he is what he has made himself; the past man was the father of the man that now is, the present man is the father of the man that will be. Each man reaps what he sows; from what he does he profits, for what he does he suffers. This is the law and chain of Karma, of action, of the work of Nature-Energy, and it gives a meaning to the total force of our existence, nature, character, action, which is absent from other theories of life."[1] He also admits the reasonableness of the Karma — thesis, that is, as is the nature of the energies, so must be the nature of the results, in other words, good must bring good results and evil must bring evil results. He believes that this fits well with the belief that there must be a cosmic justice which keeps an eye on and controls in some way the visible operations of life.

But, in spite of all this, Sri Aurobindo is not prepared to give to the law of Karma that importance and elevated position that Indian tradition normally gives to it. The originality of Sri Aurobindo's views lies in recognising the limitation of this law. He feels that this law cannot be the sole and the absolute determinant of the working of the cosmos, unless the entire process is conceived as absolutely mechanical. But, if the fundamental truth of our being is spiritual and not mechanical, it must be our self — our soul that would determine its own evolution, and the *Law of Karma can only be one of the processes that it uses for* the purpose. Sri Aurobindo says that our spirit or the self must be greater than its Karma. "All is not Law and process, there is also Being and Consciousness, there is not only a machinery but a spirit in things, not only Nature and law of cosmos but a Cosmic Spirit, not only a process of mind and life and body but a soul.... If it were not so, there could be no rebirth of a soul and no field for a law of Karma."[2]

1. Sri Aurobindo, *The Life Divine*, p. 718.
2. Sri Aurobindo, *The Life Divine*, p. 720.

Sri Aurobindo feels that the statement of the Law of Karma errs by an over-simplification and by an arbitrary selection of a limited principle. The consciousness-force of the spirit expresses itself in many forms of energies, there are inner activities of mind, of life, of senses and the body, there are things like desire, passion, impulse etc., then, there are pursuits like the pursuit of truth, knowledge, beauty, goodness, power etc., and there are activities leading to power, happiness, fortune, success, love etc. This makes the life of the spirit a complex whole. How can all this be reduced to a single mechanical principle ? How can almost a blind law of Karma account for such an immense variety of actions and dispositions ? Therefore, Sri Aurobindo says, "It is not conceivable that the spirit within is an automation in the hands of Karma, a slave in this life of its past actions, the truth must be less rigid and more plastic. If a certain amount of results of past Karma is formulated in the present life, it must be with the consent of the psychic being which presides over the new formation of its earth's experience and assents not merely to an outward compulsory process, but to a secret will and guidance. That secret will is not mechanical but spiritual, the guidance comes from an intelligence which may use mechanical processes but is not their subject....There must therefore be two elements; *Karma as an instrument*, but also the secret consciousness and will within working through the mind, life and body as the user."[1]

Ignorance, its Origin and Nature

An analysis of Sri Aurobindo's conception of Man, creation and evolution would clearly show that the concept of Ignorance has been given an important place in Sri Aurobindo's metaphysics. Creation has been described as the plunge of the spirit into ignorance, the entire world is conceived as being in the realm of ignorance and evolution is conceived as gradual progression from ignorance to knowledge. Therefore, it is essential to try to determine the nature of ignorance.

Indian Philosophers have thought on the problem and have been able to develop various conceptions about the nature of ignorance. Some of them have called it Ajñāna or Avidyā, some of these thinkers have attributed this to the principle of

---

1. *Ibid.*, pp. 720-21.

Māyā, which, according to them, is the power of the reality to produce cosmic illusion. But, almost all of them agree in believing that ignorance is the opposite — the antithesis of knowledge, and that ignorance is bondage — the cause of suffering and that the aim of spiritual activity is to free man from the state of ignorance and to lift him up to the state of knowledge. Sri Aurobindo believes in this only partially in so far as he also believes that evolution is the evolution from ignorance towards knowledge. But, he is not prepared to accept the basic thesis of these thinkers namely that ignorance is absence of knowledge. Like some of his other refreshingly original views, even here he holds that knowledge and ignorance are fundamentally similar in nature. He ridicules the Indian philosopher for emphasising the opposition between the two.

He feels that once the integral character of knowledge is accepted to be a fact, conception of ignorance as opposed to knowledge will create logical difficulties. It would, in fact, affect the integral or the non-dual character of knowledge — and it would at once raise the problem regarding the locus of ignorance. Therefore, the only proper way of conceiving ignorance is to take it as a form of knowledge.

Sri Aurobindo traces the history of the world and finds that a distinction between knowledge and ignorance is made even in the *Ṛg Veda*, where knowledge appears to signify a consciousness of the Truth, *Satyam ṛtam*, and ignorance is conceived as the unconsciousness the *acitti*, of Truth. The Vedantists took up the idea and went on to emphasise the difference between the two by highlighting the antinomy of Vidyā and Avidyā. But, Sri Aurobindo feels that this distinction creates greater problems for the Vedantic thinker than those that it solves, because it leaves the gap between the two permanently empty. Therefore, Sri Aurobindo conceives ignorance as a form of knowledge, it may be very fragmentary, very partial, but it is basically similar in nature to knowledge. Ignorance is not absence of knowledge, that is the extreme state of complete nescience. On the other extreme there is the state of complete knowledge. In between the two is the state of ignorance. As such, it is already a movement from the absence of knowledge towards knowledge.

This can be demonstrated in a number of ways. First, it can be said that the very concept of knowledge implies the concept of degree. We shall have to admit that the only complete knowledge is the knowledge of the Absolute, and therefore, knowledge of the cosmos or the knowledge of ourselves in the cosmos cannot be a complete knowledge. From the point of view of complete knowledge such a knowledge is not knowledge but ignorance. In fact, from the point of view of every superior knowledge every inferior knowledge is partial — 'a shadow of ignorance'. That shows that knowledge and ignorance are not opposed in nature. What appears to be knowledge from one point of view is ignorance from a different — a higher point of view.

Ignorance is conceived as the power of Divine consciousness itself, as its power to withhold itself partially. Ignorance is conceived not as a sign of weakness, but as a power just like knowledge. It may be the power of partially withholding itself, but this, being a Divine power, cannot disrupt or adversely affect the Divine Unity. Partial withholding of Divine nature implies partial knowledge of the Divine, and this is what is called ignorance. That also shows that ignorance and knowledge are not contrary in nature.

But, the most convincing demonstration of the similarity of knowledge and ignorance is that both are conceived as two different poises of the same evolutionary process. This process has so far been able to reach the aspects of the mental. This state is described as the state of ignorance. Now, this state is ready to take its leap into the realm of knowledge. Thus, knowledge is the natural culmination of the state of ignorance. Sri Aurobindo feels that the soul, in the state of ignorance itself, makes all the preparation required to attain the supramental state, only a Divine veil is preventing it so far from attaining that state. "In fact, what is happening is that Ignorance is seeking and preparing to transform itself by a progressive illu- mination of its darkness into the knowledge that is already conceived in it."[1] 'Knowledge that is already conceived in ignorance' — this clearly shows that ignorance is also poten- tially knowledge. Ignorance is called ignorance because in this state one is ignorant of the supramental vision and knowledge; it is knowledge from the standpoint of the mental, ignorance from the higher standpoint. Moreover, it is also a step towards knowledge, a possibility always bubbling with the potency of knowledge, waiting for the supramental descent.

1. Sri Aurobindo, *The Life Divine*, p. 446.

But then, one question still remains unanswered, the question regarding the origin of Ignorance. This problem has been a puzzling problem for the entire tradition of Indian philosophy, because it tends to affect adversely the monistic character of reality. Sri Aurobindo's solution of the problem, although similar to the Vedantic solution of the problem, is different from it in significant respects. The Vedāntist says that mind, which is the seat of ignorance, is a thing of Māyā. Therefore, they call even ignorance an illusion. Some Vedāntists call this a cosmic illusion. There are some other thinkers who make a fundamental distinction between the Absolute and individual souls by saying that the former is absolutely free from ignorance, whereas the latter is subject to ignorance. But, Sri Aurobindo cannot accept any of these solutions regarding the problem of the origin of ignorance, because they would somehow or other affect the integral unity of the reality which Sri Aurobindo is not prepared to sacrifice at any cost. He has to explain the origin of ignorance inside the integral scheme, he has to show that ignorance, instead of affecting the oneness of reality, is very much an aspect of integral unity. Sri Aurobindo views at the whole problem in this manner, "If Brahman is the sole existence, Māyā can be nothing but a power of Brahman, a force of his consciousness or a result of being, and if the Jīvātman, one with the Brahman, is subject to its own Māyā, the Brahman in it is subject to Māyā. But, this is not intrinsically or fundamentally possible."[1] Therefore he adds, "Ignorance must be part of the movement of the one, a development of its consciousness knowingly adopted, *to which it is not forcibly subjected but which it uses for its cosmic purpose.*"[2]

Sri Aurobindo tries to prove this. Firstly, Sri Aurobindo clearly demonstrates that ignorance cannot have its origin in the Absolute Brahman or in integral Saccidānanda. Then he shows that ignorance is not inherent in the multiplicity of souls also. After establishing these two conclusions, he comes to assert that there can be no original or primal ignorance, that ignorance comes in at a later stage — at a later movement when mind is separated from its spiritual and supramental basis. Finally, he tries to determine the nature of that later stage when

1. *Ibid.*, p. 506.
2. Sri Aurobindo, *The Life Divine*. p. 506.

ignorance makes its appearance. Let us try to follow the line of his argument.

Since ignorance is conceived as a stage in the development of the process of knowledge, the solution of the problem regarding the origin of ignorance must be found in an action of consciousness manifesting itself as knowledge and yet limiting that knowledge in such a way as to create the phenomenon of ignorance. Sri Aurobindo, thus, seeks to find the solution of the problem in the nature of consciousness itself. The Divine consciousness is conceived as a force or Śakti. Sri Aurobindo at times gives to this consciousness-force the name *Tapas*. If we examine the nature of this Tapas we find that it has two aspects — at least two ways of its working. This becomes evident from an analysis of our own consciousness itself. Our consciousness has an active aspect and also a passive aspect. The active aspect of our consciousness is manifested in our external or internal acts, the passive aspect produces either no action, or just mechanical or automatic actions which we perform more or less unconsciously.

This analysis of our consciousness can give us an idea of Divine Consciousness also. There must be an active aspect and a passive aspect of the supreme Consciousness-force or the Divine *Tapas*. It is the active aspect of the Divine Tapas that is expressed in creation. It is true that this is not the only aspect of the śakti of consciousness. The passive or the unexpressed aspect is the great-reservoir of Śakti which remains behind, and which is not affected by the activities on the surface. Sri Aurobindo makes it clear with the help of the analogy of ocean and waves. Waves are aspects of the ocean, its active aspect — the aspect that is in motion, but lying behind is the vast and deep ocean that is unaffected by the movements at the surface. The two are not different, they represent the same energy or force. This analogy is very useful in explaining Sri Aurobindo's ideas regarding ignorance. To a casual observer the waves may appear to represent the ocean, this is ignorance; because this is ignorance of the fact that the vaster and the greater aspect of the ocean is the ocean in passivity — the ocean lying beneath the waves. Likewise, it is ignorance to suppose that the active aspect of the Divine Tapas that is expressed in creation is the Divine. Knowledge would involve the awareness of the passive aspect of the Divine Sakti also. It is ignorance, therefore, to consider the

creation and the forms expressed in every individual expression
of creation as everything neglecting the more sublime unmani-
fested śakti lying behind. Therefore, according to Sri Aurobindo the origin of Ignorance is to be discovered in 'Some self-
absolved concentration of Tapas', which, for us, "builds a wall
of separation which shuts out the consciousness in each form
from awareness of its own total self, of other embodied consciousness and of universal being."[1]

The Sevenfold Ignorance

Sri Aurobindo is aware that any attempt to determine the
nature of knowledge must first be able to explain the various
aspects of ignorance. This is so partly because ignorance is
not absence of knowledge, but incomplete or partial knowledge,
and also because it is from the state of ignorance that one has
to grow into the state of knowledge.

Ignorance primarily is the very state of our separative existence, and therefore in order to determine the various aspects
and modes of ignorance we have to examine the state of our
ordinary existence — the way in which we normally live. Sri
Aurobindo says that such an examination will at once reveal
that·"... this Ignorance in which ordinarily we live by the very
circumstance of our separative existence in a material, in a
spatial and temporal universe, we see that on its obscurer side
it reduces itself, from whatever direction we look at or approach
it, into the fact of a many-sided self-ignorance."[2] In fact he
asserts that we can clearly discover *seven* sides of this self-ignorance. Let us describe the nature of these seven kinds of
Ignorance.

1. *The Original Ignorance* :—In our day-to-day existence, it
is customary for us to take things surrounding us as for granted.
We somehow live and move under the belief that 'objects', 'our
embodied existence', 'the temporal relations obtaining in between
things', and similar other entities are all real. Sri Aurobindo
says that this means that we are ignorant of that which is really
real. 'We are ignorant of the Absolute which is the source of
all being and becoming.' This ignorance has been called
'the original Ignorance' because it is the most basic of all

1. Sri Aurobindo, *The Life Divine*, p. 517.
2. Sri Aurobindo, *The Life Divine*, p. 583.

types of ignorance — others somehow arising from this primal ignorance.

2. *The Cosmic Ignorance* :—The original ignorance is ignorance about the 'Absolute', the cosmic ignorance is ignorance about the real nature of the cosmos. Normally we believe that the world of space and time in which we live, move and have our being is the real world. That is why the changes that appear to take place in the world appear to us as wholly real. This, according to Sri Aurobindo, is ignorance about the real nature of the universe itself, and therefore, it is called Cosmic Ignorance.

3. *The Egoistic Ignorance* :—As the expression itself suggests, this form of ignorance concerns the nature of the self itself. Somehow we feel that the embodied individual represents the real self. We take our I-sense — the ego as everything; and do not even realise that there is a basic unity underlying all forms of being and becoming. "....We take our limited egoistic mentality, vitality, corporeality for our true self and regard everything other than that as not self."[1] This has been described as the Egoistic Ignorance.

4. *The Temporal Ignorance* :—Sri Aurobindo says that we are ignorant of our eternal nature also. That is why we believe that our life-span represents the essence of existence. Every bit of space or every duration of time is taken as constituting the very basic and vital aspect of our self. We do not realise that our true nature is somehow beyond these spatial or temporal dimensions. This ignorance which is rooted in temporal conditions has been called the Temporal Ignorance.

5. *The Psychological Ignorance* :—Sri Aurobindo feels that normally we take the superficial aspects of our life and behaviour as constituting the real aspects of ourself. The sense-experience, for example, is given the maximum of importance. We do not realise that that not only is very selective and therefore limited, but is also a very negligible and superficial aspect of our existence. There are deeper realms of our being which are not open to superficial view, but which constitute our true nature. We, in ignorance, are so much occupied and almost overwhelmed by the surface activities of our life, that we

1. *Ibid.*

completely ignore 'the super-conscient, the sub-conscient, the intra-conscient and the circum-conscient. This ignorance has been called the Psychological Ignorance.

6. *The Constitutional Ignorance* :—According to Sri Auro bindo there is an Ignorance that is rooted in the very constitution of our normal existence — in such a way that this normal manner of living shadows our true constitution itself. What he means is that normally we think that either our body or our life-force, or our mind, or any two of these or all the three would represent our true constitution. The most prevalent belief (or impression) is that life, mind and body constitute the whole constitution of man. That means that we are ignorant of the fact that there are other — deeper aspects of our constitution as well. In fact we are ignorant of the fact that it is these deeper aspects of our being that nourish and sustain the bodily, the vital and the mental activities of our self. But normally we are ignorant of this. This is called Constitutional Ignorance.

7. *The Practical Ignorance* :—On account of all these, our practical life is reduced almost to a mess. In our practical activities we are invariably chaotic and aimless, because on account of the ignorance of the 'goals' and the 'ways' of being we lose the sense of direction. Sri Aurobindo says, "As a result of all these ignorances [the six mentioned above] we miss the true knowledge, government and enjoyment of our life in the world; we are ignorant in our thought, will, sensations, actions, return wrong or imperfect response at every point to the questioning of the world, wander in a maze of errors and desires, strivings and failures, pain and pleasure, sin and stumbling, follow a crooked road, grope blindly for a changing goal, — that is the seventh, the Practical Ignorance."[1]

The Supermind

We have seen that the realm of reality has been divided into two hemispheres, the higher and the lower. The triune principle of Saccidānanda (the Pure Existent, Consciousness — force and Bliss) represents the higher sphere and Matter, Life, Psyche and Mind belong to the lower hemisphere. We have also seen that evolution has reached the level of mind and is preparing for its

1. *Ibid.*, p. 584.

next leap into the realm of the spiritual — the higher hemisphere. Now a question arises : how can this leap be brought about ? how can an evolute belonging to the lower sphere transform itself in such a way that it is able to enter the higher or the spiritual sphere.

Sri Aurobindo feels that this can be possible only if a principle mediates between the two. That principle must serve as the link between the two spheres. It must, on the one hand, be similar in nature to Saccidānanda, and, on the other, it must not be the opposite of the mental. Such a link is the *Supermind*. Supermind belongs to the higher hemisphere and yet it is the end and the ideal of mind — that which mind is going to be. As belonging to the higher hemisphere it must have a full consciousness of Saccidānanda. It is not Saccidānanda itself, and yet it is akin to its nature because it is the consciousness of Saccidānanda. Likewise, it is not mind itself, and yet it is its culmination and fulfilment.

Now, it is apparent that any attempt to determine the nature of Supermind must throw light on these two aspects of Supermind : (a) Supermind as Truth-Consciousness — as the spiritual principle having complete knowledge of Saccidānanda and (b) Supermind as the ideal and the culmination of mind. In what follows an attempt will be made to explain the nature of Supermind in the light of these two characters of Supermind.

Sri Aurobindo describes the first aspect of Supermind by calling it the *Creator, the Real-idea* and the *Supreme Truth-Consciousness*. In order to understand the meaning and implication of these expressions it is essential to examine the background in the light of which these notions have been developed.

Sri Aurobindo has spoken of the reality as Saccidānanda. Now there arises a difficulty, in the very description of reality as Saccidānanda we posit three entities and unite them in order to arrive at a trinity. "We say Existence, Consciousness, Bliss," and then we say, "they are one."[1] Now, such a differentiation and consequent integration may have been all right for the faculty of mind, but how can this be true of a reality which is necessarily non-dual ? Along with this there is another difficulty, unless some sort of a differentiation is admitted in the scheme of reality the fact of creation will remain unexplained.

1. Sri Aurobindo, *The Life Divine*, p. 118.

If reality is ever in its strict monistic status, then the question of the world being created would not arise, "for, indivisible consciousness is undividing consciousness and cannot originate division and differentiation."[1]

How can Sri Aurobindo escape from these difficulties ? There can be only one way of doing it — by conceiving a principle which would be able to *differentiate,* and *yet not divide* the unitary principle of reality. Such a principle will have the consciousness of the monistic reality and yet it will be able to differentiate it in such a way that reality would appear as a triune principle in creation. This process appears to us as difficult to conceive because our ways of conceiving are mental. Mental consciousness starts with divisions and then tries to unite them, that is why real unity is missed by it. But, there may be a spiritual consciousness which, although having the consciousness of unity, may project its consciousness in a differentiated manner — differentiating it as a triune principle. The point to be noted is that these two points of view do not contradict each other, the unitary nature of consciousness is never affected, and yet, its projection appears to be triune from the point of view of creation. This principle, which has the consciousness of the non-dual reality and which can project this consciousness in creation is the principle of Supermind. That is why Sri Aurobindo describes Supermind in this way: "The Supermind...starts from unity, not division, it is primarily comprehensive, differentiation is only its secondary act."[2]

Now, we can easily understand why Supermind has been described as the *Supreme Truth-consciousness.* The universe is an expression of consciousness, which although manifesting itself in the multiplicity, is all the time conscious of the basic unity. Creation, then, is through this consciousness, which essentially sees things as basically one, which differentiates the one without actually dividing it. Therefore, it is the Truth-Consciousness. Supramental consciousness is called Truth-consciousness also to distinguish it from mental consciousness. Mind essentially makes divisions and thereby creates appearances contrary to the nature of the real. Supermind does not create divisions and does not give false pictures, it never misses the real unitary nature of the One, and therefore, it has been called Truth-Consciousness.

1. *Ibid.*
2. Sri Aurobindo, *The Life Divine,* p. 118.

It has also been called the *Creator*, or the *Creative Idea* or even, at times, the *real Idea*. Sri Aurobindo perhaps is aware that the creative principle must not be conceived as something other than or different from the ultimate reality. The Advaita Vedāntist talks of Īśvara and Māyā, and treats them as principles of creation. He finds it difficult to reconcile this additional principle with the advaita nature of Brahman; consequently, Īśvara, Māyā, and the world — all become unreal. Therefore, Sri Aurobindo feels that the creative principle must not be viewed as something over and above the one, but as something which is able to do justice both to the oneness of the one and to the world. Saccidānanda is pure, conscious, and blissful existence — beyond space and time; creation, on the other hand, is movement — a development in space and time. There must be a link in between the two, and the link must be such that it is capable of explaining both the unity of the one and its development. That is possible only if the creative principle is conceived as a conscious Idea, which, as Idea, is one, and at the same time, is capable of expression. It is not anything different from Saccidānanda, it is its own consciousness, its own Idea. As pure consciousness, it is unitary, as an Idea it is capable of development. Therefore, Sri Aurobindo says on the one hand, that "Supermind is the vast self-extension of the Brahman that contains and develops,"[1] and on the other hand, "that by the Idea it develops the triune principle of existence, consciousness and bliss, out of their indivisible unity. It differentiates them, but does not divide."[2] Thus, creation starts when Supermind differentiates the original unity of the three principles. "No doubt, it is Saccidānanda itself that is this principle [of supermind], but Saccidānanda not resting in its pure, infinite, invariable consciousness, but proceeding out of this primal poise...into a movement which is its form of energy and instrument of cosmic creation."[3]

Now, we come to consider the second basic character of Supermind, namely that *it is the culmination and consummation of mind*. Sri Aurobindo firstly makes a distinction between the two emphasising the elements that mind lacks, and then he goes on to show that mind, in fact, is a subordinate power of Super mind, not

1. Sri Aurobindo, *The Life Divine*, p. 120.
2. *Ibid.*
3. *Ibid.*, p. 134.

opposed to it, but almost a version of Supermind in the lower
hemisphere which is waiting to be uplifted to the supramental
level.

The difference between mind and Supermind consists in the
difference between their manners of apprehending reality. While
Supermind essentially gets the unitary picture of reality, mind,
by its very nature, breaks and cuts asunder a whole into its parts.
Mind essentially creates divisions not only between the knower
and the known, but also in the objects that it apprehends.

On account of this mind is not capable of having a knowledge
of the reality. Reality can be known only as one, and so, a capacity which cannot know without analysing a whole or without
resolving it into its component parts can never know that which
is partless, indivisible and essentially one. At times, even mental
awareness claims to have known 'wholes' in their wholeness. But,
that also is not true knowledge. Mind first breaks the original
unity of the object of its knowledge and then tries to synthesise
the broken parts again into a whole. Such a whole will look
artificial, at least it cannot restore the original unity of a thing.
Thus, mind fails to 'know' in the proper sense of the word 'know'.

But, this difference between mind and Supermind itself is a
pointer to the fact that mind is nothing but an urge to realise the
Supramental level. Even the fragmentary knowledge that it has,
is possible on account of the fact that the spiritual aspect of
supermind is already present in mind. It is because Supermind
has already descended into mind, that mind is capable of spiritual activities, howsoever fragmentary such activities may be.
Mind has an inherent tendency to go beyond itself, an inherent
urge to rise higher. Moreover, even when it analyses and dissects
the object of its awareness, it at once feels the need of organising
it back into a whole. All these are examples of spiritual activities,
and that shows that Supermind is somehow already present in
the mind. That is why Sri Aurobindo says that mind is actually
a fall from Supermind. This fall, according to him, is a necessary
condition of creation, because it represents the descent of the
spirit. That makes it a precondition of evolution also. If Supermind is not there already — concealed — hidden — or inside a
veil, how can mind hope to ascend to the supramental level. And,
it is because Supermind is already — potentially there in mind
that it aspires to ascend to the Supermind.

This transition of mind to Supermind is not abrupt or sudden.

Mind, after all, belongs to the lower hemisphere and it has to ascend to the higher sphere. Therefore, there must be some intermediary steps through which this transition will be brought about. The order of ascent from mind to Supermind is through the following intermediary steps : (Mind), *Higher Mind, Illumined Mind, Intuition, Overmind,* (Supermind). The passage from mind to Supermind is a passage from Nature as we know it to Super-Nature, and as such, mind must pass through some stages which would demonstrate the continuous nature of this transition. Let us try to explain the nature of these stages.

Mind, as we know, is essentially a consciousness which measures, limits and cuts out forms of things from indivisible wholes and treats them as if each were a separate element. It perceives, senses or conceives things by analysing them into their component parts. We have also seen that reality cannot be known by such a process, for that mind somehow has to rise above its normal activities and try to cultivate some capacity for unification.

The first condition for this change is that mind must somehow become aware of its own capacities and must be able to possess them — that is, to exercise some control over them. The emergence of such an observing intelligence that is conscious of its own actions is the emergence of, what Sri Aurobindo calls, the *Higher Mind.* He describes it as "the spiritual parent of our conceptive mental ideation." In the higher mind, as he says, there is no need of the analytical activities that mind normally performs, there is no longer any need of a ratiocination, 'no logical motion step by step towards a conclusion, no mechanism of expressed or implied deductions and inferences', for, according to him, this kind of activity — this limping action of our reason — is an activity in the realm of ignorance. Higher mind, therefore, is a self-aware activity towards integration, its most characteristic movement is a *mass ideation,* a seeing of the inner relation of ideas with ideas. Truths, here, are not established by logic, they are sought to be seen in their wholeness — in their pre-reflective unity. In this stage, thus, there is the initial attempt to break away from the bondage of logic and rational analysis and to enter into the realm of the ideal.

But, it is still partial understanding, it is still not free from the empirical and rational pressure. There is as yet not a *luminous* seeing which knows things in a direct grasp. For this, what is needed is *not a mind of higher thought*, but *a mind of spiritual light*. Light is essentially illuminative, and, in a special sense, creative also. Thought-process is very slow, it reveals its objects piecemeal, through gradual steps, but there is the need of a sudden and a direct insight. Therefore, the next stage into which mind can ascend is the stage of *Illumined Mind*. *The Illumined Mind does not work primarily by thought, but by vision.* Thought here is only a subordinate movement performed in order to facilitate insight. Thought only creates a representative-image of Truth. Higher mind catches something of the substance of the Truth also. Sri Aurobindo says, "A consciousness that proceeds by sight, the consciousness of the seer, is a greater power of knowledge than the consciousness of the thinker. The perceptual power of the inner sight is greater and more direct than the perceptual power of thought."[1] Thus, "As the Higher Mind brings a greater consciousness into the being through the spiritual Idea and its power of Truth, so the illumined Mind brings in a still greater consciousness through a Truth-sight and Truth-light and its seeing and seizing power."[2]

But, these two stages of the ascent of mind can get their authority and fulfilment only by a reference to a third level — that of *Intuition*. Intuition is conceived as a power of consciousness nearer and more intimate to knowledge than any of the two previous stages. When the consciousness of the subject meets with the consciousness in the object, it sees, feels and vibrates with the knowledge of that which it contacts. Sri Aurobindo says that Intuition, in fact, is the beginning of knowledge as it brings messages from the higher or spiritual realm. Describing its nature he says, "Intuition has a fourfold power, a power of revelatory Truth-seeing, a power of inspiration or Truth-hearing, a power of Truth-touch or immediate seizing of significance... [and] a power of true and automatic discrimination of the orderly and exact relation of truth to truth."[3] These are the fourfold potencies of Intuition. It is obvious from such a description of Intuition that Sri Aurobindo is trying to incorporate in its nature all the characters that Indian seers of Truth in the past are said to possess. It is the capacity to see Truth and to

1. Sri Aurobindo, *The Life Divine*, p. 839.
2. *Ibid.*
3   *Ibid.*, p. 843.

hear it in its organised form in an act of direct and immediate revelation. He admits that Intuition can perform all the functions of reason and intelligence, with the difference that its grasp of the object is direct and not mediate like that of reason. Therefore, in a rough way the process of 'integration' starts in Intuition.

But, that is not a process of complete integration. Intuition cannot be called the highest form of consciousness. Sri Aurobindo gives certain obvious reasons on account of which a need is felt for going beyond this stage of Intuition.

Intuition, firstly, is clouded by the intervention of mental faculties. Reason and intelligence distort it in such a manner that it is not normally possible to have pure intuitions absolutely free from the mental stuff. Secondly, Intuitive flashes are so sudden, quick, brief and short-lived that it becomes difficult to understand the messages that they bring. Thirdly, before intuitive apprehension gets a chance of being expressed in imitative ways of reason, it is either intercepted or replaced. These defects of Intuition are chiefly because Intuition is the culmination of mental effort, and by effort alone pure knowledge cannot be attained. For that it is essential for spiritual light — for higher powers — to descend. Therefore, the next stage of development must be a faculty which, while possessing all powers of Intuition and of other preceding stages, must be capable of receiving the light from above.

This faculty, into which Intuition has to develop, is called by Sri Aurobindo *The Overmind*. Sri Aurobindo describes it as a 'super conscient cosmic mind in direct contact with the supramental consciousness'. Such a description of overmind emphasises the two sides of its nature — it is a kind of cosmic consciousness and it is in contact with the Supermind. The expression cosmic consciousness implies that the consciousness which has been ascending through the three previous stages now expands and widens itself. To the vertical ascent is added a vast horizontal expansion of consciousness. The previous stages including the stage of Intuition are not cosmic in nature, but, the knowledge of overmind becomes global and cosmic by going beyond the representations of consciousness in particular centres. In this stage even higher mind, Illumined mind and Intuition enlarge themselves and become wider and more comprehensive. Sri Aurobindo describes this stage thus, "The Overmind...is the final consummating movement of the dynamic spiritual transformation, it is the highest possible status-dynamis of the spiritual-mind plane. It takes up all that is in the three steps below it and raises their characteristic workings to their highest and largest power. adding to them a universal wideness of consciousness and force, a harmonious concert of knowledge, a more manifold delight of being."[1]

This is possible on account of its second character — its closeness to Supermind. It is capable of receiving the light from Supreme Truth-Consciousness. In fact, Over-mind is the proper link between mind and Supermind, it performs the mental activities in a spiritual manner, and its cosmic consciousness is a result of its affinity with Supermind. Its comprehensive nature and its global or cosmic character would not have been there, had it been limited to individual's consciousness. It is due to this limitation that Intuitive consciousness does not have a universality about it. Overmind is capable of reflecting the universal light, and therefore, its consciousness is cosmic.

But then, *Over*mind is not *Super*mind. In spite of being superconscient and cosmic it lacks the integral character of Supermind. Its cognition is global, and therefore it is capable of holding together even differences and contradictions, but for the complete view of reality consciousness must be capable of apprehending the Supreme Truth — the Absolute — as a unity. Overmind cannot do this. It can view every power of the Supreme as a separate reality. It deals with separate possibilities, and so can make every possibility a separate existence complete in itself. But, the unity lying behind is missed by it. Using the concepts of Prakṛti and Puruṣa as his illustration Sri Aurobindo says that such a dichotomy or distinction is also a creation of the Overmind. To its consciousness these two would appear as ir-reconcilable realities. That is why Sri Aurobindo goes to the extent of saying that in a sense the stage of overmind is also a stage of Ignorance. Speaking in terms of evolution, this is the last stage in the lower hemisphere that mind can attain before taking its leap into the higher realm. Speaking conversely in terms of the process of Descent or Involution, it can be said that with it (the overmind-stage) the

---

1. Sri Aurobindo, *The Life Divine*, p. 846.

realm of ignorance begins. Therefore, Sri Aurobindo says, "It [Overmind] is a power,...the highest power of the lower hemisphere; although its basis is a cosmic unity, its action is an action of division and inter-action, an action taking its stand on the play of the multiplicity. Its play is, like that of all Mind, a play of possibilities; although it acts not in ignorance but with the knowledge of the truth of these possibilities, yet it works them out *through their own independent evolution of their powers.*"¹ Consequently, Puruṣa is viewed as a separate reality and Prakṛti as another reality. The integral view is completely missed.

That view would be possible only when the veil separating the two hemispheres is removed and there is a final leap into the status of the Supermind. It is true that the individual is the instrument and the first field of transformation, but an isolated individual transformation is not enough nor wholly feasible. This transformation takes place finally on a cosmic level. He says, "A Supramental change...takes place when the involved Supermind in Nature emerges to meet and join the Supramental light and power descending from Super-nature."²

Thus, Supramental consciousness is the cosmic vision which is all-comprehensive and all-pervading. It is the integral knowledge of the essentially non-dual character of reality. Almost poetically Sri Aurobindo describes the nature of Supramental consciousness, he says, "In this comprehensive knowledge there is no independent centre of existence, no individual separated ego such as we see in ourselves, that whole of existence is to its self-awareness an equable extension, one in oneness, one in multiplicity, one in all conditions and everywhere."³

The Triple Status of Supermind

We have seen that mind is a fall from Supermind, that Supermind descends down to mind, and then mind seeks to ascend back to its supramental status. The process of Involution goes down from Mind to Psyche, Life, Matter and theoretically even to Nescience. The process of evolution is a reverse process from Nescience to Supermind. Supermind cannot have the same poise through out the entire process of Involution and Evolution.

1. Sri Aurobindo, *The Life Divine*, p. 846.
2. Sri Aurobindo, *The Life Divine*, p. 855.
3. *Ibid.*, p. 55.

Sri Aurobindo speaks about its *three* general poises, which
are nothing but the three different sessions of its cosmic and
spiritual consciousness.

He describes these three poises in this way: "The first founds
the inalienable unity of things, the second modifies that unity so
as to support the manifestation of many in one and one in many;
the third further modifies it so as to support the evolution of a
diversified individuality which, by the action of ignorance,
becomes in us at a lower level the illusion of a separate ego."[1]
In order to understand this description of the triple status of
Supermind, it is essential to remember that these poises are of
the supermind as *Real Idea*, or in other words, of Supermind as
the *Creator*. The original and integral nature of Supermind
consists in its pure unitary consciousness, for that is a timeless
and spaceless concentration of Saccidānanda itself. It is only
when this consciousness casts itself out in any kind of extension,
that is, it is only when the question of creation and consequent
evolution comes up that the question of the different poises or
phases of Supermind is raised. Thus, every status of Supermind
has a definite relation with the world-process.

The first stage is the state when unity is ready to be disturbed,
and is not yet disturbed. It is the state of 'pure ideation', when
all is set for activity — for the expression of this consciousness
into multiplicity. Sri Aurobindo tries to make the nature of
this poise clear with the help of an analogy. Just as thoughts
and images that occur to our mind are not separate existences
to us, so to this poise of Supermind, individuals and the world
are not separate existences. Just as thoughts and images appear
to us as forms of consciousness, so are all forms to this primary
poise of Supermind.

In the second poise, the Supermind appears to be expressing
its consciousness in all forms. It would realise itself as one in
many and again as many in one. The process of creation has
now begun, Supermind, therefore, has to come out of its state
of inalienable unity. One very clear expression of this poise is
that the concentration in this state supporting the soul-form
would be *Jīvātman* as distinguished from the universal Divine.
Both are basically one, but whereas the individual Jīvātman
would express and realise itself in an individual centre of unity,

---

1. *Ibid.*, p. 135.

the universal Divine realises itself in all soul-forms universally. In fact, this is all a part of the universal play in which the one has manifested itself in many, although the multiplicity is regarded as having a unity behind. In the first stage everything was regarded as unity, in the second poise the multiplicity appears, and still in the multiplicity unity is perceived.

In the third poise there is a further modification. In the second poise, as we noticed, supermind is both in the movement and behind it, but in the third poise it no longer needs to stand at the back, it has to project itself in the movement and become, in a way, involved in it. Viewing all the three poises of Supermind together, we may apply our own ways of understanding upon them. We may say that the first poise is the causal state — the *Kāraṇa-avasthā*, in which everything is potentially ready for Supermind to initiate the play of creation. The second poise can be described as immediate expression or effect of the first — the *Kārya-avasthā* — in which the play has begun. The third poise can be understood as the fully manifested state — the *Pūrṇa--Vyakta-Avasthā* — in which creative processes are fully at work and consciousness is expressed in all forms and centres. In a different way the three poises can be described differently also. The first poise is the state in which the unitary character of the supramental consciousness is still intact, although it is potentially ready to be differentiated. In the second poise, the process of differentiation starts and multiplicity makes its appearance. In the third state this multiplicity is fully expressed. But, in all the stages the urge towards unity is always there, because consciousness of integral unity represents the basic character of Supermind.

The Triple Transformation

At this stage it is essential to clarify the significance of what Sri Aurobindo calls, the triple trasformation. We have already said something about these transformations in our account of Sri Aurobindo's concepts of man and ascent. We have also seen that the final transformation for man, which would take him to the higher realms is the supramental transformation. But, supramental transformation presupposes some other transformations also which prepare the ground for this final transformation. Therefore, there is the need of explaining and clarifying the nature of the various transformations as conceived by Sri Aurobindo.

He says that there are three kinds of transformation necessary for ascending to the higher realm. These transformations would first require a complete and radical change of our terrestrial existence— of the material, the vital and the mental, and then it would require a final transformation resulting from the combined forces of one's own efforts and the light from above. Consequently, Sri Aurobindo talks of a triple transformation, (a) *Psychic transformation*, (b) *Spiritual transformation* and (c) *Supramental transformation*.

(a) *Psychic transformation* :— The unfolding of the psychic soul is the first step towards supramental change. The psychic entity, as we have seen, is the subliminal aspect of our being, and as such, is veiled or hidden from outer view. But, this part of our being is imperishable and immutable. As Sri Aurobindo says, "the psychic entity in us persists and is fundamentally the same always : it contains all the essential possibilities of manifestation but is not constituted by them, it is not limited by what it manifests, not contained by the incomplete forms of the manifestation, not tarnished by the imperfections and impurities, the defects and depravations of the surface being." This psychic being does, at times, influence our conscious activities, but, our mind fails to detect the source of this influence and considers even such influences to be its own activities.

This being so, the veil which hides this inner being has to be removed. If the psychic being is the permanent and imperishable aspect of our being, we must first try to awaken this aspect of our being. This is what is called Psychic transformation. Normally this being does not reach the surface-consciousness in a clear and distinct manner. Therefore, psychic transformation would consist in locating clearly the soul-element in us and to follow its dictates. For this a change of the material, the vital and the mental is needed. All these activities must be regulated by the 'light' emanating from this Psychic being.

Sri Aurobindo admits that normally such a process of transformation is very slow. Its initial appearance on the surface is weak and indistinct, therefore, a discipline is needed for aiding the process of its expression so that the psychic being may transmit its intimations to the mind and heart and life with a greater purity, force and distinctness. Sri Aurobindo describes the method of bringing about this transformation in his Yoga. By this transformation he means an awakening of the soul and relating matter, life and mind to that awakened soul.

(b) *Spiritual transformation*:—Psychic transformation brings about changes in the ways and activities of the soul, but that is not enough. By the process of psychic transformation, matter, life and mind are purified, but there must also be an opening out of the soul to spiritual intimations. The psychic being must be turned, so to say, towards whatever seems to belong to a higher reality. This is what is meant by spiritual transformation. Sri Aurobindo feels that when the soul is awakened and is able to guide and regulate life and mind, it must try to bring about a spiritual change in its conscious life. It may, for example, seek the spiritual reality through the good, the true, the beautiful, 'through all that is pure and fine and high and noble.'

Sri Aurobindo thinks that the soul may attempt to achieve this contact mainly through the thinking mind as its instrument, it may put a psychic impression on the intellect and higher mind and intuitional intelligence and turn them in that direction. As this transformation will become more and more perfect, the spiritualised mind will move beyond all forms and figures, beyond all ideas of good or evil, or true or false, or beautiful or ugly. Such a spiritual consciousness will tend towards the apprehension of that which transcends all dualities, and is one.

(c) *Supramental transformation* :—Spiritual transformation leads the soul to the apprehension of spiritual unity. "A spiritualised consciousness is achieved and the life falls quiet, the body ceases to need and to clamour, the soul itself merges into the spiritual silence."[1] "But this transformation...does not give us the integral transformation; the psychic transformation is replaced by a spiritual change on the rare and high summits, but this is not the complete divine dynamisation of nature."[2] For that supramental transformation is necessary.

Sri Aurobindo says that psychic transformation and spiritual transformation uplift man to higher reaches of consciousness, but if the soul is left only with these, there will only be a vision of a unity above us, not a realisation of it. And, as it happens with every vision it will tend to grow fainter and weaker, and

1. Sri Aurobindo, *The Life Divine*, p. 802.
   Ibid.

consequently only a faint memory of such a vision may ultimately remain. This happens with all cases of intuitional experiences. Therefore, the vision must be transformed into a realisation. For that it is necessary that there takes place a *decent* of the higher consciousness. "The Truth-consciousness [that is, Supermind] finding evolutionary Nature ready, has to descend into her and enable her to liberate the Supramental principle within her."[1] In this descent would consist, what Sri Aurobindo calls, Supramental transformation. As the psychic change has to call in the spiritual change to complete it, so the spiritual change has to call in the supramental transformation to complete it. The final change can be brought about only through such an intervention by the supramental consciousness.

This transformation will bring to us the abiding spiritual sense and the consciousness of the Infinite, and will cause a radical change in the whole of our terrestrial existence. The supramental presence in matter, life and mind will change entirely the nature of the material, the vital and the mental. Man then will no longer move in ignorance, they will act on knowledge. They will become Gnostic beings and life in the state will become a Divine life. The complete effects of this transformation can be calculated only when an account of Sri Aurobindo's conception of 'Gnostic Being and Divine Life' is understood.

Gnostic Being and Divine Life

(1) Gnostic Being, its nature

Sri Aurobindo admits that as we reach in our thought the line at which the evolution of mind into overmind changes into an evolution of overmind into supermind, we are faced with a difficulty. We are constrained to seek for some exact or precise idea and a clear description of the supramental existence. Sri Aurobindo feels that it is difficult for mental thought to understand or describe supramental nature, it is impossible for mind to forecast in detail what the supramental change must be like. Supermind is a state beyond mind, and therefore cannot be understood in terms of mental categories. But, in spite of this difficulty, Sri Aurobindo feels that certain

1. *Ibid.*, p. 816.

deductions — at least with respect to the general nature of this change — can very well be made. For example, it may consistently be maintained in the light of the nature of the evolutionary process that supramental nature must be a perfect integration and consummation of spiritual nature and experience. This also can be said on the basis of the nature of the process of ascent that this change would involve a total spiritualisation of mundane nature. Likewise, this can also be maintained that souls that would emerge as a result of the supramental transformations would not remain 'mental men', but would become super-men or supramental men. They would not be men of ignorance, but men of knowledge — the 'Gnostic beings'. This transformation then will seek to establish a race of Gnostic beings.

Gnostic beings, then, are not ignorant souls caught in the process of evolution, they are *men of knowledge* (hence the name 'Gnostic'). The Gnostic individual would be the consummation of the spiritual man, his whole way of being, thinking, living and acting would be governed by the power of a universal spirituality. That is so on account of the nature of supermind itself, which is essentially unitary in character. Its consciousness is integral and therefore it would also harmonise and unify apparent diversities. That is why the Gnostic being will always have this sense of integral unity. This sense is so keen that the supramental Gnostic being will have not only this integral sense in his own inner or outer life, but would be able to create a harmonic unity even with the still surviving mental beings.

The Gnostic being is a perfect and complete individual. This perfection results from highest possible integration both within and without. Sri Aurobindo describes this character of the Gnostic being thus, "A complete self-knowledge in all things and at all moments is the gift of the Supramental gnosis ... with a complete self-mastery, not merely in the sense of control of Nature, but in the sense of a power of perfect self-expression in Nature."[1]

The Gnostic being always acts in awareness of the harmony of his individual self with the total self, of his individual will with the total will, of his individual action with the total action. This simply means that the Gnostic being is completely divinised spirit. Another implication of this description is that all the

---

1. Sri Aurobindo, *The Life Divine*, p. 864.

activities of the Gnostic being is based on knowledge and not on ignorance. Ignorance is a fragmentary view of reality and not its total view. Therefore, activities performed in ignorance will always lack the universal awareness of thought and action. The Gnostic being *knows*, and therefore his actions are not chaotic. Yet another implication of this description is that the Gnostic being will feel no difficulty or hindrance in performing an action. We, in our normal mental life, feel such a difficulty on account of the barriers that our ego-sense creates around itself. The Gnostic being transcends all such barriers, and therefore, becomes one in realisation with the Infinite.

Therefore, Sri Aurobindo says that an evolution of Gnostic consciousness brings with it a transformation of world-consciousness and world-action. His experience of the universe is that of one living in the universe, and at the same time that of one who carries the universe with himself. S.K. Maitra, describing this character of the Superman, writes, "He will have the cosmic consciousness, sense, feeling, by which all objective life will become part of his subjective existence and by which he will realise, perceive, feel, see, hear the Divine in all forms."[1]

Again, the supramental being performs his activities in the joyous spirit, his only aim is the delight of the manifestation of the spirit. He has no desires, no wants, nothing to strive for or achieve. Even delight is *not his goal*, it is his nature. Knowledge is not his aim, for him there is no new discovery. He knows already, and therefore, he brings out only that which is already known.

Thus, it is apparent that supramental transformation carries life, mind and body beyond themselves into a greater and a higher being. In the Gnostic individual, therefore, the powers of life, mind and body are not suppressed or abolished, but perfected and fulfilled by, what can be called, a process of self-exceeding. For example, the relation of the Gnostic individual with his body would be of a totally different kind from the relation that we have with our bodies. In the Gnostic being even the body becomes an instrument of spiritual activities and presents no problems or creates no hindrance for the Gnostic individual.

Now, we are in a position to say that the Gnostic individual is

1. S. K. Maitra, *The Philosophy of Sri Aurobindo*, pp. 89-90.

the man with an entirely changed and spiritualised outlook. We can try to understand this with the help of an analogy. If we trace the history of mankind from the primitive to the civilised man of today, we find that growth consists not in creating anything entirely new, but in bringing about a change of outlook and of a way of looking at things. When, for example, the primitive came across a gold-ore, he treated it just like any other stone, but when man came to know about its value, the entire outlook towards the gold-ore changed. Knowledge did not create an entirely new man or an entirely new gold-ore, there was only a difference in the way of looking at things. Likewise the Gnostic being will not be an entirely new individual born out of nowhere. He is the individual who has been able to acquire knowledge, and therefore, his outlook towards everything — towards matter, life and mind — completely changes. It is, as it has been said, an outlook born out of knowledge and not out of ignorance.

ii. Types of Gnostic Beings

A supramental or gnostic race of beings would not be a race made according to a single type, moulded in a single, fixed pattern. The law of supermind is the law of unity fulfilled in multiplicity-in-diversity. Therefore, although the basic consciousness invariably remains the same consciousness, there will be infinite diversity in the manifestation of gnostic consciousness.

In fact, the question of 'types' or 'kinds' of Gnostic beings has a relevance in two different contexts. The Gnostic being is the man of knowledge, the man who has risen above the realm of ignorance. But, it is quite possible that the knowledge of one is intuitional, and that of another even higher or over mental. That is to say, knowledge is not something that is attained as soon as one starts rising above the realm of ignorance. There may be different levels of knowledge which different individuals may attain. There may, therefore, be an overmental Gnostic being or an intuitional Gnostic being.

But, the second aspect of this question is more relevant, because the real man of knowledge is the *Supramental Gnostic being*. The question is, 'are there types of supramental Gnostic beings also ?' Sri Aurobindo says that even there the individuals cannot be cast strictly according to a single type of individuality.

Even Supermind has three poises or phases, and therefore it would not be correct to maintain that the level of knowledge reached by every Supramental Gnostic being would be . exactly the same. At least a difference of degree has to be there. Therefore, even in this stage, it has to be believed that every being would be a *unique* expression of the same supramental light — different from every other, not necessarily in quality, but at least in degree.

iii. Personality of the Gnostic Being

Now, a very pertinent question can be raised : is the Gnostic being a person ? Does he have a personality ? This question would involve yet another question. All through it has been emphasised that the Gnostic being, unlike the mental being, works on knowledge and not on ignorance, that in this state man's entire outlook is changed — perfected and thoroughly spiritualised. That shows that the identity of the individual being is perhaps not lost in the Gnostic state. Then the question arises, will the status and personality of the Gnostic being be similar to the personality of ordinary individuals ?

If we think of the self as the separative self — as an ordinary ego, then these questions would not arise, because then, we can very well think that the ego ceases to exist and disappears in the transcendental consciousness. In that case it would be believed that with the emergence of the transcendental consciousness personality would be finally lost, and that the question regarding its nature would not arise. But, the Supermind is not conceived in that way, on the other hand, it is conceived as the consummation of mind. The Supramental Gnostic being moves on this very earth. Should we then suppose that the Supramental individual *is a self without personality — an impersonal Puruṣa* ? But, even this supposition would create further difficulties. We shall have to suppose, then, that all the Gnostic individuals are similar in being and nature. Moreover, in that case the Supramental acts will have to be conceived as *resulting from void*, which, again, is illogical.

Sri Aurobindo solves the difficulty in a very easy manner. He feels that all these difficulties appear as difficulties only to mental consciousness. All the solutions that are generally referred to are mental solutions of the problem, and therefore, they give rise to further difficulties. But, there would remain no difficulty if the problem is viewed in the light of the Supramental consciousness. In the Supramental consciousness Personality and Impersonality are not opposite principles, they are inseparable aspects of one and the same reality. The reality is the being which is impersonal and universal in nature, but expresses itself in Nature in forms of personality. A Supramental Gnostic being, therefore, can be described as a spiritual person, but he is not a personality in the sense of a pattern of being marked out by a settled combination of fixed qualities and characters. He is not also a completely impersonal being expressing itself in various forms. The Gnostic individual, in reality, is the *inner person unveiled*, spirituality unmaked. He is not a surface-personality having the need of a mask or a persona. He is thus above the distinction of Personality-Impersonality. He is an infinite and universal being — necessarily revealing in nature, expressing and revealing itself in various forms.

Is the Gnostic Being a Jivanmukta ?

An account of Sri Aurobindo's conception of the Gnostic being would remain incomplete if it is not compared with the concept of Jivanmukta, because to a casual reader the two might appear to be the same. The general description of the Jivanmukta shows that it bears a very close resemblance to the Gnostic being. In broad terms, the Jivanmukta is he who attains liberation in the bodily state itself. He is, as it were, a citizen of two worlds. As still an embodied living being he is very much in the phenomenal world, but as a liberated being he belongs very much to the transcendental world. Even the Gnostic being, in certain respects, can be said to be a being of this description. He also represents the consummation of this-worldly nature, and attains this state under the conditions of this very life.

But, the two notions are not exactly identical. Sri Aurobindo has tried to make the concept of Gnostic being by far richer than that of Jivanmukta. One of the basic reasons for making this claim is that the Gnostic being, even after attaining supramental status, attempts to bring down the higher light and consciousness into the evolutionary process. The Jivanmukta as the liberated individual continues in existence in the body so long as the forces of Karma make the body continue. Once he is out

of it, that is, once he attains the status of 'Videhamukti', his task
is done. He now becomes fully emancipated and completely
free from the cycle of births and rebirths. The Supramental
Gnostic being, on the other hand, makes himself one with the
creative impetus and therefore, works for the emergence of
Divine life on earth by transforming others also into Gnostic
beings.

But, the most important point of difference is that, according
to Sri Aurobindo, the Gnostic being is not an entirely new
existence. He asserts that in such a being all parts of the embodied existence including even the physical are transformed and
divinised as a result of the Supramental transformation. It is not
entering into a new life or world, it is the perfecting and divinis-
ing of the earthly existence itself.

In the light of these points Haridas Choudhary suggests that
all Supermen or Supramental Gnostic beings can be thought of
as Jīvanmukta, but all Jīvanmuktas are not Supermen.[1] The concept of Superman comprehends the concept of Jīvanmukta and
is something more.

The Divine Life

The distinction between the Superman and the Jīvanmukta
itself shows that the attainment of the Supramental status is not
the ultimate destiny of man. The Supermen are also required
to work for the transformation of others, and therefore, the
ultimate goal of evolution lies still ahead. It is a life in which
all individuals would be Gnostic beings, in which there would
emerge a race of beings endowed with Supramental powers.
Explaining this in terms of Sri Aurobindo's own words, S.K.
Maitra says, ". . . from the point of spiritual evolution, this
[attainment of the Gnostic state] would be only an individual
liberation and perfection in an unchanged environmental existence : for a greater dynamic change . . . of the whole principle
and instrumentation of life and action, the appearance of a new
order of beings and a new earth-life must be envisaged in our
idea of the total consummation, the divine issue . . . for what is
wanted is the emergence of a divine life on earth, not the isolated realization by a few individuals of their true inner life."[2]

1. Haridas Choudhary, *Sri Aurobindo, the Prophet of Life Divine*, p. 160.
2. S.K. Maitra, *The Philosophy of Sri Aurobindo*, pp. 94-95.

Thus, we find that the transformation of man into Superman is only one although essential-aspect of evolution, but the process does not come to a stop with the emergence of one or a few Supermen, it has to move ahead to bring on earth a *Divine Life*. The Divine Life, then, primarily consists in a life, in which there will be a race of Supramental Gnostic individuals. Divine life means 'a perfected life on earth' — a life not of limited consciousness, a life not based on outward conditions like our normal life, but a life of inner completeness and perfection of being. So, the first description of the Divine life is that it consists of a race of Supermen. A perfect human world cannot be created or composed of men who are themselves imperfect. Sri Aurobindo is aware that it is difficult to fix up the line at which the mental life ceases and the Divine life begins. But, with the advent of Divine life a spiritual transformation becomes apparent not only in the life of this or that individual, but in the collective life of Gnostic beings.

Describing the nature of Divine life Sri Aurobindo says, *"To be and to be fully is Nature's aim in us."*[1] An explanation of the implications of this expression will throw some light on the nature of Divine life. (1) To be fully, firstly, is to be wholly conscious of one's being. Ordinary existence, that is, life in terms of the mental is ignorant living or unconscious existence. Existence in Divine life is self aware existence — existence with the knowledge of existence. (2) This means that to be fully is 'to have the intrinsic and integral force of one's being'. This implies that in the self-aware existence of Divine life the beings will be in complete possession of the force and capacities that they have been able to cultivate. Self-aware existence means complete self-possession. (3) To be fully must also mean to have the full delight of being. The delight must also be intrinsic, automatic and natural. Pain and suffering are signs of imperfection, and therefore, they cannot have any place in Divine life. (4) To be fully is also to be fully *universally*. Ordinary existence is existing in the limitation of a small restricted ego, and therefore, is an imperfect existence. Describing this characteristic of Divine life Sri Aurobindo says, "All being is one and to be fully is to be all that is. To be in the being of all and to include all in one's being, to be conscious of the consciousness of all, to be integrated in force with the

1. Sri Aurobindo, *The Life Divine*, p. 907.

universal force, to carry all action and experience in oneself and
feel it as one's own action and experience, to feel all selves as
one's own self, to feel all delight of being as one's own delight
of being, is a necessary condition of the integral divine living."[1]
(5) This implies that to be fully is also to be *transcendentally*.
This means that Supermen, existing in Divine life, somehow
transcend and are above not only their individual existences, but
also the universe. It is quite probable that this notion of 'transcendental existence in Divine life' is merely an extension of Sri
Aurobindo's idea of the Gnostic beings who have, so to say, a
transcendental attitude towards everything happening around
them.

These things, according to Sri Aurobindo, are impossible without an inward living. 'The divinity in man dwells veiled within
him', and so, an outward expression of that inner aspect does
not represent his real nature. The individual has to find himself,
his true existence, he can do this by living in inwardness. This
task of going within is a difficult task; but in Divine life such an
existence becomes normal and natural.

This inner life is not an imprisonment or confinement, it is
not being restricted to the personal self. In Divine life there will
also be a vivid and intimate consciousness of *others* — 'a
consciousness of their mind, life and physical being which are
felt as if they were one's own'. The Gnostic being in Divine life
will act not out of a surface sentiment of love and sympathy or
any other similar feeling, but out of a consciousness of an intimate oneness. He finds himself not only in his own fulfilment,
but also in the fulfilment of others. He sees Divine working
everywhere, and his actions are performed in clear awareness of
this.

Divine life, thus, is the emergence of a perfect life on earth, a
life not of separation or isolation, but one of unity and harmony,
a life not regulated by the mental and natural forces, but a life
regulated by Super-consciousness. Nature, thus, changes into
Supernature, individuals are transformed in the triple way
(mentioned earlier) by Supramental consciousness, and life becomes a life of supreme consciousness and joy. He describes
this life in the following manner, "A life of gnostic beings carrying the evolution to a higher supramental status might fully be
characterised as a Divine Life, for it would be a life in the

1. Sri Aurobindo, *The Life Divine*, p. 907.

Divine, a life of the beginnings of a spiritual divine light and power and joy manifested in material Nature. That might be described, since it surpasses the mental human level, as a life of spiritual and supramental Supermanhood."[1] Supermanhood consists in a new consciousness in which humanity itself finds its self-fulfilment.

Comparing Divine life with our ordinary mental life of ignorance Sri Aurobindo says that the new life would, in a sense, be a reversal of the present law of human consciousness and life. We, in our ordinary existence, believe that joy and grief, peril and passion, pleasure and pain, success and frustration, uncertainties of fate, the struggles and strifes of life, the worries and anxieties of existence are all inevitable and necessary aspects of the universe. We cannot conceive of life to be anything different. Any picture of life that does not take into account these is considered to be empty and even unrealistic. But, the entire outlook will become different in the Gnostic existence or Divine life. Consciousness and joy would be infinite in this life. This would open to our view more vistas, greater delight of the spirit, and would bring to our reach such immensity of existence, consciousness and bliss that we, as mental beings cannot even imagine. Such a Divine life, according to Sri Aurobindo, is going to be our ultimate destiny. He says, "this fulness of life must be the goal of development towards which we are tending and which will manifest at an early or later stage of our destiny."[2]

Integral Yoga

Divine life, then, is the ultimate destiny, the goal of evolution. But, how are we to bring it on earth ? Sri Aurobindo feels that such a state is bound to emerge sooner or later, but its descent can be expedited by spiritual activities. But, how precisely are we to expedite it ? Sri Aurobindo's answer is that this can be done by *Yoga*. It is not possible to explain the nature of Yoga as conceived by Sri Aurobindo in complete detail, partly because of the vastness of its description and partly because of its essential dependence on *Tantra*, which falls beyond the scope of our study. Even so, we can try to determine the salient features of Sri Aurobindo's Yoga in a philosophical manner.

1. Sri Aurobindo, *The Life Divine*, p. 945.
2. Sri Aurobindo, *The Life Divine*, p. 947.

Its Aim

The word 'Yoga' literally means 'Union', and therefore, the basic aim of all kinds of Yoga is the realisation of the Divine — the realisation of unity. All philosophies of Yoga presuppose that the greatest evil is the separation of the finite from the infinite, and therefore, the restoration of the original unity is the aim of Yoga. Sri Aurobindo, somehow or other, believes in some such concept of Yoga, but he makes it consistent with the general nature of his philosophy. Even a casual look at the main aspects of his thought will make it clear that there are certain basic ends that his Yoga seeks to serve.

(1) We have seen that evolution has reached a particular stage both at the individual level and at the cosmic level. We also have noticed that evolution is preparing for a leap into the spiritual or the Supramental level. 'Yoga' is needed to facilitate and expedite this leap. (2) We also know that Sri Aurobindo believes that the ultimate destiny of the process of evolution will be a Divine life in which all beings will be liberated. It is his conviction that such a state is bound to come sooner or later, but it is better if it comes sooner rather than later. Yoga is needed to expedite that. (3) Sri Aurobindo admits that life-process, in a sense, is itself a *Yoga*, because every activity is an activity towards the realisation of unity, being an expression of the infinite within us. But, ordinarily such a Yogic activity is performed almost unconsciously without the awareness of its aims. and purposes. The aim of Sri Aurobindo's Yoga is to do it in a conscious way. (d) Ordinarily, this process moves in a very slow speed. Yoga accelerates the process. "Thus Yoga implies. not only the realisation of God, but an entire consecration and change of the inner and outer life *till it is fit to manifest a divine consciousness and become part of a divine work.*"[1] That is why the aim of Yoga is variously described, sometimes it is described as 'the outflowing of the Divine in Collective Humanity'. Sometimes it is described as 'liberation in and of Nature and not simply from Nature', it is also described as, 'spiritual self-manifestation as distinguished from mere self-realisation'.

From such descriptions one special feature of Sri Aurobindo's Yoga can be brought to light. Yoga, according to him, is the

---

1. Sri Aurobindo, *Lights on Yoga*, p. 3.

realisation of divinity here — on earth — in the bodily state itself; it does not lead to a supernatural existence. It changes the entire physical, vital and mental processes. As he says, "Our Yoga is a double movement of ascent and descent, one rises to higher and higher levels of consciousness, but at the same time one brings down their power not only into mind and life, but in the end even into the body. And the highest of these levels, the one at which it aims is Supermind. Only when that can be brought down is a divine transformation possible in the earth consciousness."[1] Integral Yoga, thus aims at the Divine transformation of the whole of the embodied existence and also includes sarvamukti or the collective liberation of the mankind.

Its Nature

Describing the nature of Yoga Sri Aurobindo says, 'Yoga means union with the Divine, a union either transcendental (above the universe) or cosmic (universal) or individual, or as in our Yoga, *all three together*.'[2] That is one of the reasons why it is called integral. We have seen that Yoga helps and expedites the process of ascent, which is nothing but a process of *widening, heightening* and *integration.* Yoga helps all these aspects of evolution and therefore it is integral. Let us now try to determine some of the basic characters of his *Integral Yoga* or *Pūrṇa Yoga.*

(a) Firstly, it can be said that all other forms of Yoga, some-how or other, demand the cultivation of some special faculties or capacities, and therefore, they are not within the easy reach of everybody. Sri Aurobindo outlines the process of an inner Yoga which can be followed by everybody. That is why he does not lay much emphasis on either the breathing or postural exer-cises of Haṭha Yoga, or on the Prāṇāyāma and Āsana prescribed in Patañjali's Yoga. He does not also assert that Yoga requires the observance and performance of such religious rites and rituals that require special capacities and resources. He does not even recommend the recitation of prayers and mantras. His Yoga, as we shall see, is an inner-Yoga requiring some disciplines of purification and spiritualisation which every one can practise.

1. Sri Aurobindo, *The Riddle of the World*, pp. 2-3.
2. Sri Aurobindo, *Lights on Yoga*, p. 16.

(b) Most of the Yogic procedures adopt a negative attitude towards the world. Patañjali's Yoga aims at the attainment of Vivekajñāna which is only the knowledge of the discrimination between the self and the not-self. Sri Aurobindo believes that Yoga aims not at a discriminating knowledge, but at the spiritualisation of even the not-self. (c) Likewise, most of the Yogic philosophies believe that what is needed is a rising above the physical and the bodily. Sri Aurobindo does not recommend a complete suppression or rejection of the physical or the bodily, on the other hand, he believes that the aim of Yoga is to charge even the physical with the Supramental light. (d) Again, usually the Yogis assert that the union with the Divine takes place in a state of *Samādhi* or *ecstatic trance* in which waking consciousness completely fades out and all contacts with the ordinary world and surroundings are lost. On the contrary, Sri Aurobindo believes that the spiritual union with the Divine can take place in this body itself — in the state of waking consciousness itself. (5) All Yogic philosophies state that the aim of Yoga is the liberation of the individual. Sri Aurobindo says that that is not the only aim. In fact, even individual liberation is an aspect of the ultimate goal — the redemption of mankind and the emergence of Divine Life on earth. (6) Therefore, the *process of Yoga*, as recommended by Sri Aurobindo lays down such unique techniques that are different from usual Yogic disciplines. We have seen that the passage from the mental stage — which we have reached — to the supramental stage is through various inter-mediary steps which mind can assume on its onward march. Therefore, Yoga is the effort to move the mind along the path of ascent (through higher mind, illumined mind, Intuition and Overmind) towards Supermind. For this a *threefold process* is recommended which corresponds to the *process of triple transformation* discussed earlier. This includes (i) a process of *psychicisation*, (ii) a process of *spiritualisation*, and (iii) a process of *supramentalisation*. These three are conceived as three steps of Integral Yoga or Pūrṇa Yoga. These steps are essentially inner, and that is why, at times, Sri Aurobindo's Yoga is described as inner Yoga.

Psychicisation involves a persistent effort to realise the centrality of the psychic being — the Jīvātmā which represents the Divine in man. Normally that aspect remains veiled and in the background. Sri Aurobindo feels that the first step is to awaken it. Describing the process of psychicisation Haridas Choudhary says. "Psychicisation means psychic change of the lower nature, bringing right vision into the mind, right impulse and feeling into the vital, right movement and habit into the physical — all turned towards the Divine, all based on love, devotion and adoration — and finally, the true vision and the sense of the dynamic Divine (the Mother) everywhere in the world as well as in the heart."[1] Thus, in this step consciousness has to turn inwards, and it has to reform accordingly the physical, the vital and the mental.

Spiritualisation is the second step of Yoga, it is also described as the process of opening out. Psychic change prepares the ground by transforming the physical, the vital and the mental. Now, the mental must start its onward march by opening itself out to higher consciousness, to the Superconscient. By this process the self seeks to bring to itself peace, power, knowledge and bliss etc. and spiritualises its thought and action. Psychic change, in a way, is a change within the limits of natural aspects — surface and subliminal, spiritual change rises above and seeks to bring down into play the aspects of the higher realm.

Finally, the third step of *Supramentalisation* is needed. In this process consciousness is fully divinised and the entire point of view changes. All forces of disunity and duality are superseded and the vision of complete unity emerges. Sri Aurobindo feels that there are four different stages in Pūrṇa Yoga for 'stilling all storm and tumult of the mental'. They are *Quiet* (*acañacalatā*), *Calm* (*sthiratā*), *Peace* (*Śānti*) and *Silence* (*Nīravatā*). These four are not qualitatively different stages, they represent progressively the stages through which mind is completely freed from all disturbances. Supramentalisation brings about two changes — *universalisation*, which is nothing but expansion of consciousness and *transcendentalisation*, which is nothing but the knowledge of the identity of the Divine.

These three stages evidently represent the three transformations (discussed earlier) which are essential for the realisation of Divine Life.

1. Haridas Choudhary, *Sri Aurobindo, The Prophet of Life Divine*, pp. 88-89.

How is Yoga Integral ?

Sri Aurobindo claims that his Yoga is integral or synthetic, because firstly, it comprehends all forms of Yoga and secondly, it emphasises such aspects of Yoga-discipline that are missed by other forms of Yoga. There is for example, Haṭha Yoga, which recommends the various disciplines of the body; Rājayoga concentrates on mind, Jñāna Yoga, Bhakti Yoga and Karma Yoga recommend the ways of knowledge, devotion and action respectively. Different religions of the world emphasise either one or the other of these ways. Sri Aurobindo feels that all these ways emphasise only different aspects of the whole process and neglect the other ones. Knowledge and Devotion, for example, are not opposed to each other and yet Jñāna Mārga and Bhakti Yoga assert and lay emphasis on their own ways. Sri Aurobindo feels that what is needed is an all round and total development. The growth of knowledge alone, or the perfection and control of only the body, or the way of intense devotion will not bring about the change. What is needed is a total transformation of all the aspects of being — the mental, the vital and the physical. Therefore, only that process can be Pūrṇa Yoga which will aim at the complete transformation of every aspect of being. This is the aim of Sri Aurobindo's Yoga, and therefore, it is called integral.

CHAPTER V

KRISHNACHANDRA BHATTACHARYA

Life

K. C. Bhattacharya was born at Serampur on the 12th of May 1875. He was born in a Brahmin family of Sanskrit scholars; naturally, in his childhood itself he was initiated into an appreciation of ancient Indian wisdom. Krishnachandra had his initial school education at the local school. However, after passing his matriculation examination in 1891, he was sent to the Presidency College. He was a brilliant student through out, and so succeeded in getting the P. R. S. award of the Calcutta University in 1901.

He joined the Bengal educational service, and served as Lecturer in Philosophy in various colleges of Bengal. He retired from the educational service in 1930, when he was officiating as the Principal of Hooghly College. After retirement he was invited to work as the Director of the Indian Institute of Philosophy at Amalner. He worked there till 1935, when he was offered the post of the George V Professor of Mental and Moral Philosophy of the Calcutta University, in which capacity he worked till 1937.

He had a very keen philosophical insight and consequently he was a very cautious writer. His writings were brief, precise and full of meaning. Particularly towards the end of his life he was in the habit of writing short notes — scribbles — which he used to throw about in his room in the night only to be gathered and safely preserved by his wife in the morning. These scribbles, at times, contained profound philosophical ideas. Some of them are yet to be arranged, classified and published. K. C. Bhattacharya died on the 11th of December 1949.

General Character of his Thought

K. C. Bhattacharya had a deep study of ancient Indian philosophy — particularly of the Advaita Vedānta, Sāṅkhya, Yoga and Jaina Philosophies. He was also well-versed in classical German Philosophy — particularly the philosophy of

Kant. His vast and deep study provided the intellectual background in the light of which his profoundly original mind could
go on with the work of 'construction'. In fact, if we survey the
main writings of K. C. Bhattacharya we shall find that his work
can be classified under two heads : (a) the work of interpretation and (b) that of construction. Under the former would
come his interpretations of Vedānta, Sāṅkhya, Yoga, Jaina and
other philosophies. Even here one will find that K. C. Bhattacharya is not merely a historian or just a faithful commentator,
he will appear to be original because all the time he will be
trying to suggest new ideas, the rudiments of which provide the
basis of his own philosophical views. The editor of his *Studies
in Philosophy* says that his method is one of *Constructive Interpretation*, but the fact remains that his own philosophical insight
is so deep that it would be difficult to understand even his interpretations unless one is familiar with his own philosophical
convictions.

It is difficult to give an account of his philosophy in terms of
any accepted philosophical model, in fact, it is not safe to desig-
nate his philosophy with a name. An approximate description
of his philosophy can be given by calling it the philosophy of
Transcendental Idealism. It is not idealism in the sense of "idea-
ism", it does not seek to suggest that reality is an idea. It is
idealism in the sense of "ideal-ism." The ultimate reality is
conceived as the end of the process of realisation. His philosophy can be called transcendental in the sense that the nature
of the ultimate is not describable in terms of any accepted
philosophical epithets. Krishnachandra relates everything to
experience and reality is conceived as the ultimate presupposition of experience. It is neither subjective nor objective; to
relate the subject and object in knowledge it is very essential
that the relating principle is neither subjective nor objective.
That is why Krishnachandra conceives the ultimate reality as
transcending the distinction between the subjective and the
objective. That is why his philosophy has been called 'transcendental'. In another sense, his philosophy can be called the
philosophy of *Abstract Idealism* also. Although his ultimate
reality is not quite similar to the *substance* of Spinoza or to the
Brahman of Advaita Vedānta, it is very much abstract. It is
abstract because Ultimate Reality is arrived at by carrying the
process of abstraction to its maximum limit.

Concept of Philosophy

Usually it is believed that philosophy is an attempt to construct a world-view. In India philosophy is made to serve a practical — more accurately a religious — purpose. It aims at freeing man from suffering. The path leading to this state of complete freedom from suffering consists in a kind of knowledge. This knowledge is conceived as the knowledge of the distinction between the 'real' and the 'unreal'. That means that philosophy has to give a world-view, it has to analyse the nature of the world in order to discover the real and unreal aspects of the world.

But, Krishnachandra does not agree with this fully. In this respect his position is similar to that of Kant, or even to that of the Logical Positivists. Like them, K. C. Bhattacharya also believes that it is not an essential function of philosophy to construct a synthetic view of the world. He feels that judgments of philosophy are not factual; they are not related to facts in so far as they do not claim facticity like the empirical judgments.

Theoretic Consciousness

Judgments of science claim to have a relation with facts. Both Science and Philosophy are expressions of *Theoretic Consciousness*, because both have to deal with judgments that are speakable or at least systematically communicable. *Theoretic Consciousness* is theoretic because it is conceived apart from its expressions, it is theoretic also because it has just a 'believed content' and not a 'meant content'. K. C. Bhattacharya defines it thus, "Theoretic consciousness, at its minimum, is the understanding of a speakable."[1] At this level the speakable does not have a meaning content, it is only believed. "What is spoken must be in the first instance believed."[2] This needs a clarification. This can be illustrated with the help of an example, an example that K. C. Bhattacharya himself has used — the example of 'the square circle'. A square circle is neither believed nor disbelieved. It does not have even a spoken content. Even when it is spoken, it is spoken almost as if it has not been spoken.

---

1. K. C. Bhattacharya, *Studies in Philosophy*, Vol. II, p. 101.
2. *Ibid.*

Therefore, it cannot form part of Theoretic consciousness. Only that will form a part of Theoretic consciousness, which being a speakable, has a 'believed content'. For example, even a lie will form a part of Theoretic consciousness, because although it is a lie, when it is spoken it has a content that is believed. When a lie is spoken it gives out a suggestion of something of the type "believe me", and it is understanding of that spoken content that forms a part of Theoretic consciousness.

This consciousness, again, is not knowledge, it involves a belief that something may become known. Knowledge is an explicit awareness of an actual or possible state of affairs, the awareness in theoretic consciousness is not explicit, on the other hand, over and above its belief, it somehow gives the impression of unknownness also. Therefore, Krishnachandra says that Theoretic consciousness involves not the knowing, but the *understanding* of the speakable. It understands, it is aware, but it does not explicitly know.

Four Grades of Theoretic Consciousness

All forms of Theoretic consciousness as involving the understanding of the speakable are understood as aspects of thought. There may be *four* forms of thought, of which one is literal thought, and others are symbolic. Literal thought, technically speaking, is not thought proper or pure thought, but including that there are four forms of thought. Consequently, it is said that there are *four grades of Theoretic Consciousness.*

(a) *Empirical*:—Empirical consciousness has always a reference to the objective. This reference is not superficial or casual, it is this reference that constitutes its meaning. It is an awareness of a content that is either perceived or imagined to be perceived, and *this* reference to the object forms a part of the meaning of the content. Here, the object is understood as *fact*. In order to appreciate or grasp the content of this consciousness, namely object as fact, there is no need of referring it to thinking.

(b) *Objective*:—This consciousness is also objective. The difference between this and the empirical consciousness is that in the latter a reference to sense-perception as revealing the object as fact has to be made, but in the former such a reference is not necessary. Moreover, in empirical thought there is no reference to the subject, but in objective consciousness there is the reference of object as related to the subject. That is why empirical consciousness understands the object as fact, whereas, objective consciousness understands it not as a fact, but as *self-subsistent*.

(c) *Subjective or Spiritual*: — This consciousness has no reference to the objective, it is purely subjective. It does not have any content that is contemplated in the objective attitude, the content here is thought of or grasped in the subjective attitude, that is, in an *enjoying* consciousness. In the first two stages the content is *contemplated* — viewed as object either as fact, or as a content related to the subject. But, in spiritual thought the content is *enjoyed* in a purely subjective attitude. Its content is called *reality*.

(d) *Transcendental:* — This consciousness has a reference neither to the subjective nor to the objective, it somehow transcends their distinction. Therefore, the content of Transcendental consciousness is transcendental, and is called the Truth.

These four grades of Theoretic consciousness have to be clarified further, but before that some general remarks on the nature of the grades have to be made.

It is necessary to assert in the very beginning that, according to Krishnachandra Bhattacharya, Philosophy is not concerned with empirical consciousness, it is concerned with the last three grades of Theoretic consciousness. Empirical consciousness is literal thought, it deals with facts, therefore, its content is the concern of science, where as, the contents of the last three grades, namely, the contents of pure thought in the objective, subjective and transcendental attitudes form the subject-matter of Philosophy. It is interesting to find that an attempt to distinguish the contents of the first grade from those of the last three will also bring to light the distinction between science and philosophy.

Empirical thought as we have seen, deals with facts which form the subject-matter of science. It has a reference to object as fact, and therefore it is literal thought. Literal thought conveys some *information* about facts. In literal judgments, for example, the relation between a subject and an object is represented and it is represented as conveying some information. "x is" is a relational judgment expressing the nature of a fact. But, if 'x is' does not convey any information, and if it is something other than a relational judgment, then it can be said that 'x is' a symbol of something. In that case thought *is not literal but symbolic*. Beliefs about facts, that is, judgments in literal sense have a *meaning*, but non-informative judgments about belief have a *significance*, they signify something about which we do not have literal information. Therefore, such judgments are symbolic. It is on account of this that Krishnachandra says that science is literal thought, but *philosophy is symbolic thinking*.

Now, if "x is" is taken to be a symbolic judgment, then in the judgment "x is", 'x' may be presupposed either as *self-subsistent*, or as *real* or as *true*. Krishnachandra says, Truth is only symbolically spoken, reality is literally spoken as symbolised and the self-subsistent is literally spoken as meant. That is to say, if symbolic thought (and, for that matter, philosophical judgments also because philosophical judgments are smbolic judgments) is put in judgment-form, any of the three things can happen : (a) In the judgment 'x is' merely its form may be symbolic, the content being objective. (b) In 'x is' only 'is' may be symbolic, x remaining subjective. (c) In 'x is' even 'x' may become symbolic. In the first case thought is *contemplative*, in the second it is *enjoying* and in the third it is *transcendental*. That shows that we have *three grades of philosophy* — (a) Philosophy of the object having the self-subsistent as its content, (b) Philosophy of the subject with the speaking subjectivity as its content and (c) Philosophy of Truth having the transcendental Absolute as its content.

This needs a further clarification and explanation. But, even before that a very significant aspect of the nature of philosophical thought has to be taken note of. If 'x is' is an empirical judgment, then it represents a relation between the subject 'x' and the predicate 'is'. But if 'x' is a philosophical judgment then there is no such factual reference of the subject to some predicate. That means that the predicate has been presupposed and that it does not explicate or amplify the meaning of the subject that is already believed. Such judgments are only verbal or self-evident. That is the reason why Krishnachandra says that Philosophy is the *self-evident elaboration of the self-evident*.[1] "The self-evident is spoken, but not spoken of."[2] Therefore, the

---

1. K. C. Bhattacharya, *Studies in Philosophy*. Vol. II, p. 103.
2. *Ibid*.

self-evident is independent of the spoken belief of an individual, it goes beyond the individual's, spoken belief. That explains the transcendental nature of philosophy. Facts are not self-evident, therefore, they do not form parts of philosophy. In fact a ladder of thought with self-evident steps can be constructed in which the not-self-evident literal thought would be at the bottom, and truth as absolutely self-evident would be at the top.

Therefore, the three stages of philosophy are not entirely different from each other, on the other hand, the inner logic of each step pushes us forward to the next. It can be said that the object of knowledge in each step is the same; only we go on *misunderstanding* it in some way or the other till we reach the final stage. Each earlier stage is negated in turn and every such negation leads to the formation of the belief in the next higher stage. Every succeeding step, in a sense, is a logical implication of the previous one. The last stage, of course, is beyond negation because there is no further implication which may be drawn from it. Thus, the philosophical judgments form a continuous and progressive series, in which the negation of the previous stage leads to the next, till the final stage is reached which is beyond negation.

Philosophy of the Object

The philosophy of the object having the self-subsistent as its content is the assertion of the insufficiency of the sciences, because a negation of the 'object as fact' (which is the realm of science) leads to the objective as self-subsistent. K. C. Bhattacharya says, "It is the theoretical inadequacy of its approach to the object ... it is the irrationality of our beliefs in the ultimate truths of matters of facts that leads to the more rational belief in the pure object, or the self-subsistent."[1]

That shows that the object with which philosophy is concerned is not factual, it is just what is contemplated in the objective attitude. Therefore, it is not a 'thing' to be known, it is only a form of objectivity. Its concern is, more or less, what is called the 'Experimental Datum". Philosophy does not study the objects objectively as sciences do. It emphasises the subjective experience of the objective. It presupposes "that the concepts

1. G. R. Malkani, *Some Points in K. C., Bhattacharya's Concept of Philosophy*, Philosophical Qly. July 1950. p. 44.

of matter, life and mind must have their counterparts in certain subjective experiences and derive all their meanings from those experiences."[1] Errors of philosophy arise when a distinction is not made between 'objectivity' and 'existence' or between 'self-subsistent' and 'factual', and when it is believed that there is an object outside and independent of the individual. Even Kant made that mistake when he said that the thing-in-itself was unknown and unknowable. He said so because he thought that the thing-in-itself was objective. But, if somehow we come to realise that the thing-in-itself is not external to us, we would not say that it is unknown; on the other hand, we would feel it that is most intimately known.

Philosophy of the object, then, deals with the object that is intelligible only in relation to the subject — that is, with the self-subsistent object. What is common to such objects and facts with which sciences deal is *objectivity*. What is objectivity? It is itself not a fact, it is the occasion or the circumstance in which something is understood objectively. The objectivity of facts is factual not formal, but the objectivity of the self-subsistent is formal. That branch of the philosophy of object which deals with and elaborates the self-subsistent forms is *Logic*. The forms studied by Logic do not have a *necessary* reference to facts, and therefore Logic is not a science, it is a kind of the Philosophy of the Object. But these logical forms may have a reference to some pure objects. These pure objects are not facts, they are objective but not factual. Perhaps, K. C. Bhattacharya, while speaking about these pure objects, has Plato's *Ideas* in his mind, which are objective but not factual. These pure objects are metaphysical objects. Thus there are two branches of the philosophy of the Object — *Logic* and *Metaphysics*.

Philosophy of the Spirit

We shall be in a position to appreciate fully the nature of the Philosophy of the Spirit when we come to discuss Krishnachandra's notion of subjectivity, but it would be fruitful to have some idea of it in relation to the grade of theoretic consciousness which has the self-subsistent as its content.

Metaphysics, as we have seen, elaborates the concept or the form of he object in relation to the subject. That shows that no

1. *Ibid.*, p. 50.

metaphysical concept is intelligible without reference to the subject or the spirit. In fact, within the realm of the philosophy of the object, logic deals with pure forms which are the forms of pure object — and these pure objects form the subject-matter of metaphysics. That is to say, logical activities are symbolic — its forms symbolising the metaphysical content. Now, what do metaphysical objects signify ? Metaphysical concepts cannot be the symbols of facts, because they are self-subsistent. Thus, they can be symbols only of contents that are *enjoyingly believed*. Enjoying understanding of a content means an awareness of it as symbolised by "an objectively contemplated meaning." These contents which are enjoyingly understood are the subject-matter of the philosophy of the spirit

The whole thing can be understood in a simpler manner by emphasising the difference between 'self-subsistence' (the content of the philosophy of the object) and 'reality' (the content of the philosophy of the subject). The consciousness of the self-subsistent is consciousness of objectivity in relation to the subject; therefore, it is an awareness in the objective attitude. But, the self-subsistent is not the real. How can we have a consciousness of reality ? This we cannot have in the objective attitude, because reality can only be realised — enjoyingly understood. Objective relation between a subject and the object can give us a content which is self-subsistent, but reality can only be *felt* or *realised*. This is an *enjoying* activity of the subject, and this is what forms the subject-matter of the philosophy of the spirit.

This enjoying consciousness has always a reference to "I". Enjoying understanding of a content can be called *Introspection*. K. C. Bhattacharya feels that Introspection represents the clearest form of spiritual or subjective activity. Its content is not the body, which is factual, nor the mental, which may at least give self-subsistent forms; its content is "I", and as such it involves an abjuration of the objective attitude and is understood as what the object is not.

In fine, the philosophy of the spirit is contemplation in the purely subjective attitude in contrast to the purely objective attitude of science or the subject — related objective attitude of the philosophy of the object. We can say now that the study of all contents enjoyed in explicit reference to the subject 'I' may be called the philosophy of the spirit.

If we analyse this enjoying awareness of the spirit, we find that something else is also enjoyed along with the subject and enjoyed in reference to it. K. C. Bhattacharya speaks about its three grades : (a) first, there is the enjoying awareness of the subject as embodied, (b) then, there is the consciousness of other selves, and (c) there is the consciousness of an over-personal self. The last is, what can be called, the religious form of the spiritual or subjective consciousness.

Thus, we find that the *philosophy of the subject* with its various grades including the study of religious consciousness, constitutes the subject-matter of the philosophy of the spirit. Of course, a proper appreciation of this would be possible only after a study of Krishnachandra's analysis of the notion of subjectivity.

Philosophy of Truth

Religious consciousness, as we have seen, is the highest kind of spiritual activity, but this does not involve a theoretical denial of the subject as 'I'; on the other hand, in this consciousness, along with the awareness of the over-personal self, there is an enjoying consciousness of *I am not*. K. C. Bhattacharya speaks of the possibility of the consciousness of the denial of 'I'. The content of this consciousness is *Truth*, because this consciousness is above the subject-object distinction. This is the consciousness of the Absolute, that is of the Truth. The Absolute is not the same as the overpersonal reality that is enjoyed in purely subjective attitude. The over-personal reality constitutes the content of religious consciousness, and religious consciousness is a process of inwardising, that is, it is a process in which 'I' is not negated but enjoyed as the whole process becomes completely inner and subjective. The Absolute cannot become an aspect of the purely subjective life, it is the highest form of theoretic consciousness and therefore, although it is positively believed, it is understood only negative by way of symbolism. That is why K. C. Bhattacharya says, "The consciousness of truth as what is believed in but not understood either in the objective or in the subjective attitude, as not literally speakable at all but speakable only in the purely symbolistic way, is extra-religious or transcendental consciousness."[1] Thus, the Absolute as transcending the subjective and the objective — as the Indefinite — constitutes the subject matter of the philosophy of Truth.

1. K. C. Bhattacharya, *Studies in Philosophy*, Vol., II, p. 16.

The nature of the Philosophy of Truth will become clearer when we come to discuss Krishnachandra's concept of the Absolute.

Theory of Knowledge

Krishnachandra describes knowledge thus, "It is in introspection into knowledge ... that we realise that we believed before we knew — and that there was then no awareness of the distinction of the object believed from the belief. Knowledge as distinct from mere belief involves the awareness of distinction."[1] It is apparent that knowledge, here, has been described in terms of belief. It is true that nothing can be known unless it is believed and also that there is a difference between 'belief' and 'the object believed'. The awareness of this distinction is also an essential aspect of knowledge.

That shows that fundamentally knowledge is always a kind of an awareness. Awareness can be of two types : awareness in the objective attitude and awareness in the subjective attitude. In the former a distinction is made between the object of awareness and the subject of awareness; in the latter, it is difficult to make such a distinction. Gopinath Bhattacharya says, "Of the two types of awareness, it is one in the objective attitude that the author (K. C. Bhattacharya) primarily takes to be what is signified by the term knowledge."[2] But he himself admits that even "one's awareness of himself — an awareness in the subjective attitude — also has been called knowledge at times."[3] Again, while discussing the mutual implication of knowledge and truth, Krishnachandra says, "Knowledge and Truth have to be defined in terms of each other, the former, as what alone is true and the latter as what alone is known."[4] Again, he says, "Knowing is known only as implied in explicit awareness of truth and that truth is asserted only as a content that is known."[5] Here Knowledge and Truth have become related to each other, and Truth is conceived *not* as knowing in the objective attitude.

1. K. C. Bhattacharya, *The Subject as Freedom*, pp. 56-57.
2. Gopinath Bhattacharya, *Editor's Introduction*, K. C. Bhattacharya's, *Studies in Philosophy*. Vol II, p. xvii.
3. *Ibid.*
4. K. C. Bhattacharya, *Studies in Philosophy*, Vol. II, p. 154.
5. *Ibid.*

These descriptions of 'knowledge' create a very great difficulty for a scholar who is trying to apprehend K. C. Bhattacharya's account of the nature of knowledge. It is now clearly evident that the term 'knowledge' has not been used by him clearly in one precise sense. There appears to be some ambiguity about it. But a little reflection will show that this ambiguity is there because the term 'knowledge' itself is ambiguous. Both in ordinary discourse and in academic discussions this term is used in various and different senses. But if we take note of Krishnachandra's treatment of the concept of philosophy and view at his concept of knowledge in that light, we shall be able to determine and outline a theory of knowledge that would be free from the ambiguities mentioned above.

K. C. Bhattacharya does not conceive knowledge as a passive state of the subject. It is a sort of an activity — an activity of a free reference of the subject to the object. If this is so, sciences cannot claim *to know*, because they, in a sense, cut away this reference to the subjective and lay emphasis on the mere factness and objectivity of the object. The empirical aspect of the theoretic consciousness, therefore, is not knowledge. The awareness of the object as fact is only a non-cognitive awareness. With respect to the object as fact, "we should say that it is known simply as evident and that it is not known as related to knowing."[1]

Now, a free reference of the subject to the object might mean a free reference of the subject to the object in the objective attitude or a free reference of the subject to the subject as object, that is, a free reference of the subject to the object in the subjective attitude.

In the former, the subject relates itself to the object freely, that is, without itself getting related to it. Gopinath Bhattacharya makes this point clear by saying that, "it is rather the case that the subject has an immediate feeling of relating itself to the object without having a feeling of getting related to it."[2] This awareness is knowledge in the realm of the philosophy of the object. In this the subject is aware of the experiences and thoughts of the object without in any way identifying himself with them. This may be called knowledge in the

1. K. C. Bhattacharya, *Studies in Philosophy*, Vol. II, p. 161.
2. Gopinath Bhattacharya, *Editor's Introduction*, K. C. Bhattacharya's *Studies in Philosophy*, Vol. II, p. xviii.

objective attitude. The object of this knowledge may be either a physical fact or a psychic fact — a psychic fact because a psychic fact is not purely a mental event, it is always an aspect of the object. The object has certain modes of relatedness to the subject, e.g., knownness, feltness etc. This relatedness viewed as a character of the object is a 'Psychic fact'. This knowledge, therefore, may be called, 'awareness through psychological introspection' in the objective attitude.

This takes us to consider Introspection proper, the spiritual Introspection, which is awareness in the subjective attitude, or, in other words, which is a free reference of the subject to the subject in an enjoying consciousness. In the former case there was an awareness of the relatedness of the object to the subject. This is negated in this awareness — in spiritual Introspection. "Introspection proper is a form of the theoretic consciousness that implies an abjuration of the objective attitude."[1] This is knowing by enjoying — the enjoying understanding of the subject "I". This, then, is knowledge in the realm of the philosophy of the spirit.

That is why this knowledge is described as the free reference of the subject to the subject itself in an enjoying consciousness. But, if we analyse this enjoying consciousness still further, we find that in the act of enjoying itself something over and above the self is also enjoyed. We have seen that, according to K. C. Bhattacharya, that something else may be either a body — physical or mental, or other selves with whom the self stands in some relationship, or an over-personal self, a reference to which is made in religious consciousness.

Of these three the first two cannot be described as cases of pure subjectivity. In the enjoying consciousness of 'I', in which body is also enjoyed, there is, in a sense, an enjoyment of individuality. Such a consciousness is expressed in our saying, 'I am such and such'. The consciousness of individuality somehow gives to the self an objectivity. That means that this subjectivity is somehow infected with objectivity, and as such, does not remain pure subjectivity. Likewise, when I am conscious of other selves in my enjoying consciousness of 'I', I am aware of myself in relation to others. This again is not pure subjectivity. These two then cannot be proper or pure examples of knowledge in the

1. K. C. Bhattacharya, *Studies in Philosophy*, Vol. II, p. 113.

purely subjective sense (as a free reference of the subject to itself
in an enjoying awareness.).

A higher form of subjectivity, as we have seen, is the consciousness of an over-personal reality. The reason is obvious.
In the first two cases subjectivity is always disturbed either by
the awareness of objects or by the awareness of other selves. It is
true that in both these cases 'the body' or 'the other self', is a
shadow of 'I' because it is realised in the 'I-consciousness'; but
this also is true that the shadow does also have its effects on the
I-consciousness. But, in the enjoying consciousness where the
subject as 'I' has an awareness of an over-personal reality, the 'I'
itself becomes a shadow. The awareness of 'I', in a sense, transcends its introspective boundaries and has a consciousness of self-
fulfilment in the awareness of the super-personal reality. This
awareness can be called knowledge in the realm of the Philosophy
of the spirit, and this can be the highest form of knowledge
available to us. Clarifying this point, Malkani describes this
knowledge as knowledge *by self-abnegation* and *not by self denial*.[1]
This knowledge is possible by renouncing the self and not by
denying it.

Even self-denial is possible, but that would be beyond the
limits of knowing. When 'I' is denied, what is left is pure subjectivity — subjectivity as pure freedom, in other words, the
Absolute. The Absolute, according to K. C. Bhattacharya, cannot be an object of knowledge, because it is only negatively understood. Its contents are not literally expressible, and hence it is *not
known*. That does not mean that it is unknown and unknowable.
To say that the Absolute is unknown and unknowable is also to
say something positive about it. Kant made that mistake when
he said that reality was unknown and unkowable. According to
K. C. Bhattacharya, Truth, being indefinite, can never be an
object of knowledge. "Knowledge is primarily of a definite
object and is to be distinguished from the awareness of
the Indefinite."[2]

---

1. G. R. Malkani, *Some Points in K. C. Bhattacharya's Concept of
Philosophy*. The Philosophical Qly. July 1950, pp. 54-57.

2. Gopinath Bhattacharya, *Editor's Introduction*, K. C. Bhattacharya's
Studies in Philosophy, Vol. II, p. xviii.

Negation as the basis of his Philosophy

It can very well be said that just as the dialectical movement is at the root of Hegel's metaphysical speculation, so negation is at the root of K. C. Bhattacharya's metaphysics. In fact, he has made negation the basis of arriving at the Absolute itself. He says, "The region of Negation is the region of the Indefinite."[1] Absolute has to be conceived as absolute negation, because any known content, any attribution of a positive character would make it definite. It is only by following the process of negation to its maximum limit that the Absolute can be arrived at.

The importance of negation can be demonstrated also by showing that corresponding to different types of negation there are different philosophical attitudes. Credit has to be given to K.C. Bhattacharya for classifying the different philosophical attitudes and for finding their basis in the different forms of negation.

Krishnachandra appears to have the feeling that negation has to be discussed if not for anything else at least to find out a basis for the logic of the view that *Truth* is manifold (as Jainas, for example, believe). Truth and illusion are related and "negation is intelligible as illusion",[2] because illusion is what is actually not. Therefore, the notion of negation involves the notion of illusion.

Negation has been conceived by K. C. Bhattacharya somewhat differently from its usual conceptions. Negation means rejecting a thing as illusory. Negation is very aptly illustrated in the examples of ordinary illusions. When we deny reality of the snake appearing in the rope, we are making use of negation. The rope, in this case, has been rejected as illusory.

Now, a very pertinent question can be raised; What kind of existence is denied of the illusory ? Broadly speaking there can be two answers to this question. Firstly, it can be said that it has no *objective* existence. This answer denies the objectivity of the thing apprehended in illusion, which means that it may have some non-objective existence. Secondly, it can be said that it has got no existence at all, that is to say, it has neither an objective existence nor a subjective existence. Here every kind of

---

1. K. C. Bhattacharya, Some aspects of Negation, *Studies in Philosophy*, Vol. II, p. 208.
2. K. C. Bhattacharya, Some aspects of Negation, *Studies in Philosophy*, Vol. I, p. 207.

existence is denied to what is presented in illusion. Illustrating this K. C. Bhattacharya says, "Illusion may be regarded (1) as having some kind of abstract being or (2) contradiction itself."[1] In his interpretation of Śaṅkara's theory of Māyā, while analysing the three stages of illusion, Krishnachandra refers to these two kinds of negation.[2] The first, as we shall notice, admits of *three* kinds of demands; so, in all, there are *four* kinds of negation.

These *four* kinds of negation are illustrative of four different kinds of philosophical attitude and temperament. They have been described thus, "Illusion may be a being only to be denied, (ii) a being as positive as fact but different from it and positively related to it, (iii) identical with fact relation being that of identity, or (iv) no being at all but negation transcending all being."[3]

If this classification is combined with the different stages of positive attention and negative attention, then the whole thing can be viewed in a different way. We can say that there are four stages of positive and negative attention corresponding to the four kinds of negation. (1) In the first stage positive attention is fixed on the object alone, (2) In the second stage attention alternates between the subject and the object, they are attended to successively, (3) In the third stage attention is directed towards the subject and the object simultaneously, they are viewed as forming a unity in a complex system, (4) The fourth stage is the stage of negative attention where attention is withdrawn from both the subjective and the objective and the Indefinite is apprehended.

In the light of this we can now try to determine the aspects of negation and also the philosophical attitudes that correspond to the different aspects of negation.

(1) The first stage of negation corresponds to that kind of positive attention which is directed to an analysis of an object out of a confused mass. Here attention is withdrawn from the given mass and is fixed upon a single objective element analysed

1. *Ibid.*, p. 205.
2. K. C. Bhattacharya, Sankara's Doctrine of Maya, 4 to 6, *Studies in Philosophy*, Vol I.
3. K. C. Bhattacharya, Some aspects of Negation. *Studies in Philosophy* Vol. I, p. 235.

out of the mass. The positive, determinate and definite objective elements occupy attention, and therefore everything apart from the objective is *negated* — rejected as unreal. What is denied, therefore, is the non-object. The object is 'not-illusory', that is to say, the given is not subjective, it is objective. He says, "So to say 'this object is not illusory' is to say that this objective is not ... subjective but is self-identical."[1] This stage of attention is the basis of the philosophical view which is called *Pan-objectivism*, and negation here, means negation of the non-objective as illusory.

(2) In the second stage attention is not directed solely to the object. Attention is directed firstly to the objective and then to the subjective. The subjective and the objective — both appear as *not-illusory*, even though opposite. "The idea is conscious of not being objective but the object distinguishes itself from the idea by not being conscious."[2] So, here, when attention is fixed on the objective the subjective is negated, and when it is fixed on the subjective the objective is negated. The subjective and the objective are attended to and rejected alternatively and successively. The philosophical attitude that corresponds to this view is *Dualism*.

(3) In the second stage, as we have seen, the objective and the subjective are attended to successively, but there is a stage of attention in which it is possible to attend to them together. In this state of attention, they appear as two aspects of the same system. One peculiarity of this stage is that no aspect of thought in this stage appears as final although no aspect of thought is positively uncertain or indefinite. In this stage the object of attention is the identity of the subjective and the objective. The same thing may appear as both objective and subjective. In fact, here, the distinction between negative and positive attention vanishes. K. C. Bhattacharya says, "Each position is different from an infinity of other positions and is thus constituted by an infinity of differences, by infinite negation. Each negation too would thus be the negation of Infinite position, that is, a negation identical with infinite position."[3] Therefore,

1. K. C. Bhattacharya, Some aspects of Negation, *Studies in Philosophy*, Vol. I, p. 213.
2. *Ibid.* p. 214.
3. K. C. Bhattacharya, Some aspects of Negation, *Studies in Philosophy*, Vol. I, p. 209.

"the distinctness of a particular given position and the corresponding negation vanishes altogether."[1] The subjective may appear as the objective and vice-versa. To such an attitude of attention and negation corresponds a philosophy of Hegel's type.

These three stages are stages of positive attention. The fourth stage is the stage of negative attention.

(4) In this stage attention is not directed to any thing positive, objective or subjective, though apparently it may also appear to be positive in its approach. Here we start with 'contradiction' or 'transcendental negation' as our first principle. All determinates are negated, "being is abolished and absolute negation alone remains, not only as inexplicably definite, but also as inexplicably self-related or self-negating, that is, as a free function or activity."[2] This way of negative attention, which is the state of complete negation, is the proper way for apprehending the Absolute. The type of philosophy that corresponds to this stage of negation is the philosophy of the Advaita Vedānta type.

This fourth stage of negative attention has been given a special status in Krishnachandra's philosophy, because that is the way through which the Absolute can be realised. In fact, the importance of negation lies in the fact that the subject has to go through a series of negations and denials in order to realise the Absolute. The normal life of man is in the empirical world. Therefore, the first denial is the denial of the empirical object — the object as revealed by the senses. This denial leads to the position of a pure object that is independent of thought. Then, this pure object is denied. This second denial leads to a belief in the subjective. But, the subjective is also denied in some self-denying experience like that of religious surrender or metaphysical denial even of the 'I' : Now, this is the limit of negation, because here negation reaches its completion. No further denial is possible because here nothing has been posited and denial is possible only when some assertion is made. This denial transcends even the I-consciousness and thereby apprehends the Absolute — the Indefinite.

1. *Ibid.*, p. 215.
2. *Ibid.*, p. 210

This shows that K. C. Bhattacharya has made negation the basis of his philosophy in so far as it is through the different stages of negation that metaphysical ascent towards the Absolute is possible. The full implication of this will be clear when we come to discuss the subject's progressive realisation of freedom.

Notion of Subjectivity

(a) The Subject and the Object

K. C. Bhattacharya feels that the term 'subjectivity' has been used in so many diverse senses that it becomes difficult to determine its precise meaning. But the most normal description of subjectivity is that it is "the cult of the subject". Even this expression suggests that subjectivity primarily is a breaking away from the objective. This negative way of understanding subjectivity has at least two advantages, firstly, whenever it is difficult to determine what a thing is, it becomes more convenient to try to know what that thing is not. The positive character of subjectivity is at least difficult to be precisely determined, and therefore, its nature can be determined by trying to know initially what it is not. Secondly, as we shall presently see, this negative description of subjectivity becomes a positive factor of its nature and enables us to have a clear idea of subjectivity. Therefore, in the very beginning, we can say that the subjective is non-objective. Krishnachandra says very clearly, "The modes of subjectivity are the ways of freeing onself from the modes of objectivity."[1] He goes on to say, "This cult of the subject, as it might be called, takes various forms, but they all involve a feeling of disassociation of the subject from the object, an awareness of ‚the subject as what the object is not."[2]

Let us clarify it further. Object is 'what is meant'. Whenever we know an object, we become aware of a meaning content. The awareness of the subjective does not involve such an awareness of a meaning. The subject is not a meaningless word, but it does not have a meaning content. K. C. Bhattacharya says that the subjective is not *meanable*, it may at best be a *significant speakable*. These expressions themselves make a

1. K. C. Bhattacharya, *The Subject as Freedom*, p. 29.
2. *Ibid.*, p. 40.

distinction between the objective and the subjective, but this has to be clarified still further.

Meaning is general in character. Whatever a speaker means by a word must be capable of being meant by every hearer if he uses that word. The object has a meaning content in this general sense. Clarifying this, K. C. Bhattacharya comes to suggest that the word *this* may be taken as the symbol of the object. An individual uses the word 'this' to denote a particular object, but others also may use the word 'this' to denote that very object. The word 'this' may stand for a general meaning that is understood both by the speaker and the hearer as meaning an object. The word 'this' may, therefore, be used as the symbol for the meant object.

But, the subject cannot thus be denoted by the meaning of the word. When I, for example, use the word 'I' I, use it for myself and when the hearer uses it he uses it not for me but for himself. It is on account of this uniqueness of the word 'I' that 'I' is used by K. C. Bhattacharya as the symbol of the subject. He prefers the word 'I' to both 'you' or 'he' because the word 'I' is more unique than either of the two.

A distinction between these two symbols — 'this' as the symbol of the object and 'I' as the symbol of the subject will bring to light the distinction between the subjective and the objective. That the word 'this' can symbolise the object shows that the object has a generality about it, but the subject as expressed by the word 'I' has a uniqueness because it is neither singular nor general, or in a sense, both singular and general. It is general because *everybody* can use it, it is singular because everybody uses it *for himself only*.

Again, the distinction between the two can be shown to be a fact on another consideration also. If we analyse our consciousness of the object, we find that it is invariably through the awareness of meaning. For example, when a man from a light house reports the approach of a ship, 'the ship as approaching' is understood on the basis of the awareness of the meaning of the report. But, when consciousness of the subject is understood, it is not understood through meaning. When I call myself 'I', 'I' is understood not through the understanding of the meaning of the word 'I'. It is understood as the self speaking or expressing of itself.

Another point that appears to be significant in this connection is that the subject can, at times, be spoken as the object, although not meant as the object, but the object can never be spoken as the subject. Speaking in terms of 'I' and 'this', K. C. Bhattacharya says that "the statement 'this is 'I'" is false, while the statement 'I am this' cannot be denied.[1] We can use expressions like 'I am a father', 'I am a lawyer' and so on, but we cannot point to an object and say 'this is I — or this is the subject'.

That shows that the subject can be objectified, but that objectification cannot be a determinant of the subject. Even when the subject is referred to as 'this' or 'that' the subject does not become the object; in fact, even there the subject is felt to be disassociated from the object. That is why K. C. Bhattacharya says that the subject cannot be known except through the denial of the object. "We know the self not as object but in knowing the distinction of the object from it, or in knowing the object as distinct from it "[2]

But then this has to be accepted that the subject in his quest for self-awareness begins by relating itself to the object. That relation has to be negated. That process is only to emphasise the difference between the two — only to impel the subject to disassociate itself from the object. Even so, this initial step towards the realisation of subjectivity involves a negative relation with the objective. It is only when the subject realises its distinction from the objective that it is on its way to the realisation of complete subjectivity.

This gives the impression that the first stage of subjectivity is an awareness of the distinction of the subject and the object. But there is another way also in which the words 'subject' and 'object' have been used by K. C. Bhattacharya. In that sense there appears to be a necessary relation between the subject and the object, they appear to be essentially inter-dependent. In that sense the subject is that *which frees itself* from the object, and the object is that *from which* the subject frees itself.

This use of the words 'subject' and 'object' gives out very interesting results. First, subject and object become inter-related, one presupposes the other. Secondly, in every stage of

1. K. C. Bhattacharya, *The Subject as Freedom*, p. 6.
2. K. C. Bhattacharya, *Studies in Philosophy*, Vol. I, p. 151.

subjectivity that which would be negated would become the object, because by negating it the subject is freeing itself from it. And in relation to this object that which would free itself from it would become the subject. For example, as we would clearly see a little later, the world of objects is 'object' in relation to the body — awareness because it is through the awareness of the body that one becomes aware of the subject's distinction from the world of things. In relation to that world 'body' is the subject. Body again is 'the object' in relation to Image and Thought or, what is called, Psychic subjectivity, because it is by rejecting the bodily that subjectivity identifies itself with Psychic subjectivity. Thus, in relation to the body Psychic subjectivity is the subject. In this way, in every stage of subjectivity, the subject and the object would be relative to each other.

(b) *Further analysis of subjectivity*

Krishnachandra is aware that to specify subjectivity as non-objective is not to determine it fully. He, therefore, goes on to analyse its nature still further.

Subjectivity has so far been described as the awareness of the distinction of the subject from the object. But, K. C. Bhattacharya feels that this awareness may be due to subject's awareness of the body. I see that there is a cup of tea before me, because my body can contact this object through its senses of touch, taste, smell, sight etc. This causes an awareness of the distinction between the object — the cup of tea — and eyes and fingers or sight and touch. It is on account of this awareness of the distinction of the *body* from the object that the self becomes aware of its distinction from the object.

But, is subjectivity *bodily subjectivity* — the awareness of the self as embodied ? K. C. Bhattacharya admits that the process of subjectivity starts in body-awareness, but that is not subjectivity proper. Things are considered to be external and objective in relation to the body, that shows that the awareness of the body is also a kind of subjectivity. But K. C. Bhattacharya says that subjectivity also involves an awareness of its distinction from the body. Body-awareness is sensuous, subjectivity cannot be apprehended through the senses. Moreover, the body cannot be identified with the 'I', because in the 'I-consciousness' itself there is an awareness of the distinction between 'I' and the 'body'.

This awareness might make the subject identify itself with,

what K. C. Bhattacharya calls, the *Psychic subjectivity*. When an object is known, felt or perceived, there is also an awareness of feltness, knownness etc. This awareness is called Psychic Subjectivity. Psychic facts include *Images* and *Thoughts*, and an awareness of these is Psychic subjectivity. But, K. C. Bhattacharya says that this also cannot be subjectivity proper, firstly because the Psychic facts somehow retain their relation with the object and secondly because it is absurd to identify the subject as expressed in the spoken word 'I' with thoughts and images. Subjectivity, therefore, involves an awareness of the distinction of the subject from Psychic activities also.

The next stage of subjectivity is feeling. Feeling has an advantage over images or Thought because feeling is completely free from the meaning content. But according to K. C. Bhattacharya subjectivity must transcend feeling-awareness also, because although it is free from meaning-awareness or from the objective, it still has the awareness that it is unmeaning. In subjectivity proper even the awareness that it is unmeaning must be transcended.

That leads to Introspection, which represents subjectivity in a pure form. Introspection is awareness of the subject through the spoken word 'I'. K. C. Bhattacharya says that the subject can be best expressed by the word 'I'. Although the pronouns 'you' and 'he' also denote subjects they are not as unique as 'I'. The word 'he', for example, can be used for the same person by a number of speakers. Likewise, when I address somebody as 'you' I become aware of him through his body. If I am not aware of a body before me, I cannot address him as 'you'. It is not so with the word 'I'. I become aware of 'I' not through my body. Therefore, Krishnachandra feels that the subjectivity proper is the awareness of the subject as 'I' is 'I-consciousness'.

This I-consciousness is not understanding the meaning of the word 'I', it is the *enjoying understanding* of the subject as 'I'. It is not even *believing* in the 'I'; it is the 'I'.

But in a very strict sense even this cannot represent subjectivity proper. Even if the subject is expressed through the symbol 'I', it is *expressed* and it is understood by the hearers. Subjectivity proper cannot thus be limited by any kind of expression. Subjectivity is inwardness and as such, any attempt to determine it would generalise it. Subjectivity is complete uniqueness, and any attempt to express it will disturb its uniqueness. Moreover, when the subject is expressed as 'I' — even though symbolically, a relation with 'others' is established, and that cannot determine the uniqueness of subjectivity.

Therefore, K. C. Bhattacharya says that true subjectivity would consist in a going beyond the 'I' — in a denial of 'I'. Subjectivity proper is what even 'I' is not. That is the realm of the Indefinite — the Absolute.

(c) *A Summing up*

This analysis of the notion of subjectivity has become so complex and elaborate that it would be worthwhile to try to sum up the whole deliberation. Taking subjectivity in its normal sense, K. C. Bhattacharya describes it as an awareness of the subject's distinction from the object. Subjectivity is the cult of the subject — it is non-objectivity. This basic meaning of subjectivity has been retained through out the analysis of the notion of subjectivity. Then, taking Subjectivity in a very *wide* sense Krishnachandra enumerates three stages of subjectivity (a) *Bodily Subjectivity*, (b) *Psychic Subjectivity*, and (c) *Spiritual Subjectivity*. In the bodily stage the self identifies itself with the body. This stage consists of three substages : the body as perceived, the body as felt and the knowledge of the absence either through imaginative perception or through conscious non-perception. In this stage the self gradually goes on identifying itself with one of the three in a progressive manner. The second stage is the stage of Psychic subjectivity, which admits of two broad divisions — Image and Thought. In this stage the subject identifies itself with the psychic life and subjectivity is understood as awareness of image and thought. A negation of this stage of subjectivity leads to the third stage of subjectivity — the spiritual subjectivity. The transition from the psychic stage to the spiritual stage is on account of the subject's awareness of a demand 'pointing to the positive freedom from objective meaning'. Spiritual subjectivity has also been subdivided into three sub-grades : (a) Feeling (b) Introspection and (c) Beyond Introspection. In the first stage of feeling there is a feeling of freedom from actual thought, and in its second stage there is a feeling of freedom from possible thought or a *feeling of feeling*, as K. C. Bhattacharya calls it. Introspection is the clearest example of subjectivity, because it is the awareness of the subject as 'I'. But in this awareness itself there is the awareness that subjectivity, properly speaking, is not even expressible. Therefore the purest or the completest subjectivity would be the state beyond Introspection — the Indefinite or the Absolute.

Progressive Realisation of the Subject's Freedom

This analysis of subjectivity itself throws light on the manner in which the subject can realise its basic nature — its subjectivity or its freedom. If we combine the analysis of subjectivity with the theory of negation, we shall find that the various stages of subjectivity form a progressive way for the realisation of the subject's true nature.

This process consists of a series of steps. It is called progressive because it is by the rejection and supersession of each preceding stage that the succeeding stage is attained. This process continues till there remains nothing to be rejected or superseded.

The normal man is a subject living in the midst of surrounding objects. The objective sets a limit to his freedom. Even in that realm he is free, but that freedom is limited. In his reflections on Kant's view on freedom and morality, Krishnachandra talks about two kinds of freedom : the freedom of the elective will, which is in fact, freedom of choice and the noumenal freedom. The process of realisation is the process of the gradual growth of the first kind of freedom into the noumenal freedom.

The first step, and, as we have seen, the most positive step towards the realisation of subjectivity is the negation of the objective. The emphasis on the objects clouds the vision of the subject, and thus prevents him from realising his free nature. Therefore, the object has to be negated.

The negation of the objective, in a sense, is the assertion of the bodily. Body is closer to the subject than the object, in that sense even the body can be called subjective. It is when the objects are considered in relation to the body that they appear as external or objective. Body, moreover, does not belong to the world of the perceived objects, as it is not perceived as being there — outside. Thus, it can be said that the subject, on its way to the realisation of freedom, negates the objective and identifies itself with the bodily. That is why this stage has been described as the stage of bodily subjectivity. He says that the "first hint of freedom is reached in the feeling of the body."[1]

Krishnachandra makes a distinction between 'perceived body' and 'felt body', and says that on his way to the realisation of freedom, the subject first identifies itself with the perceived body, and then with the felt body. The perceived body is the body perceived externally, and the felt body is the body felt from within. In the next step the subject has to disassociate itself not only from the external body but also from the body as felt. "The realisation of this freedom from the felt body is the precondition of all distinctively spiritual activity."[2]

There is another subtle distinction that K. C. Bhattacharya makes at this stage. Like objective facts body can also be known *externally* or *internally* or *as absent*. The perceived body is body known externally, the felt body is the body known internally, but the subject may identify itself with the *body as absent*. The 'body as absent' is not the knowledge of the absence of the body, it is the awareness of the body having the capacity to acquire 'knowledge of absence.' Knowledge of absence, according to K. C. Bhattacharya, can be of two kinds: — knowledge of absence through imaginative perception or through conscious non-perception. These two cases can be illustrated with the help of two examples. Suppose we visit a place which we had visited sometime ago. There used to be a tree at that place, but now we notice a difference in the field without knowing the absence of the tree. We become aware that something is missing, but we do not know what is missing. Let us take another example. A person is looking for a book in his study-room, but he does not find it. He is not conscious of any empty look, but he has a cognition of an object being absent. The former is the *perception of absence* and the latter is perception of the *object as absent*. In both these two cases, we can later become conscious of non-perception. In the first example, we can come to know that the particular tree that was there is missing, in the second example, we can come to notice a difference on the table where the book was supposed to have been kept. Thus, the primary cognitions in both these cases can be called examples of knowledge of absence through *imaginative perception* and the secondary

• 1. K. C. Bhattacharya, *Studies in Philosophy*, Vol. II, p. 54.
   2. K. C. Bhattacharya, *The Subject as Freedom*, p. 105.

cognitions in both these cases can be described as examples of *conscious non-perception.*

The relevance of this emphasis on knowledge by absence is that it indicates the manner by which the subject on its onward march is able to rise above the bodily. If we compare the felt body with the perceived body we shall find that the felt body is only *half-distinguished* from the perceived body. It is not felt as entirely disassociated from the perceived body, and yet it appears to be somewhat different from it. Absence imaginatively perceived *is* on a level with the felt body, because although not fully disassociated from the external body, it is distinguished from it. In the first example when we become aware of something missing, this awareness of absence is distinguished from the body in so far as it is only imaginatively felt — the body being not able to discern the absence through its tools of senses. Thus, Absence known through imaginative perception is at par with the felt-body, but absence known through conscious non-perception is at a higher level, because it enables the subject to rise above the level of the felt-body. When, for example, in our secondary cognition, we become conscious of the 'tree' which is now missing, we do not actually become conscious of 'the tree', because the tree could have been known only through the external body and its senses. It means that we have become conscious of something that is akin to image or thought, that is, akin to our psychic life and not fully to our bodily life. Thus, knowledge of absence through conscious non-perception makes us rise above even the level of the felt body and takes us to the realm of the psychic fact. That is why K. C. Bhattacharya says, "Conscious non-perception then is a transitional stage between body-feeling and imagination with which Psychic fact begins."[1] "Psychic fact begins with the distinguishing of what the present is not. Conscious non-perception is the distinguishing of the present from the detached presentation ... and may be taken as the immediate pre-condition of the felt detachment of the presentation from the present ... [thus] the first clear hint of the subjective would be realised in the knowledge of absence through conscious non-perception."[2]

1. K. C. Bhattacharya, *The Subject as Freedom*, p. 122.
2. *Ibid.*, p. 123.

In this way the subject negates the bodily and comes to assert the psychic life. Psychic facts include *Image* and *thought*. Image is a form of presentation, but it is not given as completely distinct from the object, it is abstracted from the belief in the object. It is not known as having a space-time dimension, but as having a sort of a 'relatedness' to the object. *Thought*, on the other hand, moves in the realm of universals and abstractions, and therefore appears to be completely detached from the substantive nature of the object or the body or even of the image.

These constitute psychic life. The subject's felt awareness of his disassociation from the body leads him to identify himself with his psychic life. The negation of the bodily is the assertion of the psychic.

But, the subject soon comes to realise that this cannot be its true nature. Image has an objective look and thought invariably maintains a distinction between "content" and "consciousness". The truly subjective is above this distinction. It is both 'the content of its consciousness' and 'the consciousness of its content'.

Thus, a rejection of the psychic enables the subject to enter into the realm of subjectivity proper — the spiritual realm. Feeling, according to K. C. Bhattacharya, is the first expression of spiritual subjectivity. Therefore a negation of the subject's identification with his thought-content leads him to identify himself with his feeling-subjectivity. In feeling the process of detachment from meaning becomes complete. In thought, the meaning-awareness somehow persists, but in feeling there does not remain a distinction between 'awareness' and 'its content'. Therefore feeling appears to be akin to subjectivity proper. K. C. Bhattacharya talks about two grades of feeling. In the first grade the subject detaches itself from thought — actual or possible and enters into that realm of subjectivity which is completely free from meaning-awareness. But this stage is also negated, there has to be a feeling of detachment even from feeling itself. This feeling of not having a feeling, i.e., this feeling of detachment from feeling itself is called *'feeling of feeling'*. The subject, in his progressive march towards the realisation of his freedom, first comes to think of himself as a feeling-self; but very soon rises above this feeling and becomes detached even from feeling subjectivity.

A supersession of this state of feeling leads to the realisation of the proper subjectivity, which has been called *Introspection* by K. C. Bhattacharya. Introspection is not ordinary introspection or psychological introspection, it is not merely 'looking within'. According to K. C. Bhattacharya, it is spiritual Introspection, which is a cognitive function — an awareness. This awareness is awareness of the "I"—not as a content distinct from the subject, but, as he says, *as* the *enjoying understanding of the subjetct as "I.*" Introspection then, is not what is meant by the word "I", it is not even believing in "I", it *is the "I"*. The — "I-awareness" or the realisation of "I", therefore, is the realisation of subjectivity proper. The process of disassociation from the objective — and from meaning content is complete here. It is pure knowledge — knowledge not in terms of the *distinction* between "content" and "consciousness". It is knowing by enjoying, by rising above the distinction between content and consciousness, it is knowing by affirming the unity of the subjective.

An analysis of this state of Introspection reveals that the subject can transcend his I-consciousness in his introspective awareness. He can have an awareness of other selves or of the social self and also of an over-personal self as in religious consciousness. This shows that even the introspection of 'I' can be negated. It is thus possible to go beyond even I-consciousness.

In every stage, as we have seen, there is an inner demand for going beyond that stage. The introspective subjectivity is free from meaning-content and even from felt content, but it is still not complete freedom because it has still an awareness of itself. For the realisation of complete freedom even this awareness has to be negated, and that is not an impossibility because evidences of self-transcendence are there. In the social awareness of other selves or in the religious awareness of Super-self the self does go beyond itself.

This can be better appreciated if we view at the problem in a different way. Introspection, or the realisation of the subject as 'I' is the realisation of the subject's free nature. In it there remains an awareness of the subject's freedom. For complete freedom even this awareness must be negated. Therefore for the realisation of complete freedom even a negation of 'I'—a negation of the Introspective self becomes necessary. K. C. Bhattacharya makes a distinction between '*Subject as free*' and

'*Subject as freedom*'. The former is the Introspective stage of subjectivity — the actual state which one can attain in his progressive attempt to realise freedom. *Subject as freedom* is the ultimate state — the ideal, the subject's ultimate destiny.

But, as this state does not have any definite content, there remains nothing to be negated. This then is the *realm of the Indefinite — the Absolute*, the ultimate destiny of the subject. The question of transcending this state would not arise, as this does not contain any definite content to be negated. Transcendence, as we have seen, is possible only when some content is negated and superseded. Therefore, this stage of complete freedom is transcendental or indefinite. We cannot have an exact and definite idea of this stage, we cannot have any *definite* attitude towards this state of which even an enjoying consciousness is not possible. This region of the Indefinite, then, is the region of the Absolute.

Concept of the Asolute

We have just described the Absolute as completely indefinite. Even earlier it had been said that the Absolute of K. C. Bhattacharya can neither be described as objective nor as subjective. In fact, it is not safe to ascribe any epithets to it. Strictly speaking, it is not even thinkable. At best, an attempt can be made to have an idea about it in terms of certain symbols.

K. C. Bhattacharya feels that the western philosophers have committed the error of trying to describe the characters of the Absolute. Kant, for the first time, realised the futility of such attempts, but even he made the mistake of calling it unknown and unknowable. He did not realise that to call the reality unknown and unknowable was also to give a description of the reality.

On account of some such reasons K. C. Bhattacharya feels that the Absolute cannot be described even as reality. It is pure Indefinite, that is why it transcends the subjective and the objective. The subjective and the objective are never free from contents that are definite. Plato's *Nothing*, the *Śūnya* of the Buddhistic nihilists, the indeterminate *Elan Vital* of Bergson, the dark chamber of Hegel's Being — are all different approaches to the Indefinite, but they all fail to represent the Indefinite truly because they all place the Indefinite either in the subjective realm or in

consciousness that is indefinitely other than the content."[1] The use of the word "indefinitely" with both the alternatives is indicative of the fact that the Absolute of Feeling can be understood as that from which 'known being is distinct'. That shows that the Absolute of Feeling is indifferent to both being and non-being. It is in this sense that the Absolute is *transcendental*. We now come to an interesting result. The Absolute as knowing is such that it cannot be known, the Absolute as willing is contentless and is understood as negation of being, the Absolute as feeling is above being and non-being and is transcendental. That once again shows that the Absolute is the Indefinite. Our reflective capacities cannot know it, its freedom is untouched by any content that we can think of, it can be designated neither as being nor as non-being. Hence it is completely indefinite.

We can arrive at the same conclusion in a different way also. K. C. Bhattacharya goes further to speak about the three alternative forms of the Absolute. The Absolute may be understood as *Truth* or *positive being* that is not known, or as *Freedom* or *Reality* or *positive non-being*, or as Value or positive indetermination in an *indefinite unity*. These three correspond to the three forms enumerated above. Truth, by its nature, is self-evident; but is no content of any consciousness, and therefore it is not known. Belief in freedom is willing itself, it is not a matter of any intuition. Of value it cannot be said either that it is self-evident or that it is not known.

It is difficult to determine the mutual relation of Truth, Freedom and Value. In the Absolute their mutual relation can be described as Alternation, and each one of these may be called 'an alternative form of the Absolute'. Alternation, according to K. C. Bhattacharya, may be understood as constituting the Absolute. He says, "In one direction their identity and difference are alike meaningless, and in another direction their identity is intelligible, but not assertable. Truth is unrelated to value, value to reality and reality to truth, while value may be truth, reality value and truth reality. The Absolute may be regarded in this sense as an alternation of truth, value and reality."[2] Each of these in a sense, is the Absolute, and the Absolute alternately is all of these. Such a description of the alternative forms of the Absolute once again exhibits the inadequacy of our reflective ways to

1. *Ibid.*, p. 139.
2. K. C. Bhattacharya, The Concept of the Absolute and its Alternative Forms, *Studies in Philosophy*, Vol. II, p. 143.

apprehend the Absolute, which, in the last analysis, is indefinite.

At this point a very pertinent objection can be raised. If the Absolute is indefinite, unknown — beyond being and non-being, and if it is not even expressible in the understandable forms of reflection, then it is futile — even logically inconsistent to try to describe the triple forms of the Absolute. K. C. Bhattacharya is conscious of the possibility of such an objection being raised. He says that these descriptions of the alternative forms of the Absolute do not take away from the Absolute its indefinite character. Śaṅkara's Brahman is also indeterminate, and yet attempts are made to have an idea of the Brahman by calling it 'Saccidānanda'. This is only a proximate description of the Brahman — just an attempt to know the unknown in the best possible way. Brahman as existence, consciousness and bliss is nothing but another version of the Absolute as knowing, willing and feeling. Therefore, these descriptions do not, in any way, affect the transcendental nature of the Absolute. K.C. Bhattacharya is not trying to suggest that there is actually an Absolute having three forms. He clearly says, "it is meaningless, therefore, to *cognitively* assert that there are three Absolutes or one Absolute . . . what are here understood as *three* are only their verbal symbols."[1] The Absolute does not have a known content, and therefore no description of the Absolute can be cognitive. The need for such descriptions and elaborations is felt on account of the possibility of various kinds of philosophical theories about the Absolute. A reference to these forms will be able to incorporate all kinds of possible approaches to the Absolute. An emphasis on one of these forms, for example, will give rise to one kind of theory.

This clearly shows that the Absolute has not been conceived in an ordinary way. It is not an impersonal or over-personal reality. It is not a known content. It is meaningless to try to describe the characters of the Absolute, because such descriptions are given only of known entities. Descriptions of the Absolute should be understood as our imperfect attempts to *have an idea* of the Absolute.

The Absolute can only be believed and not known. It is a positively believed entity that can be understood only partially — that too negatively. It can be spoken of — but only in terms of symbols. It is completely indefinite.

1. *Ibid.*, p. 141-42.

CHAPTER VI

S. RADHAKRISHNAN

Life

Radhakrishnan was born on September 5, 1888, at a small place, Tiruttani, forty miles to the north-west of Madras. He was the second child of his parents. His early life was spent in Tiruttani and Tirupati, both famous as places of pilgrimage. Perhaps on account of that early influence he was naturally attracted towards religion. He admits himself that since then he developed a firm faith in the reality of the unseen world, a faith which was never forsaken. He had his school and college education in Christian missionary institutions. During this period he came to be acquainted with the main teachings of Christianity and also with the critical remarks of the Christian missionaries on the Hindu way of life. That led him to undertake a study of Hindu scriptures. He unconsciously developed a respect for such powerful religious preachers as Swami Vivekananda. His early religious orientation was a result of all these influences and impressions. His first book *Ethics of the Vedanta,* a thesis prepared in connection with his M. A. Examination, was published in 1908 when he was only twenty.

In 1909 he was appointed a teacher of philosophy in Madras Presidency College and then his academic activities started. In 1918 he was appointed Professor of Philosophy in the new University of Mysore. That gave him an opportunity of making an extensive study of Western philosophy also. Some of his books and articles adopting a comparative attitude were published at that time. In 1921, he was appointed to the most important chair of philosophy in India, the King George V chair of Mental and Moral Philosophy in the University of Calcutta. He was invited to Oxford in 1926 to give Upton Lectures on Hindu View of Life and after that teaching and Lecture-assignments abroad followed one after another. During this period he also founded the Indian Philosophical Congress in collaboration with other eminent men of philosophy in India.

By then Radhakrishnan had established himself as one of the

greatest intellectuals of the country. His vast knowledge of
ancient Indian Religion and Philosophy along with his extensive
acquaintance with the wisdom of the west created the image of
his being the only bridge-builder between the east and the
west. This coupled with his brilliant power of oration caused his
fame to spread. He was given the Spaulding chair of the Oxford
University, and then he gained an all-round recognition. All kinds
of honour started pouring in in quick succession, and he passed
through various phases of life taking upon his shoulders
responsibilities one after the other — the responsibilities of a
Professor, a Vice-chancellor, an Ambassador, the Vice-President
of India and lastly the responsibilities of the highest office
that India could offer to him — that of the President of the
Indian Union.

Nature of his Philosophy

Radhakrishnan has the rare qualification of being well-versed
in the great traditions of both the east and the west. His early
education made him familiar with the knowledge of the east —
particularly of India, and his own scholarly adventure acquainted
him with the wisdom of the west. Naturally he combines the
two traditions with perfect ease, and is able to evolve a philosophy of synthesis.

But, his fundamental convictions are deeply rooted in Indian
traditions. The root notions of his own philosophy are generally
taken from ancient Indian philosophy — particularly from the
Vedantic tradition, but he has a knack of presenting such ideas
into idioms and models of western thought. He seems to be
presenting old and traditional ideas in a refreshingly novel
manner.

Joad, in his *Counter attacks from the East*, describes Radhakrishnan's metaphysical standpoint thus, "...the function, the
unique function which Radhakrishnan fulfils today is that of a
liaison officer. He seeks to build a bridge between the traditional
wisdom of the east and the new knowledge and energy of the
west."[1] This statement does contain some elements of truth,
and that is apparent from the fact that Radhakrishnan makes
persistent efforts to bring about an east-west-synthesis.

---

1. C.E.M. Joad, *Counter attacks from the East*, p. 38.

His basic philosophical position is of a kind of a synthesis of Advaita Vedānta and the philosophy of Absolute Idealism. He takes up the monistic character of the Vedantic reality and combines it with some of the important aspects of Absolute Idealism. Like Vedānta he believes that the reality is one, like Absolute Idealism he shows that everything is a necessary aspect of the One. Consequently one finds it difficult to reduce his philosophy to any of the current metaphysical models. It can broadly be described as a philosophy of *Monistic Idealism*. It is monistic because reality is conceived as one, and it can be called Idealism for reasons more than one. His idealism is of course metaphysical, but metaphysical idealism may be either *idea-ism* or *ideal-ism*. The former means that reality is of the nature of an idea — that it is mental or spiritual. Radhakrishnan also conceives reality as spiritual, and therefore he is an idealist. Ideal-ism, on the other hand, emphasises the ultimacy and value of some ideal. Radhakrishnan prefers this sense of the word 'Idealism' and himself acknowledges that his philosophical point-of-view is an idealistic point-of-view in the sense that it believes that there is a spiritual ideal towards which the entire world-process is progressing. He analyses different senses of the words 'idea' and 'idealism' and comes to assert, what in his opinion, appears to be the real meaning of the word idea. When we ask with reference to any thing or action, "what is the idea ?" we mean to ask, what is the principle involved in it or what is the meaning or purpose of its being or what is the aim or value of the action ? That shows that in trying to determine the nature of an idea we try to determine what that thing is driving at. Thus if we assert that the universe is driving at something — that it has a meaning and a value, that it is not a blind striving or an irrational movement onwards, but is a constant and persistent progression towards some higher end, then we are an idealist. An idealist, in this sense, is a *teleologist* who believes in the ultimate meaning and purpose of the universe. An idealist, therefore, is a philosopher who "can find no rest until he gains a view or a vision of the world of things and persons which will enable him to interpret the manifold experiences as expressive, in some sort, of a purpose."[1] Radhakrishnan is an idealist in both of these two senses. He is an

---

1. Radhakrishnan, *An Idealist View of Life*, pp. 15-16.

idealist in the first sense because he conceives the ultimate reality as spiritual. He is an idealist more particularly in the second sense because he is convinced that the world-process is serving some purpose, is steadily trying to reach some goal. He seems to have the feeling that the scientific and technological advancements have made life's ways mechanical and that the materialistic competitions have almost lulled the souls of mankind to sleep. Therefore he thinks that what is required is a reawakening of the soul, a recovery of the spiritual faith. His philosophy, thus, is nothing but an attempt to illustrate that the ultimate nature of the universe is spiritual, and that unless the spiritual sense is awakened man's life will remain chaotic — a life of anguish and evil. On account of such a tremendous emphasis on the ultimate spirituality of everything Radhakrishnan at times appears to be a *mystic* also, but his mysticism is mysticism only to the extent to which idealistic thought of the monistic variety tends towards it.

Nature of The Ultimate Reality

Radhakrishnan feels that the main function of a philosophical enquiry is to find an explanation of the universe. The explaining principle has to be ultimately real because it has to provide a basis for everything real. Therefore, Radhakrishnan thinks that the ultimate reality must be able to satisfy all questions regarding the how and why of the universe.

In conceiving the nature of the ultimate reality Radhakrishnan leans heavily on the Vedānta. The Vedānta conceives the ultimate as the Brahman, which is the logical prius of the universe. In fact, according to Vedānta, the Brahman has not to be proved or established, it has got to be accepted because without presupposing it nothing can even be thought of. More or less in the same vein Radhakrishnan also says that the ultimate reality is the Brahman — the Absolute — which is the logical ground of everything real and existent.

At this point the naturalist might assert that there is no need of positing any super-natural or spiritual principle for the explanation of the universe in view of the fact that everything can be given a naturalistic explanation. Radhakrishnan feels that the naturalistic solution is based on the presupposition of the reality of time, and as such, it keeps itself confined to temporal phenomena without realising the necessity or even the need of going beyond time. "It looks upon the world as a sort of an automatic machine which goes on working in a blind haphazard way. It reduces the temporal world to unconscious forces, makes life, consciousness and value mere by-products. It believes that the world machine needs only to be taken to pieces to be comprehended"[1] Therefore Radhakrishnan asserts that the naturalistic explanation fails to appreciate the nature of the ultimate reality. It seeks to provide an explanation for the orderliness that it discovers in nature, but it forgets that the orderliness of nature is not mechanical — determinable in terms of blind material forces.

It is on account of this failure of the naturalistic explanation that Radhakrishnan goes deeper in his attempts to conceive the nature of the ultimate reality. He is aware that it is not possible to give a naturalistic description of the ultimate, but he is also aware that the ultimate must be such that it can fully account for everything — the universe and even itself. In the material world we do not have any such principle which can account for itself, everything material is explainable in terms of something other; therefore the ultimate principle must be outside the scheme of the material, must be different from the physical forces. That is why Radhakrishnan feels that the ultimate must be a *spiritual* principle.

The full implication of the word 'spiritual' will be clear in due course, but to begin with this can be understood in a negative manner; the spiritual may be understood as something different from and higher than the physical. Radhakrishnan, more or less, like the Advaita Vedantist, feels that it is not possible to give an exact description of the ultimate, but attempts can be made to understand it as nearly as possible by giving the nearest possible description of the ultimate in terms of the limited language-capacity that we possess. Therefore, an examination of the world-process itself reveals that there is invariably a point at which our physical explanation comes to stop and beyond which it cannot go. That shows that we have to seek an explanation in terms of a non-physical principle.

---

1. Radhakrishnan, *An Idealist View of Life*, p. 314.

The Absolute or the Brahman

This non-physical principle is designated by Radhakrishnan both in the Indian way and in the western manner. He at times calls it the Brahman, and at other times, the Absolute. His Absolute contains in it the elements of both — the Advaita Vedānta and of the Hegelian tradition. It is the only reality, but it is not arrived at by carrying the process of abstraction to its maximum limit.

This will be evident if we examine the strictly monistic character of the Absolute as it has been conceived by Radhakrishnan. He believes that the ultimate explanation of the universe has to be monistic. The Absolute in itself is essentially one. Like the Advaita Vedantist Radhakrishnan also believes that the Absolute does not admit even of internal differentiation — the svagata-bheda as the Vedantist calls it. The differentiations that appear to be there are so only from the point of view of creation. It is true that everything, in a sense, is an expression of the Absolute, but these expressions do not in any way affect the monistic character of the Absolute. "The same Absolute reveals itself in all these but differently in each. The ultimate reality sleeps in the stone, breathes in the plants, feels in the animals, and awakens to self-consciousness in man",[1] and yet the ultimate reality in itself is the one Brahman unaffected by all these manifestations.

In fact, the reason for Radhakrishnan's emphasis on the monistic character of the absolute is the fact that he has come to realise that the world somehow or other expresses a *unity* within its processes. The processes of the world reveal that they are not stray or casual processes, they reveal a unity. Now, this unity cannot be explained unless the ultimately real is conceived as one. Plurality tends towards differentiation and diversity. Thus, Radhakrishnan's monism has its roots in teleology.

The Absolute is conceived by Radhakrishnan as *"pure consciousness* and *pure freedom* and *infinite possibility."*[2] Whereas the first two characters have been described, more or less, in the Vedantic manner, the third character has been explained in the manner of Hegel's Absolute Idealism. The Absolute is pure

---

1. Radhakrishnan, *Reign of Religion in Contemporary Philosophy*, p. 43.
2. Radhakrishnan, *An Idealist View of Life*, p. 343.

consciousness, because consciousness is the most ineffable and the constantly existing phenomenon. We cannot think of any stage of existence without relating it to consciousness. It is always there. It is an infinite possibility because infinite worlds could arise from it; this universe is only one possibility of the Absolute. It is pure freedom because its act of actualising a possibility is not determined by anything, it is a free act. It could have created a world different in every detail from that which is actual. If one drama is enacted and other possible ones postponed, it is due to the freedom of the Absolute.

In fact, Radhakrishnan feels that the qualities of existence, order, development, purposefulness, etc. that we notice in the world, demand an ontological foundation, and that can be provided by nothing less than the Absolute. "Why is there existence? Why is there anything at all ? If everything disappeared there would be utter nothingness. If that nothingness did not provide or was not itself the possibility of being, there could not have been anything at all. The existences of the world are imperfect and impermanent and nothing that is imperfect can subsist of itself or by itself, for in so far as it is imperfect it is not. The Upaniṣads lead us from the imperfect existences in the world to the Supreme and Absolute Being...the existence of the world means the primacy of Being."[1]

This shows that the very existence of the world implies the existence of such a being from which the world is derived. It is the pure Being and as such the foundation of all existences. Radhakrishnan, at times, calls it the logical 'prius' of the universe.

This Absolute, according to Radhakrishnan *has to be spiritual in nature*. The known principles of the universe are inadequate to explain the universe. They always stop at a particular point, everything beyond which is beyond their grasp. As such, they seek to explain the known universe in terms of unknown principles. Our faint glimpses into the life of the spirit reveal to us that spiritual qualities have a power to take us beyond the known. Therefore we are constrained to think that the Absolute is a *spirit*.

It is a *free* spirit. It is free in so far as there is nothing to

---

1. Radhakrishnan, *The Recovery of Faith*, p. 79.

limit it. It has no 'other', and therefore there is nothing beyond it. Its freedom is uninterrupted.

The Absolute is described as *Infinite*. It is infinite because it cannot be finite. The finite is finite because it depends on something other than itself. The Absolute Spirit being the ultimate reality is self-grounded and is also the foundation of everything else.

It is *changeless* because it is infinite. Being infinite it is self-existent and hence *complete-in-itself*. To change means to become something which the changing thing is not. That implies that the changing thing lacks something. As the Absolute Spirit lacks nothing it is complete-in-itself.

It is *eternal* also. The character of eternity follows from the qualities of changelessness and self-dependence. But, the Absolute is eternal not in the temporal sense. It is not eternal in the sense of remaining what it is in all moments of time: it is eternal in the sense of being timeless. It transcends time in the sense that time is irrelevant to the Absolute.

Radhakrishnan calls the Absolute *the whole of perfection*. Everything else is imperfect. There may be degrees of perfection, but the wholly perfect is the Absolute.

This is why Radhakrishnan asserts that the Absolute is beyond all its expressions. Even though the world is an expression of the reality, the ultimate reality cannot be reduced to Nature. Radhakrishnan's conception of ultimate reality is not pantheistic in character, it keeps on swinging in between Pantheism and Theism.

But, all these descriptions of the Absolute are imperfect attempts on our part to understand its nature. Radhakrishnan is convinced that the nature of the Absolute cannot be fully comprehended. He says, "Pure Being which is the Absolute can only be indicated. It can be alluded to but not described."[1] This once again shows the deep influence of Śaṅkara on the philosophy of Radhakrishnan.

Absolute and God

Over and above the principle of the Absolute or Brahman Radhakrishnan also talks about the principle of God. We come

---

1. Radhakrishnan, *The Recovery of Faith*, p. 87.

across a similar account also in the Advaita Vedānta of Śaṅkara, but there the two principles are conceived as basically one, as different ways of apprehending the same reality. Śaṅkara makes a distinction between *Pāramārthika Dṛṣṭi* and *Vyāvahārika Dṛṣṭi* and the difference between the two principles of Absolute and God is ultimately reduced to these two points of view.

Radhakrishnan also distinguishes between the Absolute and God although he does not reduce their distinction to the empirical and the transcendental points of view as it has been done in the Vedānta. He feels that in order to explain the universe it is necessary to think of a principle that would account for the order and purpose of the universe. Like Whitehead Radhakrishnan also believes that one cannot account for the dynamic and creative character of the universe if the primary Being is also not conceived as creative. Like him again he feels that there has to be a principle, a God — a non-temporal and actual being — by which the indeterminateness of creativity can be transmuted into a determinate principle. This shows that the Divine Intelligence — the creative power — has to be conceived as the *Intermediary between the Absolute Being and the Cosmic process.*

That is how the principle of God appears in the philosophy of Radhakrishnan. The Supreme has been conceived as revealing itself in two ways — Absolute and Īśvara. God is the Absolute in action, it is God, the creator. The real in relation to itself is the Absolute and the real in relation to the creation is God. Radhakrishnan feels that the demands of reason have to be reconciled with the demands of experience. Metaphysical as well as religious aspirations have to be satisfied. The Absolute is the object of metaphysical aspiration, God of the religious aspiration.

This shows that unlike Śaṅkara Radhakrishnan is not prepared to reduce God to unreality by making it a product of Māyā and ignorance. God is real in so far as creation is real. God is an aspect of the Absolute, God is the Absolute from the human end. The real as infinite possibility is the Absolute, but when we limit the Absolute to its relation with that possibility which has actually been realised in the form of creation, then the Absolute appears as the Creator, as wisdom, love and goodness— as God. Radhakrishnan explains this in a very clear way when he says, "We call the Supreme the Absolute when we view it apart from the cosmos, God in relation to the cosmos. The Absolute is the pre-cosmic nature of God, and God is the Absolute from the cosmic point of view."[1]

Now all the usual attributes of God can be attributed to the God of Radhakrishnan's conception also, all the proofs for God's existence assume a validity and a significance. It now becomes very convenient for him to go through the history of eastern and western thought in order to pick up those Divine attributes and characters which have enabled the God-concept to retain its sacredness and ultimacy.

Although Radhakrishnan seems to be inclined to give credence to all forms of traditional proofs for God's existence, *the Teleological proof, the Moral proof and the one based on Intuitive experience* appear to be his most favourite arguments in God's favour. He at times talks of the *causal proof* also, but his version of the causal proof is similar to Descartes' version of this proof. Like him, Radhakrishnan also says that in order to explain ourselves — our existence, we have to think of a cause, a creative capacity which could create beings like us. Of course, such a cause will not be an ordinary cause in so far as ordinary causes depend upon some prior causes. This divine cause, therefore, has to be a self-dependent cause.

Radhakrishnan attaches great value to the *teleological proof* for God's existence. He is convinced that the world-processes are not chaotic and that they are constantly revealing some purpose — some end that has to be realised. This purposive character of the universe cannot be explained unless a divine intelligence is posited to explain it. He clearly says, "The rational purposive character of the universe gives us enough justification for presuming the reality of a spiritual environment."[2]

Explaining the moral proof he says that our moral life itself presupposes *a* moral Governor of the universe. Our moral efforts — our sense of morality itself — will lose all its effectiveness unless it is backed up by the belief that one is accountable for his good and bad deeds, that is, unless it is believed that the universe is being governed by a moral Governor, a God, who keeps an eye on everything good and bad.

But, the most important evidence of God's existence, according

---

1. Radhakrishnan, *An Idealist View of Life* p. 345.
2. Radhakrishnan *An Idealist View of Life*, p. 333.

to Radhakrishnan, is the possibility of intuitive experience of divine nature. He thinks that every body is capable of having spiritual experiences. Every attempt on our part to try to apprehend something that transcends our normal and ordinary capacities is an evidence in favour of the reality of spiritual experiences. It is these experiences that reveal to us the fact that the world is not a chaos — that it is progressively trying to attain a goal. Moreover, those who have been able to cultivate their intuitive capacities have been able to get glimpses of the spiritual reality. These experiences show that the reality itself has to be wholly spiritual so that it may cause and give sustenance to all kinds of spiritual experiences. Radhakrishnan is so much sanguine about the trustworthiness of such experiences that he says that proofs for God's existence are not even necessary, they are only convenient aids to faith which ultimately rests on the testimony of the intuitive experiences.

Let us now try to enumerate the basic characters of God. God is conceived as the *Supreme mind.* As supreme intelligence and wisdom. He actualises the possibility of creation. He is also *love* and *goodness.* Using the analogy of the Hindu trinity of *Brahmā, Viṣṇu* and *Śiva,* Radhakrishnan says, "The one God creates as Brahmā, redeems as Viṣṇu; and judges as Śiva. These represent the three stages of the plan, the process and the perfection. The source from which all things come, the springs by which they are sustained and the good into which they enter one. God loves us, creates us and rules us. Creation, redemption and judgment are different names for the fact of God."[1]

In clarifying his views on the relation between God and creation Radhakrishnan appears to be greatly influenced by Whitehead's philosophy of God. Like him he also believes that God is organic with the world, it is impossible to detach God from the world. It is not that God arranges everything in the beginning and leaves the world to grow under the control of the secondary causes, as the Deist thinks. A God who has arranged everything at the beginning of the world and can change nothing and create nothing new, is not a God at all. If the universe is truly creative then God must also remain constantly creative. God also grows with the universe by giving it a constant direction towards the goal which it ever seeks to attain. It is

1. Radhakrishnan, *An Idealist View of Life*, p. 338.

true that God is not wholly identical with the universe, it is
transcendent in so far as it cannot be identical with the universe
which constantly lacks something and which is a steady progression towards perfection. Throughout the process of creation
there remains an 'unrealised residuum' in God, which makes him
transcend the universe. Perhaps in the end this unrealised
residuum would vanish, but then the purpose of this creation
would also be complete, God then will recede into the background of the Absolute. "The beginning and the end are limiting conceptions, and the great interest of the world centres in
the intermediate process from the beginning to the end."[1]

World

With God conceived as the creative principle of the world, it
becomes convenient for Radhakrishnan to give a spiritualistic
account of creation and the world. Before detailing the salient
features of Radhakrishnan's conception of the nature of the
world, it would be fruitful to keep in mind some important
aspects of this account. Firstly, it is interesting to find that
Radhakrishnan is all the time struggling to incorporate in his
description of the world the scientific or even the materialistic
descriptions of the physical world with the constant emphasis
that the spiritualistic description, instead of contradicting the
materialistic account of the physical world, comprehends it.
Secondly, Radhakrishnan is very much against the mechanistic
explanations of the universe. He is convinced that mechanistic
explanations cannot *explain*, as they leave many gaps in their
explanation. He offers a teleological explanation of the universe
and asserts that the universe is steadily trying to realise some
purpose and is progressing towards some goal. Thirdly, One
can very clearly see that Radhakrishnan's explanation of the
world seeks to synthesise some aspects of the Vedantic explanation with some aspects of the Hegelian type of explanation of
the universe.

Radhakrishnan is against materialistic or naturalistic explanation of the universe on the ground that it asserts the ultimate
reality of time and refuses to go beyond the temporal process.
The materialistic explanations are mechanistic, they look upon

1. *Ibid* p. 340.

the world as a sort of an automatic machine which goes on working in a blind and haphazard way. That is why Radhakrishnan adopts an idealistic explanation of the universe.

The universe, therefore, is conceived as expressing an aspect of the Divine plan. God creates the world. The world has a beginning and an end. God is not separate from it. He is the past, the present and the future of the world; and yet He is quite distinct from the world, the distinction being the distinction of the creator and the created. Creation is the actualisation of one of the inherent possibilities of the Absolute. The world, therefore, is dependent on the particular choice of the creative energy. Radhakrishnan says that the Spirit enters into the spirit of the non-spirit to realise one of the infinite possibilities that exist potentially in the Spirit.

Now, if the world is the actualisation of *one* of the infinite possibilities, it follows that it is a result of *a* 'free' act—that it is not a necessity for the Creator. The world, therefore, is an *accident* of the Absolute. It is not essential for the Creator to have this very world, any of the possibilities could have been realised. Therefore the world is an accident.

This emphasis on the accidental nature of the world is very significant. Firstly, it succeeds in maintaining the monistic character of the real and also its free nature. Secondly, it enables Radhakrishnan to emphasise the difference between the Creator and the created. One can find the traces of the influence of Śaṅkara on this aspect of Radhakrishnan's thought as Śaṅkara also believes that the world is not necessary to the Brahman.

To this element borrowed from ancient Indian thought Radhakrishnan adds another taken from the Absolute Idealism of the west. Radhakrishnan says that the universe, although an accident, is real. There is, in his opinion, no contradiction involved in thinking that the accidental can very well be real. The terms 'accidental' and 'real' are not necessarily incompatible with each other. The world can very well be conceived as both real and yet accidental. It is accidental because it is an accidental actualisation of one of the infinite possibilities of the Absolute, it is real because it is the *Absolute's* accident. A character that follows from a thing accidentally is as much real as a character that follows from it necessarily. The created world is not an illusion because it is willed by God. In this connection one can make a distinction between 'non-created divine reality and 'created reality'. One is reality-in-itself, the other is the reality in the thought and being of the world, but both are real.

Radhakrishnan describes the world in terms of certain characteristics. Firstly, it is an *ordered whole*. Nature is a system of relationships intimately inter-dependent. Secondly, there is a tendency towards a greater inter-relatedness, a greater inter-action between the organism and its surrounding environment. Molecules, atoms and electrons are parts of a unity interacting with one another not fortuitously, but in relation to the material system of which they form parts. Thirdly, the expression of reality is in the world in terms of Matter, Life, and Mind. They are described as grades of experience. They are all expressions of reality, and yet they express reality in their own ways. Every matter-particle in every material system acts in unison with other ones; the adjustment and inter-relatedness are even greater in life and consciousness. Fourthly, the world is *dynamic*. This is one of the most prominent characters of the universe as conceived by Radhakrishnan. Nature is always active, "never satisfied with the levels it has reached, it always aspires to other levels."[1]

This character has two implications : (a) firstly, it gives rise to doctrine similar to that of Emergent Evolution. If conti-nuous change is the rule of the universe, then there must emerge new qualities at every moment of creation. That is what Radha-krishnan's statement 'unpredictable novelties occur' signifies. (b) Secondly, if the world is continuously changing then it can only be divided in *phases* and *not in parts*. He says, "We do not have realms or spheres of being, but only modes or phases of activity. The process of nature is one, supple and continuous, and not a constructive series of static entities with fixed attributes."[2]

But the dynamic character of the world does not indicate that the world is mechanistic. The continuous changes have a pur-pose. The world is not a futile play of meaningless atoms, it is gradually proceeding towards an end. "In spite of little ups and downs of change there seems to be a compelling drift towards better things."[3] This tendency seems to be inherent in every aspect of the creative process. Radhakrishnan appears to be so

1. Radhakrishnan, *An Idealist View of Life*, p. 313.
2. *Ibid.*, p. 225.
3. *Ibid.*, p. 313.

much impressed by the purposive tendency of the world-process that he goes on to speculate about the possible end of the cosmic process. Perhaps this teleological tendency will ultimately reach a state when the entire world-process will be spiritualised. That will be the ultimate destiny of the cosmic process.

Radhakrishnan is aware that no account of reality and creation can be complete until two puzzling questions are answered, (a) the question with regard to the 'why' of creation and (b) the question regarding the creator. Radhakrishnan answers the first question in brief and in a simple manner, but in trying to solve the second problem he is forced to develop his thought in a particular fashion. The second problem is especially significant for him because the ultimate reality has been conceived rather in an impersonal manner.

It is in reply to the second question that Radhakrishnan has introduced the concept of God in his philosophy, and it is in this context that he tries to utilise the Vedantic concept of *Māyā*. The all-embracing power that creates is called Māyā, and it is described as the creative power of God. God, as we have seen, is not something over and above the Absolute. God, is Absolute viewed from the point of view of the world. It appears to be God from the point of view of one possibility that has been actualised. In other words, when we view at the Absolute in relation to the possibility that has been actualised, it appears as power, wisdom and love, and as creator, sustainer and destroyer of the world — and to that we give the name — God.

Now, we can try to find an answer to the first question. Radhakrishnan is aware that that is a ticklish question and that almost all theistic theories begin to falter in the face of the question regarding the 'why' of creation. In the Upaniṣads creation has been described as the *Līlā* of the absolute. Līlā is described as a joyful and sporting game in which certain limitations are imposed upon oneself just for the sake of joy. Creation is conceived in some such manner in the analogy of a sporting game. Some prominent commentators of the Upaniṣads have inferred from this that creation is just an illusory game being played for the sake of joy, and that in reality there has never been a creation. Radhakrishnan once again tries to find a solution of his own in the light of his basic metaphysical standpoint with regard to the nature of the world. According to him also creation is Līlā, but he adds that this Līlā is real. Now, Radhakrishnan has to face a logical difficulty. If creation is a real Līlā, then it follows that creation is necessary to the Absolute, and in that case, the free character of the reality is affected. In reply to that it has to be accepted that it is difficult to appreciate at this point a clear-cut distinction between 'necessity' and 'accident'; but according to Radhakrishnan, such a distinction is unwarranted in the context of reality. Therefore, it can safely be said that "it is in the nature of the Absolute to grow into the world — the world is the affirmation of the Absolute."[1] In that sense creation is necessary. But it is not necessary for the Absolute to have *this very* creation, in that sense creation is an accident. Radhakrishnan suggests that the etymology of the word 'Brahma' also supports this view. The word 'Brahma' is from *Bṛh*, which means 'to grow'. Therefore he says, "The question as to why the Absolute limited itself...is irrelevant. For, there is no such thing as the Infinite which first was an Infinite and then transformed itself in the finite."[2] The infinite *is* the finite, the Absolute is its other also. "We do not have the infinite and the finite, God and the world, but only the infinite as and in the finite, God as and in the world."[3]

Nature of the Soul

In order to understand Radhakrishnan's account of the nature of the soul, it is essential to take note of two things in the very beginning. First, Radhakrishnan even here tries to remain faithful to the Indian tradition, and as such, is convinced about the ultimate spirituality of man. Second, he is realistic enough to be impressed by the present-day conditions of man. He is aware that man, as we find him in the world, is a biological and psychological individual, who is determined by his instincts, drives and motives. *Thus*, he is aware that man is a peculiar combination of egoism and self-transcendence, of selfishness and universal love. Therefore, he tries to develop his views regarding the nature of the soul in this light.

It would have been convenient for him to reject the reality of the biological or the natural man. The ancient Indian

1. Radhakrishnan, *The Reign of Religion in Contemporary Philosophy*, p. 443.
2. *The Reign of Religion in Contemporary Philosophy*, p. 443.
3. *Ibid.*, p. 442.

philosopher, at times, does this. But a modern thinker like Radhakrishnan cannot afford to be unrealistic. Therefore he seeks a way out. He accepts the ultimate spirituality of the soul, but asserts the reality and value of the biological life also, maintaining all the time that the two are not incompatible with each other. He maintains that the physical aspect of man also has a reality, but that it does not contradict the ultimate spiritual nature of the soul. This represents the fundamental outlook of Radhakrishnan's philosophy of the soul, and therefore, it is in the light of this that he develops his views on the nature of the soul.

Radhakrishnan comes to think about this because he has a very deep realisation of the present-day state of man. It is true that man today appears to be much more comfortable — at least outwardly — than his ancestors. All the means of convenience and smooth life are today at his disposal. Science has brought within his easy reach articles of comfort — even of luxury. But a little insight will reveal that in the midst of plenty, the present-day man is basically restless, even unhappy. Man appears to have lost the zest for life, a continuous boredom characterises his life's ways. He very soon gets tired of the object of his love, there is no occupation or engagement which can give him sustained joy. Radhakrishnan feels that evidence of this can be gathered from any aspect of life and experience. Our lives, both individual and social, have become so much mechanised that we ourselves have turned, more or less, into machines. An awareness of such a condition of man leads Radhakrishnan to think about the real nature of man. Why is it that he is forgetting his own manness?

He comes to feel that this is chiefly on account of an overemphasis on the scientific ways of life. Science paints a deterministic picture even of man, it claims to have known every aspect of man, it claims to have determined the functions of every part of man's body. But, it does not realise that to know the nature and functions of the physical parts of the bodily man is not to know the real man. The real man cannot be reduced to nervous or brain or bodily functions. It is on account of this that the exclusively scientific picture of man becomes a very partial and narrow picture of man. Radhakrishnan feels that the over-scientific attitude of the present-time treats everything almost in the manner in which a scientist analyses objects of his experiments.

Man cannot be known in that way, that would only lead to a dehumanisation of everything and would make even the picture of man unnatural and unfamiliar to man himself.

From this it does not follow that the scientific picture of man is a false picture. Only this has to be remembered that that is a picture only of the physical man, a very partial picture which cannot represent those aspects of man which cannot be grasped by sense or intellect.

Now, it is clear that according to Radhakrishnan there are two aspects of man — one that leads the scientist to describe man in his own scientific way, and the other that transcends the capacity of scientific analysis. It is *not* proper to characterise these aspects of man in the traditional manner by calling them 'body' and 'soul', because that gives the impression that the soul represents only such characters that are clearly absent in the bodily. It is better to call these two aspects as *the finite* and *the infinite aspects* of man. The finite aspects are by and large aspects of the bodily, but even the bodily aspects of man give the evidence of the presence of spirituality in them. Radhakrishnan uses the word 'soul' in a very wide sense, so much so that even such bodily activities that have a tendency towards self-transcendence are described as soul-activities. In order to appreciate this an analysis of the two aspects of the soul is necessry.

But, even before that certain relevant facts that are peculiar to man only, and on account of which souls are to be distinguished from other aspects of nature, have to be brought to light.

One very significant fact about the activities of man is that unlike other aspects of Nature man is not wholly determined in terms of his class-characters. In every other aspect of Nature class-characters are very important; if one knows the class-characters of a crystal or of a plant or even of a lower animal one can claim to have known it. But in the case of man that is not so. Class-characters have their own importance, but individual characters are equally important. By knowing the general nature of man-in-general we cannot know man; infact, the peculiarities of the individual appear to be by far more important. It is in this sense that man is described as unique. Radhakrishnan, more or less like Tagore, feels that no account of the nature of the soul can afford to overlook the uniqueness of every individual.

There is yet another peculiarity present in all kinds of soul-activities which also has to be taken into account in every description of the nature of the soul. An analysis of man's life makes this point clear. Man, unlike other aspects of Nature, has the capacity to reflect and to plan his moves. He does not act blindly. He can, if he likes, fix up goals from before and make systematic efforts for its attainment. Philosophically speaking, this means that man has the capacity to live ahead of himself. This is what Radhakrishnan means by the expression 'self-transcendence'. Man can go beyond himself, can aspire to heights much beyond his ordinary reach. This, according to Radhakrishnan is a very significant aspect of soul's activity. Now, we are in a position to determine the nature of the two aspects of man.

(a) *The finite aspects*

According to Radhakrishnan the finite aspects of man are those aspects that are determined by the empirical or environmental conditions. In a general way, the bodily self can be described as representing this aspect of man. It is called finite because its determining factors themselves can be determined in terms of known conditions. Let us, for example, consider those aspects of man that are determinable by Biology, Psychology or Physiology. These aspects have a naturalistic explanation and the explaining conditions are sought to be determined by these scientific studies.

The peculiarity of this aspect is that it always considers the embodied man as a subject living in an environment. There is a constant influx of stimuli from the environment and the behaviour and the character of the individual can strictly be determined in terms of the responses that the individual makes to these stimuli. All such bodily responses are stimulus-determined. Radhakrishnan gives to this aspect of man different names — the empirical man, the physical man, the natural man, the bodily individual etc.

An analysis of this aspect at once brings to light certain very interesting points. Firstly, it has to be accepted that this represents one of the real aspects of man. There have been many religious philosophies both in the west and in the east which have emphasised that the bodily propensities have to be

completely annihilated in order to give full expression to the
real nature of the soul. In India, seers of the past emphasised
the illusory character of the physical self. Radhakrishnan is
not at one with them. He says that the physical constitutes one
aspect of the soul. "The realm of spirit is not cut off
from the realm of life. To divide man into outer desire and
inner quality is to violate the integrity of human life...the two
orders of reality — the transcendent and the empirical are closely
related."[1] Radhakrishnan asserts, more or less, like a Perfectionist,
that the suppression of the physical nature will mar self-fulfilment. It is not to be suppressed or rejected, it *has* to be
perfected.

But, the bodily aspect, although real, is only a stage — a
phase that has to be superseded. Radhakrishnan says that the
finite aspects of man have a reality so long as man remains
confined to that stage, but that is not his final nature. At this
point one may experience a little difficulty in appreciating this
particular element of his thought, he may object by pointing out
that if the finite aspects of man are ultimately to be transcended
they are not after all real. But Radhakrishnan will say that such
a doubt misses the point in question. Finite aspects are real in
the senses in which 'a stage' or a 'phase' of any process of
growth or development is real. Unless the 'stages' are crossed
the goal cannot be reached. If we are travelling on a road and
crossing various mile-posts, it does not mean that the mile-post
crossed becomes unreal as soon as it is crossed. But then, this
also has to be realised that if one decides to stay at a particular
mile-post, he suspends his onward march. The mile-post thus is
a stage, not the goal.

Radhakrishnan tries to prove this in a number of ways.
Firstly, even in this stage we get an evidence of unity and order.
The bodily aspects clearly exhibit 'organisation' and 'unity'. It
is not that bodily behaviour is completely chaotic having no
rule or law behind it. Every organism, for example, grows in
and through changes, and yet it remains identical with itself and
exhibits order and harmony. Had it not been so, medical
sciences, or even the sciences of Biology and Physiology would
not have succeeded in their attempts to determine the bodily
functions. This order is not just mechanical, it is always trying
to realise certain purposes. This itself is a pointer to the fact

1. Radhakrishnan, *The Bhagvad Gita*, p. 13.

that there are 'ends' beyond the bodily stage. Secondly, the embodied individual is somehow aware that he is capable of going higher than the bodily stage. He is aware of the limitations of his physical nature, and yet he somehow realises that he can surpass the limitations. He does not fully understand this, but he has an awareness of a 'beyond' within himself. Radhakrishnan says, "man's awareness of his finiteness and temporality means his consciousness of eternity."[1] "Man's inabili y to achieve perfect contentment in the finite, his unquenchable longing for consummate happiness may be taken as indicative of his supernatural destiny."[2]

(b) *The Infinite Aspect of Man's Nature: true nature of the soul*

The finite side of man's nature consists, as we have seen, of the physical and biological aspects of the individual. We have also seen that even in that aspect man is always aware of a beyond, which impels him to surge ahead and to transcend his bodily aspects. Therefore, an analysis of this capacity of self-transcendence itself will reveal the true nature of the soul. The bodily is determined in terms of naturalistic conditions, but the awareness of one's hidden capacity of self-transcendence cannot be so determined. Therefore, it is different from and higher than the empirical. Radhakrishnan says that this is *the spirit* in man. The infinite aspect of man, then, consists in his *spirituality*.

It is difficult to give an exact or precise meaning of the word 'spiritual', but Radhakrishnan feels that at least in the context of man, an understanding of this word is not as difficult as it initially appears to be. The import of this expression can be made clear with the help of examples taken from man's life — examples of such activities that can be called spiritual.

The word 'spiritual' stands for something higher than the empirical. In the empirical realm a distinction has to be made between 'the subject' and 'the object'. Therefore, that which is higher than the empirical must transcend this subject-object dichotomy. There is at least one example in which this distinction becomes negated, that is the fact of *self-consciousness*. In self-consciousness the self is aware of itself, the subject itself is the object of its awareness. Now the spiritual must be of the nature of self-consciousness. There is, again, another very significant fact

1. P.A. Schilpp. Ed. '*The Philosophy of Sarvapalli Radhakrishnan*', p. 57
2. *Ibid.*, p. 142.

relating to self-consciousness. At least in the case of man, self-consciousness is like a chord which is able to bind and keep together all the discreet experiences of an individual. That an individual remains identical with himself—that he continues to be the same person is only on account of the fact that he is all the time conscious of his own self. Therefore, self-consciousness gives to an individual a distinct personality. Thus, by calling man a spiritual being Radhakrishnan means that he is a self-conscious person who is able to unite all his experiences and activities in his act of self-consciousness. It is on account of this capacity of unification that he can foresee his future and make plans for it. This capacity enables him to organise his moves and to bring about a spiritual growth. This then is the true nature of man.

Radhakrishnan describes this as an aspect of the Divine. The very fact that we are not satisfied with our present status and that we are constantly striving to attain greater heights shows that we bear the Divine spark within ourselves. He clearly says, "There is, in the self of man, at the very centre of his being, something deeper than the intellect, which is akin to the Supreme."[1] Radhakrishnan feels that this unity can be felt and realised within. In fact, all our spiritual activities, aesthetic or moral or religious are expressions of the fact of kinship between man's nature and Divine nature. Therefore, it can be said that in his infinite aspect man bears the stamp of his Divine origin and is capable of cultivating Divine excellences. He can exercise free choice, and can act in freedom. He can rise to great spiritual heights—and can have spiritual experiences.

Radhakrishnan substantiates his views by gathering examples of such human activities that can be cited as evidences in favour of the presence of the Divine element in man.

Let us, for example, consider such actions that are regarded as 'noble'. We help a man in distress, we practise morality in a rigid manner, we undertake pains in order to help others. How can we account for these ? Materialistic considerations cannot explain these facts. These self-sacrificing activities are possible only because we have somehow a consciousness of the Universal within us which leads us to establish an affinity—even an identity with the object of our love. Again, how can we explain

---

1. Radhakrishnan, *An Idealist View of Life*, p. 103

the facts of aesthetic enjoyment, the scientist's dedication, the religious commitment and similar other facts ? In listening to the melodious notes of a sweet music we seem to forget every-thing about this mundane world; we, for the time being, begin to soar high in a different world. This is a clear illustration of our spiritual behaviour. Again, in extra-ordinary moments of our life we do have flashes of the presence of the Divine element in us. Radhakrishnan is never tired of referring to the great intui-tive experiences of the prophets like Jesus, Buddha, Zoroaster and Mohammad, and asserts that these clearly show that we are capable of experiencing the Divine. Again, the very longing of a limited and finite creature like man for salvation is itself an evidence of the presence of spiritual element within him. One cannot aspire for anything of which he does not have any idea, or which he cannot in any way share. Salvation is the state of complete spirituality, the state of Divinity itself. One cannot aspire for such a state unless he himself is spiritual. Yet another very convincing proof of man's Divine nature is the fact that even the most immoral and the most wicked of all men can also be reformed. It is possible only on account of the presence of Divine element within him. Radhakrishnan attempts to justify this by taking recourse to facts of history and evolution. If we compare the physical nature of the primitive with that of the modern man, we do not find much difference. The differ-ence lies in their approaches to life. The history of evolution is the history of gradual unfolding of spiritual capacities latent in man. That is why, with the growth of evolution the patterns of life and behaviour begin to differ. Moreover, with the advent of man we notice a distinct and radical change in the course of evolution. Prior to that, evolution had proceeded more or less on mechanical lines, but when man appeared on the scene his efforts and behaviour started having a hand in the course of evolutionary growth. That shows that man has within himself Divine capacities.

On the strength of all these evidences Radhakrishnan comes to feel that the true nature of man is his ultimate nature, which consists in spirituality and which is, in a sense, akin to Divine nature.

Some other Characters

In trying to give an account of the nature of the soul

Radhakrishnan leans heavily on the Indian tradition, and hence concepts like karma, freedom, rebirth etc. become important in his philosophy of man also.

Karma and Freedom

One of the most important characters of the spiritual man is freedom. Freedom is conceived by Radhakrishnan as constituting the essence of spirituality. Freedom ordinarily means freedom of decision or freedom of choice, but Radhakrishnan's meaning of the word freedom is more comprehensive than this; it includes this meaning and adds something more to it. Freedom implies a particular metaphysical status of man. It means that the soul is metaphysically free, that is to say, by its very nature the soul is not determined by any extraneous factor. It means that, unlike other aspects of Nature, soul is not determined by environmental factors, it can exercise its own control, and can have a say in its growth. A simple instance of his freedom is the capacity of creation that man possesses. He can create original works of art, build structures, express his creative genius in art, science and music. Freedom also means that man is free to choose his own course of life and action, it means that the future of man depends to a very great extent on man himself.

Radhakrishnan believes in the doctrine of Karma also. More or less in the manner of ancient Indian Philosophy he believes that the soul has to pass through various embodied stages and that the tendencies of each stage are determined by the 'Karma' performed in the past. From this it follows that the Karmas performed in this life will determine the future. One may raise a doubt here by saying that the Law of Karma is the determining factor of life, and as such soul's states and tendencies are after all *determined*. Thus it may be pointed out that the belief in the law of Karma is not quite compatible with the idea of freedom. Radhakrishnan removes this doubt in a very simple manner. Firstly, he says that karma and freedom are not incompatible with each other because the karmas are karmas performed by the soul. Freedom does not mean absence of any determining conditions, it means being determined by nothing else but oneself. Freedom is *self determination* and being determined by one's own karma is nothing but self-determination. Secondly, Radhakrishnan tries to demonstrate the compatibility of **karma and** freedom in a very simple manner. He says that there are two aspects of Karma — a retrospective aspect that has a connection with the past and a progressive aspect that has its influence on the future. Man is determined by the past Karma, but is free to create prospective Karma. Radhakrishnan sums up this idea in a very profound manner when he says that choice is the assertion of freedom over necessity by which it converts necessity to its own use and thus frees itself from it. Speaking analogically he says, "The cards in the game of life are given to us, we do not select them. They are all traced to our past Karma, but we can call as we please, lead what suit we will, and as we play we gain or lose — and that is freedom."[1]

Are souls one or many ? To this puzzling question Radhakrishnan gives a very illuminating answer. If reality is one, the question of there being many souls should not arise. But, this would be so only when the reality or the Absolute is viewed in its pre-cosmic nature: in that case even the distinction between the Absolute and God would vanish. But reality can be viewed even from the point of view of the cosmos — from the point of view of the world that has been created. Viewed thus, there would appear many souls. Radhakrishnan believes in the reality of many souls as separate centres of actions. He also says that they continue to retain their individuality till the end of the cosmic process. The full implication of this doctrine will become clear when we come to consider the doctrine of Human Destiny.

The Doctrine of Rebirth

The doctrine of the plurality of selves along with the consciousness of the fact of death leads Radhakrishnan to develop a doctrine of *Rebirth* also. If souls have to retain their individuality till the end of the cosmic process, they must continue to exist in some form or the other even after death. Rebirth therefore means survival, it is continuing to exist by assuming different bodies after death. Radhakrishnan is aware that it is difficult to understand the mechanism of rebirth fully, but an awareness of the unfulfilled urges and tendencies in the purposive set-up of the universe compels us to think about some

---

1. Radhakrishnan, *The Hindu View of Life*, p. 75.

possible forms of life after death just only to provide yet another
opportunity for the realisation of the unrealised urges. We cannot, in one life, exhaust all the potentialities of life. The most
general ground for the rejection of a belief in rebirth is the fact
that there is no evidence of anybody having any memory of the
past life. But Radhakrishnan says that lack of memory about
the past life is not an adequate ground for rejecting the belief in
rebirth. No body has any memory of his existence in his mother's
womb, but that does not mean that that is not a state of existence.
Death puts an end to the memory-capacity, but sufficient evidences of the tendencies of the past are available in life. The inborn
patterns of behaviour and some of the peculiarities of the individual can be explained only by presupposing a prior birth.

Human Destiny

Man is a finite-infinite being. Even in his finite embodied existence his spirituality asserts itself. He, even in the midst of his
finite surroundings, has yearnings of a higher kind. That shows
that the 'being' of man is a continuous march towards the realisation of that higher spiritual state. The soul has to pass through
various stages of embodied life, but all these stages are only resting places for him, not his goal His various births merely
provide him with opportunities for directing his energy towards
the realisation of the goal of existence — which is the ultimate
human destiny.

Ancient Indian Philosophy describes this ultimate goal of existence as the state of complete salvation or *Mokṣa*. It is conceived
as a state free from suffering — a state in which one is able to
realise one's true nature. Radhakrishnan also conceives this state
more or less in a similar manner, but his conception of the ultimate human destiny bears the mark of his own metaphysical
convictions, and hence contains some such elements that appear
refreshingly new and original. The most distinctive feature of
his description of human destiny is that it has been worked out
in a very consistent manner, in the sense that it follows naturally
from Radhakrishnan's account of the 'reality, world and man'.
If reality is ultimately one and if man is man only *in* creation
and if man as man is finite-infinite, then the ultimate human
destiny can be nothing else but the realisation of oneness. Radhakrishnan comes to this conclusion in a consistent manner.

This has to be remembered that so long as man is in the

embodied state he cannot attain his ultimate destiny. Therefore, the first aspect of his destiny would be freedom from the embodied existence. But although that may make *him* free, that will not put an end to creation; and so long as the cosmic process does not come to an end, complete unity will not be established. Therefore, the final aspect of his destiny must be the realisation of his unity at the end of the cosmic process. Let us try to follow Radhakrishnan's description of human destiny in a more detailed and clearer manner.

The destiny of man lies in his ultimate salvation. But, in what does salvation consist ? According to Radhakrishnan, although the finite aspects of man are real, the distinctness or the uniqueness of man consists in his spirituality. Therefore salvation would mean the realisation of complete spirituality. This amounts to the realisation of Divinity. Therefore Radhakrishnan says, "The destiny of the human soul is to realise its oneness with the Supreme."[1] The goal of life is the union with God, the realisation of the complete monistic character of reality. This can be described as self-realisation also, because it is the fullest expression of the higher nature of the self. The infinite aspect of the self bears the mark of the Creator and reminds the self perpetually of his real nature. Radhakrishnan tries to describe certain salient features of this stage.

The attainment of this state opens before the self the possibility of a new kind of experience — the experience of the Universal — of the One which expresses itself everywhere. Faint glimpses of such an experience can be had in artistic or aesthetic or ethical sensibility. One of its clearest examples is the mystical experience of gifted seers. Artistic experience, for example, in a very faint way, gives us an idea of the nature of the experience of the state of salvation. In the rare moments of aesthetic contemplation we rise above the distinction of 'me' and 'thou' and have a realisation of the universal working both within us and in the object of our contemplation. Such moments are moments of peace and pure joy. What is a momentary experience in this state becomes an aspect of the life of the liberated soul.

This, according to Radhakrishnan, is an entirely new state because all the strifes and strains of the embodied state are finally silenced in this state. The individual is now able to bring

1. Radhakrishnan, *Eastern Religion and Western Thought*, p. 96.

about a perfect inner peace and a coherence with the outside world. In the realisation of unity one feels the presence of one spirit in all minds, lives and bodies, and therefore, the life of the self becomes almost as comprehensive as the universe itself.

Such a salvation can be attained even while the self is in the embodied state. Radhakrishnan seems to be impressed by the ancient Indian concept of *Jivanmukta,* but describes it in his own peculiar manner. The liberated individual is the Jivanmukta, and as such is not affected by the world. He does not have any passion or attachment left for the worldly objects, and as such acts in a selfless and disinterested manner and works simply for the good of others. This description is similar to the description of the Jivanmukta, and yet there is a difference. The ancient Indian thinker believes that the Jivanmukta becomes 'Videhamukta' as soon as he is free from the fetters of the body which, as a result of the momentum generated by the forces of the karma, has continued to exist even after the attainment of *mukti* by the self. But once this momentum is exhausted the self does not come back to assume any bodily form, he is now fully free from the forces of birth and rebirth. According to Radhakrishnan this is not necessary. He feels that even when an individual is able to attain salvation, his task is not complete; he has now to play a part in the salvation of others. Individual salvation is not the ultimate destiny of even the individul souls.

Therefore, it is not necessary for the liberated individual to be fully free from rebirth. He lives and moves in the world for the redemption of others and if for that purpose it becomes essential for him to assume different bodily forms, he will do it. The only thing is that he has become finally free from the bondage of love and passion for life and fear of death. He is now completely free from egoism and selfishness. All his actions are now guided by his realisation of the oneness of everything.

In this connection a very interesting question is raised by Radhakrishnan. It appears that even after attaining salvation, that is, even after having a realisation of the basic oneness of every thing, the individual remains *an individual.* That raises a problem that has baffled all protagonists of the theories of Liberation. Is the individuality of the individual lost in the Supreme in the state of salvation ? Or, does the individual in any way retain its individuality ? Does realisation bring about an obliteration of individuality ? It appears that Radhakrishnan does not give a categorical answer to this question, and yet his answer is both interesting and illuminating.

In a sense, it can be said that in the state of realisation individuality is more asserted than denied. He admits this when he says, "There is no question in my scheme of the individual being included in and absorbed by the Divine"[1] Realisation is realisation of one's true nature, and in that sense it cannot be a denial of individuality. Moreover, as we have seen, even after attaining salvation an individual has to stay as an individual in the world and has to work for the redemption of others. That also shows that the individuality of the individual is not obliterated. Using the upaniṣadic analogy of the river and the sea Radhakrishnan says that although the river appears to be lost in the sea, the sea and the river do not become identical with each other. That is to say, the individuality of the individual is retained even in salvation. This can be proved on the ground that although the individual after redemption realises Divinity, the Supreme does not become the individual — the identity of the two is not established in an objective manner.

But that is only one aspect of Radhakrishnan's solution of the problem, that is not the final solution because individual redemption is not the ultimate human destiny. Even when an individual is liberated, he does not become free from the cosmic process *till all others are saved*. The world-process will reach its final goal when every individual will realise Divinity. Therefore *the ultimate human destiny is not individual redemption but universal redemption — "Sarvamukti"*, as Radhakrishnan calls it.

Will the individual retain its individuality even then ? Radhakrishnan says that this question is irrelevant. The problem of man and his destiny is relevant in relation to the fact of *creation* which is nothing but an actualisation of one of the infinite possibilities of the Absolute; and therefore with sarvamukti the purpose of this creation will be realised. That will be the end of the cosmic process. When all of us will be liberated, time-process will be transcended. The ultimate destiny, therefore, is the 'end of time'. As Radhakrishnan says, "we need not assume that the cosmic process is an end-in-itself. When its end is reached,

---

1. Radhakrishnan, *Reply to Critics*, Schillp Ed. *The Philosophy of Sarvapalli Radhakrishnan*, p. 799.

when its drama is played, the curtain is drawn and possibly some other plot may commence."[1]

The Way of Realisation— Religion, its nature

How can man attain the ultimate human destiny ? Radha-krishnan's stress on 'sarvamukti' as the inevitable and ultimate human destiny creates a peculiar paradox. Man is asked to awaken a sense of Divine within him; but if all men are to be saved, and if that is inevitable, then men do not have to do anything on their part, they have only to wait patiently. *But* will he attain his ultimate destiny simply waiting ? And, if this is not so — if he has to make efforts for salvation, is there any sense in asserting the inevitability of sarvamukti ? Radhakrishnan would say that by just waiting without doing anything man will only delay his own salvation and thereby sarvamukti also. Moreover, this delay would be utterly indefinite and uncertain.

And, we cannot afford to delay it. The present-day world is heading towards destruction, and if we do not become alive to the needs of the hour, it would become a task too difficult for us to build out of the ruins. The present-day man, according to him, is in the need of a radical change in the ways of his life. Burdened and tired to death by his loneliness in the midst of everything, man is in frantic search of some means for peace for release from the anguish of existence. Therefore, at least to expedite salvation he has to do something.

"All seers, whatever be their sects or religions to which they belong, ask us to rise to the conception of a God above Gods, who is beyond image and concepts, who can be experienced but not known, who is the vitality of the human spirit and the ultimacy of all that exists. This is the highest kind of religion— the practice of the presence of God"[2] 'The practice of the presence of God' — this expression appears to be significant, but how can this be practised ?

Religious Experience

Radhakrishnan says that one must begin with a faith —a faith in *Religious Experience*. Religious experience alone is

1. Radhakrishnan, *An Idealist View of Life*, p. 310.
2. Radhakrishnan, *Occasional Speeches and Writings* (1952-59), *Religion and its place in Human Life*, 12th August, 1954.

capable of making man realise spirituality. Let us, therefore, try to determine the nature and characters of Religious Experience as it has been conceived by Radhakrishnan.

This experience is not merely a form of knowledge as other ordinary experiences are, it is not just expressible in a body of certain codes and rules of behaviour. It is all thèse and yet it is much more than all of these. It is called an experience because it produces an objective awareness — an apprehension of the real coupled with an enjoyment — a sort of an inner satisfaction. It is called *religious* because of its peculiar nature — a uniqueness that cannot be reduced to any of the other forms of experience. Its peculiarity consists in its attempt to discover eternal truths, in its effort to raise the life-spirit to some higher spiritual level. Unlike other experiences its aim is to discover the hidden and the ideal possibilities of human life, it is a quest for the emancipation of mankind from the compulsions of finite existence.

Radhakrishnan asserts that one must have a faith in the reality and value of such experiences. These days it has almost become an intellectual fashion to dismiss all talks about such experiences as purely imaginative or nonsensical. But Radhakrishnan says, "However much we may quarrel about the implications of this kind of experience, we cannot question the actuality of this experience itself."[1] He says so on account of the fact that while profound intuitions do not normally occur, their milder forms are possible in the experience of everybody, as, for example, in the case of pure aesthetic joy. "The witness to this spiritual life is borne not only by the great religious teachers and leaders of mankind, but by the ordinary man in the street in whose inmost being the well of the spirit is set asleep. In our normal experience events occur which imply the existence of a spiritual world".[2] "When we experience the illumination of a new knowledge, the ecstasy of poetry, the subordination of self to something greater; family or nation, the self-abandonment of falling in love, we have faint glimpses of mystic moods."[3] An analysis of deep and sincere love, for example, will make this point clear. In the feeling of love, or, for that matter, in any feeling of this kind, we almost forget our surroundings, and we are lost — absorbed in some

1. Radhakrishnan, *An Idealist View of Life*, p. 93.
2. Radhakrishnan, *Eastern Religion and Western Thought*, p. 61.
3. Radhakrishnan, *An Idealist View of Life*, p. 93.

experience of 'the beyond'. Whenever a man does something with sincerity or with a sense of purpose, he has this experience within himself. In his *Religion and Society* giving a vivid illustration of this kind of experience, Radhakrishnan says, "Any serious pursuit of ideas, any search after conviction, any adventure after virtue arises from resources whose name is religion. The search of the mind for beauty, goodness and truth is the search for God. The child nursing at the breast of his mother, the illiterate savage gazing at the numberless stars, the scientist in his laboratory studying life under a microscope, the poet meditating in solitude on the beauty and pathos of the world, the ordinary man standing reverently before a starlit sky, the Himalayan heights or a quiet sea or before the highest miracle of all, a human being who is both great and good, they all possess dimly the sense of the eternal, the feeling of heaven."[1] Thus, the fact that such experiences enable men to forget the ills and worries of life at least temporarily is an evidence of the fact that only through such experiences can salvation be attained.

Now, we are in a position to enumerate some of the characteristics of Religious Experience as described by Radhakrishnan.

(1) It is an experience; that means firstly that it is not anything extraordinary or super-natural, secondly that every man is capable of it, and thirdly that it involves an awareness of an objective kind.

(2) It is an integral and undivided consciousness. That distinguishes it from ordinary experience. In ordinary experience the duality of the subject and the object is always maintained. In this experience there is no subject-object differentiation. Radhakrishnan describes this nature of the religious experience in very eloquent words. He says, "It is a condition of consciousness in which feelings are fused, ideas melt into one another, boundaries are broken and ordinary distinctions transcended. Past and present fade away in a sense of timeless being. Consciousness and being are not there different from each other. All being is consciousness and all consciousness being. Thought and reality coalesce and a creative merging of subject and object results. Life grows conscious of its incredible depths. In this fullness of felt life and freedom the distinction of the knower and the known disappears."[2]

1. Radhakrishnan, *Religion and Society*, p. 47.
2. Radhakrishnan, *An Idealist View of Life*, pp. 91-92.

(3) It is autonomous in character in so far as it is an independent function of the mind. It is not in any way determined by any extraneous factors. Its inspirations are spontaneous and inner.

(4) That shows that it is essentially *inner* and *personal*. Radhakrishnan seems to be deeply impressed by Whitehead's 'Religion in the making'. Like him he also insists on the primacy of the inner life of the individual. Religious experience is an experience developed in the human inwardness, it is a life being lived in subjectivity.

(5) The peculiarity of this experience is that it somehow shows an attitude of complete indifference towards such worldly things towards which in our ordinary life we normally feel attached. This experience, as he says, shows an incurable dissatisfaction with 'the finiteness of the finite and the transiency of the transient'. It constantly aims at the attainment of perfection.

(6) Religious experience, as he says, is the total reaction of the whole man to the whole reality. The expressions 'total', 'whole' etc., that are being used here, are not without meaning, nor are they being used merely for giving emphasis on the 'whole' nature of this experience. It is implied that this experience is not partial in any way. It involves the whole of the subject, and the reaction of the subject in this experience is not towards any particular presented aspect of the reality, but to the reality as a whole. As he says, "the privacy of the individual self is broken into and invaded by the universal self which the individual feels as his own."[1] It is a vision which is the "precious possession of the soul coming out in life on every side."[2] 'On every side' — that is significant. It is not a reaction of *mere knowing* or of *mere feeling*. It is a total reaction of the total man including the intellectual, moral and aesthetic aspects of the whole man.

(7) This experience does not create a disturbed state in the individual's life; on the other hand, it brings with it a state of peace. Radhakrishnan uses the word 'Śānti' for this and defines

1. Radhakrishnan, *An Idealist View of Life*, p. 92.
2. Radhakrishnan, *Reign of Religion in Contemporary Philosophy*, p. 305.

it as "a positive feeling of calm and confidence, joy and strength in the midst of outward pain and defeat, loss and frustration."[1] In this experience, the usual heat and fret of life are quietened and the individual experiences a profoundly satisfying joy and peace.

(8) Together with joy there is also a feeling of inner freedom. The disturbance of peace and the consciousness of pain are all due to anxieties and worries of life, which, in their turn, are the results of man's making himself a slave of the worldly situation and an over-prominent ego. The religious experience enables the individual to throw the burden off and to have a feeling of relief and release. It is in this way that this experience creates a feeling of freedom.

(9) There is also the feeling that this experience is the most certain and the most ineffable possession of man's life. An experience of this kind — even if it occurs only for a moment — leaves its mark on the whole of life — a mark so deep and powerful that it is never dimmed or forgotten. "Doubt and disbelief are no more possible. He [the person who has the experience] speaks without hesitation and with the calm accent of finality."[2]

(10) But, this certitude or ineffability can neither be demonstrated nor proved. Radhakrishnan uses the expressions 'Self-established', 'self-evidencing', self-luminous' etc. to describe the nature of such an experience. Its certitude is not based on rational argumentation, the experience itself is "pure comprehension, entire significance, complete validity. It comes with a constraint that brooks no denial."[3]

(11) Against these descriptions it may be said that they are empty words signifying nothing. Radhakrishnan is aware of the inadequacies and limitations of language, he is aware that it is not possible for our modes of expressions to comprehend fully the nature of this experience. These descriptions are, in fact, *human* attempts to explain the inexplainable. With our limited forms of language it is not possible to give an exact and precise description of this experience. It transcends expressions although it does provoke them. In this experience the self *is* wholly

1. Radhakrishnan, *An Idealist View of Life*, p. 93.
2. Radhakrishnan, *An Idealist View of Life*. p. 95.
3. *Ibid.*, pp. 92-93.

integrated, the distinction between the knower and the known is transcended, and therefore it is not reducible to any intellectual description that presupposes the subject-object-duality. He says, "Conceptual substitutes for ineffable experiences are not adequate...any attempt to describe this experience falsifies it to some extent."[1] This is the reason why he goes on to say, "Deep intuition is utterly silent. Through silence we 'confess without confession' that the glory of spiritual life is inexplicable and beyond the reach of speech and mind. It is the great unfathomable mystery and words are treacherous."[2] Symbols and suggestions taken from the local and historical traditions are employed to give an idea of the nature of this experience, but this must always be remembered that they are mere symbols and suggestions that are being used for want of a better means of expression.

Essence of Religion

A life that presupposes the ultimacy and the supreme worth of religious experience is a religious life. Therefore the nature of religious experience will also determine the nature of religion itself.

In the course of history of thought religion has been identified with feeling, emotion and sentiment, or with instinct, cult and ritual or with perception, belief and faith. Radhakrishnan feels that all these views are right in what they affirm, but wrong in what they deny. Religion does contain in some form or the other the elements that they emphasise, but their positive claim, asserting that religion is only what they think it to be, is wrong. Religion is somehow a synthesis of all these. There is a cognitive element in it and also a feeling-element. Likewise there must remain ritualistic and moral elements also in religion.

In fact, Radhakrishnan feels that the conflict of different religions is only on account of the fact that emphasis is laid only on one aspect of religion in utter disregard of other aspects which are also equally important. If we try to go deep into the nature of the religions, we shall find that there is a basic — almost transcendent — unity among all religions. It is only

1. *Ibid.*, p. 96.
2. *Ibid.*, p. 101.

when a particular religion in course of time starts emphasising
one of its aspects as constituting the essence of religion that
conflicts arise. In fact, these conflicts do not touch the essence
of religion, they are the results of mutual incomprehension.
We are born or trained in certain traditions of religion. Consequently, we use our own symbols and ways to represent the
Absolute reality. These symbols and ways are determined by
our age, circumstances and upbringing. We do not realise that
at the heart of every symbolic formulation lies that which is
beyond them. We do need a form, but this should not be confused with the spiritual reality. Forms may be diverse, but the
reality is one. Religions may be many on account of the diver-
gence of the forms, but the essence of them all is one and the
same.

What is the essence of religion ? What is that common
element that every religion shares ? Radhakrishnan says,
"Religion is not a creed or a code but an insight into reality."[1]
This insight will reveal that man is always confronted with
something greater than himself which is somehow immanent in
the human soul. This is the eternal or the Absolute Reality
which is present in the soul of man as its secret ground and
forms a bridge between the finite and the infinite insight into
this truth is the essence of religion. Therefore, Radhakrishnan
says that Religion is that discipline or the way of life which
enables man to "make a change in his own nature to let the
Divine in him manifest himself."[2] Religion implies a faith in
the ultimacy of absolute spiritual values and a way of life to
realise them. This faith involves an awareness of the beyond,
and therefore a conviction that such an awareness is possible.
That is why great religions have often been prophetic, or have
been based on truths intuited or seen by gifted seers. That is
why religion is *the affirmation of the ultimacy of Religious
Experience.*

The Way of Religion

It is now clear that, according to Radhakrishnan, it is through
religious experience alone that man can attain salvation. But, it

1. Radhakrishnan, *My Search for Truth*, p. 27.
2. Schilpp Ed. *The Philosophy of Sarvapalli Radhakrishnan*, p. 59.

is not easy to have this experience. It involves a struggle within, a fight against oneself — a very difficult fight indeed. "It is easy to fight non-human nature, forests, floods and wild beasts, but it is difficult to fight the passions in our heart, the illusions that we embrace."[1] All such passions and illusions are due to an over-emphasis on the personal will; and so the fight is, in fact, against that will, against egoism, against the undue assertion of the self.

Radhakrishnan says that this fight can be carried on in two stages. The first stage is the preparatory stage and the second is the final assault. The preparatory stage consists in bringing about certain changes in the intellectual, ethical and emotional make-up of man. *Doctrine, Devotion* and *Worship* — these constitute the first stage. The second stage is the stage of *Meditation, Contemplation* and *Love.* Speaking about 'self-recognition and the way to it' Radhakrishnan says, "An absolute inward purity demanding self-mastery and self-renunciation is demanded."[2] In this statement the expressions 'self mastery' and 'self-renunciation' refer to the preparatory stage and the expression 'an absolute inward purity' refers to the second stage.

The first stage is the stage of discipline. 'Discipline of human nature is essential for the attainment of the goal. Purity of mind and body is the means for perfection'.[3] Disciplining of human nature means putting a restraint on the passions and feelings of man, 'purity of mind' implies a radical change in the intellectual standpoint, and the expression 'purity of body' stands for an ethical discipline.

Passions mislead a man. They must be put under check. The normal man is a bundle of emotions, as a result of which he develops personal attachments and strong worldly bonds. That has to be controlled. "Excited emotionalism, which seeks and strives after sensations and rapturous states of a sensual character, is quite different from perfect insight."[4] Emotion is the excited display of our sensuous nature in love, disgust and frustration. But there is a difference between this emotion which is nothing but passion and religious emotion; the former must

---

1. Radhakrishnan, *Occasional Speeches and Writings* (1952-59), pp. 361-62.
2. Radhakrishnan, *An Idealist View of Life,* p. 111.
3. Radhakrishnan, *Occasional Speeches and Writings* (1952-59), p. 205.
4. Radhakrishnan, *Eastern Religion and Western Thought.* p. 78.

give way to the latter because the latter perfects the former. The latter stands for an emotional relationship of devotion and love to the Supreme.

Passions become prominent because of an over-emphasis on ego. "The ego is the knot of our continued state of ignorance, and so long as we live in the ego, we do not share in the delight of the universal spirit."[1] Therefore, our point of view must change. We must give up our ignorance to make room for knowledge. And in order to know the truth we must cease to identify ourselves with the ego and we must come out of the shell of the body, life and mind. This is what Radhakrishnan calls 'intellectual progress'. It helps in clearing the mental atmosphere of errors and illusions, ignorance and falsehood. This wisdom, however, is not easily won, it requires effort, it demands endurance, struggle, pain and suffering. It is achieved through rigorous discipline and maximum sacrifice.

It is now evident that Radhakrishnan is talking about *an ethical discipline*. Ethical discipline consists of a series of efforts which aim at the recognition and performance of duties. Duties, according to Radhakrishnan, are "opportunities afforded to man to sink his separate self and grow out into the world."[2] Therefore, "every individual must subdue his senses which make for self-assertion; pride must give place to humility, resentment to forgiveness, narrow attachment to family to universal benevolence."[3] This requires selfless practice of love — even of self-sacrifice.

'Love of the neighbour', for example, is not merely a theoretical maxim of a moral code, it is man's attempt to practise love and sacrifice. He has to cultivate a feeling of detachment. Detachment has both positive and negative aspects in it; negatively, to be detached is not to want anything for oneself; its positive aspect consists in a free and willing giving away of everything personal. Explaining this point analogically Radhakrishnan says, "if we cannot be satisfied with the beauty or the flowers unless we pluck it and put it in our button-hole, we cannot be at peace."[4] This analogy symbolically suggests that unless we give up the attitude of 'possession' — the feeling of

---

1. *Ibid.*, p. 95.
2. Radhakrishnan, *Indian Philosophy*, vol. II, p. 614.
3. *Ibid.*
4. Radhakrishnan, *Eastern Religion and Western Thought*, p. 131.

having everything for ourselves, we cannot be at peace. To be
at peace one must renounce narrow and selfish interests. This
may lead to physical suffering, but suffering and renunciation form
the core of ethical discipline, not merely as negative creeds but
as positive principles of love.

Now, the stage is set for 'the final leap' into the realisation of oneness with the Supreme. With the hindrances removed
there must come an inward change, a 'persistent endeavour to
dwell in the Divine'. This is possible only by *silent meditation*
and *quiet contemplation*. The intellectual, emotional and moral
disciplines prepare the soul, the individual now "withdraws his
soul from all outward events, gathers himself together inwardly,
strives with concentration",[1] and 'there breaks upon him an
experience — sacred, strange, wonderous, which quickens within
him, lays hold on him, becomes his very being."[2] Thus it is a
stage of concentration — *dhyāna* — in which the soul withdraws
itself from the senses and the ego and meditates on the Supreme.
"It is the gathering up of all dispensed energies, the intellectual
powers, the heart's emotions, the vital desires, nay, the very
physical being itself, and concentrating them all on the Supreme
goal."[3]

Prayer, modes of worship, rituals, the various religious rites
and ceremonies, even idol-worship — all these may have a significance, all these may help different individuals in different ways,
but the basic thing is silent meditation. Radhakrishnan uses the
terms 'yoga', 'realisation', 'dhyāna', 'intuitive apprehension' etc.
to denote this state. Whatever these terms may signify — the fact
remains that Radhakrishnan is convinced of the ultimacy and of
the finality of this process. 'Brooding, not reasoning, meditation,
not petition, results in an enlargement, an elevation, a transformation of one's being and thus in a re-creation of the world. By
closing our eyes and looking within, by contemplation or brooding we change our inner nature.' Religious life does not consist
so much in prayer and rites as in those silent hours of self-
communion which enable us to control our character and to
build up our personality. That is why it is said that the religious

1. Radhakrishnan, *Occasional Speeches and Writings* (1952-59), p. 291.
2. *Ibid.*
3. Radhakrishnan, *An Idealist View of Life*, p. 113.

way intensifies our thoughts, purifies our emotions and creates conditions for the growth of the spirit.

Persons who develop a capacity for such meditation are able to develop a different attitude towards the world and other beings. They live in the world and yet they do not belong to it. They walk and move in the world and yet they are not affected by its ways. In a spirit of universal love and in a free, selfless and dispassionate manner they practise self-sacrifice.

The Element of Mysticism

In Radhakrishnan's account of the nature of religious experience and the way of realisation, we come to discover an element of mysticism. Radhakrishnan claims that his account is not contrary to science because it is based upon a scientific analysis of the nature, aspirations and urges of man. If that is so, there should not remain any element of mysticism in his religious views. But Radhakrishnan somehow admits that there must remain a mystical element in the religious urge, although he asserts that the presence of this element does not make religion unscientific; on the other hand, he feels that it is quite consistent with scientific thinking.

When is an element called mystical ? Radhakrishnan says that when anything is not accessible to us in the normal ways — through the ways of reason or intellect we describe it as mystical. Mysticism is a defect of thought *only* when it is negative in approach — emphasised only to cover up ignorance and the lack of capacity to explain something. Mysticism, in fact, is a natural and necessary aspect of higher thinking. This can be recognised only when the rational and the scientific ways of understanding realise their limitations and come to perceive the evidence of 'a beyond' that transcends the rational and scientific ways. According to Radhakrishnan, it is in this sense that there is the presence of a mystical element in religious experience.

It is a fact that our ordinary ways of apprehension are limited in their scope and application. There are domains and realms that lie completely beyond their range. But even in their limitations they themselves suggest that it is possible to go beyond them. No scientific inquiry can be final, whenever a new theory is discovered, it is implied that even that can be improved upon.

This is true of all our endeavours and persuits. That shows that there is a hidden capacity in man to go beyond himself. If this capacity is sufficiently developed, man can extend his consciousness far beyond his egoistic nature — possibly to universal consciousness. The nature of this capacity cannot be fully comprehended by his limited ways of understanding, but in every aspect of his life and experience he comes across its evidences and proofs. This is the mystical element of his thought. It is mystical only because it is not completely comprehensible, and yet it is a real aspect of man's life constituting the essence of all his activities. Religious experience, of course, is the result of a very clear, developed and effective working of this element. Radhakrishnan, therefore, can be described as a 'mystic' in a very special sense of the term.

Different Ways of Knowing

Radhakrishnan's epistemological study is nothing but an exploration into the possible sources of knowledge. He considers this problem to be very important, firstly because this problem is traditionally important, secondly because every system of metaphysics is based on an epistemology outlining the sources of knowledge and thirdly because Radhakrishnan's metaphysical convictions demand a faith in a particular source of knowledge — a source whose relative strength in relation to other possible sources of knowledge has to be determined. Radhakrishnan is aware that the East generally emphasises the ultimacy of *creative Intuition* and that the West lays emphasis on *critical Intelligence*. He tries to examine the relative merits of the two faculties.

According to him there are three possible sources of knowledge : *Sense-experience, Intellectual Cognition,* and *Intuitive Apprehension*.

Sense-experience is the source through which we know the sensible qualities of the object. Radhakrishnan's 'Sense-experience' is nothing different from what Psychology describes as sense-perceiving. Its function is to gather impressions of the physical objects — both outer and inner and to provide materials for every kind of study and thought.

Intellectual Cognition, on the other hand, is almost the same as Conceptual knowledge. It is knowledge obtained by a process of *analysis and synthesis*. The data supplied by the senses are

analysed by the intellect and a new synthesis is perceived.   This
knowledge is not only *indirect* but also *symbolic*.   It is indirect
because its contact with the object is not a direct contact; it deals
only with that which is given by sensibility.   From the senses it
receives only *certain representations* of the objects; that is to say,
it receives merely signs and symbols; and hence it is symbolic.

Radhakrishnan feels that sense-experience or Intellectual Cognition cannot give the knowledge of reality, although in practical
life they are useful as sources of knowledge. He thinks that both
of them are inherently limited, and in a sense, even defective. As
such they are incapable of comprehending the reality.

Inadequacy of Sense-Experience

Through the senses only external features of the objects are
known.   For example, when a rose is perceived, only its colour,
texture and similar other characters are known while its essence
remains unknown.   These sensory impressions do not touch the
core of the object, they are too superficial to be able to give an
idea of the reality.

Moreover, senses are not always reliable.   They very often
deceive us.   Illusions and hallucinations occur quite naturally
without even letting us suspect that we are being deluded.   Therefore it is not safe to pin absolute faith on the senses.

Again, sense-impressions themselves, at times, conflict with each
other. The same thing appears differently to different viewers
and also to the same viewer at different times.   The same coin
appears round from a particular distance and elliptical from a
different distance.   No two sense-apprehensions of the same object can be exactly alike.   How can then we hope to have an
impression of reality through the senses ?

Thus, Radhakrishnan feels that although sense-impressions
are otherwise useful they cannot give the knowledge of reality.

Inadequacy of Intellectual Cognition

Intellectual Cognition also is unable to give us the knowledge
of reality on account of the following reasons :
    (a) Intellectual deliberation rests on the presupposition of the
duality of the subject and the object. That which is non-dual —

the Absolute — cannot be known through a process that knows only after creating a separation between the knower and the known. (b) Intellect moves in the realm of relations only. Relations presuppose multiplicity. Thus, Intellectual knowledge is knowing by relating different entities with each other. Reality is One, and therefore above diversity and relations. Consequently, it cannot be known by intellectual or relational ways. (c) Intellectual Cognition is symbolic in nature and, as such, moves in the world of symbols. For knowing reality, on the other hand, it is essential to go beyond the symbols to the symbolised. (d) Intellect, in its deliberations, separates 'the what' from 'the that', and then by a kind of an intellectual synthesis tries to restore the unity of the two. But no amount of conceptual synthesis can restore the original unity of the reality, just as no treatment of a deep cut-wound can restore the original smoothness of the skin. (e) Intellect is not primary or original. It works on materials and data supplied by other sources. Hence, if any view of reality has to be based on intellect, it will have to presuppose not only intellect but those other sources also. (f) Intellect, in fact, is merely an aspect of our mental life; feeling, conation etc. are other aspects which also are equally important. A complete comprehension of reality will be possible only when all these aspects are taken into account and satisfied.

Intuitive Apprehension

It is on account of the fact that Sense-experience and Intelligence appear to Radhakrishnan as incapable of giving us the knowledge of reality that he comes to develop the concept of a third source of knowledge — that of Intuitive Apprehension.

Intuition is the direct realisation of its object. It is not knowledge by signs or symbols, it is a direct knowledge culminating in the highest kind of immediacy. In the Intuitive apprehension the distinction between the knower and the known completely vanishes, and their duality is completely destroyed. It is, in a sense, *knowing by becoming*. In the Intuitive apprehension the knower establishes an identity with the known. This can be illustrated by taking the example of anger. No intellectual deliberation can give us any idea of the emotion of anger. We can know it only by *being* angry. Intuition, therefore, establishes a unity — almost an identity between the knower and the known.

Explaining this point Radhakrishnan says that in Intuitive apprehension we become one with the truth, one with the object of knowledge. The object known is seen not as an 'object outside the self, but as a part of the self'.

Intuition and Sense-impression

Intuition has certain clear advantages over sense-impression and intellectual deliberations. Sense-experience can explore only external or superficial aspects of the object, whereas Intuition can apprehend its essence. Senses are liable to error. Intuition is infallible, it does not even need verification for judging the veracity of truths intuited. The need for verification is felt only when ideas are related to objects — only when there remains a difference between 'knowing a thing' and 'being a thing'.

In spite of this there is one point common to them both, which brings them closer to each other. Both of them apprehend their objects *directly* and *immediately.* Like sense-experience Intuition is knowing without the medium of anything and without the intervention of anything. That is why it is said that Intuition possesses the directness of the senses, and that Intuition is, in a sense, an extension of the process of perceiving to regions beyond the reach of the senses.

Intuition and Intellect

Intellectual Cognition also is not quite infallible. It is not free from doubt. Logical arguments are challengeable and can be rejected on the strength of equally strong arguments. Intellect studies both the outer and the inner aspects of objects, and yet it is indirect and symbolic. Its main tool is 'analysis' and so it fails to grasp the 'whole' nature of objects. *But* Radhakrishnan says that this must not lead us to suppose that intellect and intuition are quite opposed to each other.

In fact, Intuition needs intellect for the expression, elaboration and justification of its results. Intuition in itself is dumb. Its results, in order to be communicated to others have to be put in understandable and intelligible forms — and for this intellect is needed. Intellect, on the other hand, presupposes Intuition, without which its deliberations cannot start. The function of Intellect is 'analysis', but there must be something to be analysed, and that something must be a 'whole'. The whole as a whole can be grasped by Intuition alone. That gives to Intuition its primacy.

Nature of Intuitive Apprehension

It is evident from this that Radhakrishnan conceives Intuition, more or less, in Bergson's way. Intuition has the directness and unity of Instinctive knowledge and consciousness of the Intellect.

It is *direct* and *immediate* because it deals with the objects themselves and not with their signs or symbols. It deals with them without taking help from or without the intervention of anything else. Intuition is *self evident*. It is self-evident because it does not need the support of anything else for its expression. It is its own guarantee, its validity and truth become evident as soon as it takes place. Intuition gives a very *intimate knowledge* of its object because it is knowing by becoming. It is *not unpractical* or impossible, on the other hand, it is *natural to man*. Every one of us is capable of some intuition; ordinary examples taken from life can prove this.

Intuition thus conceived performs the functions of sense, instinct and intellect and does something more. It is on account of this special peculiarity of Intuition that it is capable of knowing reality.

A strong evidence of the exclusiveness of Intuition lies in the fact that certain aspects of life are open only to Intuition. The emotion of love, for example, baffles intellect. In order to know it one has to become a lover.

Judgments of value are possible only through Intuition. The worth of life, the belief in the highest good, and the belief in the moral nature of the universe are all realised through Intuition. We appreciate the beauty of Nature, we perceive moral qualities in human conduct — in these examples of aesthetic and moral sensibility we do not pause and think and then come to know; we come to know almost in a flash. Intuition, thus, makes us aware of the object in an act of sudden insight. This is evident even in the examples of ordinary Intuitions.

The general principle of life and logic and the basic assumptions of sciences are all known through Intuition. Unity, for instance, is one such assumption and we are aware of unity only intuitively. 'The deepest convictions by which we live and think', and 'the root principles of our thought and life' are not derived from perceptual experience or logical knowledge, but from intuition. Great Truths are not proved, but seen.

The knowledge of the self also is possible only through Intuition. How do I know that I am? Self-awareness, according to Radhakrishnan, is an intuitive awareness. In every act of feeling, willing and knowing the self is intuitively aware of itself as feeling, willing and knowing.

Giving a very vivid description of the nature of Intuition Radhakrishnan says, "Intuition is only the higher stage of intelligence, intelligence rid of its separative and discursive tendencies. While it liberates from the prejudices of the understanding, it carries our intellectual conclusions to a deeper synthesis. In stead of being an unnatural and mysterious process, it is a deeper experience, which by supplementing our narrow intellectual visions, amplifies it. Intuition is not an appeal to the subjective whims of the individual, or a dogmatic faculty of conscience or the uncritical morbid view of the psychopath. It is most complete experience we can possibly have. It is the experience which devout souls have in moments of spiritual exaltation or religious devotion."[1]

1. Radhakrishnan, *Reign of Religion in Contemporary Philosophy*, p. 439.

CHAPTER VII

SIR MOHAMMAD IQBAL

Life

Sir Mohammad Iqbal occupies a unique position in Contemporary Indian Thought. He is the only thinker of the recent times who tries to apply academic philosophical standards to Islamic thought. Most of the other Indian thinkers philosophise in the background of ancient Hindu tradition. Iqbal, although having the same philosophical spirit and temperament, carries the Islamic tradition with him; and yet, philosophically speaking, appears to be close to other Contemporary Indian thinkers in many respects.

Mohammad Iqbal was born in 1876 at Sialkot. He got his early education at Sialkot and Lahore. He had a uniformly good career and obtained his M. A. degree in Philosophy, after which he became a lecturer in the Oriental College. By that time his fame as a poet had begun to spread. In 1905 he went to Cambridge from where he obtained his Tripos, having carried out his studies under McTaggart. For some time he did research on Persian Metaphysics at Munich in Germany. In 1908, he returned to Lahore and joined the bar as a barrister. He never took his profession of law seriously and kept on pursuing his poetic interests which also bear the mark of his philosophical study and insight. He became very famous as a poet, but he never neglected his serious philosophical pursuits. In his old age he accepted a pension from the ruler of Bhopal, which he enjoyed till his death. He died at Lahore in 1938.

General Introduction

Iqbal himself says that the general aim of his philosophical thinking is the reconstruction of religious thought in Islam. That shows that the basic concepts and categories of Iqbal's metaphysics are derived from Islam. But, there were many other influences that determined and shaped his philosophical views. Persian Philosophy, particularly the various interpretations of Islamic thought, led Iqbal to think about the central religious themes of Islam. Then, there was the deep influence of Islamic mysticism on his views — specially of Sufism. His philosophical studies and his personal contact with great intellectuals of the West like McTaggart made a deep impression on his thought and moulded it both positively and negatively. The western philosophers whose philosophies influenced Iqbal's own thought were Bergson, Nietzsche, the British Idealists in particular and many others.

A student of Iqbal's philosophy will be tempted to raise a question at the very outset : Is Iqbal only a commentator on Islam or is he an original thinker ? There is no harm in saying almost unhesitatingly that he is both. His metaphysics is original both in its treatment of the basic metaphysical concepts, and, to some extent, in its content also. But, all the time, he is eager to point out that his metaphysics is not inconsistent with the Islamic trends of thought.

One particular aspect of his thought, which incidentally represents the fundamental project of Iqbal's philosophy will make his standpoint clear. Normally it is believed that traditional Islam is theistic in content, but pantheistic in outlook. It is theistic because the Islamic God is personal, its outlook is somewhat of the pantheistic type because extreme emphasis is laid on God's decree. The omnipotence of God and the ultimacy of Divine will have been emphasised very much. Along with this it is recommended that for salvation a complete surrender to the Divine Will is necessary. From these emphases one gets the impression that in traditional Islam there is a big metaphysical gulf between God and man. The religion of Islam tries to bridge up this gulf, but one feels that traditional Islam glorifies God so much that man relatively appears to be insignificant.

Iqbal proposes to re-surrect man. He tries to show that the entire universe (even God) is of the nature of an ego. He recommends an assertion and a development of the ego and thus comes to demonstrate that contrary to general impression God and man are not poles apart, but are akin in nature. He also tries to show that such a view is quite compatible with the teachings of Islam. Thus his intention is to remove the misunderstanding of the Quranic truths — to remove the impression that traditional Islam creates a gap between God and man. That is why he calls his own thought a reconstruction of Islamic truths. One notable feature of this reconstruction is that he moves with perfect ease in between his own notions and Islamic ideas.

This is evident from the consideration of another fact also. Although Islam is an example of theistic religion, some of its notions (for example, its extreme emphasis on monism) appear to be derived from pantheistic beliefs. In fact, some interpretations of Islam place it in between Theism and Pantheism. Iqbal shows very clearly that Islam is not pantheistic in any way, and that its emphasis on monism is like the theistic emphasis on the oneness of God. Iqbal's philosophy, then, can be described as a particular version of Theism, it emphasises those aspects of Theism, which usual Theism only broadly suggests but never clearly develops.

In trying to have an idea of Iqbal's philosophy we shall have to adopt a procedure somewhat different from the one that is usually adopted for outlining any religious or metaphysical philosophy. Iqbal tries to show that both the material world and God have to be conceived as having ego-propensities in them. Therefore, before analysing his theory of God or of Nature or of the world it is essential to explain the nature of the ego. Consequently, an account of Iqbal's philosophy of the self or the ego has to be given first. But, even before that the way in which the ego is known has to be determined. Iqbal feels that an intuition reveals to us the nature of the self. Therefore, before we take up the study of Iqbal's metaphysics the nature of intuition has to be clarified.

Nature of Intuition

Iqbal feels that the ultimate truths which religion and metaphysics seeks to emphasise are not known by us in the ordinary way. The ordinary way is the way of experience. Iqbal does not mean to suggest that the empirical way is a false way or that experience does not give any knowledge. He does give value and importance to both experience and thought, but he adds that these represent only a particular level of knowledge — the normal level. In this level whatever is known is known under space-time dimension and is useful from the empirical and pragmatic point of view. But the reality-in-itself, according to Iqbal, cannot be *directly* known in this manner. Thus, Iqbal is not in favour of denying the importance of sense-experience or of thought, but he feels that they approach reality in a very indirect manner, through the symbols of reality. But, it is possible to approach reality directly and to have a direct consciousness of reality. He says that the Quran has spoken about such a process. He gathers the Quranic ideas and develops them in the light of his own study and insight.

The Quran describes this source of knowledge — the one that can know reality directly — as *Faud* or *Qalb*, which has been translated as the *'heart'*. Iqbal describes it thus, "The 'heart' is a kind of inner intuition or insight which, in the beautiful words of Rumi, feeds on the rays of the sun and brings us into contact with aspects of Reality other than those open to sense-perception. It is according to the Quran, something which "sees", and its reports, if properly interpreted are never false. We must not, however, regard it as a mysterious special faculty, it is rather a mode of dealing with Reality in which sensation, in the physiological sense of the word, does not play any part. Yet the vista of experience thus opened to us is as real and concrete as any other experience."[1] This self-explanatory description of 'the heart' in Iqbal's own words clearly shows that 'the heart' is the faculty of *Intuition*. He feels that it is not a mysterious faculty. Intuitions, according to him, have played dominant roles in the history of mankind, they have influenced the life and behaviour of societies of all times and places, they have left enduring impressions on the mind of man. Therefore, Iqbal feels that this is not to be dismissed lightly as some persons at times try to do. This is the way through which Reality can be apprehended directly.

In order to be able to appreciate the nature of Intuition it is better to enumerate the characteristics of Intuition as they have been enumerated by Iqbal.

(1) A very prominent character of Intuition is *immediacy*. Intuition is immediate knowledge of Reality or God because it knows it without the help of any medium. Iqbal says that Intuition has the directness of sense-experience. It grasps its object directly as senses do. In this respect it is different from thought or conceptual knowledge that knows only through concepts or through an inferential process. But, it differs from sense-experience in so far as it does not need the help of any sense-organ.

1. Iqbal, *Six Lectures on the Reconstruction of Religious Thought in Islam*, p. 23.

Moreover, unlike sense-experience it always apprehends its object as a whole.

(2) The last point brings to light another characteristic of Intuition. Intuitive experience is always a whole — an unanalysable unity. Its unity can never be broken. It is knowing by being, because in intuitive awareness the distinction between the subject and the object vanishes altogether. In Intuition the knower becomes one with the known and thereby realises it.

(3) This experience, according to Iqbal, is a moment of very intimate relation with the Supreme. Iqbal says that it is an awareness of God, 'a feeling of the presence of the Divine'. Iqbal is aware of the usual criticisms of an assertion like this. It may be said that there is no evidence of the direct knowledge of the Divine presence. Naturally, the question arises, 'On what basis or ground can such an assertion be made ?' 'How, for example, do we come to know that the known being is the Divine Self ?

Iqbal says that this process is not very different from the process by which we become aware of the presence of other minds. We do not become aware of their presence with the help of any special faculty. The only ground of my knowledge of other minds is the awareness of the physical movements similar to my own, from which I infer the presence of other minds. The other minds are believed to be there on account of my awareness of some kind of 'response' in between me and the other. Similarly, in a similar realisation — in an awareness of some kind of 'response' in between me and the Supreme, I become conscious of the Supreme self.

(4) The Intuitive experience, according to Iqbal, is not a mere subjective state into which the individual retires, it is not just the private and personal experience of a particular individual. Iqbal says that this experience has an *objectivity* about it. Its object is not the fancy of an individual's intellect, it transcends the individual and causes an awareness in which the individual feels that the object — the Supreme *self* — is *there*.

(5) Intuition, according to Iqbal, is not the property of the mind or the intellect, it is the property of 'the heart'. Intellect knows its object after creating a distinction between the knower and the known, but, the heart, establishes an affinity with its object; in fact, in a sense, it becomes the object. That is why it is said that Intuition is knowledge by the heart.

(6) Intuitive experience enables an individual to realise 'eternity' in a moment. In the moment of this experience time comes to a stop — it is transcended. This experience enables the individual to forget the worries and anxieties of mundane existence and lifts him up in an entirely different world altogether. Iqbal describes this character of Intuition by saying that this experience gives to the individual a sense of the unreality of *serial time*. The mystic experience fades away very soon and the individual returns to serial time, but the moment in which he gets the experience continues to inspire him. It makes him realise that serial time can be transcended and that eternity can be realised in a moment.

(7) Iqbal unhesitatingly asserts that this experience is incommunicable. Incommunicability is taken as a defect of Intuitive apprehension by many unsympathetic critics of Intuition. On account of such a criticism many believers in the authenticity of this experience start asserting that it is not incommunicable and that it is possible to communicate the truths known by Intuition in ordinary understandable language. But Iqbal is not dismayed by such criticisms. He is frank enough to assert that these truths cannot be communicated. Its incommunicability is due to the fact that it is a function of the heart and involves feeling untouched by discursive reason. That does not mean that the person having the intuitive experience can do nothing else but practise silence. Iqbal says that the content of this experience cannot be communicated as such. But the 'mystic' can interpret his experience in terms of verbal forms, and these interpreted truths can very well be communicated. He says that feeling has an inherent tendency to grow into idea and thus to assume a cognitive significance. It is through these *ideas* that we come to have an idea of the intuitive experience.

Objections against Intuition Considered

Thus, Intuition, according to Iqbal, is the direct awareness of the reality. It knows its object not by relating it with the subject; on the other hand, it knows 'by becoming the object'. In order to clarify its nature still further and to defend it Iqbal anticipates certain possible objections against the authenticity of Intuition and meets them. He also enumerates some of the objections that have actually been raised against it, and tries to give suitable replies to them.

(1) One of the most radical objections against Intuition is that there is no ground for asserting that Intuition can know the Supreme reality or God. The question of the possibility of knowledge is raised only when the existence of the object is either established or presupposed. For example, with respect to any physical object we can say that it can be known through the senses only because the physical object is there. But, the existence of God cannot be asserted in that way. Therefore, the problem of the possibility of its knowledge by intuition does not arise. Iqbal says that an objection of this type is based on the presupposition that sense-experience is the only way of getting knowledge. The objector does not realise that this would unnecessarily limit the scope of knowledge. Over and above this, there are other levels of experience and of knowledge. This becomes evident on consideration of the fact that there are many *known* things which go beyond the scope of the senses. Besides this, the testimony of many reliable seers and prophets strengthens the conviction that it is possible to have a direct awareness (not through the senses) of the Divine.

(2) Another objection that is usually raised against Intuition is that there is nothing special or extra-ordinary about it. If we analyse the nature of, what is generally called, intuitive experience we shall find that it can very well be explained and determined in terms of physical, physiological and psychological factors. The type of training and education that one gets, the atmosphere in which one grows, the associations and habits that one forms, the mood and temperament that one is able to cultivate — all these will clearly explain and determine the so-called intuitive experience. Therefore, the objector may point out, there is no need for giving any special status to Intuition.

Iqbal says that an objection of this kind is not an objection at all. No body can deny that an experience — of whatever kind it may be — does depend on the factors mentioned in the objection. It is true that even for intuitive experience a particular kind of psychological make-up, mood, temperament etc. would be necessary. But this does not prove the unreliability or the inauthenticity of Intuitive experience. Whatever be the process for preparing an individual for the intuitive mood, the fact remains that this is capable of giving the knowledge of reality.

(3) A very usual objection against Intuition is that it is not a normal process. It is said that such experiences are the

abnormal products of disorganised brains. Persons who indulge constantly in such acts of experience can, by no standards of sanity, be called normal.

Iqbal meets this objection in a very effective way. Firstly, he says that this objection is based on the presupposition of an imaginary level of normalcy. What is the dividing line in between the normal and the abnormal ? In fact, every experience that makes us aware of something and upon which life can be based is normal. Intuitive experience easily satisfies these two conditions. It does make us aware of a reality and it brings about almost a change in the personality of the individual. Secondly, Iqbal refers to the testimony of history and says that history bears witness to the fact that the life and activities of mankind have always been based on such experiences of seers or prophets or prominent leaders of men. Thirdly, Iqbal says that if this objection is true, even a genius will appear to us as an abnormal or a neurotic. The ways and behaviour and the cognitions and experiences of a genius appear to be different from those of a normal man. That does not mean that the genius is abnormal or insane. Had that been so, there would not have been any progress in any field whatsoever.

Iqbal meets this objection in a different way also. He feels that those who raise an objection like this tacitly assume that they are great psychologists of human nature. They do not see that their so-called psychological analysis is based on the analysis of only such men whom they consider to be normal from before. They never try to investigate into the nature of the mind of the genius — or a gifted seer. How is it possible to arrive at a conclusion regarding what happens in the mind of a genius only on the basis of a study of the minds of 'normal' men ?

Thus, Iqbal says that this objection is based on the assumption that whatever normal individuals can know through their usual organs of sense and intellect is knowledge. This assumption itself appears to Iqbal as wrong.

(4) Some persons may say that mystical experiences, infact, preach escapism. An emphasis on Intuition, according to them, is negation of the value of worldly pursuits, it merely takes the individual to a world of fancy. Such imaginative satisfaction may initially appear to be attractive, but the individual is bound to be disillusioned sooner or later.

Iqbal admits that there have been religions who preach some form of escapism. But, he says that this is not the essence of religion, as it is not true of all religions. He says, "that there are religions and forms of act, which provide a kind of cowardly escape from the facts of life, I do not deny. All that I contend is that this is not true of all religions."[1]

(5) In this connection Iqbal makes a mention of and examines the objection against religion raised by Freud and others. They say that what goes in the name of religion, and for which the sanction of Intuition seems to be necessary, is nothing but the expression of such repressed wishes and desires which had remained unfulfilled, and which had been repressed and sent to the unconscious. Religion, according to this view, is an imaginary wish-fulfilment. "Religious beliefs and dogmas, according to the theory, are no more than merely primitive theories of nature, whereby mankind have tried to redeem reality from its elemental ugliness and to show it off as something nearer to the heart's desire than the facts of life would warrant."[2]

Iqbal says that it is because the Freudians fail to understand the nature of religious facts like intuitive experience that they talk about the region of the unconscious. They say that religion or intuition takes us to the world of fancy — far removed from the world of facts. But, what is 'the unconscious' ? Is it not just giving a 'name' to something that is completely unknown ? Actually these persons are over-zealous to explain everything in terms of some causal factors just because a scientific explanation is an explanation of this kind. When they are not able to explain religion thus, they posit a cause in the unconscious. They do not realise that a religious explanation is something different. Religion is not Physics or Chemistry. It is concerned with a kind of experience the data of which cannot be completely reduced to the usual ways of science.

(6) Iqbal examines the psychoanalytic account of religion still further. Freud says that the repressed wishes which are satisfied even in religious acts and beliefs are generally sexual in character. Jung does not say this; but, more or less, in the same vein maintains that religious drives are primitive in nature, some-

---

1. Iqbal, *Six Lectures on the Reconstruction of Religious Thought in Islam* p. 32.
   2. *Ibid.*

what biological, and seek to put certain restrains, ethical or
otherwise, on the impulsive character of the original drives.

Iqbal says that it is not possible to explain religious consciousness either in terms of Freudian *Libido* or Jung's *Racial Unconscious.* In fact, even an ordinary insight will reveal that the
sexual impulse and the religious urge are generally opposed,
even hostile to each other. An ordinary insight, again, will
reveal that the essence of religion is not what these people think
it to be, its aim is to come in direct contact with and to realise
the Reality, its aim is to be one with something higher. Religious
urge is satisfied not by the ways suggested by Freud or Jung,
but by coming in contact with the Supreme. Intuitive experience
is the only way in which this contact can be brought about.

Thus, Intuitive experience, according to Iqbal, is the only
possible source through which Reality can be known. This experience is strictly personal. Its *content* cannot be communicated.
That does not mean that it does not have any significance or
value for others. The seer can interpret the truths intuited by
him in his own verbal forms or propositions, and they can very
well be communicated to others.

Nature of the Self

In outlining his conception of the self Iqbal follows a particular procedure. He first states the organic view of man, and
then refers to some of the interpretations of this view by the
different sects and schools of Islam. In particular he makes a
mention of the views of Devotional Sufism, specially to the
famous expression of Hallaj — '*Anal Haq*' or 'I am the creative
truth.' He tries to organise the salient features of all these ideas
and then arrives at his own conception of the Self. 'Anal Haq'
particularly seems to have provided to Iqbal the rudiments of his
own notion of the self.

Before giving an account of this, it would be worthwhile to
determine the general meaning of the word 'self'. What is it that
the word stands for or denotes ? We shall see that Iqbal's meaning of the word is not very different from this, although he lays
emphasis on some such elements that are not ordinarily emphasised very much. Our life, in a sense, consists of a number of experiences, and the word 'self' is used to denote the entity that
somehow unifies these experiences into one unit. It is the prin-

ciple that organises the activities and the experiences of an individual, and gives them a significance different from the bodily. That is why the 'self' is generally understood as other than the body. Iqbal admits that the self is the principle of unity in the individuals, but he asserts that it is not opposed to the bodily. According to him, the self gives unity even to bodily activities.

In order to make this point clear Iqbal first states the Quranic conception of the self and then develops it by adding to it his own ideas and by giving to it newer interpretations wherever necessary. It is on account of his belief in the validity of the Islamic conception of the self that he prefers to use the word 'Ego' for the self. Both these words — 'the self' and 'the ego' are similar, but whereas the word 'self' somehow gives the impression of being something over and above the body, the word 'ego' denotes the complete individual comprehending both its passional vitality and its spiritual propensity.

Iqbal says that the Quran emphasises the *individuality* and *uniqueness* of man. According to him the Quranic conception of man lays emphasis on at least three aspects of man, (a) that man is the chosen of God, (b) that man, with all his faults, is meant to be the representative of God on earth, (c) that man is the trustee of a free personality which he accepted at his own peril. Iqbal feels that various schools of Islam overlooked the importance of these aspects of man perhaps on account of their obviousness. It is quite evident that an emphasis on these characters means and demonstrates the centrality of man. But the followers of Islam instead of developing these concepts, concentrated on some other metaphysical questions, on account of which even the centrality of man was thrown in the background and the metaphysical nature of man remained unclear. Ghazzali, for instance, conceives the self as something simple, indivisible and unmutable, as something over and above the mental states, that abides in and through changes. Iqbal does not believe in this. He says that we do not have any ground for believing in such a metaphysical entity. On what evidence can we establish soul's simplicity or immutability ? Morever, if the soul is conceived as simple many of our complex psychological phenomena, like that of Double personality, cannot be explained.

In the same way Iqbal is not prepared to accept any pantheistic account of the soul because it reduces the soul to unreality. He asserts that there is no experiential evidence in favour of the

unreality either of the soul or of the world. There are some interpreters of Islam who give even to Islam a pantheistic interpretation and make it a peculiar inter-mixture of Theism and Pantheism. They over-emphasise the monistic character of God, call
God the Supreme Reality, and by implication mean that the
world or the soul cannot have an independent reality.

Iqbal somehow asserts that we have got to accept the reality
of the self. This belief is the starting point of Iqbal's philosophy
and he feels that this belief is not inconsistent with the general
trend of Islamic thought. He thinks that even Pantheism cannot
reject the reality of the self. Such a rejection becomes self-contradictory because even to reject the reality of the self, the self has
to be accepted as the one who rejects.

Therefore, to understand this problem an insight into the
nature of the 'ego' is essential. Psychology cannot explain its
nature properly, because Psychology is concerned with the sur-
face-activities of the ego. Psychology reduces it to a flux — to
a series of processes like sensing, thinking, feeling etc. To grasp
the true nature of the ego it is necessary to have an intuition of
what is behind this flux. Iqbal is aware of the difficulties that
one faces in trying to give a description of the ego. That is because its nature can be grasped only by an intuitive insight, which
generally one does not care to cultivate.

Such an insight tells us that there is somehow a unity behind
the flux, a unity of the mental states. No mental state can exist
in isolation, there is a unity organising all the mental states.
This unity is different from the unity seen in material objects.
Parts of a material object can exist in isolation, mental states
cannot. We cannot say that my feelings have no relation
whatsoever with my cognitions or with my thought. This
principle of unity of my inner life or of the mental states is the
ego. It is the ego which keeps all experiences organised in a
unity.

The unity of the ego is unique in the sense that such a unity
is found only in the ego. Its uniqueness is revealed also by its
quality of essential privacy. The activities of the ego are essentially personal and private. For example, my desire for a certain
thing is *my* desire, and it cannot be satisfied if others get the
object of my desire. The dentist may sympathise with my
toothache, but cannot experience the feeling of my toothache.
My pleasures, pains, desires and thoughts are exclusively my own.

This description of the ego shows that various affections and experiences are felt and organised by the ego and are given a final shape and direction. Quoting a relevant verse from the Quran and expressing the significance of the words *khalq* (meaning creation) and *Amr* (meaning direction) Iqbal says, "The verse...means that the essential nature of the soul is directive, as it proceeds from the directive energy of God, though we do not know how divine 'Amr functions as ego — unites."[1]

This means that a clear line of distinction cannot be drawn in between the soul and the body. Iqbal appears to be against the doctrine of *parallelism* of the body and the soul and seems inclined to reject even inter-actionism. He feels that both these doctrines fail to explain adequately the relation between the body and the soul. Parallelism makes them passive spectators of each other. According to this theory, in spite of the fact that body and mind run parallel to each other, they remain unaffected by the activities of the other. Interactionism, on the other hand, raises the difficulty regarding the exact place or locus where interaction takes place. Therefore Iqbal conceives their relation in a different way. He says that both the soul and the body are *systems of acts* and as activities they are close to each other. The nature of the activities of the body is repetitive or somewhat mechanical, whereas the acts of the ego are spontaneous and free. But the initiation of the body also comes from the activities of the soul. Iqbal says, "the body is accumulated action or habit of the soul; and as such undetachable from it."[2]

This description of the nature of the relation between the body and the soul throws light on another character of the self. The self is a series of activities, and as such must need an environment on which it will act or to which it will react. In his actions and reactions he will utilise even the body. Thus, the egos cannot remain in complete isolation, they must have a world. The ego is confronted with the world of the non-ego, and it is through his experiences of this world of the non-ego, that the life of the ego grows and develops.

From this Iqbal deduces two other characters of the ego (a) Firstly, the life of the ego is not a mechanical life, it is steadily trying to realise some purpose. (b) The life of the ego is constituted

1. Iqbal, *Six Lectures on the Reconstruction of Religious Thought in Islam*, p. 143.
2. *Ibid.*

by the experiences, feelings and volitions of the ego. The first throws light on the teleological character of Iqbal's philosophy. This quality is apparent even in his philosophy of the self. The actions and reactions in between the ego and the non-ego enrich the life of the ego, and it is through these that the ego grows. That shows that the ego is not a mechanical product of the environment, that he is capable of meeting and facing the environment in its own way. Secondly, the fact that life of the ego is a series of activities performed in the face of some challenge from the environment shows that his cognitions, feelings and volitions determine his life. Iqbal attaches very great importance to volition because in certain respects even cognitions and feelings are the results of certain decisions taken by the individual. Moreover, the fact that the ego is also a series of activities highlights the essentially volitional nature of the ego. Iqbal speaks particularly about *desires* and says that desires have a creative power within them — a capacity to arouse us and to stir us to action. It is this *creative-capacity* or *Soz*, as Iqbal calls it, that represents the core of our ego-life. Desires have the power to arouse this *Soz*. Taking the example of *'Ishq'* (or love), Iqbal says that this is a very forceful example of intense desire, and that a simple insight into the nature of love will show how this desire constitutes the ego and gives to it a new meaning and significance.

Now, we are in a position to explain one of the most prominent characters of the self, namely *freedom*. We have seen that the ego is conceived, on the one hand, as that which is organised and disciplined by its own experiences, and on the other, as that which is determined by its relation to the environment. That raises the question, does the ego determine its own activities or is it causally determined by something else ? Modern physical theories try to show that all our activities are determined by our physical conditions and material requirements. They go to the extent of developing a theory of physical behaviourism and try to show that even consciousness and thinking can be reduced to physical and physiological processes. But, Iqbal says that this does not prove that the ego is not free in its activities. The physical or the physiological patterns do not determine the ego, on the other hand, they are the means through which ego performs its activities. It has the capacity to choose its course of action, everything ultimately depends upon its own choice and decision. Moreover, it is capable of affecting and regulating even physical behaviour as it exercises a directive control over the body. This shows that the ego is free.

In fact, mechanical causation does not appear to Iqbal as the final truth. This is evident from the fact that man can change his environment and make it conform to its own needs and purposes. Obstructions or hindrances of the non-ego or of the environment only arouse and sharpen the power and insight of the ego. In the face of obstruction the ego is capable of putting out his best.

Iqbal feels that the ego potentially is capable of infinite freedom. In his finite activities it appears to be limited, but if its powers are cultivated fully its freedom would know no bounds. Even in his finite existence he is somewhat free in taking his own decisions. An extension of this freedom will make his ego-activities overcome the obstacles that normally limit his freedom.

Another important character of the self has to be emphasised in order to clarify its nature fully. That character is *Immortality*. Iqbal believes in the doctrine of Personal immortality and substantiates his view by referring to the Quran. According to him Immortality appears to be both the nature of the self and his ultimate destiny. The self is immortal in spite of the apparent fact of death. There is no inconsistency in believing that immortality represents both the nature and the destiny of the individual. One can never become anything which he is not already. Normally, the self's sense of immortality remains shrouded by the physical and the bodily conditions, but the self survives death and is immortal.

Nature of the World

Contemporary Indian thinkers are aware that the present-day intellectual deliberations cannot afford to go against the assertions of the sciences. Iqbal also feels the same way, he also is aware that science has succeeded in determining the nature of the material world. Therefore, like other contemporary Indian thinkers, he also comes to assert the reality of the world. He has his justification for making this assertion, but his belief in the reality of the world is categorical and unqualified. He is very much a realist in maintaining that the external world exists and is real.

Iqbal says that an intuitive insight will reveal the reality of the world. One kind of intuition makes us conscious of our selves and makes us aware of a principle of unity that organises our experiences. Another intuition tells us that we are pitted against a world of non-ego. In all our actions we feel that forces other than the ego obstruct us. Thus this intuition forces us to accept the reality of the obstruction and of the environment. Iqbal feels that without accepting the reality of the world we shall not be able to explain our experiences and behaviour.

What, then, is the nature of the material world ? Normally it is believed that the physical world is the world of matter extended in space and time. It is held that there are certain basic material particles which come in association with each other in space and time and thus constitute the material world. Iqbal believes that such a materialistic account of the world is not acceptable. Neither science nor philosophical reasoning will support such a view. This view pre-supposes a particular conception of space and time, which itself is not acceptable. Therefore, before trying to understand the nature of the material world, it is essential to be acquainted with Iqbal's conception of space and time.

1. Space and Time

There have been various conceptions of Space and Time, but they can broadly be brought under two general heads: the Absolutistic or the Objective conception of Space and Time and the Relative conception of Space and Time. The most popular version of the Absolutistic notion of space and time is that Space and Time are objective frame-works in which objects exist. Space is conceived as the form and order of co-existence and Time as that of succession. It is on such a conception of space and time that the materialistic conception of the world bases itself.

Iqbal says that Kant was the first thinker to realise the defect of such a conception of space and time, and therefore he came to conceive them not as objective entities but as subjective forms of perception. Iqbal also feels that the objective conception of space and time is not tenable if not on any other ground, at least on the ground that it is inconsistent with itself. Space and time are conceived as objective frameworks in which objects exist. But it is almost obvious that it is not space or time that gives sustenance to the objects, but that space and time themselves are sustained on account of the objects. If we take out all the objects from space and time, space will shrink to a point and time to a moment. This is why Iqbal commends Kant for realising the inherent defect of the objective conception of space and time.

But Iqbal feels that Kant also made the mistake of emphasising the subjective nature of space and time instead of emphasising its character of relativity. Kant, according to him, has not been able to realise that 'being relative' is by far more comprehensive than 'being subjective', the former may include the latter. It is on account of this lapse on the part of Kant that he had to limit space and time to the phenomenal world only.

Iqbal makes a special mention of Iraqui's views on the nature of Space. According to him there are three kinds of space — that of material objects, that of non-material beings and that of God. Likewise, time also, according to him, can be of these three types. Iqbal perceives one great merit in his views. By talking about more than one space and more than one time Iraqui is able to explode the myth regarding one objective space or time. But even he makes the mistake of taking space and time as something fixed and given. Iqbal says that Space and Time are relative. For example, the view of space has to be relative to the sense-experience through which space is apprehended. If the world is apprehended by one sense only, it will give a different impression of space than what can be had if the world is apprehended by more than one sense. To the snail, for example, the world will appear as one-dimensional, to some other creature it may appear as two-dimensional, and to man it appears as three-dimensional having length, breadth and depth as its dimensions.

Thus, Iqbal comes to feel that Space and Time are relative. They are relative not only to the different grades of being, but also to the different levels of experience of the same being. The impressions of space and time that we have will be different from the impression of space and time that other animals may have. But, even in our case our impressions of space and time may vary in accordance with the different levels of experience with which we may look at them. Time, for example, will appear to be just a succession of moments if it is viewed from the ordinary level, but if we view at it from the level of reflection, its impression will be different. We shall realise that the time which appeared very long to the ordinary experience, appears to be very short when viewed reflectively. Again, as Bergson thinks, at the intuitive level we do not have the impression of time as succession. At that level we take time to be one *duration* incorporating in its bosom and advancing along with all the moments which appear to ordinary intellect as merely succeeding each other. Thus, Iqbal says that space and time are relative even to the levels of experience. They are relative to the psychic or mental capacities of the ego.

2.   *The World as an Ego*

If such is the nature of space and time, we shall not be logically justified in believing that the world consisted of fixed substances or things located in objective space and time. What, then is the nature of the material world ?

Iqbal says that it is not possible to have an idea of the material world through ordinary sense-impression or intellectual apprehension. Both these faculties work on one basic presupposition, namely, that the world before our view is there — rigid, fixed and static. When senses or intellectual deliberations apprehend the object, they work under the belief that the object continues to be in the same state in which it had been when contacted initially. Thus they view at the object in the traditional mould of space and time without realising that every object is essentially a dynamic process of growth and development.

Therefore, Iqbal asserts that it is intuition that can reveal the true nature of the physical world. Iqbal, at this place, seems to be influenced by Bergson, who says that intuition reveals reality as a continuously changing, developing and growing process and as constituting a duration. Iqbal is not completely at one with Bergson because he does not give to the ego its proper place in his philosophy of duration. Iqbal feels that an intuition into the nature of time and life-process reveals the centrality of the ego. Bergson had not realised this initially, but even he had to make room for this in his philosophy of consciousness.

What does intuition say with respect to the nature of the physical world ? Iqbal says that we have a direct intuition of the self and that a further intuition tells us that the world can be conceived in the analogy of what we have known about the self through Intuition. The self is revealed to us as a continuous and changing flow of feelings, volitions and cognitions. These states are so continuous that one cannot determine where the one ends and the other begins. Iqbal seems to have utilised Bergson's notion of duration with very great advantage. Even Bergson says that one can have an idea of duration in his awareness of intense feeling. In that state all aspects of experience inter-mingle with each other in an indistinguishable manner; and what is known is a 'whole' expressing the force of life — the *elan vital*. Iqbal goes a little further and says that such is the nature of all ego-activities. An intuition into the nature of the activities of the ego reveals pure duration in which past, present and future run into each other and appear almost simultaneously. The ego is revealed as life, as activity and as continuous growth.

The physical world is understood in the analogy of the self. Therefore, the physical or the material world is conceived as continuous movement. In fact, in his philosophy of the physical world Iqbal utilises ideas taken from Bergson, Nietzsche and Schopenhauer and synthesises them with the Islamic ideas. Like Bergson he says that the material world is life, change and movement. He further emphasises the primacy of will or volition even in the realm of the physical. This reminds us of Schopenhauer. In explaining the volitional nature of the world he speaks about the importance of 'impulses' and says that even the physical world can be reduced to certain expressions of impulses. This idea appears to be similar to some of the basic notions of Nietzsche.

Viewing these ideas in a general way Iqbal tries to present a picture of the world. He finds that the universe also exhibits a *tendency to egohood*. The universe manifests a clear tendency to grow as an individual. An individual is an organisation of all its parts. In an individual the whole-part relationship is of a special order. The parts cannot subsist apart from the whole. In a sense, it can be said that the whole is in every part of the individual. That is why an individual is an individual. Iqbal says that the universe exhibits a tendency of that sort. Although it appears that there are diverse and discreet aspects of the universe, there is an inner unity among them all; all these aspects appear as aspects of the totality.

There is yet another subtle distinction that Iqbal is able to make. An individual, in a sense, is a unity of individuals. If we survey the functioning of any aspect of an individual, we shall find that it itself functions as an individual. An interesting conclusion follows, the entire physical world may be viewed as an individual, and along with it even the different aspects of the world may be viewed as separate individuals. That is why Iqbal says that every detail of the world is an ego, and that the totality is the ego of the egos.

It necessarily follows from this that the universe is steadily progressing towards the realisation of some end or purpose. Iqbal believes in the teleological conception of the world. It is the inherent nature of the ego to grow and to rise to higher levels of its activity. In our life we fix up new ideals and make efforts to attain them. That is how we grow. The world-process also is ever striving to realise newer and newer ends.

The world, then, is of the nature of an ego, it is life and activity. It is essentially creative in nature, and as such, it is constantly growing. It has *a reason* and *a purpose* and also *a plan*. At present, we are not mentally so equipped as to be able to understand fully the reason and the plan of the universe. But, the world-process clearly exhibits a tendency towards progress, towards the realisation of some end.

One very interesting conclusion that Iqbal arrives at is that we cannot think of the end of the world-process. It is infinite progression. There are infinite possibilities that it can realise, and therefore, it will go on realising higher and higher ends. No state of the world can be final, at no stage the law of continuous growth ceases to operate.

God

Like many other prophetic religions Islam also believes in Monotheism. It conceives God as one, omnipotent, all-knowing, and supremely good creator of the world. It believes that God is a personal God. The distinction between God and the Absolute appears to be irrelevant to Islam. Iqbal tries to develop such a notion of God and shows that it satisfies not only the religious urge of man, but also his metaphysical curiosity. The nature and attributes of God have been interpreted from that point of view.

i *On the Traditional Proofs for the Existence of God*

Iqbal does not attach much value to the traditional proofs for God's existence. He feels that the Cosmological, Ontological and the Teleological proofs for God's existence are attempts on the part of our limited intellect to comprehend the nature of God. He feels that as proofs they are utterly inadequate because they are somehow based on a superficial interpretation of experience and not on an intuitive experience of reality.

Criticising the Cosmological argument Iqbal says that it is manifestly inconsistent with the nature of the Causal law. It views the world as an effect and through a series of causes and effects arrives at a first uncaused cause just in order to avoid, what is called, *infinite regress*. But such an argument is obviously defective. Firstly, the supporters of this argument do not realise that a finite effect can be caused only by a finite cause, and involves an infinite series of finite causes. Secondly, it is against the nature of the law of causation to stop at a particular step arbitrarily and to elevate it to the status of the first cause. The fear of infinite regress is too weak a ground for the rejection of the scientific notion of an infinite series. Thirdly, the cause reached by this argument cannot be a necessary cause because being a cause it is inherently relative to the effect. Thus, Iqbal feels that this argument tries to reach the infinite God by superseding the finite; but the fact remains that the infinite so reached will only be a false infinite.

Likewise, Iqbal feels that the Teleological argument for God's existence also fails to prove what it wants to prove. This proof gathers evidences of order, harmony and purpose in the world and on their basis comes to assert that there is a supreme intelligence behind the universe. Iqbal says that such an argument can only show that God is merely a contriver and a designer of the world. It does not prove that God is the *creator* of the world. But the most effective objection against this proof is the one that attacks the very presupposition of this proof. Iqbal says that the analogy on which this argument is based is a defective and bad analogy. It is based on the analogy of the work of human contrivance. It presupposes that there is a basic similarity between human creation and Divine creation. But Iqbal says that they are not similar. A work of human creation involves isolation of materials and then their rearrangement. But in God's creation (i.e. Nature) everything is inter-related with every other thing in such a way that isolation or separation of anything from others is not possible. Hence the two are not similar, and therefore an argument based on the presupposition of their similarity is obviously defective.

The Ontological argument also, in spite of its appeal is not free from defects. It tries to arrive at the existence of God on the basis of an analysis of the notion of God itself. But Iqbal says that this proof does not prove the *existence* of God. It merely succeeds in showing that the idea of God includes the *idea* of his existence. Moreover he says, "Between the idea of a perfect Being in my mind and the objective reality of that Being there is a gulf which cannot be bridged over by a transcendental act of thought."[1] Again, he says that the Ontological argument suffers from the fallacy of *Petitio Principii* in so far as it tacitly assumes what it seeks to prove. The point in question is whether a transition is possible from the ideal or the mental to the exist-ent, and this precisely is what is done in the Ontological proof; in it a transition is made from the mental to the existent.

Thus, we see that according to Iqbal 'proofs' do not give the knowledge of God. For this Iqbal leans on the authority of *Intuition.* Just as an intuition reveals the nature of the self or of the world so an intuition reveals the nature of God also. Iqbal is convinced that this is the only way in which God's existence can be apprehended. We can do nothing else but describe, interpret and elaborate truths known through intuitive experience.

ii *God as the Supreme Ego*

According to Iqbal the universe is of the nature of a free creative force. He also says that the world-process is not blind but purposive. The teleological character of the world shows that the world-process is being rationally directed. He says further that rational egos have the capacity to regulate and direct their own creative life. Therefore we are constrained to think that there is a Being directing the creative life of the universe. That Being cannot be Outside the universe, because in that case the end and the goal of the world would become

1. Iqbal, *Six Lectures on the Reconstruction of Religious Thought in Islam*, p. 42.

external. Thus, the supreme Ego is conceived as guiding the creative progress of the world.

In fact, Iqbal believes that individuality is a matter of degrees. There is a rising note of egohood through out the universe, it has not reached perfection even in human beings. Therefore, Iqbal comes to conceive God as the Supreme Ego — as the ideal of egohood. It is from this point of view that Iqbal interprets the Quranic description of God as *Light*. This analogy of light has been used not only in Islam, but also in Judaism, Christianity and Zoroastrianism. Iqbal says that the teaching of modern Physics is that the velocity of light cannot be exceeded and that it is independent of perspectives and remains the same for all observers. Thus, the analogy of light gives an impression of immense dynamism — of continuous and ceaseless movement. Iqbal thinks that light is the nearest metaphor for understanding the nature of the Absolute Ego, which is the most perfect embodiment of dynamic and creative life.

At this point a doubt may be raised : 'Is it not a fact that individuality implies finitude ?' If God is an ego, can we conceive Him as infinite ? Iqbal says that this problem appears to be a problem because we place the infinite in space-time-dimension. We have seen that space and time are not absolute dimensions that can limit the Supreme ego. The Supreme Ego is infinite in the sense that it has infinite creative possibilities within it, of which creation is only an expression. God's infinity involves an infinite series of expressions, even space and time are expressions of the possibilities of God.

iii *Attributes of God*

Now, we are in a position to discuss the main attributes of God as they have been conceived by Iqbal. The attributes are generally theistic and are taken from Islam, but the interpretations of Iqbal carry the mark of his academic philosophical training. He makes a distinction between the attributes apprehended by intuitive insight and those known through intellectual deliberations. In a sense, the former are not actually attributes, because they are apprehended as constituting the essence of God. Oneness, Egohood etc. are attributes of this type. That is why Iqbal gives a detailed analysis only of the intellectual attributes like *Creativeness, Knowledge, Omnipotence, Eternity, Immanence, Transcendence* etc.

Creativeness

This attribute appears to be a necessary attribute of God on account of the fact that God has been conceived as an ego. An ego-life is essentially a creative life. The Supreme Ego is also creative in the way in which an ego is creative. But Iqbal experiences a difficulty in arriving at this conclusion. The question of Divine creativeness raises another question : what is the manner in which Divine creativeness proceeds in the process of creation? Iqbal says that the orthodox but popular school of Muslim Theology, namely the Ashraite, hold that the creative method of Divine energy is *atomic*. The world, according to the Ashrites, is composed of indivisible atoms, the *Jawahirs*, as they have been called, and the creative energy of God keeps on creating fresh atoms every moment. Even space is regarded by them as an aggregation of atoms. Although the atomistic theory of the world has found some expressions in the recent time also, Iqbal finds it difficult to appreciate fully the Ashrites account, because he finds it difficult to reconcile it with a purely scientific point of view. Therefore, he interprets the attribute of creativeness in a different way. He says that the Supreme Ego, or God is creative in the *inner* way. This means that He creates completely from within himself. Finite creation proceeds by presupposing the reality of the other. For the Supreme Ego, there is no other, and therefore creation for him means the unfolding of his own inner possibilities. His creativeness is infinite because these possibilities are infinite.

Knowledge

Divine knowledge has also been understood in a similar manner. Knowledge, as applied to the finite ego, is discursive or intellectual knoweldge. This knowledge is based upon the distinction between the knower and the known. The finite ego, therefore, knows *the other* — the object being something different from the subject. But, God being all-comprehensive, there is no 'other' of God. The universe also is not existing in opposition to God. Therefore Divine knowledge cannot be a knowledge of the type of intellectual knowledge. Therefore, "in Him thought and deed, the act of knowing and the act of creating, are identical".[1] Divine knowledge is creational, and as there is nothing outside God He himself is the object of his knowledge. He creates as He knows, and knows as he creates. Divine knowledge, therefore, has been, understood as a *living and creative activity'* — almost as a kind of self-reflecting mirror.

Omnipotence

Iqbal says that omnipotence literally conceived means a blind and capricious power which knows no limits. But he says that the Quran does not view omnipotence in that manner. In the Quran the concept of Divine omnipotence is intimately connected with the concept of Divine wisdom. That is why whenever the Quran speaks about the evidence of Divine Omnipotence, it refers only to the instances of order and design.

The attribution of omnipotence to God raises the problem regarding the presence of evil in the world. The fact of pain is so universal and the experience of suffering is so vivid that this problem cannot be dismissed as a trivial problem. Iqbal is aware of its importance, and tries to solve this problem by making evil consistent with Divine omnipotence. He refers to the mythological stories regarding the original fall of man and interprets that story in a different way. The old Testament and also some interpretations of the Quran take the first act of disobedience on the part of Adam as the initial sin of man, and therefore, as a fall of man. They explain the presence of suffering and sin — of physical and moral evils — as the consequence of that fall. Iqbal views that legend in a different way; he feels that man's first act of disobedience was also his first act of free choice. In fact, freedom is a necessary pre-condition of goodness. Freedom does involve risks, because if man is given freedom; he can use it both ways, he can of course use his freedom rightly, but there remains the possibility of wrong choice also. Thus, Iqbal says that God has knowingly given to man a freedom. It involves a risk, but that God has made him free in spite of this risk shows that He has immense faith in man. Perhaps it is only in this way that it is possible to bring out the potentialities latent in man. In this way pain and suffering are necessary aspects of the fact of freedom. He says, "Good and evil,...though opposites,

---

1. Iqbal, *Six Lectures on the Reconstruction of Religious Thought in Islam.* p. 107.

must fall within the same whole".[1] Evil, therefore, does not contradict Divine omnipotence. Omnipotence, after all, has not to be conceived as a whimsical or arbitrary capacity capable of doing everything and anything. It must appear to be a 'resonable' concept. It must be both emotionally and intellectually satisfying. Viewed thus the presence of evil is not inconsistent with the power of god.

Eternity

Eternity has not been conceived by Iqbal as a time-concept, it is not an idea of endlessness in time. Time, as we have seen is not conceived as a series of succeeding moments. Real time is *duration*, which leaves nothing behind and which potentially is everything that is to happen. God is eternal because He is the possibility of all expressions. Time-process is one of the expressions of the infinite possibilities contained in God. It is in this sense that God is eternal.

Immanence and Transcendence

Although Iqbal's theism is not deistic, he attributes to God the property of transcendence. The attribute of immanence is normally associated with pantheistic accounts of God. Iqbal is against Pantheism because of its acosmism. That is why Iqbal emphasises the transcendence of God. But that does not mean that he rejects immanence altogether. He says that God is both. He is not immanent in the world in the pantheistic sense of the term. He is immanent in the sense that the world is His creation. That is why the world reflects the ego-nature of its Creator. God is transcendent because the Supreme Ego is not within the grasp of the finite ego. The characters of immanence and transcendence can be undestood in a different way also. God is immanent in the world because the world is an expression of a Divine possibility, it transcends the world because there are infinite other possibilities that are yet to be realised.

In this way Iqbal feels that God is able to satisfy both the religious and the metaphysical demands. By conceiving God as a unity of infinite possibilities the metaphysical demand is satisfied, and by conceiving God as personal and as the Supreme

1. Iqbal, *Six Lectures on the Reconstruction of Religious Thought in Islam*, p. 118.

Ego, a way is opened for a direct communion between God and man, and in this way the religious demand is also satisfied.

Human Destiny

Iqbal tries to follow the Quranic account of human destiny and interprets it in the light of his own views regarding the nature of the soul. It can be said that the ultimate human destiny is the realisation of Immortality.

Immortality has been understood both as soul's nature and as his destiny. According to Iqbal these two descriptions of Immortality are not inconsistent with each other. However, these descriptions are not to be understood in an unqualified manner or in the Vedantic way. Immortality means deathlessness, and it is in this sense that it constitutes the nature of the soul. Death is not the end of the soul, the soul survives death and continues to exist even after it. The forms of his after-death state may not be determinable, but his survival after death is a fact, it is his *nature*. However this is not his destiny. The soul as an ego is an organisation of certain activities and potentialities. He will *be truly immortal* only when these potentialities are fully and freely expressed. That is his destiny — the realisation of his *ego-hood*, the realisation and free expression of all the potentialities contained in the self. Iqbal says that this can be realised through persistent and continuous action. It is in this sense that Immortality is the ultimate human destiny.

Iqbal takes up the Islamic idea of immortality and reviews it in the light of a number of influences — the theological interpretations of Islam, psychological and scientific accounts of man, the views of some important western thinkers like Kant, Bergson, Nietzsche and others. He seems to have been impressed particularly by Nietzsche's doctrine of *Eternal Recurrence*. Iqbal says that Nietzsche's doctrine is based on the assumption that the quantity of energy in the universe is constant and consequently *finite*. It follows from this (a) that the number of the centres of this energy is not infinite and (b) that there is no question of the dissipation of energy. These ideas help Iqbal in arriving at his conclusion.

Iqbal says that the Quranic view of the destiny of man is partly ethical and partly biological. It is biological because it refers to certain biological statements in its explanation of the immortality of soul; for example, it speaks about the state of *Barzakh* — a state in between death and resurrection. This account is ethical because immortality is conceived as a prize that can be won by pursuing certain ethical disciplines and activities.

Interpreting the Quranic idea of immortality Iqbal says that the Quran is clear at least in emphasising three points with respect to Immortality, (a) that the finite ego has a beginning in time, (b) that there is no possibility of its return to the earth, and (c) that finitude of the ego is not a misfortune. A clarification and interpretation of these descriptions of Immortality will clarify Iqbal's own views, which, according to him, are not inconsistent with the Quranic teaching.

The first statement emphasises the finiteness and the humanness of man. The finite ego is a created being, as such it did not pre-exist before the emergence of the spatio-temporal world. The implication is that immortality must be conceived as the immortality of such a created and finite being. Immortality, therefore, does not mean attaining Godhood. The individual somehow has to remain as an individual even in immortality.

According to Iqbal Immortality does not mean obliteration of individuality. Whatever be the final fate of man (The Quran says that on the last day of judgment the final fate of man will be determined in the light of the deeds done by him in life), it does not imply the loss of individuality. The uniqueness of the individual is retained even in salvation.

The second statement mentioned above shows that immortality does not necessarily involve a belief in re-birth. It is not essential for the soul to be associated with another body after death. Once the soul is free from the fetters of the body, he is free from the bondage of birth or re-birth and awaits the final judgment with regard to his destiny.

The third statement is very significant as it gives a justification for the first statement and is able to dignify the status of the finite ego. The statement says that finitude must not be understood as a misfortune. It is because finitude is taken to be an evil that its negation is considered to be essential for the realisation of the ultimate destiny. Iqbal says that the supporters of such a view do not realise that the dignity or the uniqueness of the individual can be retained only if the individual is allowed to approach the Supreme with the irrepressible singleness of the 'individuality'. The last day of judgment as conceived by the Quran gives an opportunity to the individual to see for himself the consequences of his past actions and to face them.

Thus, the ultimate destiny of man is not a state completely free from the individuality of the self, it is not a mingling of the self into the Divine like the mingling of the river and the sea. It is a state in which the individual qua individual realises complete ego-hood. In this state all the potentialities of the ego are fully expressed, and the ego reaches the highest point of intensity. Iqbal says, "The unceasing reward of man consists in his gradual growth, in self-possession, in uniqueness and intensity of his activity as an ego....And the climax of this development is reached when the ego is able to retain full self-possession, even in the cause of a direct contact with the all-embracing ego."[1] This, according to Iqbal, is the ideal of *perfect manhood*.

Iqbal, at this point, anticipates an objection, in fact, such an objection is at times raised by the pantheistic Sufists. They say that if in the state of realisation the individuality of the ego is retained, then it would become difficult to justify the infinity of the Supreme Ego. Thus, the objection assumes the form of the question : how can the Infinite Ego and the finite egos remain distinct from each other ? Will this not affect the infinity of the Infinite Ego ? Iqbal meets this objection by saying that this objection is based on a misunderstanding of the true nature of the Infinite. The objection presupposes that infinity is infinity in extensity. Infinite extension absorbs and embraces all its finite expressions. True Infinity consists not in extensity *but in intensity*. Intensiveness of ego-activity expresses itself in its infinite form in the Supreme Ego; but that does not mean that the Supreme Ego will absorb within its bosom all the finite egos. Extensively regarded every individual is an aspect of the Spatio-temporal order, but regarded intesively every ego is a unique and distinct individual, is itself a centre of concentrated energy, although intimately related with that on which it depends for sustenance. We find an example of the intensive life of the ego in the state of intense passion or deep emotion; in that state the energy of the ego is concentrated in one direction. This concentration of energy is infinite in the Supreme Ego, but it does not rule

1. Iqbal, *Six Lectures on the Reconstruction of Religious Thought in Islam*, p. 163.

out the possibility of there being other centres of energy, which, although finite in relation to the Infinite, are themselves *distinct* centres of ego-activity.

One may, at this point, raise another doubt. He may say that this description is not in the line of the Islamic conception of God and man. In Islam very great emphasis is laid on God's decree, and a sort of a surrender to Divine will is recommended. That is why some faithful interpreters of Islam say that there is an element of *fatalism* in Islam. That shows that Iqbal's emphasis on the uniqueness of the ego and on the fact that the individuality of the ego is never obliterated is not consistent with Islamic teachings. If God's decree is supreme, and if our fate is to be decided by Him, then how can we assert the ultimacy of the individuality of the finite egos. Iqbal admits that this kind of fatalism has remained in Islam for centuries. Islam talks of *kismat* or fate almost in a helpless manner. Iqbal says that such an interpretation of Islam was given on account of the fact that powerful people wanted to kill the initiative of ordinary individuals by emphasising the value of *kismat* just in order to maintain and retain their own powers. In fact, the fatalistic tone of the Quran serves the purpose of emphasising the intensive character of the ego life. Prayer, for example, is one of the best illustrations of intensive living, it is not fatalism or a complete surrender to the forces of destiny. It is an expression of the power of the ego, not an acceptance of triviality on the part of the individual. That is why Prayer can be offered with perfect ease and concentration even on the battlefield.

Importance of Prayer

Iqbal's analysis of 'Prayer' becomes significant in relation to another question, 'how can the ego develop his ego-capacities'?

Iqbal believes that the world provides a field for ego-activity, an opportunity for the ego to express its potentialities. In fact, all activities performed in the world are ego-sustaining or ego-developing activities. Even the pleasure-giving or pain giving acts unfold and enrich the ego-capacities. Man has accepted at very great risk the trust of personality and freedom. How can he justify this trust ? How can he use his freedom in the right way ? He must have a respect for the ego and a faith in its capacities. This requires *patience* — patience in all kinds of situation, even in the midst of hardships and suffering. Patience hardens the self against every kind of ills, and enables him to cultivate the capacity of applying concentrated energy to every situation that confronts him. The purest example of concentration of patience is *prayer*.

Prayer or the act of worship intensifies life. It is the way by which the ego is able to affirm itself even in the midst of adversity. Describing the power and the characters of prayer Iqbal says that it is through prayer — the act of worship, that the ego can lead a life of intensity and develop his manhood. (a) Prayer deepens emotion and activates the will of the ego. (b) It is natural to man as it is an instinctive act of the heart. (c) It is the practice of intense patience and of concentration of energy. (d) It is the means of spiritual illumination. Iqbal says, "Prayer as a means of spiritual illumination is a normal vital act by which the little island of our personality suddenly discovers its situation in a larger whole of life."[1] (e) It enables the individual ego to affirm itself in the world, and thereby to discover its own worth and value in the life of the universe. (f) Prayer, according to Iqbal, has to be regarded as a necessary supplement to the intellectual activity of the individual. The intellectual and scientific apprehensions give a hazy picture of reality. Prayer makes this picture clearer and brings about a deeper vision of the reality. (g) That is why Prayer is conceived as a synthesis of *Power* and *Vision*. It is a vision of the reality, and as a result of the vision, there emerges a power in the ego. (h) Prayer, thus, is not the acceptance of the insignificance of the individual — it is a yearning for the possibility of a new experience, and of gaining new power for the ego. (i) Iqbal feels that the object of prayer is better achieved when it is congregational. The Spirit of true prayer is social. Congregational prayer enables the individual to perceive the ego in others and thus to develop a respect for other egos. This respect for others is essential for self-development. Secondly, congregational prayer implies that different egos have come together animated by the same aspiration, and guided by the same impulse. This gives a new energy to the individual egos.

---

1. Iqbal. *Six Lectures on the Reconstruction of Religious Thought in Islam*, p. 124

Prayer, thus, is a mode of worship through which the ego can develop itself and march ahead in its quest for immortality.

Immortality is not ours as a matter of right, it has to be won — achieved. The ego must continue to struggle through concentrated ego-activities till he wins his resurrection. *Immortality, therefore, is the consummation of the life-process within the ego.*

BIBLIOGRAPHY

(of Books in English)

I SWAMI VIVEKANANDA

Vivekananda, Swami, —*Complete Wórks of Swami Vivekananda*, Vol I-VIII. Mayavati, Almora, Birth Centenary Edition, 1963.

—*What Religion is* ? Ed. John Yale, Int. by C. Isherwood. Advaita Ashram, 1962.

—*Jnana Yoga*. Advaita Ashram, Mayavati, Alamora, 1930.

—*Karma Yoga*. Advaita Ashram, Mayavati, Almora, 1930.

—*Selections from Swami Vivekananda*. comp. Swami Pavitrananda. Advaita Ashram, Almora, 1946.

Nikhilananda, Swami, *Vivekananda, A Biography*. Ramkrishna Vivekananda Centre, New York, 1953.

Rolland, Roman, *The Life of Vivekananda and the Universal Gospel*. Tr. Malcolm Smith. Advaita Ashram, Almora, 1965.

Sharma, D. S., *The Master and the Disciple*. Sri Ramkrishna Math, Madras, 1947.

Tejasananda, Swami, *Swami Vivekananda and his Message*. Ramkrishna Mission. Belur Math, Calcutta, 1965.

Yogeshwaranand, Swami, *Teachings of Swami Vivekananda*. Advait Ashram, Mayavati, Almora, 1953.

II RABINDRANATH TAGORE

Chakrabarti, Amiya, and others, Ed. *Rabindranath*. Calcutta, Book Exchange, 1944.

Estborn, Sigfrid, *The Religion of Tagore in the Light of the Gospel*. Wesley Press and Publishing House, Mysore, 1949.

Narvane, V. S., *Rabindranath Tagore, a Philosophical Study*. Allahabad Central Book Depot, 1947.

Radhakrishnan, S. *The Philosophy of Rabindranath Tagore*. Macmillan and Co. Ltd, London, 1919.

Ray, B. G., *The Philosophy of Rabindranath Tagore*. Hind Kitab, Bombay, 1949.

Sykes, Majorie, *Rabindranath Tagore*. Longman's. Calcutta, 1943.
Tagore, Rabindranath,

—*Creative Unity*. Macmillan and Co. Ltd., (Indian
    Edition) 1950.

—*Crisis in Civilization*. Shantiniketan, 1941.

—*The Diary of a Western Voyage*. Tr. Indu Datta.
    Asia Publishing House, Bombay, 1962.

—*Fire Flies*. The Macmillan and Co., New York, 1928.

—*Fruit Gathering*. Macmillan and Co. London, (Indian
    Edition) 1927.

—*The Gardener*. Macmillan and Co. London, (Indian
    Edition) 1919.

—*Gitanjali*. Macmillan and Co., London. (Indian Edition)
    1924.

—*Lectures and Addresses*—Ed. Anthony Soares. Macmillan
    and Co., London, 1928.

—*Lover's gift and Crossing*. The Macmillan and Co.,
    London, (Indian Edition) 1927.

—*Man*. Andhra University, Series No. 16. Waltair, 1937.

—*My Reminiscenses*. Macmillan and Co. (Indian Edition)
    1923.

—*Personality*. Macmillan and Co., (Indian Edition) 1948.

—*The Religion of Man*. 3rd Impression. George Allen and
    Unwin. London, 1949.

—*Sadhana*. Macmillan and Co., London. 1947.

—*Stray Birds*. Macmillan and Co., London, (Indian Edi-
    tion), 1923.

—*A Tagore Reader*. Ed. Amiya Chakrabarti. The
    Macmillan Co., New York, 1961.

—*A Tagore Testament*. Ed. Indu Datta, Meridian Books,
    London, 1953.

—*Thought Relics*, Macmillan Co., New York, 1921.

—*Towards Universal Man*. Tr. Various Hands. Asia
    Publishing House, Bombay, 1961.

Tagore, Saummendranath., *Rabindranath Tagore and Universal
    Humanism*. St. Vaccum Co., Bombay, 1961.

III Mahatma Gandhi

Ashe, Geoffrey, *Gandhi, a Study in Revolution*. Asia Publishing
    House, Bombay, 1968.

Bose, N. K., *Studies in Gandhism.* Second Edition. Indian Association Publishing Co., Calcutta, 1947.

Datta, D. M., *The Philosophy of Mahatma Gandhi.* University of Calcutta, 1968.

Dhawan, G. R., *The Political Philosophy of Mahatma Gandhi.* Navajiwan Publishing House, Ahmedabad.

Fisher, Louis, *The Life of Mahatma Gandhi.* Jõnathan Cape., Thirty Bedford Square, London, 1952.

Gandhi, M. K., — *An Autobiography or the Story of my Experiments with Truth.* Navajiwan Publishing House, Ahmedabad, 1948.

—*The Art of Living* —Bharatiya Vidya Bhavan, Bombay, 1961.

—*Non-Violence in Peace and War.* 2nd Edition, Navajiwan Publishing House, Ahmedabad, 1944.

—*Satyagrah, Non-Violent Resistance.* Navajiwan Publishing House, Ahmedabad, 1951.

—*Selections from Gandhi,* Ed. N. K. Bose. Navajiwan Publishing House, Ahmedabad, 1948.

—*The Law of Love.* Ed. T. Hingorani. Bhartiya Vidya Bhavan, Bombay, 1962.

—*The Mind of Mahatma Gandhi.* Ed and Comp. R. K. Prabhu and U. R. Rao. Navajiwan Publishing House, 1967.

—*My Non-Violence.* Navajiwan Publishing House, Ahmedabad, 1960.

—*Hind Swaraj or Indian Home Rule.* Navajiwan Publishing House, Ahmedabad, 1958.

—*My Religion.* Navajiwan Publishing House, Ahmedabad, 1958.

—*Sarvodaya.* Navajiwan Publishing House, Ahmedabad, 1958.

Gregg, Richard B., *The Power of Non-Violence.* Navajiwan Publishing House, Ahmedabad, 1949.

Jones, Stanley, *Mahatma Gandhi, an Interpretation.* Holder and Stoughton, St. Paul's House, London, 1948.

Kripalani, J. B., *The Gandhian Way.* Bera and Co., Bombay, 1945.

Mahadevan, T.M.P. Ed., *Truth and Non-Violence*. Unesco Publication, Gandhi Peace Foundation., 1970.

Mukherji, Hiren, *Gandhi, a Study*. National Book Agency, Calcutra, 1958.

Prasad, Mahadeva, *Social Philosophy of Mahatma Gandhi*. Vishvavidyalaya Prakashan, Gorakhpur, 1958.

Radhakrishnan, S. Ed., *Mahatma Gandhi*. Essays and Reflections, George Allen and Unwin Ltd., London, 1949.

IV KRISHNACHANDRA BHATTACHARYA

Bhattacharya, K. C., *Studies in Philosophy*, Vol. I, Ed. Gopinath Bhattacharya. Progressive Publishers, Calcutta, 1956.

—*Studies in Philosophy*. Vol II. Gopinath Bhattacharya. Progressive Publishers, Calcutta, 1958.

—*Studies in Vedantism*. Calcutta University Studies No. 3. Calcutta, 1909.

—*The Subject as Freedom*. Indian Institute of Philosophy, Amalner, 1930.

Maitra, S. K. and others, Ed. *Krishnachandra Bhattacharya Memorial Volume*. Indian Institute of Philosophy, Amalner, 1958.

Also in — George Burch, *Contemporary Vedanta Philosophy*, Review of Metaphysics, March 1956. pp. 485-96. Ras Bihari Das, *Krishna Chandra Bhattacharya*, The Modern Review, April, 1934, pp. 435-39. Basant Kumar Lal, *Existentialism and the Philosophy of K. C. Bhattacharya*. The Philosophical Quarterly, April, 1959, pp. 31-42. G. R. Malkani, *Existence*, The Philosophical Quarterly, October 1937 (pp. ˙163-73 and January 1938 (pp. 231-55). G. R. Malkani, *Some Points in K. C. Bhattacharya's Concept of Philosophy*, The Philosophical Quarterly, July 1950, pp. 41-60.

V SRI AUROBINDO

Aurobindo, Sri — *The Life Divine*. Pondichery, 1955

—*Savitri, a Legend and a Symbol*. Pondichery 1951.

—*The Human Cycle*. Pondichery, 1949.

—*Foundation of Indian Culture*. The Sri Aurobindo Library, New York, 1953.

—*Lights on Yoga,* Arya Publishing House, Calcutta, 1948.
—*More Lights on Yoga,* Pondichery, 1948.
—*The Riddle of this World.* Arya Publishing House, Calcutta, 1946.
—*The Ideal of Human Unity.* Pondichery, 1950.
—*Bases of Yoga.* Arya Publishing House, Calcutta, 1947.
—*Future Evolution of Man: The Divine Life upon Earth.* George Allen and Unwin Ltd., London, 1963.
—*Synthesis of Yoga.* Pondichery, 1948.
—*The Supramental Manifestation upon Earth.* Pondichery, 1952.
—*Sri Aurobindo on Himself and on the Mother.* Pondichery, 1953.
—*Lights on Life-Problems.* Ed. and Comp. Kishor Gandhi. Sri Aurobindo Circle, Bombay., 1961.
Choudhary, Haridas, Ed., *The Integral Philosophy of Sri Aurobindo.* George Allen and Unwin Ltd., London, 1960.
—*Sri Aurobindo, the Prophet of Life Divine.* Sri Aurobindo Path Mandir, Calcutta, 1951.
Das, Adhar Chandra, *Sri Aurobindo and the Future of Mankind.* Calcutta University, 1934.
Langlay, G. H., *Sri Aurobindo, Indian Poet, Philosopher and Mystic.* David Marlow Ltd., 1949.
Purani, A. B., *Sri Aurobindo, Some Aspects of his Vision.* Bharatiya Vidya Bhavan, Bombay, 1966.
Roy, Anil Baran, *The World Crisis* (Sri Aurobindo's vision of the future). George Allen and Unwin Ltd., London, 1947.

VI S. RADHAKRISHNAN

Joad, C.E.M., *Counterattacks from the East.* George Allen and Unwin Ltd., London, 1933.
Marlow, A. N., Ed., *Radhakrishnan, an Anthology.* George Allen and Unwin Ltd., London, 1952.
Radhakrishnan, S., — *An Idealist View of Life.* George Allen and Unwin Ltd., London, 1947.
—*East and West.* George Allen and Unwin Ltd., London, 1955.

—*Eastern Religions and Western Thought.* Clarendon Press, Oxford, 1939.

—*East and West in Religion.* George Allen and Unwin Ltd., London, 1954.

—*The Hindu View of Life.* George Allen and Unwin Ltd., London. 1954.

—*The Reign of Religion in Contemporary Philosophy.* Macmillan and Co., London, 1920.

—*Religion and Society.* George Allen and Unwin Ltd., London, 1947.

—*The Recovery of Faith.* George Allen and Unwin Ltd., London, 1956.

Raju, P. T. and others, Ed., *Contemporary Studies in Philosophy.* George Allen and Unwin Ltd., London, 1951.

Schilpp, P. A. Ed., *The Philosophy of Sarvepalli Radhakrishnan.* Tudor Publishing Company, New York, 1952.

Singh, Jagannath, Ed., *S. Radhakrishnan* (Commemoration Volume) Leader Press, Allahabad, 1953.

VII SIR MOHAMMAD IQBAL

Dar, Bashir Ahmad, — *A Study in Iqbal's Philosophy.* Shaikh Mohammad Ashraf. Kashmiri Bazar, Lahore, 1948.

Fyzee, Asaf. A. A., *Modern Approach to Islam.* Asia Publishing House, Bombay, 1963.

Hassan, Ishrat, — *The Metaphysics of Iqbal.* Lahore.

Iqbal, Mohammad, *Six Lectures on the Reconstruction of Religious Thought in Islam.* Kanpur Art Printing Works, Lahore, 1930.

—*Reconstruction of Religious Thought in Islam.* Oxford University Press, London, 1934.

—*Speeches and Statements.* Comp. Shamloo. Al-Mahar Academy, Lahore.

—*The Secrets of the Self* (Asrar-i-Khudi). Tr. Reynold A. Nicholson. Macmillan and Co. Ltd., London, 1920.

—*The Complaint and the Answer* (Shikwah and Jawab-i-Shikwah) Tr. Altaf Hussain, Lahore, 1943.

Sinha, Sachchidananda., — *Iqbal, the Poet and his Message.* Ram Narain Lal Publishers, Allahabad, 1947.

Vahid, Syed Abdul, — *Iqbal, His Art and Thought.* Shaikh Mohammad Ashraf, Kashmiri Bazar, Lahore, 1948.

General

Behari, Bankey, *Sufies, Mystics and Yogies of India.* Bharatiya Vidya Bhavan, Bombay, 1962.

Farquhar, J. N., *Modern Religious Movements in India.* Macmillan and Co., New York, 1918.

Frazer, R. W., *Indian Thought, Past and Present* T. Fisher Unwin Ltd., London, 1915.

Macmunn, Sir George, *The Religions and Hidden Cult of India.* Sampson Low, Marston and Co., London.

Morrison, John, *New Ideas in India.* Macmillan and Co. Ltd., London, 1907.

Narvane, V. S., *Modern Indian Thought.* Asia Publishing House, Bombay, 1964.

Radhakrishnan, S. and Muirhead, J. H. Ed., *Contemporary Indian Philosophy.* The Muirhead Library of Philosophy. George Allen and Unwin Ltd., London, 1952.

Radhakrishnan, S. and Raju, P. T. Ed., — *Concept of Man.* A Study in Comparative Philosophy. George Allen and Unwin Ltd., London, 1960.

Radhakrishnan, S. and Moore, Charles A. Ed., *A Source Book in Indian Philosophy.* Princeton University Press. 1957.

Raju. P.T., *The Idealistic Thought of India.* George Allen and Unwin Ltd., London, 1953.

Ray, Benay Gopal, *Contemporary Indian Philosophers.* Kitabistan, Allahabad, 1957.

Schweitzer, A., *Indian Thought and its Development.* Tr. Mrs. Charles B. Russell. Henry Colt and Co., New York, 1936.

Sirkar, M. N., *Hindu Mysticism.* Kegan Paul, London, 1934.

Underwood. A. C., *Contemporary Thought of India.* Williams and Norgate Ltd., London, 1930.

INDEX